FAMILIES IN CRISIS

Readers in Social Problems

DONALD R. CRESSEY, CONSULTING EDITOR
UNIVERSITY OF CALIFORNIA, SANTA BARBARA

FAMILIES
IN
CRISIS

EDITED BY
PAUL H. GLASSER
AND
LOIS N. GLASSER
THE UNIVERSITY OF MICHIGAN

HARPER & ROW
Publishers
NEW YORK, EVANSTON, AND LONDON

Gould Intro

Contents

PART I / FAMILY CRISIS THEORY

PART II / POVERTY

PART III / DISORGANIZATION

PART IV / ILLNESS AND DISABILITY

FAMILIES IN CRISIS

Part I

Family Crisis Theory

Introduction

As UNDERGRADUATE students we were liberal arts majors. We were fortunate in being able to take courses in all of the social and behavioral sciences and in many of the physical and biological sciences as well. Each instructor was a specialist in his field but tended to view the world from the limited perspective of his expertness. Class discussions often were concerned with the problems of the community and society around us. Many touched every student personally in one way or another. Each professor had his own orientation to an understanding of the issues. Frequently the same issues were discussed in classes in different departments, and explanations were not only different from one another but also sometimes inconsistent with one another. When solutions were proposed, similar difficulties emerged.

Maybe this is somewhat unavoidable in a complex society in which there has been a knowledge explosion requiring specialization in training. Faculty colleagues complain, with some justification, about the difficulty of keeping up with new material focused on their specific interests in their discipline. The real world is very complicated indeed. That which confronts us and with which we have to deal every day has many explanations and many solutions. While the vast increase in knowledge has enabled us to better understand and sometimes have greater control over what is happening around us, it also has enlarged the complexity of the society and the problems its members face. While we have many more interpretations of the phenomena that affect us, these are not always well integrated in a way that allows us to fully comprehend the issues or make decisions. We now know that there are multiple causes for any single problem and that there are usually multiple solutions.

All sciences require that similarities in the real world be abstracted and related to each other. This process is called conceptualization and leads to the development of theories.

These conceptualizations are nothing more than ideas, for which a vocabulary is created, enabling us to describe consistencies in what we see better than we have been able to before. On the basis of these descriptions, we are sometimes able to predict certain future events. Concepts and theories do not elucidate the totality of our experience but only allow us to better approximate our understanding of its various aspects.

This is the problem. The real world is so complex that we can conceptualize only small parts of it at any one time. Too often we forget that the family is a product of many factors: what goes on inside the heads of each of its members, which in itself is a product of physiological and social experience; the present interpersonal relationships and experiences of each of the individuals within and outside the family; the history of the group and the rules it has established; the physical environment in which the group finds itself; the pressures placed upon it by the social, political, economic, and educational institutions that surround it; and the norms of the culture in which it resides. Each of these factors interpenetrates one another, but most of our conceptualizations are limited to one factor only. There is some overlap among these areas but there is some inconsistency too. Therefore, our knowledge of the family is like a giant picture puzzle in which some pieces are missing, other pieces do not fit together well, and only a few sections provide clear images.

Our fascination for this social unit in which most of us grew up and in which we continue is almost unending. This has led to the study of the family by scholars in all the social and behavioral sciences. The flow of popular literature in this area in newspapers and magazines never ceases. The reasons for our interest in this institution are numerous and varied, although two seem of prime importance. Most of us have more and more continuous contact with this social group than with any other in society. Second, most scholars would agree that during the first six years of life certain behavioral dispositions are laid down that affect each of us forever after, and the child's most extensive and almost inclusive contacts during this period are with parents and siblings in the home.

For a while many of the experts believed that the family was diminishing in importance; some even predicted its demise.[1] Others, who took a more optimistic view, were saying that the personal functions of the family (affection, security, guidance, and sexual gratification) were becoming more important while the social functions (reproduction, physical maintenance, placement or status, and socialization) were becoming less meaningful.[2] The most recent evidence indicates that neither prediction is true. If anything, the family is increasing in importance. Both personal and social functions of the family have become enlarged and more significant, but this was not readily recognized because they have changed drastically. Further, the family has been required to learn to adapt quickly to the increasingly rapid rate of change experienced by almost all the other institutions in the society. The family, as the most flexible group which performs tasks that maintain the stability of the society in a way no other institution can, is now just beginning to be recognized again not only as a unit requiring study but also as one needing heightened attention by those who set social and public policy.[3]

The lively interest shown in the family by professionals and laymen has led to a great many and often conflicting points of view about the way it operates, what its problems are, and how these problems should be solved. With this in mind, in this volume we have tried to provide the reader with a great variety of orientations from the social and behavioral sciences. Almost all the disciplines are represented, and differences within academic areas are portrayed. When theoretical positions are different, or even appear inconsistent, the student has a right to know this so that he may form his own opinion.

We have tried to provide multiple views of the three problems in the family around which the book is organized—poverty, disorganization, and physical and mental illness. Differences in understanding frequently lead to dissimilar solutions at both the interpersonal intervention and the social policy levels. Variations among helping professionals as well as policy setters are wide, and as the reader will learn, there is even disagreement about how much disagreement there is. Nonetheless, there is also a good deal of agreement, which directs us to change the ways we might help families in crises through both personal intervention and legislation. Our hope is that this selection of articles will not only provide the reader with information but also challenge him to think through what the material means and question some of his own attitudes and values in the process.

The three types of family problems discussed in this reader are considered crises. But what is a crisis? *Webster's New Collegiate Dictionary* defines it as a "decisive moment, turning point. A crucial time. . . ."[4] This provides focus but no content.

A crisis occurs when some stressor or event produces stress or disequilibrium for the unit under discussion.[5] While these concepts originated in the physical sciences, in the social and behavioral sciences they have been applied to individuals, small groups, and institutions. Much of the early development of concepts in the latter disciplines was in family sociology.[6]

The event leading to a crisis may have its source outside the family itself, such as a war bombing, political or religious persecution, or a flood, tornado, or hurricane. It may also have its source within the family, as with illegitimacy, non-support, a mental breakdown, infidelity, a suicide, or alcoholism. The event may be some unexpected change in the composition of the family through the loss or gain of a member, because of death, illness, war, pregnancy, adoption, etc. For example, a parent or child may die or become ill, or aged grandparents may find it necessary to move in with children and grandchildren.[7] Or the event may occur in the minds of citizens of the community, such as regarding a family member as deviant and labelling him delinquent, retarded, or mentally ill, for example; or in the minds of individuals in the family, such as not wanting a pregnancy or considering a divorce. Often a crisis is precipitated by some combination of these events.

The presence of stress means that some internal difficulty or strain is experienced by the group. Family stress sometimes is accompanied by psychological stress but this need not always be so. Family demoralization frequently is a sign that stress is present. For stress to be relieved, the present method of family functioning must be changed; alterations in group structures and processes are needed to handle the difficulty. For example, shifts in the family power structure, means of communication, affectional relationships, tasks assigned members, or ways of solving problems and resolving conflicts may solve or ease a crisis. Without such modifications, disequilibrium will continue and family functioning is likely to become less effective and less efficient.

All forms of abrupt or disjunctive changes are likely to cause crises. Therefore, unless family members are adequately prepared, family developmental changes may result in crises. Le Masters describes parenthood as a crisis from this point of view.[8] For the family to handle such variations in the situations they must deal with, role restructuring is usually essential.

A similar event may be a crisis for one family but not for another. Hill has identified three variables that

. . . help to determine whether a given event becomes a crisis for any given family: (1) the hardships of the situation or event itself; (2) the resources of the family: its role structure, flexibility and previous history with crisis; and (3) the definition the family makes of the event; that is, whether members treat the event *as if it were* or *as if it were not a threat* to their status, goals and objectives.[9]

While these three categories are closely related to one another, note that the first focuses on the event or social and physical situation, the second on past and present family functioning, and the third on the psychological reactions of individual members and the family as a group. Some families are known to be crisis-prone, that is, almost any out-of-the-ordinary event precipitates considerable family stress. In these cases it seems clear that neither the internal organization of the family nor the psychological strength of its members is adequate to deal with change.[10]

On the other hand, a review of the research literature reveals that three features seem to characterize families that are able to respond adequately to stressor events—involvement, integration, and adaptation. The first refers to commitment to and participation in family life by the members of the group. Integration has to do with interdependence of the instrumental and socioemotional roles of individuals in the group. When each person in the family requires the help of the others in achieving group and individual goals and in maintaining psychological equilibrium, particularly if the members work well together, the family is likely to handle adequately internal and external difficulties. The third factor refers to the ability of the family group and each of its members to change their responses to one another and the world around them as the situation demands—flexibility of the family in group structure and individual behavior.

The community response to stressor events, however, is equally important but has had little study. Hansen and Hill have identified four types, based on positive and negative positional (institutions) and personal (friends and neighbors) responses of the community.[11] The *therapeutic* response is represented by the disaster victim, for whom aid is provided by agencies and individuals in the community. The *social welfare* response is illustrated by the illegitimately pregnant mother. Aid is generally provided by health and welfare agencies, but many persons in the community may make known their disapproval of the woman's condition. The *repressive* response is represented by the income tax dodger. Sanctions are applied by government institutions, but those close to the person who committed this offense often avoid accusation and may even defend and sympathize with the tax dodger. Finally, there is the *persecutive* response, represented by the American Communist. Legal sanctions are applied, neighbors see him as deviant and potentially dangerous, and the family is under considerable pressure to change. If the family cannot escape and will not change, it is likely to become more cohesive as a defense against personal and legal persecution.

Crises are not necessarily bad for the family or its members. The disequilibrium that develops requires new methods for handling problems. Out of this situation may arise new and creative solutions for organizing activities that are superior to those that were present before the crisis occurred. This experience may enable the family to handle future crises in a superior manner. In addition, it may result in greater individual and group satisfaction with family life.

Each of the crises analyzed in this volume is somewhat different from the other. In affluent America poverty confers minority and inferior status, particularly when accompanied by black skin color. This deviant position, associated with a style of life closely related to the poor person's almost continual concern about having enough food, clothing, and shelter to maintain himself, serves as a constant set of stressors on the underprivileged family. Even the best of internal organizational arrangements bolstered by considerable psychological strength of each member of the family group may prove inadequate under these circumstances. As some of the articles reveal, among the poor, crisis may be a monthly, weekly, or even daily affair, and to expect families to maintain themselves indefinitely in this situation may be asking too much.

While the literature on poverty has focused on the effects of external events on the family, the literature on disorganization has given central attention to the internal organization of this primary group. The emphasis has been on the development of crisis events because of inadequate and inflexible structural arrangements and problem-solving and conflict-resolving processes. These deficits frequently are related to the psychological weaknesses of the spouses. However, the selections will point up that the impact of cultural and socioeconomic factors should not be ignored if the reader wants to understand fully why some families break up and others seem to be in a constant state of civil war.

Serious illness—mental and physical—often creates stress in the family but also can be a product of such stress. This stressor is internal to the family, involving the temporary or permanent loss of a family member, and therefore serves as a contrast to the other types of problems discussed. In this section, more than in the other two, concern is with interpretation of the hardship or how the family members treat the event. Thus, each of Hill's three variables receives special attention.

Despite the differences in emphasis, as previously implied, the three types of problems cannot easily be separated from one another. For example, Levinger points out that the major cause for divorce among that population group for which the rate is highest—the lowest socioeconomic stratum—is inadequate or unsteady income by the husband.[12] Similarly, Haley takes the position that marital difficulties and mental illness may both be closely related to organizational problems in the family group, psychological problems of the family members, or both.[13]

The differences in emphasis in Hill's three variables described earlier were one reason for selecting these three problems for analysis in this book. There were two other reasons as well.

The next is that each problem is a major social issue today. Poverty and civil rights, which are closely linked, are probably the two most important domestic concerns. Although Murdock and Goode have demonstrated that the majority of societies have higher divorce rates than ours,[14] family instability and its concomitants (notably delinquency and crime) are written about in the newspapers and magazines every day. The problem of illness is increasingly in the limelight as monetary costs have risen and the social costs have become more apparent, especially among the poor.

The last reason for our choice is that all these problems touch each of us in our daily lives. If we have not yet experienced the crisis of acute or chronic illness in our family, it is highly likely that we will in the not too distant future. We are gradually learning that we must work hard at marriage and family life to achieve the success and satisfactions we want from them, and this requires basic knowledge and understanding of their dynamics. In that way we may prevent the disorganization in our own family that is so prevalent in modern society. Finally, we all face the issues of income redistribution and services to the poor. The functions of those who are about to enter the health, education, and welfare professions will be shaped by the ways in which we attempt to meet the very apparent needs of the lowest income group in our population.

The articles have been selected to provide a range of perspectives on the three crisis situations, and each section is arranged in a systematic manner. The first reading is intended to provide the student with a subjective view of the problem. In each case the author serves as a type of participant observer, using description in a way that helps the reader to "experience" or "feel" the problem as well as understand it intellectually. These are difficulties facing real families, that we ourselves may have to deal with some day. Therefore, it is important that we have some identification with the emotional components of the issues that follow.

This sets the stage for the second type of selection in each section, an ecological or demographic review of the problem. The crisis event is surveyed, through statistical or other means, providing an overview of the questions involved. In addition, the stressor is analyzed from the sociological or social psychological perspective.

Next there are a number of pieces that deal with specific aspects of poverty, disorganization, and illness in families. Each tends to provide a different interpretation of the problem, although a few try to integrate various approaches. Many imply or suggest solutions to the crisis, although this is not the central emphasis of this set in each section. We have tried to select articles that do more than describe—that reveal a penetrating analysis of the crisis from the author's perspective.

The last group of articles in each of the three areas focuses on solutions to the crisis. These are at both the interpersonal intervention and social policy levels. Often the resolution advocated is dependent upon the theoretical orientation of the author. Differences among scholars point up the complications of the real world and should give the reader an opportunity to think through his own priorities and approaches for himself and others.

The articles have been selected from material in the disciplines of psychology, social psychology, and sociology and the professions of social work, education, and medicine. A few are purely descriptive; many are theoretical or analytical reviews of the literature in a specified area; some are summaries of the author's own empirical studies. The mix is again purposeful, in order to provide the student with experience in reading different types of social science and professional literature.

This set of readings is intended to serve as a complement to the text in a variety of classroom situations. Instructors who teach undergraduate courses in marriage and the family and family life education will find it very useful. Since the selections deal with three major issues in our society today in the context of family life, the volume will have much utility as supplementary material for liberal arts and sciences students who elect to study social problems. Finally, helping professionals, novices, and those with considerable experience, especially in social work, education, and public health, are increasingly being required to work with the total family in trouble. For them this reader will provide new understanding and new approaches to effective and efficient service.

The book is not directed at answering all questions about

families, families in crisis, or the three social problems discussed. Rather we hope it will challenge the reader's established convictions and stereotyped responses to the world around him. Our aim is to change—even in small ways—the student's views and behavior in some aspect of his personal or professional life. If this is achieved, we will consider our efforts worthwhile and the volume a success.

Part II

Poverty

Preliminary Comments

WHAT IS it like to be poor? For many of us in the comfortable middle class it is hard to imagine. As a middle class person who lived among the poor for fifteen months, the author of the first article describes for us her own awakening concerning the problems of family life among the lowest socioeconomic group in this country. This selection is taken from a book that is part of a larger study on poverty directed by Hylan Lewis.

Mrs. Jeffers and her four-year-old son lived in a low-income public housing project in Washington, D.C., for fifteen months. As a social anthropologist she was a participant observer. As a warmly human person she was a neighbor and friend to those around her. She became a part of their lives just as they became a part of hers, and she describes with empathy and understanding the difficulties they faced and the ways they went about trying to solve them.

This piece from the short volume was chosen not only because of its emphasis upon family decision-making processes but also because of its relevance to recent public and Congressional interest in hunger. Two families are pictured. Mrs. Todd has four children and a husband overseas in the armed forces. Mrs. Martin separated from her husband after he refused to pay the bills and ran around with other women. The youngest of her four children is not legitimate, but she receives regularly monthly payments from the father and subsists on this, the payments her husband makes through the courts, and welfare supplementation. Throughout the volume the author points to the many variations in family functioning despite similar socioeconomic and living conditions.

The second selection is taken from the *Report of the National Advisory Commission on Civil Disorders*. This well-known and very important report has received little attention from elected officials despite the excellent documentation of its findings and conclusions by many social scientists. Perhaps because the report cannot be easily attacked and there does not seem to be public clamor for change in the social structure of the United States population, our representatives have decided to try to make slow progress rather than confront the issues.

Although the total report focuses on blacks, this short piece describes the relationship between unemployment, family life, and antisocial activity for both races through statistical analyses. It indicates how fatherless families, illegitimacy, crime, delinquency, and drug addiction are all related to low wages and unemployment for blacks and whites. Family problems and deviant behavior cannot be divorced from the community and society that surround the nuclear group and its members.

On the other hand, S. M. Miller believes it is important to distinguish between economic deprivation and style of life. By dividing poor families into those that are economically secure and insecure and those that are stable and unstable, he describes four relatively different styles of life. About the economically insecure, unstable poor he says, "Lower-class life is crisis-life, constantly trying to make do with string where rope is needed."

He then goes on to discuss strategies of intervention through interpersonal, economic, and political means. Each family type requires somewhat different and multiple approaches.

There are many views of the meaning of poverty. The authors of the next article look at what it is like to be a member of a poor family from a variety of perspectives—those of the public assistance client, the public assistance worker, and diverse social and behavioral scientists. These points of view are not necessarily inconsistent with each other but together form a comprehensive and integrated view of the nature of this problematic situation, revealing the circular quality of its causes and effects. With this in mind the authors suggest a varied policy and practice approach to its solution.

Since education is the traditional and most legitimate upward mobility channel for the underprivileged, an analysis of their learning problems is essential to helping them achieve upward mobility. Cultural, organizational, primary group, and individual factors are discussed by Radin. At each level the family mediates the experiences of the preschool child, and this implies a need to work with the family as well as with the school and with the child. This well-organized summary of research will suggest to the reader many intervention possibilities for raising the knowledge and skill level of the present generation of poor children as a means towards increasing the opportunities for them to enjoy the full benefits of an affluent society.

The last article in this section reviews the advantages and disadvantages of present and proposed plans of government aid to the poor. Fauri covers not only the public assistance programs but also the federal-sponsored social insurances. As a congressional consultant he emphasizes what seems likely to receive approval by the House and Senate. As a humanitarian he favors those plans that will provide the largest financial benefits to those on the bottom of the socio-economic ladder, so that poor families can be rehabilitated as quickly as possible.

LIVING POOR: A PARTICIPANT OBSERVER STUDY OF PRIORITIES AND CHOICES

Camille Jeffers

PROVIDING THE BASIC NECESSITIES: PRIORITIES AND PROBLEMS

My experience at the housing project taught me that it is no small accomplishment for low-income families to provide "decent food, clothing and shelter." I came to realize why so many mothers in and outside the project considered the provision of adequate physical care a major, if not the major, aspect of good motherhood. Adequate physical care could not be taken for granted, and seeing that the children got food, clothing and shelter was sometimes quite a feat. Different mothers had different physical-care problems, and these differences usually affected priorities.

With Mrs. Todd, rent had first priority among physical-care categories. She was determined to keep the roof over their heads until her husband got back. The rent bill was the first thing she paid when she got her allotment, even though she did not always have enough money left to meet other needs.

Clothing was one of these needs. Trying to keep her four children clothed was a critical problem. One way of easing it was to develop different styles of dress to fit varied situations. For example, Mrs. Todd had four clothing levels for her children, ranging from complete undress to Sunday best.

One day I knocked on Mrs. Todd's door and found her five-year-old daughter in charge of what looked like a small nudist colony. Since it was somewhat chilly, I asked Elsie if she didn't think it was too cold for the baby and, without

Reprinted with permission of the author and Louis D. Ferman from *Living Poor: A Participant Observer Study of Priorities and Choices,* Ann Arbor, Mich.: Ann Arbor Publishers, 1967, pp. 67-75, 91-95.

hesitation, she replied, "That's the way my mother wants her."

Mrs. Todd, like other mothers, frequently let her children run naked around the house. Sometimes the reason they were stripped was that it was wash day and there was nothing extra to put on while their clothes were being washed. At other times, the nakedness of a small child could be due to the heat or to efforts to save clean clothes for more public occasions.

Now and then I found the children, particularly baby Shirley, in semi-dress, wearing an undershirt but no panties. This was a pervasive pattern of dress for small children. As first I did not know how to interpret this semi-dress; I found mothers, who exhibited high standards for their children's welfare, dressing (or not dressing) their children in the same way. The more I saw of Mrs. Todd and other families, the more a relatively simple explanation for the practice began to take shape in my mind. Families just did not have the quantity of diapers and training pants needed for children who were not yet completely toilet trained. When funds were limited, priority had to be given to the purchase of outer clothing rather than underwear.

One result of this semi-dress was frequent urine puddles on the floor and I heard one exasperated mother cry, "I'm sick of wiping up this pissy floor." One mother had an alternative to floor wiping; she passed this job on to her children. Once when this mother's four-year-old son reported in an alarming voice that the baby had "made doo-doo" on the floor, the mother said, "Well, you know what to do; get a rag and clean it up."

Sometimes Mrs. Todd's children were dirty and disheveled. I never knew whether their appearance on these occasions was due to a lack of money to buy soap powder or to Mrs. Todd's low spirits. Either explanation could have been right. I observed, however, that when the children were dirty, Mrs. Todd was careful to see that they stayed in the building and played only in the house or in the hall. Going outside was a different matter; she always made them more presentable then. As she put it, she wanted them to look decent enough so people wouldn't talk about the way she kept her children.

This concern about what other people had to say about

their children was pervasive among the mothers. In general, children who came into the court to play looked presentable. I noticed, for example, that raggedy and unkempt children were much more in evidence within a block or two of the project, in areas that were still physically deteriorated.

Proximate living in the project appeared to have been a factor in many efforts to conform to better standards of public dress for their children and, to a lesser degree, for themselves.

When Mrs. Todd's children left the grounds of the housing project, she made a special effort to dress them as well as she could. Once Mrs. Todd refused an invitation to take Phillip on an automobile trip to the airport because he had "nothing to wear." When she was pressed for an explanation, she said that the clothing he had was not suitable enough for him to go. It was only after a neighbor lent him some pants and socks that she let him go. When she took her children to visit relatives, they would be clean and neat. She took special pains to see that they looked their best whenever they went to her mother's house in a middle class residential neighborhood. For their out-of-town vacation trip to visit relatives in a nearby state, she bought each child a completely new outfit.

Mrs. Todd managed the problem of clothing the children as well as she did only because of help from family and friends. She received hand-me-downs for her daughters from a sister who had several girls. When Phillip, her older son, outgrew the few clothes he had, they were passed down to Nicholas. Keeping Phillip adequately clothed was Mrs. Todd's biggest clothing problem; she had no ready-made or easy source of hand-me-downs for him. Occasionally her mother-in-law furnished items of clothing for the various children, particularly for Elsie, who seemed to be her favorite. From time to time, Mrs. Todd's mother gave her dresses for the girls. Friends in the project would also give her clothing that their children had outgrown. Despite her children's clothing needs, Mrs. Todd thought about helping others. She asked if I might know some family among those in CRS's study group that could use her youngest daughter's hand-me-downs.

Ranking second among the basic things Mrs. Todd wanted for her children was "decent food." This was a chronic need and made for continuing frustration. She tried to stay abreast of things by juggling the regular expected income and the hoped-for extra money from her husband. One month she would pay all the bills with her allotment and buy food with any extra money that her husband sent. The next month she would use her allotment to store up on food and rely on the extra money expected from her husband to pay bills. However, this juggling act failed when no extra money came from Mr. Todd.

Mrs. Todd's food standards and tastes were relatively high as measured by the cheaper and inferior fare offered in some neighborhood stores. She scorned the neighborhood stores that regularly slipped handbills under the apartment doors advertising their weekly specials. The prices sounded more like Depression prices than 1960 prices—for example, four pounds of fish for $1, five pounds of chicken backs for 59 cents, three pounds of chicken wings for 98 cents, pork chops at 39 cents a pound, liver at three pounds for 49 cents. For 89 cents, you could get a breakfast special consisting of one pound of sausage meat, one dozen eggs, one stick of margarine and one can of biscuits.

Mrs. Todd said that she would not buy any old thing to feed her children as neither they nor she were used to cheap foods. Describing a breakfast that the Todds had one day when a visiting friend purchased the food, she said, "We had bacon, eggs, grits and biscuits," and added, "One day my children eat like kings, and the next day they have nothing."

Her children liked to have two eggs apiece, and, with her income and its ups and downs, it took too many eggs for one such breakfast. She said that, occasionally, she gave them each one egg, but it took her a day or two to make up the expense for this kind of breakfast. The children were much more apt to get a dish of cereal or grits.

Mrs. Todd preferred to do her shopping at a commissary for service men and their families where food was cheaper. Unless she had someone to drive her there she could not save enough to make a trip to the commissary worthwhile because the round trip taxi fare wiped out any savings. Several times when she was offered a ride, she refused, saying that she had so little money to spend that it was not worth going so far.

Their diet was generally starchy, with emphasis on beans, spaghetti, noodles and potatoes. The children were particularly fond of canned meat balls and spaghetti; she gave this to them quite frequently. Another frequent meal was frozen fish sticks and frozen French fries. It was not that Mrs. Todd did not know how to prepare a balanced meal; it rather was that she chronically lacked the money and, frequently, the incentive to do it.

Often, Mrs. Todd went without meals herself because she did not like the food that she gave the children. Now and then, long after the children had gone to sleep, she would treat herself to a small, treasured piece of steak.

Numerous, undramatic little events taught me the meaning of hunger. Some lessons in hunger were provided unwittingly by the Todd children. For example, a bowl of fruit usually stood on my dinette table. When Mrs. Todd's children came over to play, they would eye it longingly and sometimes ask for an apple or a banana. As we became more friendly, their requests increased with the frequency of their visits. First, I tried to regulate demand and supply by keeping the fruit elsewhere. I began to notice that when the children came over, they would eventually make their way to the kitchen; and there, their eyes would roam around the room as though looking for something. It began to dawn on me that the fruit was less a snack or treat than a supplement to, or even a substitute for, a meal. It was an important means of appeasing the hunger that was such a constant part of the lives of many children in the project.

One day I found Mrs. Todd's nine-month-old Shirley picking dirt off the wheels of a child's tricycle and eating it. I was so startled that I shouted at her to stop. Mrs. Todd came to see what the trouble was. Her daughter did not stop for me nor did she stop the first time her mother spoke to her. Finally, Mrs. Todd had to pick the dirt out of the girl's mouth. When I asked if Mrs. Todd had ever seen her daughter eat dirt before, she said that she had seen her pick the dirt off her brother Phillip's tricycle and eat it. She was at a loss to explain Shirley's behavior.[1]

On one occasion Mrs. Todd described a food fantasy she often had, one involving her teen-age brothers and sisters: she imagined she had taken them on a beach picnic and had so much hot food cooked up that they were able to eat all they wanted.

She followed this image with: "Can you imagine a loaf of bread lasting two days with six children?" When I showed some doubt, she said, "Well it did in my house because my mother wouldn't permit us to touch it unless she gave it to us. We would get a beating if we did."

Such expressions of Mrs. Todd's feelings, thoughts, and memories involving food helped me understand better what seemed to be a contradiction in her behavior toward her children. Relying on what I thought I knew about Mrs. Todd, I had fully expected her to get angry when I saw her children go into the groceries she had brought home one day and eat a loaf of bread before she got a chance to put the rest of the purchases away. Instead of anger or annoyance, she showed the opposite, pleasure and permissiveness. It appeared that hunger was one of her children's expriences with which she readily identified. This same permissiveness and lack of anger, in matters where food for her children was involved, showed in her amusement when a three-layer cake she had baked disappeared in two hours.

One of her often repeated wishes was to be able to set one loaf in front of each of her children and let them eat until they had had their fill of bread—at least once.

Despite the trouble she had providing adequate food, Mrs. Todd was reluctant to acknowledge how bad at times the situation was for her. Some of the facts and many of the dimensions of her family's food story came out only gradually. Some were revealed in situations like the following:

One day she interrupted a conversation to ask if I had ever heard of anybody filling up on ice cream when hungry. When I asked why anybody would make such an odd choice, she replied, "Well, when that's all you can get on your Central Charge Account, ice cream is better than nothing, and with a few cup cakes you can make a meal."

When I pressed to find out whether she was saying obliquely that she had no food, she insisted that she had food. The next day she mentioned that she was thinking about asking to be referred to Surplus Foods by the agency from which she was asking help with the beds. I told her that she could make an application to Surplus Foods without an agency referral and offered to take her there. She said she could do this the following week since she had to remain at home for a few days, waiting for a visit from a social worker with information about the beds.

The following day when I came home from work, Mrs. Todd was waiting for me. Hearing my key in the latch, she poked her head out of her door and asked if I was too tired to do her a favor: she wanted to go to a Peoples Drug Store. Recalling her comment about filling up on ice cream, I immediately offered my services and took her to the drug store. The bulky bag she came out with looked like it might contain ice cream, and I also caught a whiff of tomato soup. Mrs. Todd offered no explanations.

On our return home, I mentioned that I was going to the A&P grocery and asked if she wanted anything. "I don't have any money," she said. "I'm expecting some tomorrow. If I don't get it, I will probably have to go over to my mother's." I asked what she needed but she replied, "Nothing. I have things at home. It's just that I never have everything at one time to make something."

I asked her what she needed in order to make something. She again refused to acknowledge any need at first, but after a pause she blurted, "You can bring me a loaf of day-old bread." I said that I didn't know what she planned to make out of the bread but there must be something else she needed. She delayed answering and then said, "Well if you just want to be real nice, bring me anything!"

As we separated, she asked if my son could come over and have some ice cream.

Mrs. Todd did receive some money from her husband the next day. The following week she asked me to take her to apply for surplus food. Perhaps some of the significance this trip had for her—and for me—came through in her wry but warm remark when we returned home: "Thank you, Mother, for taking me there."

When she eventually got her first supplies from Surplus Foods, she immediately offered some to me. The following week, however, she was in the doldrums again. I did not see her or the children for two successive days. The second evening of her two days of being incommunicado, she telephoned to say that she had decided that she had better call her mother (meaning me) and tell me where she was as she knew that I would be worried. She had no food in the house so she had taken all the children and gone to her mother-in-law's home.

These incidents and exchanges give some idea of the inconsistent way things went for Mrs. Todd—a good meal, a slim meal, no meals. But, somehow, she made it; and, despite circumstances, bursts of enthusiastic creativity would occasionally flare up.

One Easter, I shared some Easter egg dye with her. She later came over to borrow "any kind of flavoring" I had and invited me to see the cake she was making. When I went to Mrs. Todd's apartment, the children were gathered around the table, intently watching as she put finishing touches on the cake. She had tinted some coconut brown and formed it into a basket which nested in grass of green-tinted coconut on white icing. In the basket were several jelly beans representing Easter eggs. In addition to the cake, there was an impressive roasted turkey. The children were looking on excitedly and anticipating their out-of-the-ordinary meal. Everything was pleasant and harmonious.[2]

In general, Mrs. Todd was very interested in food and its preparation. She could watch someone prepare a dish she had never cooked before and then duplicate it with no difficulty. She used to joke that her husband would not know what had happened when he returned home, and she would prepare new dishes like chili and chop suey she had learned to prepare as a result of watching and listening to me.

Mrs. Todd was also interested in the proper service of food. One day she was present when I was setting the table for guests and began helping me. When she asked me where the salad plates were, I told her that I did not feel like dirtying so many dishes and was not going to use them. With a disdainful grunt, she overruled me, got out the salad plates and, as if to silence any protest I might have had, told me that she would come back and do the dishes.[3]

PROVIDING THE BASICS:
PRIORITIES AND REALITIES

Naming the things that she thought were important to children, Mrs. Martin said: "Food, clothes, medical care, a mama and a daddy."

Unlike Mrs. Todd, she gave priority to food rather than to rent. During my stay in the projeect, I witnessed one of her crises involving the basic necessities in which a food problem loomed large. I was a direct participant in this crisis, as I was in other incidents.

Mrs. Martin's husband had not been making the court-ordered support payments regularly. Since she had been using her $80 monthly supplement from the Welfare Department primarily for food, she fell a month behind in rent payments. She managed to borrow one month's rent from her father when she received a dispossess notice, but, by that time, two months' rent was required. After she paid the rent for two months, she was left without money for food.

She reported her financial difficulties to the Welfare Department and was told that nothing could be done until the following month, June. Her husband would have to be taken to court first, and this would take some time.

Confronted with this rule and response, Mrs. Martin sarcastically said, "And what am I supposed to do? Starve in May?"

To complicate her financial problems further, Mrs. Martin's two-year-old daughter, Tootsie, had just returned from a hospital stay for treatment of pneumonia. The doctors said her illness was due to the lack of proper food. Mrs. Martin understood and did not try to evade the doctor's diagnosis. She pointed out that she did not have enough money to feed her children properly, much less to buy vitamins.

When I offered to help, she accepted. I was again in intimate contact with hunger.

Mrs. Martin decided first to apply to a welfare agency for emergency help in getting food for her family. After unsuccessful attempts to make satisfactory, workable baby-sitting arrangements in the project for her four children, she suggested that we take a chance on finding one of her sisters at home. Taking the children with us, we traveled to a different section of the city. We found her sister at home and willing to look after the children.

Leaving the children with her sister, we drove to an office of the welfare agency. Despite her apparent brashness in many areas, Mrs. Martin was fearful of going into the agency's office alone because she had never been there before. She wanted me to accompany her; with a little encouragement, she went in by herself. We agreed to meet at the car; I told her I had some business of my own to attend to elsewhere.

When I returned from my errand, Mrs. Martin was already in the car. She sat slumped dejectedly in the corner. Her agency mission had taken only a few minutes. She had been told immediately that she could not be helped without a referral slip from her public assistance caseworker.

I gave Mrs. Martin a dime to call her caseworker. After the call, Mrs. Martin returned to the car, disappointed again. She said that her caseworker promised to call the welfare agency but told Mrs. Martin she could not see her until the following day, at which time she would give her a referral slip, provided the welfare agency agreed to help.

Annoyed at this delay, Mrs. Martin said that if her caseworker had had any consideration she would have called the welfare agency while she was near the agency, especially since she knew Mrs. Martin's plight. A good bit of her annoyance was due to her hunger. Before entering the agency's office, she had wistfully expressed the hope that the agency would be serving sandwiches; she had heard they did this. However, there were none.

After she had given her account of the agency visit, I asked what food she had at home. She had some chicken backs and rice for the children's dinner. She remarked, "That will do them for tonight as they are not bad; they understand the situation and know that I don't have anything." As far as the next day was concerned, she said, "I'll just have to let tomorrow take care of itself." It was then I let her know I would provide food to tide her over until she found out whether she was going to get help from the agency.

We returned to her sister's house for the children. As we drove up, her sister called from the window to ask if Mrs. Martin wanted some herring. Mrs. Martin's quick rejection of the offer surprised me. It developed that the herring was part of their father's fishing catch of the day before. He had already brought some to Mrs. Martin, but the fish had been too bony for the children.

Mrs. Martin's sister came down to the car with the children. In her hand was a large brown paper bag which contained day-old bread that her boyfriend had brought from the bakery where he worked. Mrs. Martin's face lighted up as she thanked her sister and told her that the children had just eaten the last pieces of bread before we left. I witnssed this scene: Mrs. Martin had poured syrup on a slice of bread for each of the three older children, who folded the bread, sandwich style, to eat it. Brenda, the lively, aggressive one, bolted hers down quickly and grabbed the last piece of bread, on which she poured more syrup. Then Dorothy and Tootsie clamored for more bread.

Mrs. Martin pleadingly and tenderly asked them to be patient; she explained that she was trying to get some food for them. The children quieted down. Seeing and hearing this led me to return to my apartment for some apples to take with us on our trip to the agency.

After our return to the project, I took the Martins enough food for the next morning. I found the children seated around the table eating syrup sandwiches made from the day-old bread their aunt had just given them.

The next day Mrs. Martin told me that she had not been successful in getting help from the agency. The reason she had been given was that the agency's funds had been exhausted in helping the unemployed.[4] Neither would she be able to get additional help from the Public Assistance Division until after the court hearing of nonsupport charges against her husband—a month away.

Mrs. Martin said that her friend, Mr. Tompkins, was due to make his $16 contribution the next day, and she was sure she could count upon him. In the meantime, she thought she could get some help from her oldest sister. She telephoned this sister and briefly explained her predicament. After she finished talking with her sister, she said excitedly that her sister had said that she would "fix me up if I come over."

This time search for food took us to a public housing project in still another part of the city. We took the children with us.[5] After we reached the sister's house and the sister went to the kitchen to pack the food, Mrs. Martin seemed deliberately to refrain from intruding; she confined her attention to her nieces and nephews, all of whom seemed quite fond of her.

Once in the car, Mrs. Martin could contain her curiosity no longer. She began rummaging through the box of food her sister had given her to see what was there.

"I hope she gave me some meat," she said wistfully. "Yes!

There's some hamburger," she answered. "She always has hamburger."

Gleefully, she enumerated the other items as she discovered them. "There's tuna fish, bread, puffed wheat, shredded wheat—but where's the sugar? There's no sugar! I wonder what she expected me to put on the cereal? I guess she forgot."

When we returned home I took Mrs. Martin some sugar. She was unpacking her box of food and the children were again eating syrup sandwiches.

I checked with her the morning after the baby's father was expected to bring his money contribution. He had brought it. The Martins were breakfasting on eggs and scrapple. While Mrs. Martin and I talked, Brenda hurriedly finished her breakfast. Then she eyed her mother's half-finished plate of food and asked for more.

"Don't you be asking for my food!" exclaimed Mrs. Martin in mock anger, sensing Brenda's intent. "What do you think this is!" In predictable fashion, she continued, "Give me your plate. You can have some."

As Brenda handed her mother her plate, Dorothy began crying, "I want some too," and with this, Brenda tried to snatch her mother's plate for herself. Holding securely onto her plate, Mrs. Martin pulled it away from Brenda and divided its contents between the two girls.

"I never get to have my breakfast!" she grumbled.

Mrs. Martin used the $16 brought by Mr. Tompkins to stock up on baby food, milk, staples and meat. When asked how far the money went, she said that by the time she had made these purchases, she did not have enough money left to get all the vegetables she needed. When I gave her some vegetables, the food crisis was over, for a while anyway.

Mrs. Martin wanted to repay me in some way, just as Mrs. Todd had wanted to do. I gently but firmly discouraged her idea of buying a present for me when she received her public assistance check. It was hardly a surprise when, on the day surplus food was distributed, Brenda appeared at my door with a half pound of butter her mother had sent me.

UNEMPLOYMENT, FAMILY STRUCTURE, AND SOCIAL DISORGANIZATION

National Advisory Commission on Civil Disorders

Subemployment in Disadvantaged Negro Neighborhoods

In disadvantaged areas, employment conditions for Negroes are in a chronic state of crisis. Surveys in low-income neighborhoods of nine large cities made by the Department of Labor late in 1966 revealed that the rate of unemployment there was 9.3 percent, compared to 7.3 percent for Negroes generally and 3.3 percent for whites. Moreover, a high proportion of the persons living in these areas were "underemployed," that is they were either part-time workers looking for full-time employment, or full-time workers earning less than $3000 per year, or had dropped out of the labor force. The Department of Labor estimated that this underemployment is two and one-half times greater than the number unemployed in these areas. Therefore, the "subemployment rate," including both the unemployed and the underemployed, was about 32.7 percent in the nine areas surveyed, or 8.8 times greater than the overall unemployment rate for all U. S. workers. Since underemployment also exists outside disadvantaged neighborhoods, comparing the full subemployment rate in these areas with the unemployment rate for the nation as a whole is not entirely valid. However, it provides some measure of the enormous disparity between employment conditions in most of the nation and those prevalent in disadvantaged Negro areas in our large cities.

The critical problem is to determine the actual number of those unemployed and underemployed in disadvantaged Negro areas. This involves a process of calculation which is summarized in the following table:

Reprinted with permission of the publisher from the *Report of the National Advisory Commission on Civil Disorders,* New York: Bantam Books, Inc., 1968, chap. 7, pp. 257–263.

Nonwhite Subemployment in Disadvantaged
Areas of All Central Cities—1967

Group	Unem-ployment	Underem-ployment	Total Subem-ployment
Adult men	102,000	230,000	332,000
Adult women	118,000	266,000	384,000
Teenagers	98,000	220,000	318,000
Total	318,000	716,000	1,034,000

Therefore, in order to bring subemployment in these areas down to a level equal to unemployment alone among whites, enough steady, reasonably-paying jobs (and the training and motivation to perform them) must be provided to eliminate all underemployment and reduce unemployment by 65 percent. For all three age groups combined, this "deficit" amounted to 923,000 jobs in 1967.

THE MAGNITUDE OF POVERTY
IN DISADVANTAGED NEIGHBORHOODS

The chronic unemployment problems in the central city, aggravated by the constant arrival of new unemployed migrants, is the fundamental cause of the persistent poverty in disadvantaged Negro areas.

"Poverty" in the affluent society is more than absolute deprivation. Many of the poor in the United States would be well-off in other societies. Relative deprivation—inequality—is a more useful concept of poverty with respect to the Negro in America because it encompasses social and political exclusion as well as economic inequality. Because of the lack of data of this type, we have had to focus our analysis on a measure of poverty which is both economic and absolute—the Social Security Administration's "poverty level"[1] concept. It is clear, however, that broader measures of poverty would substantiate the conclusions that follow.

In 1966 there were 29.7 million persons in the United States—15.3 percent of the nation's population—with incomes below the "poverty level," as defined by the Social Security Administration. Of these, 20.3 million were white (68.3 percent), and 9.3 million nonwhite (31.7 percent).

Thus, about 11.9 percent of the nation's whites and 40.6 percent of its nonwhites were poor under the Social Security definition.

The location of the nation's poor is best shown from 1964 data as indicated by the following table:

Percentage of Those in Poverty in
Each Group Living In:

Group	Metropolitan Areas in Central Cities	Outside Central Cities	Other Areas	Total
Whites	23.8%	21.8%	54.4%	100%
Nonwhites	41.7	10.8	47.5	100
Total	29.4	18.4	52.2	100

SOURCE: Social Security Administration.

The following facts concerning poverty are relevant to an understanding of the problems faced by people living in disadvantaged neighborhoods.[2]

1. 30.7 percent of nonwhite families of two or more persons lived in poverty compared to only 8.8 percent of whites.

2. Of the 10.1 million poor persons in central cities in 1964, about 4.4 million of these (43.6 percent) were nonwhites, and 5.7 million (56.4 percent) were whites. The poor whites were much older on the average than the poor nonwhites. The proportion of poor persons 65 years old or older was 23.2 percent among whites, but only 6.8 percent among nonwhites.

3. Poverty was more than twice as prevalent among nonwhite families with female heads than among those with male heads, 57 percent compared to 21 percent. In central cities, 26 percent of all nonwhite families of two or more persons had female heads, as compared to 12 percent of white families.

4. Among nonwhite families headed by a female, and having children under 6, the incidence of poverty was 81.0 percent. Moreover, there were 243,000 such families living in poverty in central cities—or over 9 percent of all nonwhite families in those cities.

5. Among all children living in poverty within central cities, nonwhites outnumbered whites by over 400,000. The number of poor nonwhite children equalled or surpassed the number of white poor children in every age group.

Number of Children Living in Poverty (millions)

Age Group	White	Nonwhite	Percent of Total Nonwhite
Under 6	0.9	1.0	53%
6–15	1.0	1.3	57
16–21	0.4	0.4	50
Total	2.3	2.7	54%

Two stark facts emerge:

6. 54 percent of all poor children in central cities in 1964 were nonwhites;

7. Of the 4.4 million nonwhites living in poverty within central cities in 1964, 52 percent were children under 16, and 61 percent were under 21.

Since 1964, the number of nonwhite families living in poverty within central cities has remained about the same; hence, these poverty conditions are probably still prevalent in central cities in terms of absolute numbers of persons, although the proportion of persons in poverty may have dropped slightly.[3]

THE SOCIAL IMPACT OF EMPLOYMENT PROBLEMS IN DISADVANTAGED NEGRO AREAS

Unemployment and the Family

The high rates of unemployment and underemployment in racial ghettos are evidence, in part, that many men living in these areas are seeking but cannot obtain jobs which will support a family. Perhaps equally important, most jobs they can get are at the low end of the occupational scale, and often lack the necessary status to sustain a worker's self-respect, or the respect of his family and friends. These same men are also constantly confronted with the message of discrimination: "You are inferior because of a trait you did not cause and cannot change." This message reinforces feelings of inadequacy arising from repeated failure to obtain and keep decent jobs.

Wives of these men are forced to work, and usually produce more money. If men stay at home without working, their inadequacies constantly confront them and tensions arise between them and their wives and children. Under these pressures, it is not surprising that many of these men flee their responsibilities as husbands and fathers, leaving home, and drifting from city to city, or adopting the style of "street corner men."

Statistical evidence tends to document this. A close correlation exists between the number of nonwhite married women separated from their husbands each year and the unemploy-

Unemployment Rate and Participation in Total Labor Force, 25 to 54-Year-Old Nonwhite Men, by Marital Status, March 1967

	Unemployment Rate Nonwhite	Labor Force Participation (%) Nonwhite
Married, Wife Present	3.7	96.7
Other (Separated, Divorced, Widowed)	8.7	77.6

ment rate among nonwhite males 20 years old and over. Similarly, from 1948 to 1962, the number of new Aid to Families with Dependent Children cases rose and fell with the nonwhite male unemployment rate. Since 1963, however, the number of new cases—most of them Negro children— has steadily increased even though the unemployment rate among nonwhite males has declined. The impact of marital status on employment among Negroes is shown by the fact that in 1967 the proportion of married men either divorced or separated from their wives was more than twice as high among unemployed nonwhite men as among employed nonwhite men. Moreover, among those participating in the labor force, there was a higher proportion of married men with wives present than with wives absent.

Fatherless Families

The abandonment of the home by many Negro males affects a great many children growing up in the racial ghetto. As previously indicated, most American Negro families are headed by men, just like most other American families. Yet the proportion of families with female heads is much greater among Negroes than among whites at all income levels, and has been rising in recent years.

Proportion of Families of Various Types

| Date | Husband-Wife | | Female Head | |
	White	Nonwhite	White	Nonwhite
1950	88.0%	77.7%	8.5%	17.6%
1960	88.7	73.6	8.7	22.4
1966	88.8	72.7	8.9	23.7

This disparity between white and nonwhite families is far greater among the lowest income families—those most likely to reside in disadvantaged big-city neighborhoods—than among higher income families. Among families with incomes under $3,000 in 1966, the proportion with female heads was 42 percent for Negroes but only 23 percent for whites. In contrast, among families with incomes of $7,000 or more, 8 percent of Negro families had female heads compared to 4 percent of whites.

The problems of fatherless families are aggravated by the tendency of Negroes to have large families. This is characteristic of poor families generally. The average poor, urban nonwhite family contains 4.8 persons, as compared with 3.7 for the average poor, urban white family. This is one of the primary factors in the poverty status of nonwhite households in large cities.

The proportion of fatherless families appears to be increasing in the poorest Negro neighborhoods. In the Hough section of Cleveland, the proportion of families with female heads rose from 23 to 32 percent from 1960 to 1965. In the Watts section of Los Angeles it rose from 36 to 39 percent during the same period.

The handicap imposed on children growing up without fathers, in an atmosphere of poverty and deprivation, is increased because many mothers must work to provide support. The following table illustrates the disparity between the proportion of nonwhite women in the child-rearing ages who are in the labor force and the comparable proportion of white women:

*Percentage of Women
in the Labor Force*

Age Group	Nonwhite	White
20–24	55%	51%
25–34	55	38
35–44	61	45

With the father absent and the mother working, many ghetto children spend the bulk of their time on the streets— the streets of a crime-ridden, violence-prone and poverty-stricken world. The image of success in this world is not that of the "solid citizen," the responsible husband and father, but rather that of the "hustler" who takes care of himself by exploiting others. The dope sellers and the numbers runners are the "successful" men because their earnings far outstrip those men who try to climb the economic ladder in honest ways.

Young people in the ghetto are acutely conscious of a system which appears to offer rewards to those who illegally exploit others, and failure to those who struggle under traditional responsibilities. Under these circumstances, many adopt exploitation and the "hustle" as a way of life, disclaiming both work and marriage in favor of casual and temporary liaisons. This pattern reinforces itself from one generation to the next, creating a "culture of poverty" and an ingrained cynicism about society and its institutions.

The "Jungle"

The culture of poverty that results from unemployment and family disorganization generates a system of ruthless, exploitative relationships within the ghetto. Prostitution, dope addiction, casual sexual affairs, and crime create an environmental jungle characterized by personal insecurity and tension. The effects of this development are stark:

1. The rate of illegitimate births among nonwhite women has risen sharply in the past two decades. In 1940, 16.8 percent of all nonwhite births were illegitimate. By 1950 this proportion was 18 percent; by 1960, 21.6 percent; by 1966, 26.3 percent. In the ghettos of many large cities, illegitimacy rates exceed 50 percent.

2. The rate of illegitimacy among nonwhite women is closely

related to low income and high unemployment. In Washington, D.C., for example, an analysis of 1960 census tracts shows that in tracts with unemployment rates of 12 percent or more among nonwhite men, illegitimacy was over 40 percent. But in tracts with unemployment rates of 2.9 percent and below among nonwhite men, reported illegitimacy was under 20 percent. A similar contrast existed between tracts in which median nonwhite income was under $4,000 (where illegitimacy was 38 percent) and those in which it was $8,000 and over (where illegitimacy was 11 percent).

3. Narcotics addiction is also heavily concentrated in low-income Negro neighborhoods, particularly in New York City. Of the 59,720 addicts known to the U. S. Bureau of Narcotics at the end of 1966, just over 50 percent were Negroes. Over 52 percent of all known addicts lived within New York State, mostly in Harlem and other Negro neighborhoods. These figures undoubtedly greatly understate the actual number of persons using narcotics regularly—especially those under 21.

4. Not surprisingly, at every age from 6 through 19, the proportion of children from homes with both parents present who actually attend school is higher than the proportion of children from homes with only one parent or neither present.

5. Rates of juvenile delinquency, venereal disease, dependency upon AFDC support, and use of public assistance in general are much higher in disadvantaged Negro areas than in other parts of large cities. Data taken from New York City contrasting predominantly Negro neighborhoods with the city as a whole clearly illustrate this fact.

Social Distress—Major Predominantly Negro Neighborhoods in New York City and the City as a Whole

	Juvenile Delinquency[4]	Venereal Disease[5]	ADC[6]	Public Assistance[7]
Brownsville	125.3	609.9	459.0	265.8
East New York	98.6	207.5	148.6	71.8
Bedford Stuyvesant	115.2	771.3	337.1	197.2
Harlem	110.8	1,603.5	265.7	138.1
South Bronx	84.4	308.3	278.5	165.5
New York City	52.2	269.1	120.7	60.8

In conclusion: in 1965, 1.2 million nonwhite children under 16 lived in central city families headed by a woman

under 65. The great majority of these children were growing up in poverty under conditions that make them better
candidates for crime and civil disorder than for jobs providing an entry into American society.

THE AMERICAN LOWER CLASSES:
A TYPOLOGICAL APPROACH

S. M. Miller

IN RECENT years, increasing attention has been directed to
"the lower class"—those existing at the economic and social
margins of society. The current concern with the limited
economic prospects of dropouts,[1] the discussions of "hardcore" and "multi-problem" families,[2] the casualties of the
welfare state,[3] the analysis of the numbers living below the
"poverty line" in America[4] and the conditions of the "submerged fifth" in Britain[5]—all reflect the growing awareness
of the "underprivileged" in presumably affluent welfare societies of high industrialization.

Much confusion exists in these discussions. Those concerned with psychological and social dislocations ("disorganization" is the commonly used word) tend to understress the
importance of economic pressures, and those interested in
economic deprivation frequently discount the role of social
and psychological problems in preventing people from coping
with their difficulties. Who is or is not "lower class" is a moot

Reprinted with permission of the author and publisher from *Social
Research*, vol. 31, no. 1 (Spring 1964), pp. 1–22. As edited in the
volume entitled *Mental Health of the Poor*, Frank Reissman, Jerome
Cohen, and Arthur Pearl (eds.), Glencoe, Ill.: The Free Press, 1964,
pp. 139–154.

The author is indebted to the Louis M. Rabinowitz Foundation for
financial assistance. He has benefitted from the suggestions and
comments of Frank Riessman, Bernard Kramer, Bernard Goldstein,
Helen Icken Safa, and Jerome Cohen. A version of this paper was
presented at the annual meetings of the American Sociological Association, Los Angeles, August, 1963.

point, as different axes of demarcation are utilized. As I have explained elsewhere, I prefer to use terms like the "new working class" rather than that of the "lower class." Since most of the literature is couched in terms of the "lower class," I have used this term despite my objections to it.

A way of classifying a population is a way of thinking about them. A frequent practice is to classify that large number of people who are members of households where the breadwinner is not involved in some kind of white collar (i.e. middle class) occupation as "lower class."[6] This category is then considered to have high homogeneity and treated as though it constituted a group with great centrality of attitudinal and behavioral patterns. This orientation has probably led to much of the confusion and conflict in discussions of the characteristics of those at the lower end of the social structure. For example, the inconsistent child-rearing results may be due to the variations from study to study in those who are sampled as members of "the lower class."

It is becoming more common, though not a consistent practice, to mark off distinctions within the manual category. Frank Riessman and I[7] have argued that a working class of skilled and semi-skilled regular workers should be distinguished from unskilled, irregular workers who might be called "lower class." Preferably, the latter group might be called by less invidious terms like "the unskilled," "marginal workers" or "underprivileged workers," restricting this latter term of Allison Davis' to a narrow scope.[8] But even where a distinction is made between the "working class" and the "lower class," the criteria of classification are frequently obscure or conflicting.

Two approaches, not always clearly noted, are employed in defining the "lower class." One approach emphasizes the definition of groups in terms of "class" characteristics, especially economic role or income. The other employs "cultural" or "status" criteria such as style of life. The Hollingshead index—occupation, education, place of residence—is in the tradition of the first approach.[9] Walter Miller's discussion[10] of "the lower class subculture" is along the lines of the second. Social workers' discussions of "the lower class client" and the "multi-problem family" almost always employ style-of-life indicators.

The two approaches intertwine but seem to make independent contributions to elucidating the characterisics of the "lower class" or the poor. Consequently, I have brought them together in an effort to move away from a broadly and vaguely defined "lower class" into a specification of types of lower-class individuals. The effort is to utilize class and status variables in categorizing a population. The combination of the two produces problems, but these may be over-weighed by the difficulties and obscurities produced by the current shifting between the two sets of dimensions in discussing groupings and issues: Walter Miller's "lower class"[11] is not Lee Rainwater's.[12]

Obviously other dimensions like education or region should also be employed. Class and status dimensions should be more carefully marked off than in the following discussion. Unfortunately the material to do an adequate job is lacking. The purpose here is to show one way of approaching the problem of differentiation within the poor. The intent is to direct more attention to the recognition of variations among the poor.

THE CLASS CRITERION

The advantage of using an economic indicator in defining the lower class is that it specifies a political-economic category to which legislation and other remedial programs could be devoted. Emphasis on style-of-life indicators can be confusing because the meaning of an attitude or behavior or what it leads to can be quite different for the rich, for the middling well-off, for those "getting by" and for the poor. The same behavior may have different roots and consequences in varying milieus.

On the other hand, the class or occupational criterion is not as clear-cut as it appears. Some unskilled workers have stable, fairly well-paid jobs and are thus not a pressing social or economic problem. (This is particularly true where the unskilled worker is employed in a unionized, mass-production factory.) Many semi-skilled and fewer skilled workers suffer some degree of irregularity of employment, especially due to seasonal factors. Another problem is that a considerable number of poor families (35 per cent to 50 per cent) have no member in the labor force.[13]

Consequently, I would suggest that an income criterion is

more useful today than an occupational criterion in the definition of the lower class. The recent analyses of poverty in the United States can be employed for this purpose.[14] They show remarkable agreement, despite their different procedures, in estimating that one-quarter to one-fifth of the United States population lives below the poverty line. The level of income defining poverty varies depending on family size, composition, age, region, type of community. For our purposes, we can ignore these complexities and put the poverty line at $4,000 family income, following Keyserling. It is this population which, if we want to use the term, could be called "lower class" or "low income" or "the poor."

The advantage of utilizing the economic criterion, and particularly the income definition, is that it specifies a socioeconomic category towards which policy can be directed. For example, Morgan reports,[15] following Lampman's earlier lead, that 10 billion dollars would bring all spending units now below the poverty line to an income level above poverty. Questions of the distribution of income and of social services can be pinpointed then in terms of how they affect this particular population.

Obviously, income levels and sources of income vary considerably among the "low-income" population. Keyserling distinguishes between the very poor, the poor, and a higher income group who suffer what he terms "deprivation" but not outright poverty. What income level is used affects deeply the characteristics of the poor. Lampman uses lower income limits than Keyserling or Morgan. Consequently, he describes a poor population with 50 per cent of the heads of households out of the labor market, while the others, using a higher income level to define poverty, report only 35 per cent of the heads as out of the labor market. We do not have data but it is reasonable to deduce that a higher percentage of Lampman's poor are on welfare than is true of Morgan's or Keyserling's.

Clearly, different income cutoff points shape the characteristics of the "low income." The lower the income level used, the more economically and socially different are the poor.

Definitions of poverty and the poor are not technical problems but social and ideological issues. The low income are not basically a "welfare poor." Only one-fifth of Morgan's poor receive welfare assistance. The social scientists and social service specialists who write of the "welfare poor" are discussing only a slice of the poor; those concerned with "hard-core" and "multi-problem families" are, in turn, analyzing only a very thin wedge of this small slice.

The income criterion has several components: the level of income, the stability or regularity of income, the source of income (employment or welfare). A number of observers believe that it makes a difference, holding income constant, whether a family is supported by welfare or not. The knowledge to make a fine classification of these components is lacking. I have resorted therefore to combining them into one indicator of economic security (roughly combining income and stability), and then dichotomizing this indicator into the two simple dimensions of high (security) and low (insecurity). Lumping together these components and dichotomizing them is inadequate.[16] But we cannot at present describe each of the cells of what should be an 8-fold or 16-fold table. I think, however, that the cells of a 4-fold table can be usefully discussed. This capsulated table should rapidly be expanded as we acquire more knowledge and understanding.

THE STYLE-OF-LIFE CRITERION

The style-of-life variable also offers difficulties. It refers at least to attitudes and behavior in the areas of family relationships and consumption patterns. A major difficulty is that the content of the "lower class style-of-life" is debatable. Further, evaluative judgments (as implied in the concepts of "family disorganization," "social disorganization" or "family instability") are invariably involved. As yet, it is not possible to formulate a clean-cut classification which avoids cultural biases and still is able to render a judgment about the impact of life style on individuals. For example, does the absence of a permanent male figure mean that the family is inevitably "unstable" and that children are necessarily psychologically deformed by living in such a family? Assessments such as these are difficult to make because much of our knowledge and theorizing about fatherless families is based on middle-class situations.

I employ the notion of "familial stability/instability," a dichotomization of style of life, to summarize a variety of elements. Familial stability patterns are characterized by families coping with their problems—the children are being fed, though not necessarily on a schedule; the family meets its obligations so that it is not forced to keep on the move; children are not getting into much more trouble than other children of the neighborhood. These are not satisfactory indicators; they are, at best, suggestive of the kind of behavior which is characteristic of stability among the "low income." The aim is to be able to describe the degrees of effectiveness of different styles of life in handling the same environment. Our vocabulary is inadequate for this task.

CLASS AND STATUS

The two approaches can be welded together by crosstabling the two dimensions of the two variables of economic security and familial stability in a 2 × 2 table:

Types of Economic Security and Familial Stability

		Familial Stability	Familial Instability
		+	−
Economic	Insecurity +	+ +(1)	+ −(2)
	Security −	− +(3)	− −(4)

Cell 1 is referred to as the stable poor; cell 2, the strained; cell 3, the copers; and cell 4, the unstable.

To some extent, life-cycle stages may be involved here, as some young people escape from cell 4 via cell 2 or cell 3 to cell 1, a more stable pattern, and beyond. Or families may drop with age from cell 1 to cell 3, where they have lowered economic security but maintain family stability.

Each of the cells contains many variants. While I believe the four types are an improvement over analysis in terms of "*the* lower class," it is important to recognize that each type has many variations. One difference, of course, is whether the family is stationary in its particular pattern or moving to greater or less security-stability. *My general orientation is to emphasize flux rather than assuming a permanent position in a pattern.*

THE STABLE POOR

Cell 1 (*the stable poor*) is characterized by stability, economically and familially. This cell points to the regularly employed, low-skill, stable poor families.

Farm, rural and rural non-farm persons undoubtedly make up the bulk of the stable poor since they are the majority of the American poor: a re-calculation of Morgan's data suggests that only 30 per cent of the poor live in metropolitan areas. The majority of all the poor and of the stable poor are white rural Southern populations. In addition, the non-urban poor are probably represented in this cell to a greater extent than they are among all the poor. Aged persons are also over-represented and constitute a large part of the downwardly mobile poor since most of them were better off at earlier points in their lives. Leftover third generation immigrant populations in large cities are probably under-represented.[17]

A number of Negro families are of the stable poor. They have higher social status in the Negro community than their economic counterparts have in the white community because of the general scaling down of incomes and occupational levels of Negroes in the United States. For reasons discussed below, Negroes and other discriminated groups are probably becoming more important politically as well as in relative size among the urban stable poor.

The children of cell 1 families are most likely of all the children of the poor to be educationally and occupationally mobile. Cell 1 might be the "takeoff" cell, the phase necessary before many can really make a big advance. But this is a dangerous metaphor for obviously many youth from families in more difficult circumstances are able to make considerable gains.

The stable poor, then, are a varied group; one component, the aged, has a poor economic future, except to the extent that social security and old-age payments improve, and a declining future as an intact family unit.

THE STRAINED

Cell 2 (*the strained*) portrays a secure economic pattern, but an unstable family one. This might be a life-cycle problem, i.e., at certain points, the families of low-wage, unskilled workers are likely to exhibit unstable patterns. Examples might be "wild" younger workers or alcoholic older workers who disturb family functioning. Or, the pattern could manifest the beginning of a move into cell 4, as a low-income family finds increasing difficulty in maintaining its economic security because of family and personal problems or the economic situation. Obviously, the two possibilities may be closely connected.

Movement may be viewed inter-generationally as well as in terms of life-cycle patterns. Many of the offspring of strained families "may fail to match the economic security of their parents" and experience inter-generational skidding.[18]

Strained familial relations may not, however, result in skidding. In earlier periods, immigrant groups faced considerable internal strain arising from the conflict between the younger and older generations in the course of acculturation. Nonetheless, the second generation generally improved its economic circumstances. The instability of today's strained families is regarded as more "pathological" than that of the immigrant populations, although some social work accounts of families at the turn of the century differ little from current reports of "poor family functioning." The current stress is on fighting and drinking among parents, illicit sexual relations of parents, and neglect or brutality towards the children. Whether the economically secure and familially unstable are characterized by these patterns is not clear. If they are not, then, the offspring of the strained family may not be as prey to skidding. Further, not all children of deeply conflicted or hostile families are inevitably unable to maintain or improve their economic position.

I have looked at cell 2 as a transitional condition. This view may be misleading: many families persist with a low but steady income and a great deal of internal strain.

THE COPERS

The copers of cell 3 manifest economic insecurity and familial stability—families and individuals having a rough time economically but managing to keep themselves relatively intact. This group probably increases considerably during extensive layoffs. Probably a considerable number of Negroes are in this group and their children are more likely to be mobile than those living in cell 2-type situations.

This cell probably contains a disproportionate number of families which have been downwardly mobile. Both Morgan[19] and I[20] have shown the sizable number of sons of nonmanual workers who end up in manual (and sometimes low-income) positions. In Great Britain, 40 per cent of those born in non-manual families move into manual occupations. Many of these downwardly mobile are probably more likely to retain a stable family style than others in the same economic predicament. As in many other situations, however, a minority of the downwardly mobile may manifest extreme familial instability, which would place them in cell 4. Limited data suggest that children of downwardly mobile families have a better chance of rising occupationally than children of families which have been at this low level for some generations.[21]

THE UNSTABLE

In cell 4, *the unstable* have neither economic nor personal stability. It is this group which is probably most generally called "the lower class," and Jerome Cohen has suggested to me that the term "lower class" might be usefully restricted to this group. Since this recommendation is unlikely to be consistently utilized by social workers, economists, sociologists, political scientists and others interested in low-income populations, I have not adopted it, preferring to focus attention on the varied segments of the low-income population. Within the unstable group, there are degrees of stability and strain—*not every family is a "hard-core case" or has a "multi-agency problem."* Nor do we have sufficient longitudinal data to assert that once in cell 4, always in cell 4. It may be that families and individuals occasionally manifest both economic and personal instability, then overcome these problems for a while. Later they may again suffer from illness, unemployment, emotional upset, or familial instability.

As important in some ways as distinguishing cell 4 from the other three cells which make up the "lower class" is to note that cell 4 is a very varied grouping. In it are partially urbanized Negroes new to the North and cities, remaining slum residents of ethnic groups which have largely moved out of the slums, long-term (intergenerational) poor white families, the *déclassé* of Marx. Also included are the physically handicapped and the aged who have dropped through the class structure. *The low-income class generally and the unstable in particular is a category of unskilled, irregular workers, broken and large families, and a residual bin of the aged, physically handicapped, and mentally disturbed.*

In some cases, social characteristics handicap the low-income groups: recent rurality (unfamiliarity and lack of skills with urban problems) and discrimination. These groups —Negroes, former mountaineer whites—would have the worst problems. They would also have perhaps the greatest potential because removing their social limitations would lead to big change. Their handicaps are less self-inflicted and self-sustaining. This may not be as true for mountaineer whites as for Negroes. Aside from people dropping into the poverty class along the life-and-physical-cycle, the whites in the lower class who have no good, i.e., social, reason for being there are most likely to be intractable to change.

Hylan Lewis[22] has suggested the categories of clinical, pre-clinical and sub-clinical to delineate patterns among the poor. I would substitute the word "chronic" for "clinical." The chronics refer to the long-term dependents, part of whom would be the "hard-core"; the pre-chronics would be a high-risk group which are moving toward a chronic situation but have not yet become chronically dependent. The sub-chronics are those who have many characteristics of dependence but have a greater ability to cope with their problems.[23]

A number of forces can lead individuals into chronic dependence. *"Lower-class" life is crisis-life, constantly trying to make-do with string where rope is needed.* Anything can break the string. Illness is one of the most important—"Got a job but I got sick and lost it"; "We managed until the baby got sick." The great incidence of physical afflictions among the poor—frequently unknown to the victim—is obvious to any casual observer. Particularly striking are the poor teeth of many. The tendency of lower class people to somaticize their emotional difficulties may be influenced by the omnipresence of illness.

Familial and personal instability may be the sources as well as the consequences of difficulties. While some frequent concomitants of low income life such as matrifocality do not inevitably produce grave difficulties in family life, they frequently do. Alcoholism, an inability to handle aggression, hostility or dependence—one's own or others' toward one— can deeply disturb family functioning. A variety of direct personal aid may be necessary.

Sophistication along these lines of analysis has frequently tended to denigrate the importance of structural factors in producing "personal inadequacies," "social disabilities," "familial instability." The work of Raymond Smith[24] and Edith Clarke[25] strongly suggests that illegitimacy is related to economic conditions—the better the economic conditions among the "lower class" Negroes of the Caribbean, the lower the rate of illegitimacy. Kunstadter[26] similarly argues that matrifocality as a "lower class" trait is related to a particular set of economic characteristics.

Prolonged unemployment, irregular employment, low income are important forces leading to a chronic pattern. Low-paid and irregularly employed individuals do not develop an image of the world as predictable and as something with which they are able to cope. Controlling or directing events appears (and frequently is) an unattainable achievement. When they suffer long-term unemployment, they are less likely than other unemployed who have had the experience of fairly regular employment, to maintain a personal stability. (Maslow[27] has argued that those who have had a stable past are more able to manage in disastrous circumstances than those who have had considerable prior deprivation.) A high-employment economy has relatively fewer "hard-core" cases than a low-employment economy. The American community studies suggest that the "lower class" is smaller in numbers in times of prosperity than in periods of depression. Peter Townsend in an informal lecture recently declared that during the 1930's in England it was believed that 500,000 to 1,000,000 of those not working were "unemployable." In 1940 with the pressures of the war, it was discovered that only 100,000 were really unemployables. Structural change would be of great importance in reducing chronic dependence.

STRATEGIES

Three basic policies are possible: (1) direct economic change, such as providing better employment, or directly raising incomes through the provision of a national minimum level of income; (2) direct services, such as case-work activities to strengthen the ego-functioning of the individual or family assistance through home-maker help; (3) indirect change by affecting the climate—social, psychological, political—of the neighborhoods in which the poor live.

What would lead one type of a low-income population in a given direction would not work at all for another type. A panacea does not work because there is no one thing which will have a pervasive impact in all cases if changed. What is dynamic for one type may be insignificant for others.

I find the concept of elasticity useful here.[28] It points to the extent of change resulting from input of additional services or income. Some types of the poor have high income elasticity—a little change in income produces a big change in behavior; other types may have low income elasticity but have high education elasticity or high casework elasticity. Still other types will respond rapidly and deeply to new housing, to a steady job, to counseling, or a package of such ingredients rather than to, say, casework. The concept of elasticity introduces frontally the issues of variable remedies for different types. The issues of costs, substitution and choice of different services or resources are made vivid by the notion of elasticity and productivity (the return per unit of expenditure).

The stable, those in cell 1, would be immediately helped if their incomes were raised so that they came closer to the American standard of life. Unionization of their industries (especially in service trades and occupations), shifts from low productivity land and industries to high productive industries, and occupational retraining would be important. In some situations, individuals have to be prepared for retraining (where, for example, the level of literacy is low) or aided in moving to new localities where opportunities are greater. They may need help in adjusting to new urban conditions, but this adjustment would probably not be very difficult where jobs and housing are adequate. The stable poor, in short, would have a high income elasticity, rapidly improving and adjusting to increases in their income.

The inadequacy of social services and payments in the United States forces many into cell 1. Improving and extending social security, which keeps many in penury and does not help a substantial number in noncovered occupations and industries, would move many from cells 2, 3, and 4 into cell 1 and lead many of the stable poor into the main society. Harrington[29] and Titmuss[30] have pointed out that social services in the United States and Britain do not seem to be benefitting the poor as much as the middle income. Obviously, changes in social policy are necessary here.

Some of the strained of cell 2 might require some casework help in improving family conditions and operations, but other approaches might be effective. If they live in a locality that manifests high rates of disturbances, they might be helped by moving to new areas. For some, an improvement in economic conditions may be necessary in order to get deeper family changes. Undoubtedly, a number are not sensitive to income changes or to neighborhood climate change and sustained casework help would be necessary.

Familial instability may be a carryover from an earlier period when the family suffered from economic insecurity; the family has not caught up with its economic improvements. But, as Seymour S. Bellin and Jerome Cohen have pointed out, in some families where economic conditions have improved after a long period of economic deprivation and family difficulties, withdrawing the stress of economic insecurity may be insufficient. The toll of the stress frequently must be overcome. Special help may be necessary to bring about familial changes of great importance. The adaptation of social agencies would be important so that they are able to meet the requirements of these families at the time of need and to provide aid in ways which fit the outlook of these families.

The copers of cell 3, who maintain family stability in the face of grave economic difficulties, obviously need economic aid. Many of them would be helped by improvement in welfare payments and practices; others, where there is a working head of household, would be advanced by regularization of work and/or shifting to more remunerative fields. The needs of the stable and the copers would seem to be similar. Improvement on the economic dimension would push more of the copers into the mobility possibilities of the stable poor of cell 1 and beyond.

Cell 4, the unstable, is the most discussed grouping of the poor today. Many, if not most, are on welfare allotments; women head many of the family units. A general improvement in economic conditions would not have much economic impact on the unstable because they are largely out of the labor force and out of the economy. It is widely believed that unstable families do not have a high income elasticity but the evidence is not strong. Specific programs aimed at this group would be important. Present-day welfare services are insufficient since they have largely been budgetary and policing activities. Concentration on improving the educational achievement of the youth of these families would be more important perhaps than a diffuse effort to achieve better family functioning.[31] A number of interesting and aggressive casework services have been offered; their degree of long-term success is unclear. A variety of direct services may be effective with some of these families —including continuous homemaking and baby-sitting services, provisions of nurseries, all-day schools, and consumer buying protection.

It may be that a less direct approach would be effective. It would involve trying to mobilize politically the communities in which the unstable live with the more stable poor so as to provide greater feelings of strength and control. The anticipated but side effect would be the improving of family conditions. A general change in a low income community precipitated perhaps by the mobile, the strained, and the copers may spread to affect the unstable of the community. The social actionists, of whom Saul Alinsky is the best-known, have this implicit strategy.

In all of the strategies it is necessary to be clear about who exactly is the target population. This is frequently determined on the basis of the numbers involved, though there is always the delicate choice of helping a lot of people a little or a few people a lot. The second step is to discover what works with whom. There is probably nothing that will help all "lower class" people in one move although, as suggested above, a steady, meaningful, well-paid job as a general base of action should not be underestimated. A decent level of living as the minimal responsibility of an affluent society, no matter what people do around this level, may be an important point to maintain in a period when government welfare payments are under criticism. But there are some things that will help certain types. We have to find the right things for the right groups at the right time.

POLITICAL ACTION

The poor are not rapidly declining; income and wealth inequality appear to be increasing in recent years; the incomes of Negroes are no longer advancing relative to those of whites; pension and assistance schemes are maintaining many in poverty rather than providing a "Welfare State" standard. The decline in the number of poor between 1947 and 1957 has been due, Lampman contends, to general economic advance rather than to a redistribution of income and wealth in favor of the poor. Improvements in social services and a decrease in inequality would require a shift in the allocation of national product towards improving the relative position of the bottom 20 per cent.

These issues are political ones. They will be affected by the possibility that the present American poor may prove to be more politically active than is usually true of the poor. If this happens, it will be because a large slice of the urban poor is made up of Negroes who have ethnic as well as economic forces moving them. Samuel Lubell[32] has argued that Negroes in large cities will furnish a new base for Democratic ward machines. They are becoming more and more politically active and demanding. This self-organization is not only important in getting changes from the government, but it is also serving to change "lower-class" Negro communities from within. Local leaders are developing and the orientation of many community agencies to provide leadership and direction to "lower-class" communities will become increasingly ineffective. The conservative orientation of gaining change and social advance through an harmonious arrangement with local power forces is being superseded by disadvantaged groups themselves actively pressuring for the kinds of changes—in housing, in schools and the like—that they believe to be important.

In the course of these pressures, it is likely that the *desegregation issue will emerge as a social class issue* affecting all "lower-class" persons, and not only as a racial issue affecting Negroes alone. Mexican-Americans and Puerto Ricans, who with Negroes increasingly make the poor of the large metropolis a "colored poor," are increasingly moving into the stable and coping patterns and beginning to develop political effectiveness. Poverty may not be treated as a racial issue affecting only Negroes. *Even where Negroes operate alone, the impact of their demands will affect all the poor as they achieve better schools, better housing, better jobs, better social services.*

CAUSE AND CONSEQUENCE

A good deal of the tone of discussions of the "lower class," even by sociologists, has a negative quality. On the other hand, a few seem to have a romantic feeling about the "lower class," particularly their juvenile delinquents, and see them as rebels against the horrors of middle-class, conformist America. The former view suffers from the assumption that they have little potential for change; the latter, that there is nothing better in present-day America to which they can change.

Among other things, the glorification theme ignores, as Riessman has pointed out, the impact on the "lower class" of its limited education.[33] The negative view frequently confuses, as Keyserling has noted, cause and consequence. The personal instability of many "lower-class" persons may be a consequence of economic instability as well as a cause of it. The chain of cause-and-effect over time frequently becomes blurred. Where is there an effective way of cutting into the chain so that change will occur?—that becomes the issue. My feeling is that structural forces have been underplayed recently as a mode of change, as "the culture of poverty" has been overstressed.[34]

The negative view has the danger of not seeing positive elements in "lower-class" life. By ignoring these elements, social policies can frequently worsen them. For example, in

an exciting study of a Puerto Rican slum, Helen Icken Safa
has reported the community and familial solidarity of the
residents of a slum barrio. When families were moved into
public housing, community ties were weakened. The project
social workers centered on the wife. The husband's role and
responsibility in the family and community diminished.[35]

It is perhaps a "heuristic" fallacy, as Frank Riessman has
said, to believe that "lower-class" people are willing and
capable of positive change. This is not always true, but if
professionals and social reformers lack confidence in the
poor, little can be accomplished in the social services or in
political action. One might fail with this optimism—as we
frequently do—but without it, it is doubtful if anything can
be moved. Frequently, disenchantment and cynicism capture
accurately a slice of life. They are also immobilizing, for
they ignore the constructive and energizing role of hope.[36]

CONCLUSION

A clearly defined "lower class" does not exist—it is a
varied, changing group as Peter Townsend has noted:

A misconception is that in a relatively prosperous society most
individuals have the capacity to meet any contingency in life.
Only a poor and handicapped minority need special protection or
help. This ignores the infinite diversities and changing conditions
to be found in any population. Men gain or fall in status and
living standards; at one stage of their life their dependencies
are minimal, at others unduly numerous; sometimes they need
exceptional help to achieve qualifications and skills held to be
desirable by society; and at all times they are susceptible to the
vicissitudes of prolonged ill health, disability, redundancy of
unemployment, and bereavement which they are usually powerless to control or even resonably anticipate. Unanticipated ad-
versity is not the peculiar experience of one fixed section of the
working class.[37]

In England, Dahrendorf contends,[38] the unskilled category
is a temporary position—individuals at various stages of the
life cycle may drop into it, but for only a comparatively few
is it a permanent position. In the United States, this is not
as true, and if caste pressures grow, it will be even less true.

The changing economy of America is producing new property relations; at the same time it is producing new working

classes and lower classes.[39] The analysis of data and the development of our concepts have not kept up with the increasing differentiation within these populations. Many pressures and counter-pressures exist in any stratum. Despite a modal pattern, considerable variety in values and behavior occurs. Since cross-pressures affect the "lower class" to a considerable extent,[40] we should look for *types* of behavior patterns even among people apparently very similar in objective characteristics. Those at the social bottom see only a vague and ill-defined "them" up there—and those above believe that those below are all rather similar. But the tops know how much differentiation within the top actually takes place; the bottoms are aware of much more differentiation than are the outsiders looking in. In particular, what has been taken as typical of the most unstable bottom-group has been generalized to apply to all who are poor or manual workers.

The label—"the lower class"—increasingly distorts complicated reality. We must begin to demarcate types of poor people more sharply if we are to be able to understand and interpret behavior and circumstance and to develop appropriate social policies. Evaluations of commentators are frequently masked as description. *Ways of coping with hard reality are interpreted as normatively prescribed when they frequently are weakly dissanctioned behavior.*

The resurgence of interest in the poor augurs well for a re-thinking of the new kind of poverty in the "Welfare State," which is unlike the mass unemployment of the 1930's or the grinding poverty of the employed workers of the 19th century. Our "received wisdom" should be superseded by new categories and concepts. New wine is being poured into old conceptual bottles and the specialness of the new is being lost.

THE PROBLEMS OF FAMILIES
IN THE AFDC PROGRAM

Paul H. Glasser and Elizabeth L. Navarre

MRS. SMITH is the 42-year-old mother of 13 children. Born and reared in the Deep South, she migrated to the Detroit area in late adolescence in search of work during World War II. Despite only a fifth-grade education, she readily found employment during this period of labor shortage and continued to work in an unskilled job until after the war ended and she began having children.

Her children range in ages from 3 to 25. The first six were born when Mrs. Smith was married to a man whom she later divorced because of his drinking. A passing flirtation led to the birth of her seventh child. However, the last six children are all the children of the same father. This man, now no longer in the picture, has never contributed more than intermittently to the family's support.

Mrs. Smith receives the maximum allowance given in the Federal-State aid to families with dependent children program (AFDC) of the Michigan State Department of Social Welfare. This grant is supplemented by the general relief and surplus foods programs of the local welfare department. Nevertheless, Mrs. Smith still has a hard time making ends meet. The family lives in an old and crowded tenement building in need of repair, in a neighborhood where there is much crime and delinquency. The children are not always properly clothed or fed, and some of them are badly in need

Reprinted with permission of the authors from *Children*, vol. 12, no. 4 (July–August 1965), pp. 151–157.

A report based upon research sponsored by Children's Bureau Grant No. D–16. Reprinted with the permission of the authors and the United States Children's Bureau. This analysis is the responsibility of the authors, and not of the Michigan State Department of Social Welfare or its staff.

of medical or dental care. Often they do not have enough money for their school supplies and laboratory fees.

Poverty is obviously an omnipresent problem in the Smith family. But poverty in this family, as in many of the 9.3 million families in this country with incomes under $3,000, is a reflection of a complex of other problems. Some of these have been noted in a congressional report:

A closer examination of the statistics regarding poverty shows the scars of discrimination, lack of education, and broken homes. Of the poor, 22 per cent are nonwhite and nearly one-half of all nonwhites live in poverty. The heads of over 60 per cent of all poor families have only a grade school education. . . .[1]

While sharing the complex problems of poverty with a host of other families, the Smith family experiences these problems in its own ways, and has its own strengths and weaknesses to help or impede its effort to break out of the poverty chain. In addition to money, it needs services to tip the balance in favor of the strengths—services based on an understanding of the family's own perceptions of its problems and how these may be overcome, as well as on the perceptions of the experts.

In preparation for the development of a special service program for families in the AFDC program in Detroit, the University of Michigan School of Social Work has undertaken an exploration in the mothers' perceptions of their problems and how well these correspond with the view of the public welfare workers and social scientists. The undertaking is part of a project being carried out in the department by the school, with a federal grant from the Children's Bureau, to demonstrate the utility of the social group-work method in a public welfare setting.[2]

In this project, mothers in the AFDC program were invited to form discussion groups, each group to focus on one area, such as the mother's employment opportunities, the adjustment problems of families with incapacitated fathers, child-rearing difficulties, and school problems. The groups met weekly for 6 to 12 sessions. Leaders, drawn from the agency's personnel and students of the School of Social Work, were closely supervised by an experienced social group worker.

We quickly learned that in order to provide an effective service, we need to know more about the families' problems and their origins from the viewpoints of clients, workers, and social scientists. The following findings are based on preliminary data gathered during 1963–1964 and a review of the literature. More complicated data, gathered in 1965, are now in the process of analysis.

THE CLIENTS' VIEW

We constructed an open-end, probe-type questionnaire eliciting information about the immediate problems of applicants for and recipients of AFDC (hereafter called clients) and their plans for solving them. Included were such questions as "What has worried you most during the past few weeks?" and "What have you been trying to do about this problem?" The questionnaire was administered to 16 applicants to the program after the completion of the regular intake interview. A similar questionnaire was administered during the same period to 17 mothers in the group sessions focused on the mothers' employment problems.

The problems mentioned by mothers in the two samples were similar, except that employment problems, as would be expected, were mentioned more often by those attending the group meetings.

As anticipated, many of the participating women described concrete problems. Fifty-eight per cent of the problems mentioned involved the need for money, either in general or for specific purposes such as medical care or school clothes. This percentage included the 16 per cent of the problems mentioned that were concerned with the mothers' own employment difficulties or those of their husbands, and the 13 per cent that were concerned with poor living quarters or the necessity of living with relatives.

One-quarter of all the problems delineated had to do with children. (Some of these were also included in the 58 per cent involving the need for money.) Among the specific difficulties mentioned were dressing children adequately for school, locating a good baby sitter, and the effects on a child of living in a crowded home with quarreling relatives. In addition, a good deal of general anxiety about the children's future was expressed, especially in relation to the lack of a father in the home, the mother's inability to give children the things they needed or wanted, and fear of not being able to rear the children properly.

Somewhat less expected was the degree of concern about health, the focus of 19 per cent of the problems mentioned. Many women expressed worry about specific conditions and the out-of-reach cost of needed medical or dental care. Some mentioned their own and their husband's inability to work because of ill health, and some expressed worry about having nobody to care for their children if they became ill. Four of the women said they had a "nervous" condition. Women whose husbands were incapacitated saw problems in the effect of the man's illness upon relationships within the family and in their own ability to accept the role of household head and breadwinner.

Few of the respondents said much about marital problems, possibly because of the shortness of the interviews. In general, when marital problems were mentioned they were expressed as hurt over divorce or desertion, hope for reconciliation (though the husband may have been gone for several years), or unhappiness over the actions of an estranged husband. One woman said flatly that if she could remarry, all her problems would be solved.

While much anxiety was expressed about specific areas of social functioning, almost one-fourth (23 per cent) of the problems mentioned indicated the existence of a more or less generalized anxiety about the present or the future. Nevertheless, few respondents indicated having plans for alleviating their problems or any idea where they might get help with them. Even the few who said they had made plans or knew where they could get help expressed little hope of improvement. It is possible that the client's very anxiety about her problems prevents her from doing anything about them.

In summary, our inquiry indicated, not unexpectedly, that the mothers involved saw the scarcity of money as their major problem. They apparently felt helpless about the situation they were in and knew of no way to get out of it. They revealed little awareness that a part of their problem might have been their own inability to call on the personal and

situational resources at their disposal. However, they did
show concern about the effects of their present circumstances
on their children.

THE WORKERS' VIEW

Workers' perspectives are colored both by agency policy
and the attitudes of the public at large. At times their views
reflect the inconsistencies of both these frames of reference,
particularly since the emphasis in the program is changing
from income maintenance to rehabilitation.

In the study, the opinions of the agency's caseworkers and
supervisors were sought in two staff meetings. The lists of
problems turned in by the caseworkers, when recommending
clients for participation in the social group-work meetings,
constituted another source of information.

We found that the caseworker tends to see most clearly
what the client sees least clearly: that in many instances
the client's inadequacy in using her resources led to her present problems and is at least partially responsible for her
inability to get out of the situation she is in. The caseworkers
describe the clients as living from day to day, or even in the
past, as if their ambitions and hopes had ended with the
crisis that led to the application for public assistance. Some
are described as immature, emotionally unstable, alcoholic,
or unmoral, some as being pleasure-bent with little or no
interest in their children, their homes, or employment. Others
are described as tending to give their children excessive protection, but, paradoxically, seeming unaware that irresponsible behavior in other areas of life may also affect their
children. Other problems mentioned were poor budgeting of
funds, unwise buying, poor housekeeping, and carelessness
in the physical care of children.

At the same time, the caseworkers recognized the fact that
most of the women in the program have problems that are
unrelated to their morals and values. They also recognized
that those women with questionable values have never experienced, and do not now see evidence of, any other kind. They
pointed out that many clients in seeking employment are
handicapped by real problems, such as inadequate child-care
facilities, transportation difficulties, poor personal appearance, chronic ill health, and lack of education and skills.

They pointed out that, for many clients, employment offers no real economic advantages unless it is steady and secure and the money earned is budgeted for an unmet need rather than deducted from the assistance grant.

The workers expressed particular concern for the children in the program, most of whom are living in broken homes. They mentioned the lack of appropriate opportunities for male identification for boys in fatherless homes. They expressed somewhat less concern about the psychological effects that divorce, desertion, or illegitimate pregnancy may have upon the mothers themselves or about their difficulties in trying to do a job generally carried out by two persons. However, they did point out that the women in the AFDC program are lonely women who have few social outlets. One caseworker suggested that society may be expecting higher moral standards of these women than are common in the general population. Many others expressed concern not only for the children in the program but also for their mothers, and gave evidence of wanting to help them.

SOCIOLOGICAL FACTORS

From the sociological point of view, a mother who receives public aid is a deviant in several ways. She is a member of the lower class in a society where middle-class values predominate. She is supported by public funds in a society in which self-support is the tradition. Unless she is one of the mothers who is in the program because her husband is incapacitated, she is rearing children without a father present in a society whose acceptance of the broken home is much stronger in print than in actuality. She is apt to be poorly educated and may be of less than average intelligence. With all these strikes against her, she is expected to live on an income which is no more than minimal by any standards and less than minimal by many.

Social scientists point out that one of the strongest determinants of an individual's chances in life is his position in the class structure.[3] In a sense, social class defines the individual's responses to the major social pressures. Lacking the partial protection that money, power, or personal influence can give, the child born into a family poor in money, education, and skills is more vulnerable than others to the vicissitudes of life. His chances for getting a good education are poor for several reasons. He receives less than normal encouragement and enrichment in the home, and possibly also less than normal in school, for cultural deprivation may give an appearance of stupidity even to a bright child. In addition, the school system may be dominated by middle-class values to such an extent that neither the content nor methods of the teaching are effective with a child from a different background.[4, 5]

The poorly educated person finds few employment opportunities open to him, and these decrease as technological advances eliminate more and more unskilled jobs. Such jobs as are open to him are the least desirable ones in terms of pay, job security, working conditions relevant to health and safety, and fringe benefits, such as insurance and sick leave. Frequent layoffs are likely, and savings to tide the family over a crisis are almost impossible to come by.

Having less access to adequate medical care throughout his life than most people, the person of low socioeconomic status is more prone to illness. Since his employment often requires physical labor, he can become incapacitated by a physical condition that would not be incapacitating to persons in more sedentary work. His poor education and lack of skills make him less adaptable to new occupations after an economic crisis.[6]

The income of the families in the AFDC program is at the lower limits of low incomes. Housing is, of necessity, usually in cheap rental units where the condition of the building may create problems in housekeeping and in efforts to make the home attractive. Drab and deteriorating housing, depressing both adults and children, often discourages women from any effort to improve their homes. Overcrowding in the homes of relatives, not uncommon in families in the AFDC program, not only requires greater physical effort in housekeeping but also creates problems in family relations.

Thus, economic need affects every part of daily life.

Receiving support from public funds is not an unmixed blessing. This is particularly true for the mothers in the AFDC program, a program long the target of much public disapproval. The uniform minimum standards of need limit the amount of any additional income they may receive without having their AFDC payments reduced. Thus, a mother cannot raise her family's economic level above poverty standards unless she is able to take on the entire burden of the family's support.

PSYCHOLOGICAL FACTORS

Among the most pervasive effects of social class status are the attitudes and values instilled in children. Not only are differences in opportunity perpetuated in each succeeding generation, but a style of life and a value system commensurate with the realities of the position are also perpetuated. Many studies have shown class differentials in child-rearing practices,[7] health practices,[8] living patterns,[9] and attitudes toward sex.[10] Current theories of child development indicate that such differences experienced as children will produce psychological differences in adults, differences which tend to maintain adults in the socioeconomic status of their childhood.

Rainwater, Coleman, and Handel have studied the attitudes of women of lower socioeconomic status.[11] Presumably, the AFDC clients are similar to these women, with two important exceptions: the AFDC recipients must live on an income considerably below that of the women these investigators studied, and most of the women in the AFDC program have gone through marital crises.

The women studied by Rainwater and associates regarded themselves as acted upon rather than acting. They saw the world as unchangeable. Such a woman responds only when she is approached in terms that are "specific, clearly defined, and readily understood." She feels helpless in the face of a chaotic world; she does not reach out to it. Seeing what happens in life as based on luck or fate rather than on her own actions, she has a "fairly pervasive anxiety over possible fundamental deprivations."

Such a woman does not lack hope, for luck may also be good, but she does not expect to be personally successful against forces she cannot control. Her gratifications tend to come from her own limited world of husband and children. She likes to be "needed." Yet, again, she does not see herself as having effective power over her husband and little over her children after their babyhood. She greatly fears loneliness.

What then must be the psychological state of the AFDC recipient who divorced from or deserted by the father of her children, is in the midst of a crisis of the type most feared by women of low socioeconomic status? Surely the sense of a chaotic world, of personal inadequacy, and of anxiety over future catastrophe must be increased.

One may assume that the dissolution of a family unit is a traumatic experience whatever the emotional relationship of the adults involved. Regardless of any other emotions, the very fact that the relationship has failed tends to lower the self-esteem of both husband and wife. Social disapproval often complicates the adjustment. A woman who has been deserted or divorced against her will might be expected to have a sharp sense of personal failure and inferiority as well as a good deal of bitterness, which may be turned either outward upon the former spouse or inward upon the self. When the woman has to depend upon public funds for support, the sense of inadequacy may be aggravated and may, in turn, heighten the helpless and dependent attitudes fostered by the lifetime experiences encountered by persons of low socioeconomic status.

MOTHERS AS FAMILY HEADS

The mother who has become head of the family through divorce, widowhood, or the incapacity of the husband is a focal point for many of the conflicts in the value system of society. Society's expectations of her, as well as her own, are apt to be confused and contradictory. A woman should work to support herself, rather than become dependent, but a mother should stay home and take care of her children. A woman should help her family in any way possible, but her role in marriage should be that of a dependent and relatively subordinate partner. A woman may work so long as her children are well cared for, but society is not obligated to help her arrange for the day care of her children. A woman alone must be strong enough to take over the paternal role of breadwinner and disciplinarian while maintaining her own role as housekeeper and mother; yet she must remain feminine enough to prevent her children from receiving a distorted conception of the feminine role in social relationships.

Women of low socioeconomic status who are heads of families face additional difficulties. Some have many children whose care leaves them little time for a companionable and educational relationship with them. However, such women are apt to look for gratification from their children in present affection rather than in future achievement.

Such women tend to be interested in broad categories of behavior such as "being good" and "being healthy," but feel helpless about influencing the details of their children's behavior. When there is no father in the home, their tendency to protectiveness, rather than the fostering of development, becomes further exaggerated. Since the home is the source of the woman's satisfaction, the attention once given to the husband may be transferred to the children. The paradox of overprotectiveness and extreme permissiveness often found in the homes of women of low socioeconomic status may be due to the passive attitudes of the mother toward life in general and toward the children's behavior in particular.[12, 13, 14]

Women of low socioeconomic status are not joiners; the world must come to them. Such tendencies toward isolation intensify the loneliness of the female head of the household. A woman without a man is a proverbial fifth wheel in many social activities. Yet a mother who goes out with a man must be extremely circumspect in her activities, particularly if she is a recipient of public aid, or the suitability of her home may be questioned. Even when the social activity is irreproachable, the problem remains of finding a baby sitter she can afford.

In addition, mothers in the AFDC program who are raising their children alone face the same problems confronting any woman in this situation. How can they provide male identification for their children? What priorities must they set upon their time and energies? In short, how does one play two full-time roles concurrently?

The conflicts implicit in the social role of a mother in the AFDC program, and the contradictory and often ambiguous demands society makes upon the woman who is rearing children without a father in the home, are likely to create a paralyzing level of anxiety in the individual. Studies have indicated that persons subject to conflicting forces are likely to react not with "goal-directed activity" but rather with "restlessness, a desire to leave the field, aggressive feelings, toward himself and others and so on."[15]

Such a level of anxiety may become a problem in itself. It may be the source of the tendency to live in the present, and of the pleasure-bent behavior noted by the caseworker in our study. It may prevent clients from making greater use of the resources available to them.

THE PRACTITIONER'S PROBLEM

The views of the client, the social worker, and the social scientist overlap, although there are differences in emphasis both within and among groups. Nevertheless, all three groups have the same goals for the family in the AFDC program: financial independence and emotional security.

The problem the practitioner faces is to find a way to help the family to achieve these interlocking goals. The clients' complex, interrelated problems cannot be reduced to a simple cause-and-effect formula. All of the major factors seem to be both causes and effects, like the chicken and the egg. However, the circular cause-effect relationship may well mean that changes accomplished by intervention in one area of life will, in turn, affect many other areas. Therefore, the practitioner needs an integrated view of the family, adding to his own observations the perspectives of the client and the social scientist.

With these perspectives, he will find that each family requires a somewhat different rehabilitation plan. He may need to deal with pressing situational factors by helping parents and children secure the clothing, housing, and medical care necessary for maintaining the kind of standard in their daily living under which they can build the self-confidence required to help themselves in other ways. He may need to help parents and children to improve their education and skills by referring them to training or retraining programs or working with school personnel. He may also find need to deal, through referral or directly, with the many psychological factors impeding the family's solution of its problem. Some mothers may require counseling through group-work and casework methods in order to change attitudes and values that are detrimental to themselves or to their children's development. Some may also need help in learning how best to carry out the dual role of mother and family head and in weathering the unusual stresses this entails. Some children may need special help with emotional problems.

This review suggests several foci requiring special attention. One is the problem of psychological passivity, which in so many families in the AFDC program not only inhibits efforts toward solving immediate problems, but also affects the quality of parental control over children and the quality of the self-image internalized by the children. Another is the need for helping families develop techniques of living in a manner acceptable to society and advantageous to the physical health and the well-being of the family, techniques their past experiences have not given them an opportunity to develop. A third is the need for defining the appropriate role for lone parents and for recognizing the structural limitations as well as the psychological elements in the one-parent family.

Effective intervention at the individual or family level requires a framework of appropriate public social policy. It must be adequate to the need and involve a strategy that takes account of the complexity of the problem. Whatever the nature of the problem it attacks—sociological, psychological, or social-psychological—the problem areas are so interrelated that intervention in any one can affect the others if it is planned from an all-encompassing perspective.

The important thing is to build on the family's strengths, for, with the help of appropriate community resources, many families in the AFDC program have succeeded in improving their situation. For example, let us take another look at the Smith family:

Mrs. Smith gives her children the best physical care possible in her circumstances. Her oldest son is a college graduate and her two older daughters are presently in college. The family is closely knit. When told that he was not obligated to help his half-brothers and sisters, the oldest son said that he paid no attention to that: "They are my brothers and sisters and I will help them as much as I can."

Mrs. Smith has been a member of one of the mothers'

groups focused on helping parents maximize the school experience for their children. She has contributed generously to the formation of more useful attitudes on the part of other group members while receiving a good deal of support for her own efforts.

SOME IMPEDIMENTS TO THE EDUCATION
OF DISADVANTAGED CHILDREN

Norma L. Radin

IN OUR industrial society, the educational institution is virtually the only legitimate channel to upward mobility for young people from families of very low socioeconomic status. Literacy and an understanding of the basic mathematical functions are the minimum requirements for any but the most dead-end jobs. Self-restraint, reliability, and punctuality are also expected and the most conclusive proof of their existence to employers is a high school diploma. Thus, if children of the extremely poor are to share in an affluent society's material and symbolical rewards as adults, plans for their future must include a high school education.

The foundation for academic success at high school age is laid by the time the child is 8 or 9 years of age. If the foundation is week, the edifice constructed upon it will be extremely shaky. The tragedy is that the public school system is often far from effective in laying this foundation in children from families of very low socioeconomic status. I refer here and throughout this article not to families of blue-collar workers such as the man on the automobile assembly line, but to families characterized by chronic unemployment, underemployment, and disorganization—the problem-ridden

Reprinted with permission of the author from *Children,* vol. 15, no. 5 (September–October 1968), pp. 171–176.

Preparation of this article was partially supported by grant No. 67–042490 from the Office of Education, under Title III, Elementary and Secondary Education Act of 1965.

families who live in dilapidated, overcrowded housing and suffer from poor health, powerlessness, and despair. Even then I do not mean to imply that all such families are alike, and that none of their children can surmount the educational difficulties presented. I recognize, too, that in the past few years State and Federal funds available to the schools for compensatory education—especially those appropriated under Title I of the Elementary and Secondary Education Act—are producing some changes, but it is still too early to determine how effective or pervasive these changes are. However, the statements that follow probably still apply to most of the schools in this country that are in neighborhoods where large numbers of seriously disadvantaged children live.

Many discerning educators and research workers are focusing their efforts on strategies for making school programs more effective generally with the children of such families. These efforts, however, have been directed in many different directions, sometimes producing contradictory results. Rosenthal and Jacobson have found that the teacher's initial expectations about a child's achievement correlate with the child's subsequent achievement.[1] Coleman and associates found that mixing children from middle-income families with children from very low socioeconomic backgrounds in school classrooms seems to increase the school performance of the latter.[2] Clark believes that if teachers raise their standards for children of very low socioeconomic status their performance will improve.[3] Cloward found that using children from low socioeconomic backgrounds to tutor young students of similar backgrounds improves the achievement of both groups.[4] Suppes sees a need for computerized instruction.[5] Bereiter noted 20-point gains in the IQ's of children who were included in a highly structured preschool program focused on language development.[6]

Schafer has found that the structure of the school system pushes children out of the classroom.[7] The Flint (Mich.) school system is trying out community schools as a solution to the problem. Litwak and Meyer suggest that linkages between the school and the child's family are needed. Others attest to the importance of a small pupil-teacher ratio, remedial reading programs, better teacher training, better pay for teachers, and community control of the school.[8]

Where is the pattern in all of these findings and suggestions? Can *an* answer be found to the problem presented by children who are educationally handicapped by the time they enter school? My contention is that there is no *one* answer to the problem. The basis for the school's ineffectiveness in educating children of very low socioeconomic status is not to be found in any one area or segment of our educational institutions but in a whole complex of factors.

This paper will attempt to delineate some of these factors. They arise from many aspects of our society and from the intrapersonal and interpersonal realms of the child's life, and they can be grouped under four general heads: cultural factors; social organizational factors: primary group or family; and the individual child.

CULTURAL FACTORS

Five points about our society in general affect our educational system and its relevance to young people growing up in our inner-city slums.

1. Of prime importance is the nature of our technology. As machines become increasingly complex and pervasive, little room remains for the unskilled laborer. Even floor polishers and lawn mowers today necessitate some ability to handle delicate and potentially dangerous machinery. In addition, there is every indication that the trend to mechanization and automation will increase as the use of computers grows and invades more sectors of our economy. Thus, there is little gainful employment available today for the unskilled, the unreliable, or the semiliterate in contrast to the past. Even entry jobs often require high school diplomas as evidence of diligence and a fair degree of competence.

2. Value is placed primarily on instrumental, goal-oriented activities. Although a poet, an artist, or a philosopher is occasionally honored, this happens rarely. Thus children who are artistically gifted but who find academic work dull are likely to run into trouble in the classroom.

3. The "Protestant ethic" of hard work and self-sacrifice, as delineated by Weber,[9] is highly respected while indulgence in sensual pleasures without concern for the future is generally denigrated.

However, in describing a subculture found among people

of very low socioeconomic status, Walter Miller[10] has emphasized two aspects that conflict with the value system dominant in our society: (1) the attribution of great value to
toughness (endurance, physical prowess, bravery) rather
than to cognitive abilities; (2) the belief that luck or fate—
not hard work—is responsible for success. While these views
have survival value for disadvantaged people, they can prevent a child from adapting to the classroom.

4. The mass media, particularly TV, are ubiquitous, even
in the homes of families of very low income. Through such
media children of the poor are constantly and vividly re-
minded of the comforts and luxuries enjoyed by children
of more affluent families. As a result they often develop a
sense of bitterness, frustration, and self-denigration. The
relation between self-rejection and poor academic performance appears to be a close one.[11]

5. The generally racist nature of our society has an additional detrimental effect on Negro children. Clark and Clark
have shown that such children absorb at an early age society's
view that a black skin is demeaning.[12] The militant civil
rights movement may be altering the picture of self-hatred
among Negroes, but the effects of the movement on personality
development have yet to be researched.

No discussion of the cultural effects on educational achievement is complete without an exposition of the relevant
aspects of knowledge and technology that are missing. We
do not really know how young children learn. We know very
little about the appropriate techniques for fostering the development of the cognitive structure. We know very little
about the best way to present new material so that it will
be comprehended and integrated into knowledge already
absorbed. We do not really know how to help children organize the information they have already accumulated.

We *do* know that some children will learn regardless of
how the material is presented; other children, of normal
intelligence, will have severe difficulties no matter what we
do. Because teachers "teach" is no guarantee that students
learn. We also do not know what specific child-rearing practices are related to specific types of behavior. Much research
is now being carried on in all these areas, but much remains
to be done.

ORGANIZATIONAL FACTORS

The school system, the major organization with which the child has contact, affects him as soon as he enrolls in kindergarten. The demands on the child as a student in the typical public school are rather subtle and never clearly spelled out. Usually if the student is to perform adequately, he must display initiative and curiosity in relation to subject matter but be complying and passive in relation to school authorities. He is expected to interact with the other students in a positive fashion, exerting leadership when he can; yet he must never overstep the bounds of approved verbal behavior or become physically aggressive. If he wishes to fight, he must wait until he gets off the school grounds.

In school the child is encouraged to stand up for himself, but verbally not physically. He must follow rules, yet understand how to use his own judgment as to when the rules do not apply. He must accept his teacher as his superior, yet feel free to think for himself and express his own thoughts. He must use language that his teacher considers appropriate for school in sentences she can comprehend. However, at home he is free to talk in any way acceptable to his parents. Thus the child meets with many expectations and restrictions requiring different and seemingly conflicting responses.

In middle-class families, the mother is familiar with the demands made on the child in his role as a student, having herself internalized them—that is, made them part of her own expectations of herself—and performed the role adequately herself. Thus she has little difficulty in explaining the complexities of the role to her children. In contrast, in a family of very low socioeconomic status, the mother may never have internalized the demands of the role and may not understand them completely.

One aspect of the student's role is to communicate in a complex language structure, which Bernstein has likened to an elaborate code.[13] The child of very low socioeconomic background may never have learned this means of communication and may use what Bernstein calls a restricted code exclusively. An elaborate code must be attended to carefully, for it transmits a number of particular messages adding up to detailed information. A restricted code fosters in-group cohesion, but it transmits only stereotyped messages that are very familiar to all the members of the group.

According to Bernstein, children from middle-class families can "switch codes," using the restricted code with their friends or members of their family on some occasions and the elaborate code when they want to transmit specific information. The disadvantaged child can use the restricted code only. Thus, when the child from the low-status family enters school, he is unaccustomed to the linguistic code his teacher is using and is unable to comprehend what she is saying— for example, when she is giving a complex set of directions. Even more serious is his inability to communicate his own bewilderment to her.

The role of the teacher also creates an obstacle to effective teaching of disadvantaged children. Throughout their training, teachers are taught that the goals of education are not measurable, that teachers are educating the "whole child," and that the degree of their success therefore is not researchable. They are told that the teacher "knows" when she is doing a good job, but no one else can really tell. This orientation has created two difficulties. It prevents the teacher from attempting to delineate her specific goals in operational terms that are measurable on a daily, weekly, or monthly basis rather than in general terms. It also has impeded research in the field of education. Only recently, with the introduction of programmed instruction, have educators begun to analyze the tiny steps that are necessary for children to develop skill in arithmetic, spelling, or reading, or to comprehend the complex concepts presented in geography and science.

The role of the school administrator has similarly impeded effective education of the disadvantaged child. It involves errors of omission as well as commission. A serious omission is that neither the principal, assistant superintendent, nor superintendent is required to form linkages with the community or with the student's parents. The parent-teacher association is the only formal avenue for involving people other than educators in the schools' efforts and generally its structure has become so rigid that its original function of serving as a two-way communication channel between the school and the parents seems unlikely ever to be restored. The errors of commission involve the use of school administrators as building managers, book rental-fee collectors, milk machine repairmen, and the like, thus cutting into the time and energy they have for serving as curriculum experts and supervisors of the instructional staff. In too many schools, the principal does little to deal with the fact that many children are having severe learning difficulties or that the curriculum is inappropriate for some students.

The usual structure of the school itself interferes with learning in children of low socioeconomic background. Students are taught in large groups of 25 to 35 children, making it impossible for the teacher to attend to their individual needs so that each child can progress at his own pace. They are promoted or retained a full grade except in a few schools that have experimental ungraded programs. Even in these programs, the teachers do not have the training or the material to be able to teach each child at his own level.

Nearly all teachers have tenure rights after a probationary period of a year or two. Removing a teacher once he has tenure is almost impossible. So teachers may remain in the school system who are not sympathetic to children from the slums or who are sympathetic but do not understand either their emotional or cognitive needs.

Interpersonal relations between teacher and student are critical in determining whether progress will occur. Rosenthal has shown that the expectations teachers have of their students affect student performance.[1] Other studies have shown that the student who feels his teacher likes him does better. Other less definitive findings suggest that children of very low socioeconomic background generally need a more firmly controlled classroom than other children because they have not developed the kind of self-discipline required for learning.

Most school systems provide little or no inservice training for teachers to help them understand the behavior and needs of the disadvantaged child. Teachers tend to resist supervision, but even if this were not so there is no time during their working day for participation in a continuing education program, for in the hours they are not teaching, they must plan their work and grade papers. Many teachers also resist working overtime to increase their skill or knowledge. Hence, if inservice training is to be offered, time for it must be made available either by closing school, which is not in the student's interest, or by paying teachers to attend the program after hours, on weekends, or during the summer.

Few school districts can afford to do this. Other methods of inducing teachers to continue their education, such as offering them higher pay for taking additional university courses, do not motivate all teachers and do not direct the teachers to the kinds of courses they need most.

Few, if any, school systems have training programs built into their structure specifically focused on how to deal with disadvantaged children and required of all teachers who have such children in their classrooms. Moreover, few teacher training institutions offer such courses and even fewer offer student teacher assignments in schools in the city slums, where many of their graduates will teach.

The teacher's role, like the principal's, is deficient in failing to demand that a linkage be formed with the students' parents. Most teachers welcome parents to the school when they come for conferences at times designated by the teacher. But they tend to regard parents who do not show up for such conferences as uncooperative no matter what may be preventing them. Teachers today rarely, if ever, visit parents at their homes; they have no time during their regular working hours for making such visits even if they wished to do so. The absence of a two-way channel of communication between teachers and the parents of low socioeconomic status creates two problems: the teacher is unaware of the kind of environment the student lives in and the parents are unaware of what they can do to reinforce and support the child's efforts to learn in class.

THE PRIMARY GROUP

Of all the influences on the child's educational achievement, the primary group in the child's life—his family—is perhaps the most critical. It is in the family that the beliefs of a culture are transmitted. It is also in the family that the attitudes, skills, and motivation essential for academic achievement are or are not fostered.

Too often, families of low socioeconomic status lack role models of successful students for the child to emulate. But there are more specific differences between most middle-income and very low-income families that tend to effect differences in their children's school performance. My own research has indicated that mothers in families of low socioeconomic status often do not foster the development of internal controls in their preschool-age children.[14] They try to protect their children from the dangers they see in the external world and to suppress the dangers they feel are arising from within the child, such as aggressiveness and sexuality; but they do not prepare their children to cope with problems. For example, they set down specific rules for behavior, but do not explain the reasons for the rules. The child is taught to follow the orders of recognized authority, not to make judgments for himself.

One consequence of this pattern of child rearing may be seen in the classroom among children who are passive in the presence of the teacher and obstreperous when there is no teacher in the room or when they have a substitute teacher whose authority they do not recognize. Even more important are the consequences for cognitive development. The child does not learn to inquire, to doubt, to think for himself.

The importance of cognitive stimulation for future intellectual development is well known. Hunt highlighted this factor in his famous book, "Intelligence and Experience."[15] Children of low socioeconomic backgrounds generally have few intellectually stimulating experiences before entering school and they generally do not have the advantage of the kind of "hidden curriculum" commonly present in middle-class homes. Parents in middle-class families are constantly teaching their children, in the normal course of their family life. Shapes, colors, numbers, names of objects, words on signs are all part of a continuous input of information to the child. Books are read, stories are told, intellectual curiosity is rewarded, and efforts to learn are praised. Thus the mother in the middle-class family incorporates components of the teacher's role in her own functioning as a parent; but the mother of low socioeconomic status tends to confine herself to meeting the child's physical and emotional needs.

Hess and Shipman's work has emphasized another generally differing aspect of parent-child relations in the two socioeconomic groups:[16] the mothers' teaching styles are not the same. Mothers in middle-class families usually try to help a child solve a new problem by first explaining the entire problem and the goals to be achieved. They then respond to the child's specific moves, correcting errors and explaining why they are errors. Mothers of low socioeconomic status tend merely to give the child specific directions without any explanation. Again they rely on specific rules rather than principles.

The physical conditions in most homes in low-income families also impede the children's education. A recent study in which I was involved indicated that the homes of such families are not only far more crowded than those of the middle-income families but they also are usually very poorly lighted.[17] Often the TV din is continuous and there is no surface on which to write, making it practically impossible for a child to read or do homework.

THE INDIVIDUAL CHILD

Hunt[15] and others have found that the developing intellectual ability of the child is not solely the result of constitutional factors but is derived from the interaction of hereditary characteristics with the environment. Piaget postulates that the more learning the child has already assimilated, the more new material he is able to assimilate.[18] Rosenzweig and associates have shown that distinct anatomical differences exist in the cortex of rats raised in a stimulating environment and those raised without access to stimulating "toys."[19] Hence there is reason to believe that raising a child in an unstimulating environment produces a youngster with more limited intellectual ability than he might otherwise have had. According to Bloom, a large fraction of the intelligence of the child is already fixed by the age of 5.[20] He doubts that environmental change beyond that point can raise a child's intellectual ability appreciably.

One characteristic frequently found in preschool children of low socioeconomic status is an inability to engage in social-dramatic play, to pretend that an object is present that is not, or to take on another's role in a reciprocal relationship. This inability to pretend has been found by Smilansky among children in Israel as well as by teachers in compensatory preschool programs in this country.[21] It may be related to the lack of games of pretending between mother and child at home. The ability to imagine situations which do not exist is critical for understanding in reading, geography, history, and many other subjects. Piaget finds it essential for concept formation.[22]

The school problems of children from low-income families, however, are not derived solely from their lack of skills other children develop at home. They also are derived from special skills such children possess that interfere with academic achievement. One is an ability to tune out undesirable words and sounds—a very useful ability in a crowded home but a distinct impediment to learning in the classroom. Another is an ability to express one's emotions in movement rather than words—a source of much of the discipline problem in schools, which are not geared to this mode of expression.

There is some disagreement among researchers as to whether or not motivation to achieve exists at all among many children from the lowest socioeconomic groups. The suggestion has frequently been made that such children *do* want to achieve but in the realm of toughness, physical power, and athletic skill rather than in academic work. But Cohen and associates found that when delinquent boys of low status were offered concrete rewards for academic achievement, their will to learn eventually became internalized.[23] This suggests that a rechanneling of the motivation to achieve can be induced much later than most psychologists once believed possible.

To summarize, many factors are impeding the effectiveness of schools in educating children from the lowest socioeconomic groups. Some of these factors are societal in nature; some, organizational; some, familial; and some, individual. No one remedy will be sufficient to resolve the problem, nor will an attack on any one aspect of it. What is clearly needed is a massive attack on all the factors involved, along with the opening of new legitimate channels of upward mobility for the few children who even then would be unable to advance educationally. The costs of such a program would be enormous but not so great as the cost of doing without it.

PROPOSED CHANGES IN AMERICAN SOCIAL WELFARE

Fedele F. Fauri

INSTITUTIONS and programs valid at the time they are established are slow to adapt as conditions change. This is no less the case with social welfare institutions than with those in health, education, government and business. There must be understanding and acceptance of social welfare services and institutions for a healthy America. Where change is needed, changes must be brought about. Our social welfare programs should be designed to enable those suffering from economic or social deprivation to attain decency and health.

Throughout the history of our nation social welfare programs have been given a low priority by the Congress and the State legislatures, except in the depression period of the 1930's when these programs were so important to a large proportion of the population. But in the last few years we have seen a renewed interest in social welfare. A number of new programs have been established and some of the old ones have been improved. However, the accomplishments to date fall far short of affording a standard of decency and health for millions of Americans—both black and white—who find themselves at the bottom of the economic ladder. One-fifth of the population continues to live in poverty during a period of unsurpassed affluence when the average annual family income is over $8,000.[1]

Until recently many were of the opinion that all that was needed to abolish poverty was a prolonged period of prosperity. America has discovered, however, that millions of Americans have not benefited from the economic growth of the 1960's, which has continued without a setback for 99

This is an updated edition of a paper given by Dean Fauri while serving as Visiting Scholar at Western Michigan University, Kalamazoo, March 25–26, 1968. Reprinted with permission of the author.

months, with an unemployment rate below 4% and the gross national product at an all time high.

With this discovery has come the enactment of a number of new programs. But as yet mass programs in the public and private sectors to eliminate poverty are in the study and talk stage. Most of the programs that have been launched are limited in scope and inadequately financed. The Office of Economic Opportunity Act was started with a good deal of fanfare and publicity. It was to wage an all out attack on poverty. Yet in each year of its existence it has been allotted less than $2 billion a year by the Congress. A Model Cities Program has been established to inaugurate a comprehensive approach to human problems involving jobs, education, health facilities, and housing. But limited financing means that only a beginning can be made in resolving the problems of our cities. A rent supplement program to enable low in- come families to obtain better housing is on the statute books but the appropriations limit it to being a token program. Our training programs make provision for only a fraction of the adults and youth of the nation who are unemployed or underemployed who could benefit from such programs.

I think it is clear that vastly greater commitments of re- sources must be made by the public and private sectors of the nation if we are to succeed in eliminating poverty. We must not only continue but greatly expand the training and educational programs for the disadvantaged—the Head Start program to give dependent youngsters a better start in life, the work-study programs to enable needy young people to continue in college, the rent supplement, public housing and other programs that have been adopted in recent years.

The interest that has been demonstrated in the last few years by the leaders of industry in training and employing the hard core unemployed indicates that we may be enter- ing a new era of cooperation between government and busi- ness in an effort to resolve some of our social problems. The National Advisory Commission on Civil Disorders endorsed this cooperation and recommended the creation of two mil- lion new jobs in the next three years—one million in the public sector and one million in the private sector. Moreover, it called for on-the-job training by both public and private employers with the latter being reimbursed for the extra costs of training the hard core unemployed.

I hope that these recommendations and others of the Commission, such as the one to provide six million new and existing units of housing for low and moderate income families within five years, will be attained in the periods of time that are specified in the report. But the adoption of new and comprehensive high cost plans is often delayed or discarded. Moreover, in times such as the country now finds itself in, and when a "program of national austerity" is being advocated, it is likely that broad scale social reforms will be postponed.

I suggest that regardless of what may happen as to the adoption of new comprehensive social welfare programs, that we no longer should postpone modifications in our income maintenance programs. Changes are needed and changes should be brought about without delay in unemployment insurance, in old-age, survivors, and disability insurance and in our public welfare system. An updating of these programs will enable the needy in the population to attain a standard of living compatible with decency and health.

I think the worst indictment that can be made against our affluent society of the 1960's is that we permit children and adults to live in stark poverty. In 1965 and 1966 I chaired a 12-member Advisory Council on Public Welfare that was established by the Congress to investigate and make recommendations concerning the public welfare system. The Council held hearings in six areas of the country and received oral or written testimony from more than 300 witnesses. We found that some needy people had to exist on diets near the starvation level. The Senate Poverty Subcommittee, made up of Senators Clark of Pennsylvania, Javits and Kennedy of New York, and Murphy of California, confirmed these findings in 1967. *Time* magazine of April 21, 1967, reviewed some of the conclusions arrived at by the Subcommittee after it visited the State of Mississippi and quoted Senator Murphy as saying: "I didn't know we would be dealing with starving people."

I think the fastest and most feasible way to correct these conditions among the poor is through revision of the social insurance programs and the public welfare system.

Our often maligned public welfare system has the potential for eliminating without delay these deplorable conditions that exist among a substantial segment of the poor, provided the system is modernized and altered to afford protection to all the needy of the nation.

Before presenting the specific changes that I believe necessary in the social insurances and the public welfare system, I want to comment briefly on the negative income tax and children's allowances. The establishment of the negative income tax or children's allowances is being advocated for the purpose of correcting present conditions among the poor. Sometimes these programs are cited as the way to eliminate the shortcomings in the public welfare system without mentioning the extremely high costs of these programs if they are to provide even the average inadequate public assistance payments of today.

The negative income tax based on an annual payment in the neighborhood of the $3,335 poverty level for a family of four is just not politically feasible. A more modest negative income tax that would provide an annual payment of $1,500 for a family of four and would permit the family to retain $1 for each $2 of outside income up to a total income of $3,000 would entail a net increase of $6 billion a year over present welfare costs. This proposal would benefit greatly those poor who are employable but does little for many of the poor who cannot for one reason or another enter the labor force. Moreover, a negative income tax at the $1,500 level would have a very limited impact on the public welfare rolls with the result that two systems for payments to the needy would have to be maintained. In more than half the States a family of four currently receives more than $1,500 a year under the Aid to Dependent Children program.

In my opinion a children's allowances program which would provide monthly payments to all children regardless of need would have less effect on reducing the public welfare rolls than a negative income tax.

Even children's allowances at the low rate of $150 a year per child would cost $10.5 billion as there are 70 million children under age 18 in the United States. A program that would allow $150 a year for a mother and one child or $300 a year for a mother and two children would have little impact on the ADC rolls. A children's allowances program of $600 per year or $50 per month for 70 million children would cost $42 billion, and if the allowances were included in income under the income tax, the cost would be about

$35 billion. Cash payments for public assistance total less than $6 billion a year.

Dr. Harvey Brazer, Chairman of the Department of Economics at The University of Michigan, has devised a plan for children's allowances that is more feasible than any other that I have seen. His plan provides for a children's allowance of $50 per month per child or $600 per year. He estimates the net cost to be in the neighborhood of $12 billion by including the allowances in income for income tax purposes, eliminating the $600 dependent tax exemption for children receiving an allowance, and requiring taxpayers to add to their tax liabilities as otherwise computed an amount equal to a proportion of children's allowances received.

This plan has many advantages over some of the others that have been proposed but it is not a substitute for ADC as a household with one child, without any other income, would receive only $50 a month and a household with two children, only $100 a month.

Now I would like to outline the changes I believe should be made in the social insurances and the public welfare system.

First, as to unemployment insurances. This program has provided economic security for millions of people. Before it became effective in the late 1930's, unemployment meant liquidation of savings and assets and accumulation of debt. This is no longer true for members of the labor force covered by unemployment insurance. These workers and their families have been protected against distress and insecurity, community purchasing power and labor standards have been better maintained, and they know that they will have some income to help pay their bills when unemployment strikes.

Despite these accomplishments, however, our unemployment insurance system could do a better job and reduce the need for public assistance. At any given time usually less than one-half the unemployed receive benefits under the program.

A number of needed improvements in the system could be cited. But I shall only mention two. First, Federal standards for benefit levels should be established so that more adequate and more uniform benefits would be provided on a nation-wide basis. When benefit levels are set by fifty states without Federal standards the result is low benefits, primarily because each state wants to reduce costs to its industries so they can remain competitive with industries in other states. Secondly, and perhaps most important, is extension of coverage. Fifteen million jobs remain excluded from the protection of the system. Many of the individuals in these excluded jobs receive low wages and are seasonal or part-time employees who often must turn to public welfare when they are unemployed. These excluded workers are being discriminated against.

In the early days of the system it was claimed that it was not administratively feasible to cover these excluded workers. Years of experience with old-age and survivors insurance, which now has close to universal coverage, have shown conclusively that it is possible to include practically all the employees of the nation under social insurance.

There is no valid reason to continue to exclude millions of workers from unemployment insurance. They should be given the same protection against the risks of unemployment that is now afforded the vast majority of American workers.

Now I want to turn to old-age and survivors, and disability insurance, to discuss some of the changes I think are needed in that program to make it more effective in reducing poverty. This program has made possible the well-being of a larger segment of the American people than any other social welfare program ever enacted by the Congress. But retired workers receive payments averaging only $98.75 per month, and the minimum benefit for a worker retiring at age 65 or older is $55 per month under the new benefit schedule approved by the Congress in December 1968.[2] These OASDI benefits are the major source of income for the vast majority of beneficiaries, and in states having low public assistance standards, the $55 minimum monthly benefit is not supplemented by the welfare departments.

The result of low OASDI benefit levels means that four million aged still live in poverty—many in stark poverty—even though this program has been improved more often by the Congress than any other social welfare program. It affords excellent protection for middle class Americans. It does not, however, afford adequate protection for those beneficiaries—children and adults—whose benefits are based on the earnings of a worker who has not had steady employment and who has worked for low wages. Benefit levels for these workers should be increased substantially even though such action would require a government subsidy to meet the additional costs to the system.

Improvement in the OASDI program such as I have suggested would also reduce the public welfare rolls. Two million aged are receiving old-age assistance—33 years after enactment of a national old-age insurance system. About one-half of these recipients also receive old-age insurance benefits. Benefit levels for OASDI have a direct bearing on old-age assistance expenditures and to a lesser extent on other public assistance programs, such as ADC, when the head of a family dies and the insurance benefits payable to his survivors are not sufficient to meet their needs under public assistance standards.

I hope we are approaching the day when the number of people on the public welfare rolls will be greatly reduced by having the insurance benefit structure provide greater protection for low paid workers and those who have frequent gaps in their employment records. Then they will not have to turn to public welfare in their old age, or if they are disabled, or in case of their premature death their children and widows will not require supplementation from public assistance.

I do not think it is sound social planning to continue the present practice of *dual* administration and *duplicate* monthly payment for nearly a million individuals. If these individuals, and those with similar circumstances who would become eligible for assistance in the future, could be supported under social insurance, public assistance expenditures and the responsibilities of public welfare departments would be greatly reduced.

I think it is essential that the social insurances (Unemployment Insurance and OASDI) be improved so that they will become more effective weapons against poverty. But even with major improvement in the social insurances, radical revision of our public welfare system is required.

Public welfare over the years has had few friends. Its limitations and shortcomings are well known to everyone. As President Johnson said when he signed the Social Security Act Amendments of 1967 and announced the appointment of the Commission on Income Maintenance, "The welfare system today pleases no one. It is criticized by liberals and conservatives, by the poor and the wealthy, by social workers and politicians, by whites and by Negroes in every area of the nation." Critics of the system are numerous. But no one has come forward with a plan to *replace* the welfare program—and note I said replace—that, in my opinion, has a chance of adoption by a Congress in the near future. I am proposing, therefore, that we need more concerted efforts to improve public welfare so that it will provide adequate assistance payments for *all* the needy of the nation in a way that will enable them to maintain dignity, decency, and health.

As you know, there is great variation in assistance levels and coverage of programs among the States. This variation bears no patterned relationship to the fiscal ability of States to finance public welfare. Some 30 years of leaving the implementation of public welfare programs largely to the fiscal ability and willingness of the States has not worked. The adequacy of money payments to those who are eligible for assistance depends upon where a recipient may happen to live instead of the extent of his needs. Average payments for a dependent child vary from a low of $8.50 per month to a high of $67.85.[3] For aged recipients the variation by States for cash payments ranges from a low of $39 per month to a high of $104. Seven States provide average old-age assistance payments of less than $50 a month.[4]

Unbelievable conditions exist in some States for needy individuals who do not qualify for the State-Federal public welfare categories. In some communities such individuals have nothing but surplus commodities and in a few instances even surplus commodities have not been available. In fact until recent changes in federal policy there were 200 counties that did not provide for distribution of surplus commodities or for the food stamp plan.

The National Advisory Commission on Civil Disorders has pointed out the shortcomings of our welfare system. It said in its recent report:

Our present system of public welfare is designed to save money instead of people, and tragically ends up doing neither. This system has two critical deficiencies:

First, it excludes large numbers of persons who are in great need, and who, if provided a decent level of support, might be able to become more productive and self-sufficient. No Federal funds are available for millions of men and women who are needy but neither aged, handicapped nor the parents of minor children.

Second, for those who are included, the system provides assistance well below the minimum necessary for a decent level of existence, and imposes restrictions that encourage continued dependency on welfare and undermine self-respect.

A welter of statutory requirements and administrative practices and regulations operate to remind recipients that they are considered untrustworthy, promiscuous and lazy. Residence requirements prevent assistance to people in need who are newly arrived in the state. Regular searches of recipients' homes violate privacy. Inadequate social services compound the problems.[5]

Perhaps this indictment and the call for sweeping reforms in our welfare system by the "Riot Commission" will bring action. Its recommendations and those of the Advisory Council on Public Welfare that filed its report in 1966 are similar and have the same objectives.

Among the Advisory Council's recommendations are three major areas.[6] These are:

(1) Establishing a national minimum standard for public assistance payments.

(2) A new and more realistic plan for the financing of public welfare programs.

(3) Providing comprehensive assistance and service on the basis of the one imperative of eligibility—need—and as a legally enforceable right of the individual.

Briefly stated, these recommendations would build upon what we now have, yet move to a new method of Federal-State cooperation under which the Federal government would set nationwide minimum standards for financial assistance, social services and program administration, variable by *objective* criteria concerning costs and economic conditions in the States and regions, and, secondly, the Federal government would assume responsibility for making implementation of the standards possible, by financing all costs over and above an *objectively-determined* State share. The State share would be expressed as a percentage of State personal income and thus would vary between States.

What are the advantages for States and the nation in adopting this new pattern of Federal-State relationships for public welfare programs? Some of them are obvious. In any given year States would know the investment they must make to achieve at least minimal maintenance for their needy citizens—a figure determined by *one* clear and equitable formula, and not dependent upon the results under several formulas. The use of one eligibility factor—need—coupled with eligibility determination by affidavit would free staff to do the job they presumably are hired to do—help people become adequate, functioning and contributing members of society.

My experience over many years convinces me that only by Federal action will the issue of inadequate assistance payments be resolved. A national floor, a minimum standard measured in dollars, with regional and urban and rural cost differences, as a Federal requirement *will make possible* more equitable treatment of needy individuals regardless of the States in which they happen to live; *it will make possible* more adequate payments in many States; and *it will make possible* a simplification in the process of the determination of need.

Under the Council's plan present expenditures by the Federal and State governments would be retained as a base. Additional financial support could be made available over a period of years to move the national floor of assistance upward to a level of adequacy. I think it is much more likely that there would be favorable action by a Congress, in any given year, to improve payments to the needy by one or two or three billion dollars than to provide a new program costing six or eight or twelve billion dollars.

In conclusion may I say that I hope no plan is adopted (like the negative income tax) that would provide an annual payment of $1,500 for a family of four and which would reduce public welfare expenditures somewhat. Such a plan would improve conditions for that segment of the poor able to help themselves by employment in periods of a tight labor market but would neglect to provide adequately for the neediest of the poor—those who cannot because of family responsibilities, or, for other valid reasons, should not, become a part of the labor force. For the former group it is my hope that greater opportunity will be afforded to them for employment in the private sector, and that the day will come that those who cannot be absorbed in private employment will be afforded employment by the government. And those who cannot or should not be part of the labor force will be provided with adequate money payments.

Part III

Disorganization

Preliminary Comments

WHAT EMOTIONS and what problems are present during and following divorce proceedings? This section begins with the answers to these questions in a classic piece by Waller as a way of pointing up the importance of the decision to marry. The choice of a marital partner is probably one of the two or three most important decisions in the life of each man and woman. As this part of the volume will document, despite our greater tolerance for divorce today, an unfortunate marriage will disrupt the lives of both spouses and their children, whether or not divorce is sought.

Waller's pioneer study, first published in 1930, combines available social psychological theory and Freudian psychoanalytic thought into a new form of the subjective interaction approach, which was developed and used extensively in later generations. The large majority of Waller's findings, summarized in the second half of the selection found here, have been substantiated by later studies. However, no other author has been able to present as well generalizations about behavior with the depth of feeling associated with that behavior, so that the reader experiences while he understands. This combination of insight, together with the emotion that makes it meaningful, still stands as an ideal rarely achieved in the social sciences.

In the next selection Levinger asks the questions that precede the one Waller attempted to answer. What are the factors that maintain a stable and successful marriage, and what are the factors that lead to its dissolution? The author uses modern social psychological theory to review a very large body of literature primarily concerned with prediction of marital success and marital satisfaction.

Organizing research findings around the concept of small-group cohesion, he summarizes data related to factors of (1) interpersonal attraction, (2) interpersonal repulsion, and (3) restraints and barriers to marital dissolution. At the end it is pointed out that some kinds of changes are much more easily accomplished than others if one wishes to save marriages or lower the divorce rate.

The second piece by Levinger discusses some of his own research data, extending and emphasizing certain aspects of the literature survey. It is an empirical study of the reasons men and women give when applying to the court for divorce. The justifications given by each sex are relatively different. An equally important finding, however, is that there are statistically significant variations between lower class and middle class responses. Interpersonal attraction can only be maintained in the context of an adequate and stable income. Love, respect, and self-actualization can only become goals in a marriage after subsistence and safety have been achieved.

Goode has a very different perspective on family disorganization from many other social and behavioral scientists. He points out that divorce is only one of many indications of marital instability in a society, and the good or bad effects of such instability on the society are unknown. The author takes issue with much of the research reviewed by Levinger. He believes that it is ideological and value-laden rather than objective and that its predictive potency is very low.

His study is a cross-cultural sociological analysis of divorce rates. His hypothesis is that the rate of divorce, particularly by class, can be accounted for by the ease with which such marital dissolution can be attained. Among Western nations divorce among the middle and lower classes becomes easier with increasing industrialization. Among non-Western nations (China, Japan, India, and Arab Islam) where divorce rules, especially among agriculturalists in the past, have been looser than in Western countries, it is likely that divorce rates may drop with industrialization. He uses divorce statistics from a large number of countries to demonstrate these patterns.

Goode attempts to account for, rather than be influenced by, values. His cross-cultural statistical approach in many ways is analogous to that used by Durkheim. He provides a refreshing and interesting means of looking at problems in marriage and the family.

The last three articles in this section deal with methods

of helping families that are having interpersonal problems. The author of each uses a somewhat different theoretical orientation in viewing the difficulties, but all see the family as a system and make use of the new method of treatment generally known as family therapy.

Tharp and Otis think that problems in family functioning and individual psychopathology are closely related. Their treatment technology is developed directly out of small-group theory and research. System problems are analyzed in role terms. In treatment concentrated attention is given to each member's interpersonal functioning in one or more of five role areas, in the presence of all other family members. Historical material is used for understanding, but intervention is focused on the here and now.

Stuart uses a modified learning theory approach to marital problems. As in the preceding article, the theoretical assumptions lead to a distinctively different method of treatment. The author-therapist reverses the husband-wife cycle of mutual punishment to mutual reward by helping each spouse to specify what he or she wants from the other and by providing immediate gratification in the form of tokens when wishes are granted. Measures of change are made throughout the treatment process and after it in order to monitor its success or failure.

The final article summarizes a number of family treatment approaches and points to the similarities and differences between these and traditional psychoanalytic psychotherapy. The recency of the family therapy movement is indicated by the date of publication of this paper—1962. Only seven years ago many therapists feared that their view of the family as a social system rather than as individuals with internal psychological problems would be seen as heresy. For this reason Haley has few references to refer to and does not make use of footnotes.

The first part of the paper is a facetiously humorous but very insightful description of various forms of family therapy. Variations on these themes continue today. This is followed by a summary of the dynamics of disturbed family functioning. Central to the analysis is a description of the play for power that often goes on in families with interpersonal problems. One prominent method is the use of paradox. An example is multilevel communication (metacommunication), in which two or more incongruent messages are communicated simultaneously from one person to another. The author refers to this as the "double-bind." Thus, the person who is expected to respond is always a loser—wrong every time.

Haley goes on to demonstrate that traditional individual-oriented psychotherapists and family treatment advocates use essentially similar techniques. They both place patients in paradoxical situations not unlike those found in their families, but this time to get individual members and the family system to change. This understanding of both the dynamics of disturbed family functioning and the dynamics of treatment technology has been extended by Haley and others and has led to much more fruitful approaches to interpersonal intervention.

This material serves as a useful transition to the final section in the volume. While the dynamics of problematic family functioning and physical and mental illness can be seen as separate and different phenomena, they are also highly related to each other. While neither can be considered the single cause of the other, each can be seen as playing some part in the difficulties families and individuals experience. As we shall continue to see, the person brings to the family physical, social, and psychological characteristics that influence the development of the system; yet the system leads to changes in these characterisics in time.

THE OLD LOVE AND THE NEW: DIVORCE AND READJUSTMENT

Willard Waller

"DECREE GRANTED"

She sits amid her tears. There is solemn judicial business up in front. . . . It concerns her . . . her and her . . . divorce. Her divorce! She divorced!

She is showing him!

She achieves that agony of complete and yet detached attention with which we witness a bad dream.

She sees her attorney standing before the judge. . . . He is reading the charges. . . . That on the 20th of August the defendant, in the presence of four witnesses. . . . He ought to read that louder. . . . Oh, why does he read it so loudly? . . . The judge leans toward the attorney. He moves his right hand. Then his left. He balances his weight against the desk exactly. Listening. . . . The low voice of her attorney . . . droning. . . . That on the night of the 13th of September, 1926, at or about seven o'clock in the evening. . . . Somehow, it is still the 13th of September . . . the said defendant. . . . Each word throws a scene, sharp, vivid, upon the screen of memory. Each sentence is a drama. She reenacts them all, and loses not a word, not a gesture. The judge moves each hand about an inch toward the ends of his desk. He squirms slightly and settles himself again.

She sits perfectly still. . . . She must sit still. The judge is still listening.

She is numb, as if the central spark of her being had gone out and the fire of life were slowly dying from her limbs. Her legs are cramped. It is because she has been sitting so

Reprinted with permission of the publisher from Willard Waller, *The Old Love and the New: Divorce and Readjustment*, New York: Horace Liveright, 1930, pp. ix–xiv, 3–14.

very still so very long. . . . Strange that all these men and all these people should be occupied with her affairs. Misery is in her viscera, and agony in her chest. She experiences that elementary emotion that is no emotion but all emotions melted into one torturing confusion.

The woman's thoughts fly backward, forward. They rush off tangentially, crisscross, collide, and go hurrying apart. She jumps centuries, and returns underground to her starting point. She listens and stares. . . . The lawyer talking, the judge listening. . . . The judge asks a question . . . nods his head. . . . Time is endless. Time is now. There is no *then*. . . . The time machine has broken and all time is one, one anguish. The lamentation of Cain.

She has a thousand impulses and follows none. . . . The judge and the lawyer are conferring. . . . She watches them . . . suspended . . . suspended . . . disembodied. . . . How warm it is! That beating drum . . . her heart!

She no longer has any control over her impulses, nor they over her. . . . Every nerve-cell in her brain and every atom of her body has revolted. They are all going to go their own way now. She assumes a dozen attitudes at once. Her thoughts and her desires strike out in contradictory ways. She is a trampled place in the cross-roads and over her march her own desires and the deeds of other people.

All is now fused in a vast expectancy. The lawyers are conferring before the judge. . . . The lawyers! . . . A feeling of confidence in her lawyer. . . . They speak so low she cannot hear them. The crowd grows restless and begins to talk in low tones. . . . A bailiff quiets them. . . . He assumes an exaggerated importance in her eyes. . . . She is suddenly very grateful to the bailiff. . . . The air of the courtroom is heavy upon her chest, and weights it down. She imagines that she is in a glass case and some one is gradually pumping compressed air into it.

She understands that the judge is about to perform that act of legal magic which makes her no more a married woman . . . which makes her . . . a divorcée. . . . Divorcée! . . . The judge is going to cut that knot which binds her to her husband. . . . Husband? . . . Strange word. . . . May I knot? She snorts at the remembered joke and her father looks anxiously at her.

The judge is going to sever that link . . . a slave bracelet

. . . long ago . . . memories . . . mental tears . . . no time for them now.

The agony in her intestines wells up and engulfs her chest and lungs. With an effort she keeps breathing. . . . Her breath is loud in her ears and irregular . . . as it was when . . .

The judge is going to lift his gavel. . . . He is going to lift his gavel and bring it down again. . . . How she has longed for this moment! How she hates it! . . . God help her now! . . . She repeats an absurd nursery prayer. . . . She wishes she believed in God so that she might pray to him!

She sees the judge's hand and arm get set to reach for the gavel. . . . The clock ticks relentlessly, piling tick upon tick through the centuries. . . . The judge is wearing a bow tie. . . . His eyes focus upon the gavel. . . . The woman knows Achilles never caught the tortoise, for time is infinitely divisible.

The judge takes hold of his gavel. The lawyers stand erect, apart. They are slightly tense before the anticipated materialization of the majesty of the law. . . . The woman hangs upon the moment. She knows one moment of entire selflessness. . . .

The judge lifts the gavel. He holds it poised. The woman watches him while he holds it in the air during ten eternities. . . . She turns her head. Her ears prepare for the devastating noise the gavel will make when it descends. . . . She wants to scream. . . . She is going to scream. . . . She does not scream. . . . She has heated up this Moloch of a law and now she must throw her marriage into it.

The gavel descends. A little noise, objectively speaking. A slight noise, hardly more than the closing of a book or the dropping of a pencil. . . . But it is a noise that shatters dreams. A little noise, but it will reverberate in one woman's ears on the far edge of time. The judge speaks. The gavel punctuates his speech.

A voice so stiff that it crackles like heavy brown wrapping paper. A voice so dry that it generates static electricity in the air it passes through.

"Decree granted!"

Voice, words and the sound of the gavel falling repeat themselves endlessly. They are metamorphosed into titanic drama. A drama in the heart of just one woman. A drama mad as madness, senseless as an idiot's dream.

She experiences that relaxation and sinking of the viscera which is grief.

She is weeping upon her father's shoulder. . . . Upon his old coat that smells of tobacco and perspiration. Her whole being flows out into tears. She floats upon the sea of sorrow and cherishes each warm wave that laps her face.

The reassuring words of her father and her lawyer bring her back to a realization of herself. Still weeping, but softly, now, she submits while her attorney leads her from the courtroom. A bailiff is about to yawn.

Some friends join her. They assure her that she will feel better "now that it is over."

"Now that it is over?" Is it over? Is it ever over? Is this the end? Is this an end? Is it an end or a beginning?

To-day the woman feels that it is an end. Tomorrow she will know that it is a beginning. Tomorrow she will know that it is an episode in a life that has become a new life and a new struggle.

Strange, is it not, that people have troubled themselves so over this woman before her divorce, and never stopped to wonder what she thought about the next day and the next? Strange that no one cares to take account of all those multitudinous and meaningless, desperate and disconnected days that follow each other when time stops?

There were always enough peculiarities and enough dramatic possibilities to incite one to wonder about the psychology of divorced persons. Dido, if you grant her authenticity, was an abandoned woman, and she came down to us amid fire and smoke. Hosea put away the faithless Gomer, and transmuted his agonies into prophecy. Napoleon was a suicide for three days.

If it takes things near at hand to make you curious, you have only to pick up this morning's newspaper. There it is: *Crazed Husband Slays Estranged Wife.* Or perhaps, *Man and Divorced Mate Die in Suicide Pact.* Again: *Divorcée Takes Own Life, Leaves Note Blaming Former Husband.* The tabloids will tell it in pictures.

There is the evidence. Divorce is one of the serious crises of life. Birth, death, marriage, divorce—these are events so great that it is difficult to reckon with them. And divorce is as important as any of the others for those to whom it occurs.

PROBLEMS OF THE DIVORCÉ

The world that loves a lover does not love a divorcé, although it may like to read about him in the newspapers. Preference for the tender emotion is not difficult to understand. Love is simple, direct, and beautiful. The lover knows what he wants and goes after it. Frustration, usually the lot of the divorcé, is complicated, circuitous, and ugly. The divorcé does not know what he wants and is not sure that he wants it anyhow. He has got what he wanted and found it was not good for him. The divorcé, further, has rendered himself vaguely indecent by violating a marriage taboo which, although consciously repudiated by the half-enlightened multitudes, yet remains a powerful element in determining their behavior. The very word divorcé, to say nothing of its more vulgar synonyms, smacks of sexual irregularity.

In the explanation of popular prejudice against divorced persons, there is another factor, of the most subtle, to be considered. People do not like divorced people because they have personal problems. A woman may lie, steal, murder, even lose her virtue, and there will still be those who say that there is some hope for her. But let her admit some difficulty in controlling her thoughts and arranging her life and she is forever damned. She has problems, personality problems! Away with her! A man may carry tales, libel, seduce, betray, he may yet rise to a position of power and trust, but if he ever admits any subjective difficulties he is branded as an impossible person. It is not a crime to have problems; if it were, the attitude could be faced and evaluated. It is simply impolite, and no gentleman would do it! And then, in these post-Freudian days, there cluster about the person who is not quite at one with himself splotches of masturbation and stains of incest.

The problems that the divorcé must face are of a sort well calculated to make him preoccupied and subjective, and therefore perhaps a bit harder to understand than he would otherwise be. They are of such a compelling nature that his energies are likely to run long in internal channels, so that all his acts are enfeebled with thought. It is not possible to imagine more thorough-going reorganization than is in extreme cases necessary after a divorce. One must reorganize his love life, he must salve over his wounded pride, he must rechannelize his habits, he must reestablish himself in his social group, and he must settle the conflict with himself, always present, sufficiently well that he can go on living effectively. The divorced woman must in most cases face also the problem of economic rehabilitation; she must learn to pay her own way. The most casual consideration of these necessities of reorganization will suffice to suggest the explanation of the fact that real reorganization is rare.

This process by which one marriage partner is split from the other and learns to live apart is one process. It neither begins nor ends with divorce. Marriage relations are carried over into the post-divorce period, indicating that there is much vitality in a relationship after the legal break has occurred. In other cases, the relationship is dead long before any mention is made of a legal step. It is the process with which we should be concerned, regardless of its location in time and space. And, though it be swift or gradual, this process must always take place whenever a marriage breaks up, and it must include, at one time or at separate times, reorganization along all the lines mentioned.

There are cases, it is true, when the divorce seems to represent only welcome relief from inhibitions. In these cases the marriage perhaps never had a strong psychic and social foundation, or it was broken by a gradual process of which the mates were unaware before the final severance. We must mention also some few very disorganized persons who do not mind the additional complicating factor of divorce. They were not integrated before marriage and do not expect to be afterwards; divorce means nothing to them. Their very unadjustment to society, by keeping marriage from being meaningful, has protected them against its dangers. Being weak, they seem strong; they have the strength of ten, because their hearts are inaccessible. But there are many other people who insist that their divorce has caused them no particular conflict and has given rise to no problems. Their very insistence upon this is usually diagnostic of some urgent conflict which would be revealed by further study, if indeed the problem does not obtrude itself while the person is in the very act of denying its existence.

It is worth while to consider at length the necessities of reorganization with which the divorcé is confronted.

(1) Probably the most pressing necessity is that of reorganizing his love life. Habits of sex expression formed in the marriage are at some stage in the process of breaking up rudely interrupted, and either new outlets must be sought, or an arrangement must be made so that one can dispense with an outlet. If the former alternative is more frequently chosen, the latter is not unusual, at least for a while. Effects of blocking the sex impulse will be observed from time to time in the course of this study, and will not be expanded upon here.

Certain alternative courses which present themselves to the divorced person who does not wish to give over sex entirely, aside from the very common practice of continuing sex relations with the mate after the divorce, are as follows:

(a) An attempt to cheapen sex, to satisfy one's self with merely physical love objects, doing away with all idealization. This is in general regressive, a rebellion against the demands of the highly complicated ego and a reversion to the elemental. In its extreme form it may be accompanied by a revival of masturbation or by definitely explosive expressions of the sex impulse. This sort of adjustment may be consciously worked out, or unconsciously adopted. It verges over into

(b) Bohemianism, or promiscuity on a high level. In the previous form of adjustment, only the sex act is contemplated, perhaps without reference to the person or the circumstances, perhaps even with these purposely made degrading in their nature. In promiscuity on a high level one considers the act, the person, the circumstances, and the subjective concomitants of these, but is not ready to answer with his whole personality for the consequences of the affair, nor to give any assurance of its continuance. In its very highest form it approximates a marriage terminable at will; in its lowest it represents hectic enjoyment of sex affairs and drinking bouts with persons not of the very lowest levels of society. The point will be made again and again in this book, and may well be stated for the first time here, that both these first two adjustments, however satisfactory they may seem to the casual observer, usually indicate a considerable degree of inner unhappiness. They indicate at best an expression of only one side of an ambivalence, and a flight from the other.

(c) The third alternative is to find a real substitute and really to transfer one's affections completely to the second love object, giving to the second mate full emotional equivalence with the first. This is more easily said than done, of course, and many things conspire to make it dangerous. There is the danger of those rebound phenomena which the novels talk about, there is the danger that the second affair, produced by some inner compulsion and subjective need, will burn out its feverish life more rapidly than the first. There is the danger that no real transference will ever be made, for it is hard to put aside the love of one's youth. There is the danger that in choosing a second mate one will make a neurotic choice allowing him to perpetuate his madness. There is the danger that one may marry a second time without being as willing to make adjustments as he was on the occasion of his first marriage. There is the danger that security-seeking mechanisms set into operation by the dissolution of his first marriage will make him unable to hold the affections of a second mate. All this and much more stands in the way of finding an acceptable substitute, but this is not to say that the thing is impossible.

The divorcé who attempts to dispense with sex expression altogether may be successful for a short period of time, during an interim when it seems that the impulse has died down under the impact of other compelling emotions. Alcoholism, gambling, card-playing, social diversions, work, athletics, religion, and art may constitute in some cases substitute outlets.

(2) A second necessity no less compelling than the first is that one repair the wound to his pride which has been inflicted by the fact of divorce. For however completely rationalized it may have been, divorce is always a blow to pride. On this point we should not be deceived. If one justifies the divorce by repudiating the mate, then he has a lingering sense of shame that he should have failed so badly in his choice of a marriage partner, humiliation that he has placed his heart so ill. If one takes the blame him-

self, then he cannot avoid a sense of failure. If one simply says that the twain could not get along, and agrees to disagree, there is still a modicum of injury to one's ego feelings because better insight was not used in the process of living together. But people rarely agree to disagree; nearly always there is one or the other of them who takes the lead in bringing about the divorce, and one's reorganization afterwards is conditioned by whether he played the active or the passive role in this process. The real extent to which conscience and the current moral code have a hold upon the most disorganized persons is not commonly realized—indeed this is one of the prime factors in causing such disorganization—and the wound caused by the violation of the monogamic code by divorce is deeper than it seems.

If one escapes the deep trauma of the experience of divorce itself, he is not yet free, but must encounter innumerable opportunities to have his tender sensibilities lacerated by being treated as people think that a divorcé should be treated. If not the divorce, then perhaps his status as a divorced person wounds him. Thus a woman who experiences no unease in living away from her husband still stands to have her feelings hurt by frequent and casual solicitations to intercourse.

These injuries to one's pride must be dealt with in some fashion, and in dealing with them one frequently reorganizes himself quite completely. Defense reactions, whose function is to guard against the infliction of further trauma, and to avoid the further exacerbation of wounds already suffered, and compensatory drives, intended to offset and neutralize, in one's own mind at least, the effects of the trauma, are the answers which one makes to ignominy's poisoned darts. In this matter as well as in the love-life reorganization is rarely complete.

(3) One's habits are usually disturbed by a marital break. Let us here overlook the fact that love is something of a habit and that one's sexual life is regulated by habit, especially in marriage, and the fact that one usually has a habitual basis for the satisfaction of his ego drives. Habits of all sorts accumulate rapidly in marriage, and upon them and their smooth operation the institution depends much for its stability. When the marriage goes, these myriad little habits go with it, and their struggles to find expression again

account for part of the vague unease and restlessness which obsess the person whose break has been recent. This adjustment is of course easier where the marriage has been of short duration or where the break has taken place gradually over a long period of time.

There is a certain division of labor in matrimony which breaks down when the couple separate. Tasks in which one formerly had a certain erotic pleasure, since they were performed for the love object, are no longer necessary. One thinks at times with regret of even the unwelcome tasks of marriage, and would be glad if they could be performed again. It is not easy, when one's life has included another person, to reorganize on the basis of life which is to be lived to and for one's self. One may miss the material comforts to which marriage accustomed him, a car with a husband who acted as chauffeur, a home with a wife who acted as cook. The very compromises of marriage, compromises which in their accumulation made the marriage acceptable to both parties but satisfactory to neither, crystallized in habit, carry over after one is free to do just as he pleases. A man who once quarreled with his wife because she set the alarm clock for a time a quarter of an hour in advance of that at which the couple had to arise, so that she might prepare herself slowly and luxuriously for the ordeal of getting up to dress, ended by contracting the habit himself and carrying it through some years of life as a divorcé. Sex habits tend to establish themselves as a result of compromises between the marriage partners, and there is a special impulsion to carry these over.

(4) Because of necessities both internal and external to himself, the divorcé must reorganize his social relationships. He has lost the one person who was more meaningful to him than any other, and he has not the solace of the bereaved person of allowing that one person to go on being meaningful. The divorcé must rearrange his whole system of relationships in such a way that other people who were not previously important may become so, and that the one person who was more important than any other may be held at a distance.

Because of things external to himself, because he no longer knows whether he belongs to certain groups or not, because the attitude of his friends is likely to be changed by the fact of his divorce, the divorcé has to work out a new status in his circle of friends. We have no clear definition of the situation with regard to divorce, and one who has just broken up his marriage does not know what his friends will think of him. Sometimes the group of friends centering around the married pair is split, part of them siding with one of the mates and the rest taking the part of the other. One does not always know who is who, or where anybody else is standing. The influence of other, and more subtle, factors is also traceable. Perhaps one's friends want to sympathize, and force their benevolent sentiments upon one who is too proud to take sympathy. Or perhaps one's friends have become somehow involved in the unfortunate circumstances of the break. Many divorcés do not attempt to salvage the remains of their circle of friends, but break completely with the people they have known or remove to another locality— a heroic remedy, but one which people often feel that they must use.

There is throughout the danger that the divorcé, because of his preoccupation with his own conflicts, will actually give some of his friends cause for offense, or that he will, through the familiar mechanism of projection, put thoughts in their heads that are really only in his own, thereby disrupting his system of social relationships. There is the further fact, mentioned at the beginning of this chapter, that the divorced person is shunned because he has personal problems, which debar their possessors from respectable salons as thoroughly as lice.

Not the least unfortunate effect of divorce is that it exposes anyone who occupies a position of trust or dignity to criticism from his enemies and rivals. Malignant tongues may make of divorce itself an indictment of an entire life and all its achievements, and the revelations as to the details of one's private life which a divorce suit may bring forth may furnish material for endless scandal and ridicule.

(5) Often with women, and sometimes with men, there appear certain problems of earning one's living. By women this is sometimes regarded as the most difficult problem. It has some intrinsic difficulty, and is made in addition to represent the objectification of many inner conflicts. It is not, as they think, the whole of their unhappiness, but it is a symbol of it. Women are still not accustomed in our culture to self-support, and are often timorous when they as-

sume that burden for the first time. Furthermore, there is involved in many cases a reduction of the standard of living in the readjustment after divorce, and in such cases one always wonders just how he is going to get along.

Compensating for this and other worries, women frequently plunge into any work that offers itself with great singleness of purpose, and overreact by an excessive devotion to their tasks for a considerable period of time. They are sincerely worried about whether they are going to make both ends meet[1] and the work in addition furnishes an outlet for their energies. Men in certain professions, such as the ministry, or to a lesser extent teaching, find their professional careers interrupted by divorce. Both doctors and lawyers are hurt a bit by a divorce; Soames Forsythe did not fail to consider the economic consequences of the step that he was taking.

(6) Most important, most intangible, and most subtle of the necessities of the divorced person's new life is that of settling the rebellion within himself, of defending the central government against the various minor insurrections and the one or two great ones in process. In a sense all this volume is concerned with this single problem, which is not separable from any of the others, but which looms up as such an important single aspect of reorganization that it will be given extended treatment. It may be briefly indicated that the conflicts of the divorced person, although having multitudinous variety, concern mainly the lines of readjustment which have been previously indicated.

The task of settling one's conflicts is at first one of learning to live with one's self and with one's wounds, and only later does positive reconstruction become possible. What divorced people usually do is to work out a technique of living with their problems; sometimes it seems that they want these problems to endure. As real reorganization after divorce is rare, the problem of the description and analysis of the mental conflicts of the divorcé becomes exceedingly complex.

MARITAL COHESIVENESS AND DISSOLUTION:
AN INTEGRATIVE REVIEW

George Levinger

WHAT MAKES a marriage "stick"? And what breaks it apart?
Such questions have answers, but the answers do not yet
rest on an explicit theoretical base. There is an abundance
of descriptive findings and of empirical generalizations, but
as yet a scarcity of conceptual construction.[1]

Consider the following instance. In a review of "willed
departures" in marriage, Goode[2] has summarized a number
of variables related to divorce proneness "which seem to be
based on good evidence": urban background, marriage at
very young ages, short acquaintanceship before marriage,
short or no engagement, marital unhappiness of parents,
nonattendance at church, mixed religious faith, disapproval
by kin and friends of the marriage, dissimilarity of background, and different definitions by spouses of their mutual
roles. Goode also notes that husband's occupation and income are inversely related to divorce proneness.[3] Other writers have shown associations between divorce proneness and
childlessness,[4] low conventionality,[5] disjunctive affiliation
networks,[6] and a series of other factors.[7]

It seems reasonable to seek a common conceptual base
that will assist in explaining those findings. This paper
presents such a conceptual frame, in which marriage is
conceived as a special case of all two-person relationships.
Marital cohesiveness becomes a special case of group co-

Reprinted with permission of the author and publisher from *Journal
of Marriage and the Family*, vol. 27, no. 1 (February 1965), pp. 19–28.

This paper was written in connection with research on marital relationships, supported by a grant from the Cleveland Foundation and
by Grant M–4653 from the National Institute of Mental Health. The
author is indebted to William J. Goode, Sidney Rosen, Steven E.
Deutsch, Irving Rosow, Dorwin Cartwright, and Edwin J. Thomas for
their reading of an earlier version.

hesiveness in general. The findings from some major studies of divorce and of marital adjustment are interpreted according to this framework.

COHESIVENESS IN MARRIAGE

The marriage pair is a two-person group. It follows, then, that marital cohesiveness is analogous to group cohesiveness and can be defined accordingly. Group cohesiveness is "the total field of forces which act on members to remain in the group."[8] Inducements to remain in any group include the attractiveness of the group itself and the strength of the restraints against leaving it; inducements to leave a group include the attractiveness of alternative relationships and the restraints against breaking up such existing relationships. Thus the strength of the marital relationship would be a direct function of the attractions within and barriers around the marriage, and an inverse function of such attractions and barriers from other relationships.

In marriage, a spouse is attracted to his mate because of her intrinsic worth, her love, her charm, her ability to please his wants, or perhaps because she gains him external prestige or will further extrinsic goals. Barriers against a breakup emanate from other sources: the emotional, religious, and moral commitments that a partner feels toward his marriage or toward his children; the external pressures of kin and community, of the law, the church, and other associational memberships.

Thus marital strength is a function of bars as well as bonds. Yet the strength of barriers matters little if the partners' attraction is high enough. In many marriages, the barriers have trivial importance. The spouses' close attachment precludes that either one would seriously consider breaking the relationship.

In other marriages, though, barriers have crucial importance. In the absence of positive feelings, they maintain outward signs of marital togetherness. Goode has called the latter case an "empty shell" marriage:

. . . The atmosphere is without laughter or fun, and a sullen gloom pervades the household. Members do not discuss their problems or experiences with each other, and communication is kept to a minimum. . . . Their rationalization for avoiding a divorce is, on the part of one or both, "sacrifice for the children," "neighborhood respectability," and a religious conviction that divorce is morally wrong. . . . The hostility in such a home is great, but arguments focus on the small issues, not the large ones. Facing the latter would, of course, lead directly to separation or divorce, but the couple has decided that staying together overrides other values, including each other's happiness and the psychological health of their children.[9]

This illustration of an "empty shell" family evokes contrasting images of "full shell" and "no shell" families. To carry Goode's metaphor farther, a "full shell" marriage would be one in which not only the boundaries but also the attractions are strong for both partners; a marriage in which there is warm emotional interchange. In contrast, the "no shell" couple is in a state of dissolution; it consists of two disconnected individuals, living separate lives. In this latter instance, boundaries as well as attractions have been eroded by the events over time, until eventually alternatives to the marital state are preferred. Goode's metaphor is appropriate. It implicitly refers to two underlying continua: fullness-emptiness of attraction, and strength-weakness of boundaries.

Finally, consider the attractions and barriers outside the marriage. These are forces that pertain to relations with parents, children, lovers, friends, enemies, employers, employes, or any of a host of alternate persons. Husband or wife may be more or less attracted to any of these relationships, and he or she will have a varying sense of obligation to maintain them. Such alternate relationships can be fully compatible with the existence of a strong and stable marriage. The maintenance of relations with in-laws or employers, for example, does not necessary conflict with the primary marital bond. However, an extreme commitment to such a relationship would interfere with the marriage; as would also, of course, a commitment to a third party that fully excludes the spouse.

COHESIVENESS AND DIVORCE

In studying marriage, high cohesiveness is far harder to detect than low cohesiveness. The privacy of the marital relationship prevents outsiders from judging how "truly happy" a particular union might be; even insiders, the spouses themselves, cannot be fully aware of all the attractions and restraints that they feel.

On the other hand, the extremes of low cohesiveness eventuate in the dissolution of the relationship. If divorce is the result, it is a public index that can be studied. For this reason, it is useful to give particular consideration to research on divorce to illustrate how the present framework can be applied.

Yet consideration of such research must note the distinction between divorce and separation. In certain groups of our society, *de jure* separation (divorce) is a less likely occurrence than *de facto* residential separation. Undoubtedly, the less socially visible a couple is, the more likely it is to resort to informal procedures of separation. The less clear a family's ties to stable norms of kin and community, the less necessary it is to make a break formal. Thus desertion has been a far more common phenomenon in the lowest socioeconomic stratum than in the higher strata. This point must be remembered in interpreting findings on divorce rates.[10]

Possible differences in the forces affecting the two partners. The term *cohesiveness* is drawn from a physical analogy. The cohesiveness of a physical bond between two nuclei in a molecule may be indicated by the amount of energy required to break it. The physical model, though, assumes homogeneity in the forces among the nuclei. A social group model of bond strength cannot assume such homogeneity. Feelings of attraction and restraint can and do vary among the members of a group.

In marriage, too, the two partners' feelings are not identical. One spouse may consider separation, while the other remains fully bound to the relationship. Nevertheless, by definition, both partners must value another alternative over that of the present marriage before both will agree to a separation. Usually, the wife is plaintiff in divorce proceedings. Nationally, the figure is about 70 per cent.[11] The preponderance of wife-initiated divorce suits results in part from cultural prescription, yet some of the author's unpublished evidence indicates that the balance of the wife's feelings is more important than the husband's as an indicator of divorce proneness.[12]

REVIEW OF FACTORS ASSOCIATED WITH DIVORCE

How do findings from actual studies illustrate the framework? Attractions that act to secure a marriage derive from love and money. The rewards that spouses receive are linked to their affection for each other, to their financial income and social position, and also to the degree that husband and wife share similar characteristics. Barriers against a breakup can be coordinated to the partners' feelings of obligation to their family, to their moral values, and to external pressures exerted on them from various sources—these are the sorts of pressures that serve to maintain the boundaries of their marriage. Finally, one can consider alternate sources of affectional and financial reward; these serve as a contrast to the internal attractions and have a potentially disruptive effect.

Table 1, together with its accompanying discussion, organizes published findings that pertain to marital cohesiveness under the three headings of attraction, barrier, and alternate attraction.

Attractions in Marriage

Esteem for spouse. It appears obvious that marital cohesiveness is positively associated with the spouses' mutual esteem and affection. Yet in what areas is esteem most apparent, and in what forms is it present or absent? Locke (24)[13] has found that spouses in happy marriages described their partners' traits in a far more positive way than did divorced persons; the former were far more likely to report the mate's traits as superior or at least equal to their own. Kelly (17) also has reported that this tendency is positively related to marital happiness. Regarding negative esteem, Goode (11), Harmsworth and Minnis (14), and Locke (24) have reported a far higher incidence of complaints about the partner among divorcees or divorce applicants than among normally adjusted spouses.

Desire for companionship. In some cultures, such as the Japanese, marriage does not promote companionship with the spouse. However, two studies of American marriages by Blood and Wolfe (4) and Kirkpatrick (20) found that desire for companionship is strongly related to marital adjustment.

Sexual enjoyment. Locke (24) has reported that happy

and divorced spouses differed significantly, both in their enjoyment of actual intercourse and in their desire for it. Terman (32) found that the most adjusted couples had the highest ratio of actual/preferred frequency of sexual relations. To qualify this finding, one should note Kephart's report (18) that concern with sexual incompatibility was found primarily among divorce applicants from the higher social strata. (The present author, in an unpublished study, has obtained a similar finding.) Sexual gratification is one vital source of marital attraction, but its lack apparently is less keenly felt among spouses who have not achieved a satisfactory material standard of living.

Husband's income. In Western nations, as Goode (12) has recently pointed out, divorce rates were greater for high-income than for low-income marriages until the advent of industrialization. However, since some unspecifiable transition point during the early part of this century, divorce rates have been negatively associated with husband's income (12). It would appear that the attractions within the marriage are lowest for the poor, and that attractions outside the marriage are relatively greater. With the reduction of legal obstacles and of economic costs of divorce, there has occurred a large increase in divorce among low-income couples.

These reasons, then, explain the inverse relation between income and divorce found in modern studies. One of the first studies to suggest this was Schroeder's (31) analysis of divorce rates in Peoria; by an ecological technique, he found a correlation of $-.32$ between divorce rates and average income in different districts of that city. Locke (24), in his comparison between happily married and divorced spouses, found that an income "adequate for the needs of the family" lessened the likelihood of divorce. Burgess and Cottrell (5) also found a moderate positive relationship. In contrast, neither Bernard (2) nor Terman (32) found such an association; however, their samples were probably too restricted in the range of financial income. When wide ranges of income and marital satisfaction are considered, as in studies of the entire U.S. population by the Census (34), there is a clear inverse correlation between income and divorced status, and even more between income and separated status.[14]

Home ownership. The proportion of couples who obtain a divorce is lower for owners than for nonowners of a home.

TABLE I. *Factors Found to Differentiate Between High and Low Cohesive Marriages*

Sources of Attraction	Sources of Barrier Strength	Sources of Alternate Attraction
Affectional rewards: Esteem for spouse[11, 14,17,24]*	*Feelings of obligation:* To dependent children[11,15,27]	*Affectional rewards:* Preferred alternate sex partner[11,14,18, 24]
Desire for companionship[4,20]	To marital bond[25]	
Sexual enjoyment[18,24,32]	*Moral proscriptions:* Proscriptive religion[8,21,30]	Disjunctive social relation[1,24]
Socio-economic rewards:	Joint church attendance[9,11,24,31]	Opposing religious affiliations[21]
Husband's income[(2), 5,12,24,31,(32),34]	*External pressures:* Primary group affiliations[1]	*Economic rewards:* Wife's opportunity for independent income[12,16,23]
Home ownership[5,24,31]	Community stigma: rural-urban[3,5,7,31,37]	
Husband's education[10,28,35,36]	Legal and economic bars[16]	
Husband's occupation[11,19,26,33,38]		
Similarity in social status:		
Religion[4,6,8,21.29, 30,38]		
Education[4,13,20,39]		
Age[4,5,24]		

* Numerals pertain to positive findings in the corresponding references listed below. Numerals in parentheses indicate which studies reported an absence of a difference between High and Low cohesive couples.

1 Charles Ackerman, "Affiliations: Structural Determinants of Differential Divorce Rates," *American Journal of Sociology,* 69 (July 1963), pp. 12–20.

2 Jessie Bernard, "Factors in the Distribution of Success in Marriage," *American Journal of Sociology,* 40 (July 1934), pp. 49–60.

3 Robert O. Blood, Jr., *Marriage,* Glencoe, Ill.: Free Press, 1962.

4 Robert O. Blood, Jr., and Donald M. Wolfe, *Husbands and Wives,* Glencoe, Ill.: Free Press, 1960.

5 Ernest W. Burgess and Leonard S. Cottrell, Jr., *Predicting Success or Failure in Marriage,* Englewood Cliffs, N. J.: Prentice-Hall, 1939.

6 Ernest W. Burgess and Paul Wallin, *Engagement and Marriage,* Philadelphia: Lippincott, 1953.

7 Hugh Carter and Alexander Plateris, "Trends in Divorce and Family Disruption," *HEW Indicators* (September 1963), pp. v–xiv.

8 Loren E. Chancellor and Thomas Monahan, "Religious Preference and Interreligious Mixtures in Marriages and Divorces in Iowa," *American Journal of Sociology,* 61 (November 1955), pp. 233–239.

9 Eustace Chesser, *The Sexual, Marital, and Family Relationships of the English Woman,* New York: Roy, 1957.

10 Paul C. Glick, *American Families,* New York: John Wiley, 1957.

11 William J. Goode, *After Divorce,* Glencoe, Ill.: Free Press, 1956.

12 William J. Goode, "Marital Satisfaction and Instability: A Cross-Cultural Analysis of Divorce Rates," *International Social Science Journal,* 14:3 (1962), pp. 507–526.

(Continued)

This finding is reported by Schroeder (31), by Burgess and Cottrell (5), and by Locke (24). Much of the association may be a function of family income and of length of marriage. However, even if the influence of those two variables is controlled, home ownership itself probably contributes to the stability of family life.[15] It would seem that home ownership is not only a source of attraction, but also helps to stabilize the boundaries that hold the marriage together. All else being equal, the mere fact of owning a home probably increases a couple's reluctance to dissolve their relationship.

Husband's amount of education. The amount of the husband's education is higher for durable than for dissolved marriages. This is indicated by data reported by Glick (10), by Monahan (28), and by U.S. Census reports (35, 36). One would speculate, *ceteris paribus*, that a wife's attraction varies with her spouse's educational status. These findings, of course, are linked to variations in other variables, such as husband's income or prestige. His years of education un-

13 Gilbert V. Hamilton, *A Research in Marriage*, New York: Boni, 1929.

14 Harry C. Harmsworth and Mhyra S. Minnis, "Nonstatutory Causes of Divorce: The Lawyer's Point of View," *Marriage and Family Living*, 17 (November 1955), pp. 316–321.

15 Paul H. Jacobson, "Differentials in Divorce by Duration of Marriage and Size of Family," *American Sociological Review*, 15 (April 1950), pp. 235–244.

16 Paul H. Jacobson, *American Marriage and Divorce*, New York: Rinehart, 1959.

17 E. Lowell Kelly, "Marital Compatibility as Related to Personality Traits of Husbands and Wives as Rated by Self and Spouse," *Journal of Social Psychology*, 13 (February 1941), pp. 193–198.

18 William M. Kephart, "Some Variables in Cases of Reported Sexual Maladjustment," *Marriage and Family Living*, 16 (August 1954), pp. 241–243.

19 William M. Kephart, "Occupational Level and Marital Disruption," *American Sociological Review*, 20 (August 1955), pp. 456–465.

20 Clifford Kirkpatrick, "Community of Interest and the Measurement of Adjustment in Marriage," *The Family*, 18 (June 1937), pp. 133–137.

21 Judson T. Landis, "Marriages of Mixed and Non-Mixed Religious Faith," *American Sociological Review*, 14 (June 1949), pp. 401–406.

22 Richard O. Lang, *A Study of the Degree of Happiness or Unhappiness in Marriages as Rated by Acquaintances of the Married Couples*, M.A. thesis, University of Chicago, 1932; cited in Goode (11), p. 57.

23 J. P. Lichtenberger, *Divorce*, New York: McGraw-Hill, 1931.

24 Harvey J. Locke, *Predicting Adjustment in Marriage: A Comparison of a Divorced and a Happily Married Group*, New York: Holt, 1951.

25 Thomas P. Monahan, "How Stable Are Remarriages?" *American Journal of Sociology*, 58 (November 1952), pp. 280–288.

26 Thomas P. Monahan, "Divorce by Occupational Level," *Marriage and Family Living*, 17 (November 1955), pp. 322–324.

doubtedly are correlated positively with prestige, with the husband's relative superiority over his wife, and with his ability to maintain a masculine role. If the husband's education is lower than his wife's, there is more likely to be a reversal in the male-female power balance with an ensuing loss of the husband's attractiveness as her marital partner.

Husband's occupation. Numerous studies have shown that divorce proneness is also inversely related to husband's occupational rank. Thus, Goode (11), Kephart (19), Monahan (26), and Weeks (38) have each shown that couples in which the husband's occupation ranks high have less divorce proneness than those where it ranks low. Part of this result may be attributed to the contribution of income, another part to the higher prestige of the professions and managerial occupations.

A third reason for the difference in divorce proneness among occupational groups relates to the stability of the

27 Thomas P. Monahan, "Is Childlessness Related to Family Stability?" *American Sociological Review*, 20 (August 1955), pp. 446–456.

28 Thomas P. Monahan, "Educational Achievement and Family Stability," *Journal of Social Psychology*, 55 (December 1961), pp. 253–263.

29 Thomas P. Monahan and Loren E. Chancellor, "Statistical Aspects of Marriage and Divorce by Religious Denomination in Iowa," *Eugenics Quarterly*, 2 (September 1955), pp. 162–173.

30 Thomas P. Monahan and William M. Kephart, "Divorce and Desertion by Religious and Mixed-Religious Groups," *American Journal of Sociology*, 59 (March 1954), pp. 454–465.

31 Clarence W. Schroeder, *Divorce in a City of 100,000 Population*, Peoria, Ill.: Bradley Polytechnic Institute Library, 1939.

32 Lewis M. Terman, *Psychological Factors in Marital Happiness*, New York: McGraw-Hill, 1938.

33 U. S. Bureau of Census, *Marriage and Divorce: 1887–1906*, Bulletin 96, Washington, D. C.: Government Printing Office, 1908, pp. 25–27.

34 U. S. Bureau of Census, *U. S. Census of Population: 1950*. Vol. IV, *Special Reports*, Part 2, Chapter D, Marital Status, Washington, D. C.: Government Printing Office, 1953, Table 6, pp. 47–48.

35 U. S. Bureau of Census, *U. S. Census of Population: 1950*. Vol. IV, *Special Reports*, Part 5, Chapter B, Education, Washington, D. C.: Government Printing Office, 1953, Table 8, pp. 63–64.

36 U. S. Department of Health, Education and Welfare, *Vital Statistics–Special Reports*, 45: 12 (September 9, 1957), p. 301.

37 U. S. Bureau of Census, *Current Population Reports*, Series 20, No. 87 (November 14, 1958), pp. 11–12.

38 H. Ashley Weeks, "Differential Divorce Rates by Occupations," *Social Forces*, 21 (March 1943), pp. 334–337.

39 Edith W. Williams, "Factors Associated with Adjustment in Rural Marriage," Ph.D. Dissertation, Cornell University, 1938, p. 98; cited in Goode (11), p. 99.

husband's home life, as associated with his occupation. Thus Monahan (26) reported that physicians have a higher divorce rate than dentists, taxicab drivers a higher rate than truck drivers. One would hypothesize that the divorce rate of general practitioners or internists, whose home life is constantly disrupted, would be higher than that of doctors with regular working hours (e.g., pathologists, radiologists, or X-ray specialists); that it would be higher for long-haul truckers than for intra-city truck drivers. High degrees of instability would tend to reduce the attractiveness of the relationship and also to erode the boundaries that contain it.

Occupational differences may also be linked to differences in susceptibility to alternate attractions. Members of certain occupations (e.g., internists, taxicab drivers, or masseurs) have a greater than average probability for extended intimate contacts with members of the opposite sex. Thus they will have a greater opportunity to explore alternate attractions that would compete with their current marital relationship. In contrast, members of other occupations (e.g., clergymen or politicians) are particularly vulnerable to externally imposed norms about boundary maintenance, which would restrain any proclivity toward divorce.[16]

Such additional considerations are important in weighing the impact of occupational factors in affecting marital stability. Future empirical studies may be able to distinguish among the separate influences of each of these components.

Similarity in social status. Many studies have linked marital adjustment to similarity of religious preference— particularly Chancellor and Monahan (8), Landis (21) Monahan and Chancellor (29), Monahan and Kephart (30), and Weeks (38). Burgess and Wallin (6) noted that frequency of broken engagements was lower for same-faith couples. Hamilton (13), Kirkpatrick (20), and Williams (39) have indicated that marital attraction is positively related to similarity in education. Burgess and Cottrell (5) and Locke (24) found that it is significantly associated with age similarity, particularly when the husband is older. Blood and Wolfe (4) have found that all three kinds of similarity relate positively to marital satisfaction. Undoubtedly, these are all different aspects of status similarity. Communication between the spouses would tend to be enhanced by relative likeness on these characteristics.

Sources of Barrier Strength

Sources of barrier forces exist both inside and outside the individual. The following examples of restraints against marital dissolution include some cases where the restraints are primarily internal, others where they are mainly external, and still others where their source is difficult to locate.

Obligation to dependent children. It is widely held that as long as there are no children involved, divorce is the couple's own affair. For that reason, one might expect that husbands and wives with children would feel a greater restraint than those without children—particularly minor children.

Early writings on divorce gave the impression that childless couples have indeed a vastly higher divorce rate,[17] but those studies neglected to adjust divorce rate by *duration* of marriage. More sophisticated analyses by Jacobson (15) and by Monahan (27) have shown, that if length of marriage is controlled, the difference in separation rate between childless and child-rearing couples is much smaller, but still noticeable. According to Jacobson (15), between 1928 and 1948 this disparity decreased to a ratio of less than 2:1. Even the most skeptical analysis of this difference by Monahan (27) showed some excess of divorce frequency in the childless groups.

The real question is, perhaps, what obligations do the parents *feel* toward their children? To what extent do they feel that divorce of an unattractive marriage would either damage or promote their children's well-being? If parents believe the former, then the existence of children will create barrier forces; if they believe the latter, then they would be likely to be attracted to an alternative other than the present marriage. Goode (11), for example, has taken the position that, in an inevitably conflicted home, children may actually benefit from the divorce.

So far, there is no published evidence which differentiates between parents' feelings of obligation to children as *barriers* that prevent a breakup and such obligations as sources of *negative attraction* to the marriage. Until such evidence is obtained, the issue will remain unresolved.

Obligations to the marital bond. In a large proportion of marriages, both partners are firmly committed to respect the marital contract, and divorce is not considered as a possibility. Each partner has certain qualms against even thinking of such a thing. On the other hand, if one or both have previously experienced a divorce proceeding, then either partner would be more likely to consider divorce. Thus, the barriers against the dissolution of the present marriage would be weaker. A study by Monahan (25) has indeed shown that first marriages are more resistant to dissolution than are second or later marriages. His data were confined to population statistics and did not pertain longitudinally to particular individuals. Nevertheless, it would be hypothesized that marriages of divorcees tend to have weaker boundaries than those of first-married spouses; further evidence is needed, however, to arrive at any sound generalization.

Proscriptive religion.   It is popularly believed that Catholics are less likely to break their marriages than persons of other religious persuasions. This is only partly true. A more correct statement is that like-faith marriages in which both members are either Catholics, Jews, or reasonably strict Protestants have the lowest probability of divorce. This has been pointed out by studies of Chancellor and Monahan (8), Landis (21), and Monahan and Kephart (30). Such studies have also shown that persons of unconventional religious convictions are most prone to use divorce as a solution to their marital problems.

Joint church attendance.   Various studies have shown that divorce proneness is inversely related to joint church attendance. Joint membership and regular attendance at church places a couple in a network of connected affiliations and exposes them to conventional values. One would assume that membership in such a net is a source of powerful external pressures. If necessary, such pressures would come into play to prevent the marriage from breaking up.

Reports by Chesser (9), Locke (24), and Schroeder (31) each indicate that, in their samples of couples, marital dissolution was less frequent among regular church attenders than among nonattenders. In his study of divorcees, Goode (11) found that (in his group of Catholics) regularity of church attendence was positively associated with duration of marriage before separation.

Primary group affiliation.   Affiliation with a church or with other sorts of organizations is one source of barrier forces; affiliation with kinfolk is another vital source. In a recent paper, Ackerman (1) has proposed that divorce rates vary across different cultures to the extent that the culture encourages "conjunctive" as opposed to "disjunctive" affiliations with kin. Ackerman defines the former case as one where husband and wife share a common network of kinfolk and friends; in the latter, their loyalties go in different directions. One would suppose that a conjunctive net of affiliations acts to restrain marital dissolution more than a disjunctive net. Ackerman's analysis of cross-cultural data shows empirical support for this supposition.

Community stigma. Another source of barriers against divorce is community disapproval. Such disapproval seems more characteristic of rural than of urban communities, which leads to the expectation that rural divorce rates are lower than urban ones. This expectation is borne out by 1955 Census data (37) and by 1960 Census data cited by Carter and Plateris (7). Also, studies by Schroeder (31) and by Burgess and Cottrell (5) have reported that divorced persons are less likely to be born and reared in a rural setting.[18]

Blood (3) has drawn attention to the importance of the visibility of the marriage relationship in the community where the couple lives. When both partners are known, when their behavior is observed, there are greater restraints against social transgressions such as extramarital affairs. Life in the country would seem more restrictive than that in the city; relations in the suburb more constraining than in the urban center.

In describing life in the modern suburb, Whyte has noted that it exerts a "beneficent effect on relations between husband and wife. The group is a foster family." Whyte quotes a minister as follows: "The kind of social situation you find here discourages divorce. Few people, as a rule, get divorces until they break with their groups. I think the fact that it is so hard to break with a group here has had a lot to do with keeping some marriages from going on the rocks."[19]

Legal and economic bars. It goes almost without saying that legal and financial considerations exert restraints against a breakup. The wide differences in divorce rates among different states can, in part, be accounted for by differences in divorce laws—as Jacobson (16) has pointed out. And, when considering differences between high- and low-income husbands, one notes that a high-income husband is likely to pay more, both absolutely and proportionately, to support his ex-wife after separation. Thus both legal and financial factors provide important restraints against going through with a divorce.

Sources of Alternate Attraction

Popularly, it might seem that alternate attractions are the chief or the only reason for broken marriages. This impression is sustained by legal fiat, which emphasizes adultery as a reason for divorce. In one state, New York, adultery is the only legal grounds for dissolving a marriage contract.

It is logically necessary that the alternative environment be more attractive than the marital relationship, if the partners are to be willing to undergo the costs of divorce. However, it is not necessary that the attraction be "another woman" or "another man." The marital relationship itself may be so unattractive that any alternative condition—with or without another partner—is preferred.

Preferred other sex partner.   Aside from reports on official complaints lodged with the Court, which frequently are colored to sustain the legal fiction, relatively few studies contain data about spouses' alternate attractions outside the marriage. It is difficult to inquire about this without asking the parties to a divorce action to compromise their personal and legal position vis-à-vis their spouse. Nevertheless, several published studies have reported that preference for an outside sexual partner does play a part in a significant proportion of divorce actions. The proportion may vary anywhere from 15 to 35 per cent of all cases—e.g., Goode (11), Harmsworth and Minnis (14), Kephart (18), and Locke (24). Complaints about external sexual attachments are more frequently reported by wives; but when the husband reports them in a divorce suit, they may be even more serious.[20]

Disjunctive kin affiliations.   Another source of outside attraction forces would be the loyalty towards one's kin or friends. If these ties conflict with those of the spouse, they will at the least lead to strain in the marriage. As mentioned earlier, Ackerman (1) has suggested that competing primary group affiliations are associated with divorce proneness. Locke (24) found that his "happy" couples frequently reported "a little" conflict with their own parents, i.e., (alternate) attractions to parents were at less than maximal strength. This source of marital disruption is worthy of fuller exploration in future studies of divorce.

In cases of disjunctive affiliation, one would hypothesize that the marital bond would be strengthened if the couple increases its physical and psychological distance from *both* sets of alternate affiliation groups, reducing thereby the disruptive forces. For example, partners in a heterogamous marriage that involves antagonistic in-laws would strengthen their relationship by moving away from the community where either set of parents resides. No systematic evidence to support this hypothesis can be cited, but it does coincide with informal observation.[21]

Opposing religious affiliations. What are the effects of obligations toward alternative competing relationships? Little direct study of this question has been made. However, one bit of evidence indicates the direction in which the answer may lie.

Landis' study (21) of divorce rates in Catholic-Protestant marriages showed clearly that mixed-faith unions were less durable than same-faith marriages of Catholics or Protestants. However, Catholic-Protestant marriages were three times more likely to break up when the wife was Protestant than when the husband was Protestant.

This result is explainable by the framework as follows. Assume that both partners are attracted to their own religious group, but that the wife's feelings are stronger. Assume, also, that the children in each of these marriages are to be raised as Catholics, as is the usual agreement in Catholic-Protestant marriages. Finally, assume that the wife takes prime responsibility for child-rearing. It follows, then, that the Protestant mother is exposed to more conflict—negative attraction toward spouse's religion and disruptive pressures from own religion—than is the Protestant father. The strength of this conflict would depend on the strength of her religious identification—probably weakest in the lowest strata and strongest in the middle or higher strata. This line of reasoning has clear-cut empirical derivations and may well be testable in Landis' existing data. Additional studies of this question are desirable.

Wife's opportunity for independent income. One other important source of alternate attraction or repulsion lies in the possibility of the wife's separate financial maintenance.

The more readily she can support herself outside the marital relationship or can be assured of such support from other means (including her ex-husband's), the more ready she would be to break the marriage.

In most cases where the husband's income is extremely low, and where the wife's earnings are a substantial proportion of family income, these conditions would seem to be met. In the upper economic strata, however, income differentials between wife and husband are large, and the wife has more reason to maintain the marriage (see Goode, 12, p. 516). In other words, wives in the lower strata appear to have less to lose and more to gain from a divorce. Economic sources of alternate attraction for the wife require further attention in research on divorce. Today, when certain forms of relief payment are contingent upon proof of the husband's nonsupport, it is particularly likely that economic factors exercise an influence on divorce proneness.[22]

Considering the wife's attraction to alternate relationships, one may also note interesting differences in divorce rates between the Eastern and Western states. Both Jacobson (16) and Lichtenberger (23) have reported that the Mountain, Southwestern, and Pacific states have had high rates, while the Middle Atlantic and New England states have had low rates. Traditionally, there has been a scarcity of women in the Western states, leading to greater opportunity for remarriage and also to greater female power.

CONCLUSION

This paper introduces an elementary framework for integrating the determinants of marital durability and divorce. The framework is based on merely two components—attractions toward or repulsions from a relationship, and barriers against its dissolution. The former correspond to Lewin's concept of "driving forces," which are said to drive a person either toward a positively valent object or away from a negatively valent one.[23] The latter correspond to Lewin's concept of "restraining forces," which act to restrain a person from leaving any particular relationship or situation.[24] These components can be used to subsume a large diversity of published findings. For example, findings about the effects of both income differentials and kinship affiliation could logically be fitted within the same scheme. Marital cohesiveness was thus interpreted as a special case of group cohesiveness.

Both the limitations and the advantages of the present analysis should be noted.

Limitations. First, the scheme is based on a hypothetical conception of the attractions and barriers that affect the partners in a marriage. These influences can rarely be inferred directly from changes in overt indices. This is one reason why this paper has not attempted to examine the complex interaction effects between different sets of such influences.

Second, the concept of group cohesiveness, from which this scheme is drawn, is itself the subject of critique and reformulation.[25] Theoretically, it is difficult to define cohesiveness so that it describes under the same rubric the forces that act on both the group and the separate individuals who compose the groups.

Third, the present review of earlier studies has been illustrative rather than comprehensive. Some pertinent studies were omitted. The discussion was often limited to single findings of available studies that were occasionally taken out of their wider context.

Advantages. At this time, it is *not* intended to offer either a general theory or to present an entirely complete review. It *is* intended to understand existing studies at a more general level of abstraction. It is suggested that marriage research can fruitfully be linked to small group research, that simple general hypotheses can be derived in the beginning stages of such a linkage, and that existing evidence about marital dissolution is suitable for documenting such hypotheses.

The present approach draws on the insights of Goode and other writers on marriage and divorce. Yet it aims to go farther in several ways. First, it points to the development of a general framework, congruent with theories about all social groups. It avoids *ad hoc* theories about "marriage" or "family," but aims to integrate the subject with knowledge of social relationships in general.

Second, the scheme intends to deal not only with actuarial rates of divorce nor only with a particular cultural milieu. Its social-psychological concepts are, in principle, applicable to any given marriage in any society. Although marriages and societies differ in the constellation of forces that determine cohesiveness, it is assumed that these determinants ultimately will be measured and precisely described.

Third, and most important, the components of the present scheme are derived from one basic assumption about the existence of psychological and social forces. Such "forces" are hypothetical. They are not easily accessible to measurement. Yet the present statement aims to prepare for eventual measurement.

Previous attempts to explain divorce have sometimes precluded a clear operational assessment. For example, Goode recently accounted for differences in divorce rates in terms of *both* "social pressures from kinfolk and friends" and a culture-based "equalitarian ethos."[26] Yet his two concepts, kin pressures and cultural ethos, are on quite different levels of conceptualization; the former is vaguely contained in the latter. In contrast, the presently proposed framework offers an opportunity for describing the relations among such concepts. To obtain a precise estimate of the various factors which influence divorce, one would need eventually to establish some common measuring unit that would indicate the magnitude of each force.

The present interpretation does not aim at novelty, but it does attempt to prepare the ground for more advanced derivations. Consider one example of a derivation from the scheme. To increase the durability of a marriage, one can (1) increase its positive attractiveness, (2) decrease the attractiveness of alternate relationships, or (3) increase the strength of the barriers against a breakup. What would be the consequence of each of these?

Increase of marital attractions would renew the partners' interest in and affection for one another. It would further the spouses' turning toward each other for their gratification, and would promote the mutual consummation of the marital bond.

Decrease of external attractions would lessen the distractions of the outside environment; therefore, it would encourage the spouse to look toward his partner as an object of need gratification. Yet this is only an indirect way of enhancing marital satisfaction. It is neither a necessary nor a sufficient means for creating positive consequences for the relationship.

Increase of the barriers is the least likely means of making a lasting increase in marital cohesiveness. Without an increase of internal attraction, barrier maintenance does not heighten the satisfactions that partners gain from their marriage. In the absence of adequate marital satisfaction, high barriers are likely to lead to high interpersonal conflict and tension. In fact, the very severity often found in cases of marital conflict may derive from the high restraints society places against breaking up a marriage. Yet this method of keeping a marriage together is society's usual prescription for dealing with low marital cohesiveness.

If the above points are logically correct, then they should lead to empirical investigation of marriage relationships to verify them. For example, one might study marriages with equal degrees of marital satisfaction that differ in boundary strength; under conditions of low satisfaction, lower tension would be predicted in those relationships where the barriers are relatively low. Or it is possible to conceive longitudinal studies in which indices of attraction and barrier forces depict the course of the partners' relationships? Additional illustrations can be developed.

The generality of the present scheme makes it suitable also for analyzing friendship or quasi-marriage relationships. For example, relationships that emerge during courtship and engagement can be examined in these terms. What, for instance, are the determinants of broken engagements? How do broken engagements differ from broken marriages in the constellation of factors that influence the partners? These questions can be investigated by asking what the attractions and barriers are as seen by the partners, and by developing criteria to indicate the stability or persistence of such influences.

To summarize, a conceptual framework has been outlined for integrating research on marital cohesiveness and dissolution. The concepts are the same as those employed for understanding the cohesiveness of other social groups. The strength of the marital relationship is proposed to be a direct function of hypothetical attraction and barrier forces inside the marriage, and an inverse function of such influences from alternate relationships. The scheme was then applied to a review of some major findings about divorce, and its implications were discussed.

SOURCES OF MARITAL DISSATISFACTION
AMONG APPLICANTS FOR DIVORCE

George Levinger

To PARAPHRASE Jean Jacques Rousseau, man's dissatisfaction results from an excess of his wants over his abilities. This simple formula appears both sensible and valid, but it covers a complex topic. On the one hand, satisfaction and dissatisfaction are ever present qualifiers of human existence. On the other hand, they are diffuse effects of a variety of often poorly understood determinants.

Marital satisfaction, too, is the composite of numerous factors, some permanent, others temporary. It not only depends on what one partner wants and can give, and the needs and capacities of the other spouse, but it also depends on the impact of the environment. Nevertheless, one may try to demarcate certain broad parameters, to outline some reasonably stable determinants or correlates of satisfaction.

In an earlier paper, based on a study of 60 urban middle-class couples, it was reported that husbands' and wives' marital goals and criteria for satisfaction were remarkably similar.[1] For example, both husbands and wives were equally prone to rank "companionship" and "affection" as the most important goals for a good marriage. And both spouses' actual happiness bore a far higher association with the fulfillment of social-emotional roles than that of success in work.

Reprinted with permission of the author and publisher from the *American Journal of Orthopsychiatry*, vol. 36, no. 5 (October 1966), pp. 803–807.

Revision of a paper presented at the 1965 annual meeting of the American Orthopsychiatric Association, New York, New York.

This work was supported in part by grants from the Cleveland Foundation and the National Institute of Mental Health (MH–04653).

Appreciation is owed to officials of the Court of Common Pleas, Cuyahoga County, Ohio; particularly to Dr. Mandel Rubin, director, and the other staff of the Department of Marriage Conciliation. Strict anonymity of applicants' names was ensured.

Nevertheless, evidence from a previous study by Farber[2] indicated that husbands and wives in a lower socioeconomic stratum tend to show some systematic dissimilarity in marital goals. Farber's husbands were significantly less concerned than their wives with the achievement of affection and companionship.

Further, dissatisfaction with marriage need not stem from the same determinants as does satisfaction. Both spouses may agree about the potential and actual rewards, but each may suffer from distinctively different problems when complaints do arise. The most extreme case of marital complaint occurs when partners are seeking dissolution—when a husband and wife are applying for divorce.

The present paper will deal with two general questions. First, to what extent do such husbands and wives differ in the bases of their marital dissatisfaction? Second, what differences can be noted across socioeconomic lines?

METHOD

The findings are based on a sample of 600 couples who were divorce applicants, representing marriages at the brink of dissolution. All these people were residents of Cuyahoga County, Ohio (i.e., greater Cleveland). All had one or more children under 14 and had been seen jointly by an experienced marriage counselor at the Conciliation Department of the Domestic Relations Court of Cuyahoga County. The interviews were of a mandatory nature, required by rule of Court for all divorce applicants with children under 14. The interview records of the marriage counselors were kept according to a standardized printed schedule.

The counselors' records were made available to us for analysis and a large number of characteristics were coded. Among the codable data, there was considerable information about each spouse's complaints about his partner.

Spouses' complaints were coded in one of the following 12 categories, with an intercoder reliability of 88 per cent:

1. *Neglect of home or children:* frequent absence, irregular hours, emotional distance.
2. *Financial problems:* either inadequate support (by husband) or poor handling of family's money.

3. *Physical abuse:* committing overt physical hurt or injury to other partner.
4. *Verbal abuse:* profanity, name-calling, shouting.
5. *Infidelity:* attachment to an alternate partner, frequently sexual in nature, which excludes spouse; adultery.
6. *Sexual incompatibility:* reluctance or refusal of coitus, inconsiderateness and other sources of dissatisfaction.
7. *Drinking:* drunkenness or excessive drinking.
8. *In-law trouble:* interference or pressure by in-laws, spouse's excessive loyalty to parental kin.
9. *Mental cruelty:* suspicion, jealousy, untruthfulness, and vague subjective complaints.
10. *Lack of love:* insufficient affection, communication, companionship.
11. *Excessive demands:* impatience, intolerance, strictness, possessiveness.
12. *Other:* miscellaneous category.

RESULTS

Let us examine the findings of the study. First, did husbands and wives differ in the number and nature of their complaints?

Concerning the number of complaints, wives' reports exceeded husbands' by a ratio of almost 2:1. The 600 wives averaged 3.05 separate complaints; the husbands expressed a mean of 1.64 complaints.

As to the nature of complaints, Table 1 shows that wives complained 11 times more frequently than husbands about physical abuse. That is, 36.8 per cent of the wives and only 3.3 per cent of the husbands said that their partner hurt them physically. Wives complained four times as often about financial problems and about drinking; three times as much about their spouse's verbal abuse. Wives' complaints significantly exceeded husbands' on three other categories, neglect of home and children, lack of love, and mental cruelty, but these ratios were less one-sided.

Husbands' complaints exceeded those of their mates on two counts. They were more apt to mention in-law trouble, by a ratio of 5 to 2; and they more often brought up sexual incompatibility in a ratio of 3 to 2.

Let us now look at some social-class comparisons. Did

complaint patterns differ across socioeconomic lines? The answer is a clear "yes."

TABLE 1. *Marital Complaints among 600 Couples Applying for Divorce, Classified by Sex and by Social Position of Respondents*

Complaint	*Proportion of Complaints by Respondent Groups*					
	Wives Total[a]	*Hus-bands* Total[a]	*Social Position of*			
			Wives		*Husbands*	
			Middle[b]	Lower[c]	Middle[b]	Lower[c]
Physical abuse	.368[d]	.033	.228	.401[e]	.029	.035
Verbal abuse	.238[d]	.075	.200	.245	.048	.082
Financial problems	.368[d]	.087	.219	.402[e]	.124	.079
Drinking	.265[d]	.050	.143	.294[e]	.048	.051
Neglect of home or children	.390[e]	.262	.457	.374	.200	.276
Mental cruelty	.403[e]	.297	.372	.408	.267	.306
In-law trouble	.067	.162[e]	.038	.074	.200	.153
Excessive demands	.025	.040	.057[f]	.018	.057	.035
Infidelity	.240	.200	.324[f]	.223	.114	.198[f]
Sexual incompatibility	.138	.200[e]	.124	.141	.267	.188
Lack of love	.228[e]	.135	.324[e]	.206	.200[f]	.120

[a] N = 600; all husbands or wives.
[b] N = 105; "Middle" refers to Class I–III on Hollinghead's Index of Social Position.[3]
[c] N = 490; "Lower" refers to Class IV–V on the Hollingshead Index. Note that 5 cases could not be categorized for social position, by dint of insufficient information.
[d] $p < .001$, indicating a significant difference in favor of the lettered number in the pair, by t test (two-tailed).
[e] $p < .01$.
[f] $p < .05$.

To examine the matter, frequencies of complaints from 490 lower-class pairs—Class IV and V, according to Hollingshead's Two-Factor Index (4)—were compared with adjusted frequencies for 105 middle-class pairs (Class I-III).

In mean number of *total* expressed complaints, there was no difference between spouses from lower and those from middle socioeconomic position. However, Table 1 indicates that lower-status wives were considerably more likely than middle-status wives to complain about financial problems, physical abuse and drinking. Middle-class wives were significantly more prone to complain about lack of love, infidelity and excessive demands. Middle-class husbands paralleled the wives in their significantly greater concern with lack of love; on the other hand, they were significantly *less* likely than lower-class husbands to complain of the wife's infidelity.

Considering the sexual relationship, one may note that "sexual incompatibility" was a more frequently voiced complaint by middle-class than by lower-class husbands, while the reverse was true for wives. The opposite was found for "infidelity."

In general, the evidence indicates that spouses in the middle-class marriages were more concerned with psychological and emotional interaction, while the lower-class partners saw as most salient in their lives financial problems and the unsubtle physical actions of their partner.

DISCUSSION

The essence of the results suggests the following interpretation. When things are going well and the relationship is fruitful, husband and wife tend to obtain very similar satisfaction. After all, their marital satisfaction is derived from one another; it is a matter of mutuality and of reciprocation,

When matters are going badly, if positive mutuality breaks down, then husband and wife complaints may still be mainly directed toward their joint relationship, but the verbalized sources of friction are different for the partners. Wives complain about the lack of love, neglect, physical or verbal abuse, or other matters included under the catch-all term of "mental cruelty." While husbands are also disturbed by neglect, lack of love, and emotional cruelty, they are more prone to express complaints about in-law interference or sexual mismatching.

These conclusions are similar to those in one major recent study of this general topic. From their 1958 national survey of mental health in America, Gurin, Veroff, and Feld[4] noted no dramatic differences among men and women in evaluating their marital adjustment. Married men and women were equally likely to mention some aspect of their interpersonal relationship, as opposed to their external environment. In that survey, women were also prone to acknowledge a somewhat higher proportion of marital problems, while men were more likely to deny the existence of such problems.

The survey findings have a second interesting implication for understanding our own results. In their random national sample the authors reported that the perceived source of marital problems was significantly connected with the educational level of the respondent. In other words, almost twice as many highly educated respondents as those with low education mentioned relationship-based problems or inadequacies in their marriage. This result accords with our own finding that occupational and educational status was linked to the nature of the spouses' goals, satisfactions and problem admission.

A study by Komarovsky,[5] published quite recently, underlines this issue in another way. Her research dealt intensively with 58 married couples, all with a "blue-collar" background. In her sample the high school educated spouses showed themselves to be more oriented toward marital communication and feeling disclosure than did the less educated persons. And the entire sample tended, on the average, to be less companionship-oriented than couples with white-collar socioeconomic status.

Some Interpretations

What integrating conceptions might help to deal with such facts? First, consider a quote from a recent paper by the economist Galbraith on "Economics and the Quality of Life"; and then let us turn to some notions about need hierarchies by the psychologist Maslow.

Galbraith[6] says: "In the poor society, not only do economic considerations dominate social attitudes but they rigidly specify the problems that will be accorded priority." (p. 117)

Maslow[7] has stated that each human being desires to fulfill a variety of needs, but he postulates the following categorical order in which they can be gratified. First and most basic are the subsistence needs of hunger, thirst and other physiological requirements. Second, there are the needs for safety and protection from external harm. Third, the individual wants love, belongingness and interpersonal warmth. Fourth are the needs for esteem and respect from other persons. Fifth, and only after the previous needs have been satisfied to a minimal extent, can the individual actively seek and achieve self-actualization.

Putting together the notions of Galbraith with those of Maslow, one may note that a large proportion of individuals, not only in the world at large, but also in the United States of America, are so heavily engaged with coping to satisfy needs at the first and second level (desire for subsistence and safety) that they are unable in their adulthood to worry about the achievement of mature love or interpersonal respect, not to speak of that rare quality of self-actualization.

The implications for preventive or curative treatment would be that our current verbal therapies, already known to be relatively unsuccessful with nonverbal people, may be not merely unsuccessful, but largely irrelevant to the needs of individuals striving at the basic levels. It may be important to consider the psychological hunger of a financially secure clientele and to learn to improve treatment practices. It is equally important to learn how other members of our population can be helped to satisfy their more basic needs, so that verbal therapy eventually might become relevant to them.

MARITAL SATISFACTION AND INSTABILITY: A CROSS-CULTURAL CLASS ANALYSIS OF DIVORCE RATES

William J. Goode

BECAUSE family experiences arouse so much emotion and social philosophers continue to believe that the family is a major element in the social structure, the field has for over two millennia attracted more ideologists than theorists and has been the object of much speculation but little rigorous research. Personal acquaintance with a family system has

Reprinted with permission of the author and UNESCO from *International Social Science Journal*, vol. 14, no. 3 (1962), pp. 507–526.

Completed under NIMH Grant No. 2526–S. I am indebted to Nicholas Tavuchis for his help in locating relevant materials for this article.

usually been confused with valid knowledge, and journalistic descriptions of the past have been the main source of information for the analysis of family changes.

The past two decades have witnessed important changes in this situation. We have come to agree that theory is not opposed to fact but is a structure of interrelated empirical propositions.[1] Good theory not only orders known facts; it also leads to new ones. In this sense, good theoretical work on the family has been rare,[2] and the younger generation of theorists does not enter the field.[3] However, we have at least come to understand the necessity of adequate theory even in this field. In addition, anthropologists—whose work is all too often neglected by sociologists—are no longer content to report that a tribe prefers some type of cross-cousin marriage but attempt to find out how frequently such marriages occur.[4] Moreover, the ideologist who sermonizes for or against some family behaviour, such as egalitarianism for women, is no less free to pursue his taste, but we no longer believe that his value-laden expositions should be given the same respect we pay to responsible research.

These changes do not imply that we should ignore ideological writings about the family. On the contrary, they are phenomena—like political or economic changes or public attitudes about morality—that affect family behaviour, and therefore must be taken seriously without being regarded at all as scientific reports. Moreover, an ideological position may determine a man's choice of the scientific problem he investigates. Nevertheless, we must keep clearly in mind that the ideological bases from which a scientific problem is chosen are essentially irrelevant to the truth of the research findings. We are properly suspicious when the author's aim seems to be to persuade us of his ideology, rather than to demonstrate, by a precise exposition of his methods, the accuracy of his data. On the other hand, the work itself is to be judged, not the motives of the researcher. We evaluate the importance of the research by its fruitfulness, and its validity and reliability by methodological canons; if it is adequately done, it is a contribution to science even if we deplore its policy sources and implications.

Finally, it is obvious that ideological positions can sometimes point to good research problems. For example, egalitarianism is certainly one motive for investigating how culture determines sex roles.[5] In general, however, ideology is a poorer compass than good theory for discovering important facts, and is at times successful only because it may happen (in the social sciences at least) that what is at the centre of ideological debate is also a key to understanding how a social pattern operates.

In any event, we are now better able to distinguish what is from what ought to be, and even the ideologist may gradually understand that without good science, policy is inevitably misguided.

Marital adjustment and happiness. Salon sociologists have talked and written much about the modern "right to marital happiness," but it is not clear that spouses even in the United States really accept such a norm. Society does not seek to create the conditions which would assure its achievement, or punish anyone who fails to make others happy. On the other hand, all societies recognize the desirability of marital contentment and the intimate misery of marital discontent. The scientific problem of studies in marital adjustment was to try to predict whether certain types of couples were more or less likely to be content in their marriages. The ideological impulse was simply, as in the field of medicine, that it would be good to advise couples beforehand not to marry if they seemed ill-suited to one another. The pragmatic basis was simply that the wisdom of elders, who have in all societies made such predictions, might be systematized, standardized, and made more precise. The first published predictive instrument in this country was developed by Jessie Bernard,[6] but at that time Burgess and Cottrell had already begun (1931) their larger study, growing out of Burgess' creation of an instrument for parole prediction. The psychologist Lewis M. Terman utilized some of their findings in a similar study, but the Burgess-Cottrell work remained the most sophisticated attempt at developing a marital prediction instrument until the Burgess-Wallin study in 1953. Locke tested its discriminative power, and various men have tried the instrument in one form or another on other populations (Chinese, Swedes, Southern Negroes).[7]

Unfortunately, this line of research seems to have come to a dead end. Widely used by marital counsellors in this country, the instrument has not improved so as to achieve greater predictive power and its power was never great.

Successive studies have confirmed the relevance of only a few items: for example, most show that if the couple's parents' marriages were happy, if the couple have been acquainted for a long time, and if the engagement was long, there is greater chance for marital success; but most other items are not confirmed by various researches. Most of the variance is not accounted for by the items that have been singled out as important.[8] In short, no new, and only few corroborating, findings have emerged in recent years.

The theory of complementarity. The primary key to this sterility can be found in the picture of the contented couple which emerges from these studies: it is the conventional bourgeois couple, meeting for the first time under respectable auspices, coming from non-divorcing families, not venturing far toward intimacy during acquaintanceship, holding steady jobs, enjoying a relatively higher education, and so on. Since, to a perhaps increasing degree, modern couples do not always come from such backgrounds, the instrument cannot estimate their future success relative to one another. To a considerable extent, the instrument in its various forms merely discriminates the old-fashioned from the modern couple, but does not discriminate from within the population of modern couples those who will be more or less successful.

One line of theory has emerged which might be helpful in gauging which men and women might live in harmony with one another, after granting that "modern" couples are less prone to be happy in marriage. The "Theory of Complementarity" was developed by Robert F. Winch to explain why, within a given pool of marital eligibles (leading to homogamy), certain people fall in love with one another and marry.[9] No one, unfortunately, has attempted either to verify this theory on a substantial random population, or even to extend it to other areas of courtship and marriage.[10]

This theory, developed with considerable rigour, accepts the wide range of findings which show that couples who marry are usually of the same religion, ethnic group, occupational background, education, and so on. However, the specific attraction between socially homogamous couples[11] is the heterogamy of their basic psychological needs.[12] For example, those who need to show deference are attracted by those who wish to achieve; those who seek abasement by those who seek dominance, and so on. Whether X falls in love with Y seems a trivial enough scientific issue, but precisely because this is a theory, it has further implications, pragmatic, sociological and psychological. It suggests, for example, why some divorcees continue to marry precisely the kind of spouses who will make them unhappy. It points to the structurally determined misperceptions of others in the courtship situation—the Western male should, for example, exhibit a relatively dominant personality, seeking achievement and autonomy, but the woman who is attracted to him may find later that he is quite different in his real needs. Winch himself denies that the theory applies to marital happiness,[13] but such an application seems worthwhile. Essentially, it is the pleasure that the young man and woman give to one another by the mutual satisfaction of their basic personality needs which determines their serious emotional involvement and commitment. To the extent that this need-satisfaction continues after marriage, the union should have greater stability and happiness (other things being equal). That is, if need-satisfaction continues, then so should the attraction between spouses. A further implication is that the new situational elements of marriage may be very different from those of courtship, and thus frustrate (or perhaps enhance) the satisfaction of each other's needs. In addition, it is of psychological importance to ask, with reference to both courtship and marriage, just how much need-satisfaction of what kind (abasement, autonomy, deference, achievement, etc.) may outweigh a failure to get satisfaction of other needs. Next, one or the other spouse may eventually obtain some of these satisfactions outside marriage, e.g., in his or her work, thus posing a new set of questions to be answered.[14] Finally, the theory seems to elucidate to some extent the attraction between very close friends.

Marital instability. I have suggested elsewhere that happiness is probably not a strategic variable in the analysis of marital institutions. Marital strain and instability, however, or the stability of the family as a boundary-maintaining social unit, may well be because at such points the individual has an option and must decide among several sets of consequences (mostly difficult for him to predict) on the basis of a complex set of value and situational elements. By contrast, there can be no problem of moral choice as between happiness and unhappiness, or "happiness and duty." Happiness would always win. Moreover, happiness cannot be built into the structure of any marriage and kinship system as a statistical likelihood or a moral norm. Again by contrast, the stability of the family unit can be, and often is.

As fruitful as the view that marital instability is the failure of boundary-maintaining forces is the view that the family is made up of role relations. Then instability can be defined as the failure of one or more individuals to perform their role obligations.[15] The major forms of instability or disorganization could thereby be classified as follows:[1]

1. The uncompleted family unit: illegitimacy. Here, the family unit did not come into existence. However, the missing individual obviously fails in his "father-husband" role-obligations as defined by society, mother, or child. Moreover, a major indirect cause of the illegitimacy is likely to be the role-failure of both mother and father.

2. Instability when one spouse wilfully departs: annulment, separation, divorce, and desertion. Instances of "job desertion" might also be included here, when the individual stays away from home for a long period of time on the excuse of a distant job.

3. The "empty-shell" family: in which individuals interact instrumentally, but fail essentially in the role-obligation to give emotional support to one another. Here, of course, there is no public dissolution or instability but the unit is in effect dissolved.

4. The crisis and strain caused by "external" events such as the temporary or permanent unwilled absence of one of the spouses because of death, imprisonment, or some impersonal catastrophe such as flood, war or depression.

5. Internal crises which create "unwilled" major role-failures: mental, emotional, or physical pathologies; severe mental retardation of a child, psychoses, chronic and incurable physical conditions.

Such a conception poses nearly impossible problems of data collection under present conditions, but does offer one way of conceptualizing the strains and options in certain kinds of marital instability. Indeed, precisely because at the present time we have no way of knowing, in any country, how many families fall into one or another of these categories at a given time, I shall in a moment limit my perspective somewhat and consider only certain problems of divorce rates.

For the moment, however, it is at least useful to keep in mind certain distinctions in this area of analysis. A primary distinction is that between the instability of the family unit and the instability of the family system in a given society. Both of these in turn must be distinguished from social change in the family system, as well as from disorganization. With respect to the first distinction, it is evident that all families do end, but this need not affect the family sysem. It is likely that high divorce rates have been common in Arab countries for many generations, as they are now, but there is no evidence that this has been until recently a changing family system. That is, the Arab family system creates—and, within limits, copes with—the problems of a high divorce rate and its essential structure remains unchanged. As we shall note in a moment, this may be also said of the Japanese Tokugawa family system. With respect to change, it is evident that if the rates of occurrence of major family happenings, such as the percentage eventually marrying, percentage married at certain ages, divorce rates, fertility patterns, and, so on, are changing, then it may be that the family system is also changing and that at least some parts of it are dissolving or undergoing disorganization. On the other hand, some of these changes may actually reduce the rates of occurrence of some phenomena classically called "disorganization," such as divorce, separation, illegitimacy or desertion. Thus, for example, the rate of desertion has been dropping in the United States. In Latin American countries in process of industrialization, with all its predictable *anomie,* the rate of illegitimacy has been dropping. Japan's family system has been undergoing great changes over the past generation and thus by definition certain parts of it must have been "dissolving," but the divorce rate has steadily dropped. Finally, even though the old family patterns may be dissolving, they may be replaced by new ones which control as determinately as the old.

Returning for the moment to a publicly recognized form of marital instability, divorce, we ought at least to ask the ideological question of whether a high divorce rate is "good" or "bad." Doubtless, there is more marital disharmony in a period of great social change than in periods of stability (assuming one can find such periods). However, marital disharmony is probabily ubiquitous, and one may ask the sociological question, what are the institutional patterns that cope with that potential or real strain? All family sysems include some mechanisms for keeping the hostilities between spouses within limits. A primary pattern is, of course, to lower expectations of emotional performance on both sides, so that neither side expects great happiness or love but does expect a minimal set of behavioural performances. A second obvious pattern noted by many is to place the greatest social value on the kin network and to reduce the importance of the husband-wife relation. As a consequence the tensions between the two are less likely to build to an intolerable level. Thirdly, all groups have patterns of avoiding marital tensions, by suppression, by defining certain types of disagreements as unimportant, and by seeing to it that husbands and wives have similar social backgrounds so that the areas of disagreement will be fewer.

Nevertheless, despite such mechanisms of prevention, disharmony is bound to arise. Societies differ, however, as to how much strain should be tolerated, just as they also differ in their solutions of problems when the level of tension seems intolerable.

Of course, divorce is one of the major solutions for an intense degree of marital disharmony and is to be found in most societies and nations. Yet I know of no contemporary society, primitive or industrialized, in which divorce is actually valued.[16] Divorce has its consequences for the society, the kin networks, and the individual; and these are tedious when not awkward, and burdensome when not destructive. On the other hand, we cannot say as yet why one society develops the pattern of divorce rather than separation or taking on an additional wife or concubine. Its primary difference is that it permits both partners to remarry. In societies without divorce, it is ordinarily only the man who is permitted to enter a new union. Thus in Western nations such as Brazil, Italy, Spain, and Portugal, the public attitudes opposing a wife's entering an unsanctioned public union are very strong while the husband is usually permitted to have a mistress outside his household. Viewing these alternatives, it seems false to speak of divorce as a "more extreme" solution than other patterns. We do not know at present whether the introduction of a concubine into a Japanese or Chinese household created more unhappiness than a divorce might have done. And whatever the answer might be, the judgement as to its desirability would still remain a matter of personal or social evaluation.

THE OBJECTIVE AND IDEOLOGICAL EVALUATION OF MARITAL INSTABILITY

One's ideological position primarily determines the evaluation of marital instability, and evidently the "rising tide" of divorce in Western nations arouses dismay even among objective social scientists—the dismay arising mainly from the peculiar historical place of divorce in Church dogma. Adequate assessment of the costs of marital instability, by any ideological standards, is hampered by the lack of a good measure of "total marital instability" in even the most statistically sophisticated countries, if we are to include in such a rate all the five major types of instability listed above. In fact, we know neither the total rate nor the psychological or social costs of any one of the five types.

We do not even know the effects of divorce although more analysts have busied themselves with this than with any other form of marital instability.[17] Moreover, such costs must always be assessed by reference to the genuine alternatives open to the participants. For example, children of divorce suffer many disadvantages compared to those who live in a happy home. But the divorcing couple cannot choose between creating a happy home and getting a divorce. They can will a divorce or not; they cannot will (and achieve) marital harmony. And, unfortunately, at least in the United States, the best opinion and data insist that children of discord or separation suffer greater disadvantages than those whose parents actually divorce.[18]

DIVORCE DIFFERENTIALS

Lacking a total rate of marital instability, I should like to explore further a question which I dealt with some years ago and which seems to relate the family in several interesting ways to the larger social structure: class differentials in the divorce rate. A fuller inquiry would be introduced by an analysis, which I am attempting elsewhere, of the broader social-structural concomitants of divorce rates. At present, we have no good study of the problem. Instead, current writers seem to be guided by the clichés, partly wrong in important theoretical and empirical respects, that urbanization and industrialization necessarily increase the divorce rates and that low divorce rates are only to be found in pious, peasant, patriarchical family systems. In addition, a good inference from anthropological data may be noted, that matrilineal societies are prone to a high divorce rate.[19]

CLASS DIFFERENTIALS: UNITED STATES

Postponing such a necessarily extended discussion of the structural conditions creating high divorce rates, let us confine ourselves instead to class differentials in the divorce rate, beginning with the United States, which seems to foreshadow so many of the changes which later take place in other countries.

Prior to the first world war, social analysts had guessed that the social relations of certain occupations created a greater proneness to divorce: the travelling salesman because he lived much of the time away from the social control of his neighbours; the bartender and entertainers because of the temptations to which their lives exposed them; the physician because of the emotional responses ("transference phenomenon" in the modern psycho-dynamic vocabulary) he aroused; and so on. Occupational data were indeed collected at that time although registration procedures were poor.[20] Most American textbooks that dealt with the topic in succeeding decades repeated these findings in one form or another. But though predictions could be made from a few specific occupations (clergymen, physicians, teachers, dancers), our knowledge of most occupations permitted no prediction at all, and occupation was soon dropped from most records.

By contrast, it seems likely that class position, with its concomitant patterning of social relations and styles of life, might affect divorce rates in at least a rough fashion. Popular belief, and to some extent that of social scientists, supposed until recently that United States divorce rates were higher among the upper strata and lower among the lower strata, where desertion was and is a common occurrence. However, a summary of the available data extending over half a century, together with new calculations from national surveys and censuses, shows that in fact there was an inverse correlation between class position and divorce rates. These findings may be summarized briefly:

1. The findings do not negate the hypothesis that specific occupations in any class position may have high or low divorce rates. Thus clergymen and professors will have relatively low rates, while psychiatrists, surgeons, and perhaps general practitioners may have higher rates.
2. Negroes have a higher divorce rate than whites.
3. When occupation is used as an indicator of class, roughly following the Alba Edwards system used by the Census Bureau, the upper occupational groups have lower rates of divorce.
4. When income is used as an indicator, the upper income groups have lower rates of divorce.
5. When education is used as an indicator, the upper groups have lower rates of divorce.
6. However, the relationship between the education of non-whites and divorce rates is positive: the higher the education, the higher the proneness to divorce.

CLASS AND A MODEL OF DIVORCE DECISION

If we avoid the pitfall of attempting to analyse divorce through so-called "cause" and focus instead on rates, a simple model of divorce decision clarifies the inverse correlation between class and divorce. We would need at least these items:

1. Predispositions in the economic and social stratum in favour of or against divorce: values and attitudes.
2. Internal strains in, or satisfactions from, the marriage.
3. Alternatives outside marriage.
4. Supporting or dissolving pressures on the part of relevant social networks.

It seems likely that ideologically the upper strata in the United States are more tolerant of divorce than the lower strata. However, the following factors would seem to create a somewhat lesser propensity to divorce toward the upper socio-economic strata:

1. The network of social relations and of kin relations is more extended, more tightly organized, and exercises greater control over the individual.
2. The income differentials between the wife and husband in the upper strata are greater than in the lower strata; consequently the wife has more reason to maintain the marriage if she can.
3. Toward the upper strata, far more of the husband's income is committed to long-term expenditures, from which he cannot easily withdraw to support an independent existence.
4. The husband in the lower strata can more easily escape the child-support payments and other post-divorce expenditures because his life is more anonymous and legal controls are less effective.
5. The strains internal to the marriage are greater toward the lower strata: marital satisfaction scores are lower, romantic attachment between spouses is less common, the husband is less willing to share household tasks when the wife is working, and so on.

CLASS DIFFERENTIALS IN OTHER SOCIETIES: PHASES OF DEVELOPMENT

The relationship between social structure and divorce seems general enough to apply to other societies. Let us explore the matter. Where there is a well-developed stratification system it would seem likely that the lower class does not count on the stability of the marriage, that the marriage itself costs less, less is invested in it than in the upper strata, the kin ties are less important and therefore the ambiguity created by divorce would not be taken so seriously as in the upper strata.

In the past, on the other hand, without any questions the divorce rate (as distinguished from the general rate of instability) was higher in the upper strata of the United States. In some states' jurisdictions, an act of the legislature was necessary to obtain a divorce and generally divorce was costly. Consequently at some unknown point in American history, the lower strata began to surpass the upper strata in the divorce rate, just as happened with respect to the Negro-White divorce differential. Thus a fuller exploration must at some point introduce the notion of phase in these considerations. In other words, the lower strata may generally have a higher rate of marital instability, but their divorce rate may not always be higher until some stage of development in the marriage and divorce system occurs.

This general theory of the relationship between the larger social structure and class divorce rates may correctly apply to the Western culture complex, where Church dogma with respect to the family was translated into State laws in every nation, and where the administration of these restrictive laws was until recently in the hands of the *élite*. However, those laws have been altered greatly over the past half-century in most Western States. Moreover, if the theory is to be generalized, it must be modified to fit those cultures such as China, India, Japan and Arab Islam, where marriage and divorce were not generally under the jurisdiction of State officials (except for extreme cases) and where marriage was not primarily a sacred affair (Japan, China).

Finally, the use of occupation as a class index, perhaps the best in view of the necessarily crude data available for cross-national comparisons, may at times introduce a new variable into the analysis, the peculiar style of life of certain occupations. For example, clergymen and teachers (in the West) will have low divorce rates but physicians and artists will have high ones—yet in most national tabulations of divorce these will all be classified together. In the West, farmers have lower divorce rates, but in Japan a special pattern of "trial marriage" creates high divorce rates among agriculturists—though many of these are never recorded.

If these necessary modifications are integrated, several inferences can be tested. (a) In the pre-industrial or early industrialization period of Western nations the upper classes will have higher divorce rates. Indeed, there may be almost no lower class divorces. (b) As a Western nation industrializes, its divorce procedures are gradually made available to all classes. Since family strain toward the lower strata is greater, the proportion of lower strata divorces will increase, and eventually there should be an inverse relation between class and divorce rate, as in the United States. (c) In China, India, Japan and Arab Islam, where the power to divorce remained in the hands of the groom's family, no such set of phases will occur. Indeed—though very likely precise data do not exist—I hypothesize that the relation between class and divorce rate moves in the opposite direction: that is, though the lower strata will continue to furnish more than their "share" of the divorces, the class differential will narrow somewhat as the upper strata begin to divorce more. (d) Finally (though here again the data will very likely never become available) since the dominant pattern of respectability was set by the urban *élite*, and the rural marriage and divorce patterns seem to have been looser, it is likely that in China, Japan, India and Arab Islam any modern changes would be toward a decline in the divorce rate of agriculturists.

Let us look at the data that bear on the first of these three hypotheses.

New Zealand. The ratio of divorced to married by income distribution shows clearly that toward the lower strata the divorce rate is higher.

Ratio of Percentage of Divorced to Percentage of Married, Within Income Groups

Income Group	Ratio[a]	Income Group	Ratio[a]
Under £100	1.78	£400–£449	.67
£100–£149	1.84	£450–£549	.58
£150–£199	1.86	£550–£649	.56
£200–£249	1.50	£650–£749	.48
£250–£299	1.10	£750 and over	.34
£300–£349	.96	Not specified	2.01
£350–£399	.87		

[a] Figures higher than 1.00 indicate that the income group concerned contributes more than its numerical "share" to the total number of divorces.

SOURCE: A. J. Dixon, *Divorce in New Zealand*, Auckland, Auckland University College Bulletin No. 46, 1954, p. 42 (Sociology Series No. 1).

The same relationship shows by occupation; the ratio of comparative frequency of divorce to numbers in each of various occupational groups being:

Proneness to Divorce by Occupation, New Zealand

Occupation	Ratio[a]	Occupation	Ratio[a]
Architect, dentist, lawyer,		Mechanic	.96
lecturer, doctor	.07	Railway employee	.80
Engineer	.72	Clerk	.55
Farmer	.17	Salesman	1.17
Manager (not company)	.32	Barman	4.73
Carpenter	.78	Labourer	2.30
Butcher	1.05		

[a] Figures higher than 1.00 indicate that the occupation concerned contributes more divorces than its numerically proportionate "share" within all occupations.

SOURCE: *Ibid.*

United States. Although an extensive summary of the relevant data is available for the United States,[21] it may be relevant to note that a more recent summary has corroborated these findings, and from one of these the following table has been taken.

Ratio of Divorced to 1,000 of Ever-Married Men by Occupation of Civilian Labour Force, 14 Years and Over, 1950 United States Census

Occupations	Number Divorced per 1,000 Ever-Married Men
Professional technical and kindred workers	18.49
Managers, officials and proprietors (excluding farm)	16.59
Clerical and kindred workers	25.70
Craftsmen, foremen and kindred workers	24.15
Operatives and kindred workers	26.18
Farm labourers and foremen	40.76

SOURCE: Karen G. Hillman, *Marital Instability and Its Relation to Education, Income and Occupation: An Analysis Based on Census Data,* Evanston, Illinois, Northwestern University, 1961, p. 19, mimeographed.

Australia. In Australia, too, the relationship holds:

Ratio of Divorced to 1,000 Married Males by Occupational Class, 1947 Census of Australia[a]

Occupational Level	Number Divorced per 1,000 Married Males	Occupational Level	Number Divorced per 1,000 Married Males
Employer	9	Employee (on wage)	15
Self-employed	9	Helper (not on wage)	23

[a] Calculated from: *Census of the Commonwealth of Australia, 30 June 1947. Statistician's Report,* Canberra, 1952, p. 268.

Sweden. A similar ratio may be found in the 1950 Swedish census:

Ratio of Divorced per 1,000 Married Men, by Occupational Category[a]

Category	Number Divorced per 1,000 Married Men	Category	Number Divorced per 1,000 Married Men
Employers	12	Wage-earners	28
Salaried employees	21		

[a] Calculated from: Personal correspondence, Central Bureau of Statistics, Sweden. Statistiska Centralbyran, Folkräkningen, Den 31 December 1950, V, VI, Totala Räkningen, Folkmängden Efter Yrke. Hushall. Utrikes Födda Och Utlänningar: Tab. 8., "Förvärvsarbetande befolkning efter näringsgren (huvudoch undergrupper) och yrkesstallning i kombination med kön, alter och civilstand den 31 december 1950" [economically active population by industry (divisions and major groups) and occupational status, and by sex, age and marital status], pp. 162–3 (males only).

Belgium. In the following table calculated from the 1947 Belgian census, a similar relation appears, although here the differences are very small.

Ratio of Divorced per 1,000 Married Men,
by Occupational Category
(Excluding Agriculture, Farming and Fishing)[a]

Category	Number Divorced per 1,000 Married Men	Category	Number Divorced per 1,000 Married Men
Employers	13	Skilled and unskilled	
Salaried workers	14	workers	15
		Auxiliary personnel	31

[a] Calculated from: Institut national de Statistique, *Recensement Général de la Population, de l'Industrie et du Commerce au 31 Décembre 1941*. Vol. 8: *Répartition de la Population d'après l'Activité et la Profession*. Tableau 18—Répartition de la population active masculine de nationalité belge d'après l'État Civil, l'État Social et les Sections d'Activité, pp. 34–5.

France.   The relationship also holds here.

Ratio of Divorced per 1,000 Married Men,
by Occupational Category[a]

Category	Number Divorced per 1,000 Married Men	Category	Number Divorced per 1,000 Married Men
Liberal professions and		Skilled and unskilled	
senior cadres	17	workers	24
Intermediate cadres	20	Domestic servants	78
Salaried workers	21		

[a] Calculated from: *Résultats du sondage au 1/20e, Institut National de la Statistique et des Études économiques*, Presses Universitaires de France, 1960 (Recensement général de la Population de Mai 1954), p. 61, p. 62, p. 63.

England.   A special study of the occupational structure of the divorcing and the "continued married relations population" in England and Wales in 1951 reveals that the proportions of the divorcing population in the selected occupational categories were almost exactly those of the proportions in the continued married population. Thus the "professional and managerial class" accounted for 13.5 per cent of the divorcing sample and 13.9 per cent of the continuing married.

Much more instructive, however, and strongly confirming our second hypothesis is the change in the distribution of the husband's occupation at divorce. Such a comparison is presented below, showing how the "gentry, professional and managerial workers" dropped from 41.4 per cent of the total divorcing population, to 11.4 per cent between 1871 and 1951. During the same period, the proportion furnished by the manual workers increased from 16.8 to 58.5 per cent.

Husband's Occupation at Divorce, 1871 and 1951,
England and Wales[a]

Year	Gentry, Professional and Managerial Workers	Farmers and Shopkeepers	Black-coated Workers	Manual	Unknown Occupation	Total of Occupations
	%	%	%	%	%	
1871	41.4	12.7	6.3	16.8	22.8	285
1951	11.4	6.7	7.6	58.5	15.8	1,813

[a] Calculated from: Griselda Rowntree and Norman H. Carrier, "The Resort to Divorce in England and Wales, 1858–1957," in: *Population Studies*, No. 11, March 1958, p. 222.

South Africa. Up to the time of writing, I have been unable to make a similar comparison for South Africa because the categories used for occupation and divorce do not correspond to one another in the sources available to me.[22]

Netherlands. The data from the Netherlands do not fit the hypothesis because of the extremely high divorce ratio among the free professions, which include both the established professions of medicine and law, and such occupations as musician, artist, writer and so on. Teaching is separate and of course has a low ratio. Unfortunately, skilled workers seem to be classified with manual labourers. Thus, although the extreme categories in the Netherlands do fit our thesis, the "free professions" do not fit.

Ratio of Divorce per 1,000 Married Male Heads of
Households, Netherlands 1955–57 (Excluding Agriculture)ᵃ

Categories	Number of Divorces per 1,000 Male Household Heads	Categories	Number of Divorces per 1,000 Male Household Heads
Heads of enterprises	18	Teaching	15
Free professions	50	Other bureaucrats	37
Civil Service and office employees	21	Manual workers	30

ᵃ Calculated from: Number of households taken as of 30 June 1956; divorces as of 1955–57.
SOURCE: *Echtscheidingen in Nederland*, 1900–57, Central Bureau Voor De Statistick, Zeist, W. de Haan, 1958, Appendix II, Table D, p. 63.

Yugoslavia.   Yugoslavia has recently begun to industrialize, and our hypothesis would suggest that the divorce ratio would be higher towards the upper strata. If education is used as an index, this appears to be so as of 1959.

Ratio of Divorce to 1,000 Married Males, by Education

School Achievement of Husband	Number of Divorced per 1,000 Married	School Achievement of Husband	Number of Divorced per 1,000 Married
Without school	124	Secondary school (completed)	148
Primary school	124		
Secondary school (incomplete)	144	Faculty, high and higher school	144

SOURCE: *Statistical Yearbook of the Federal People's Republic of Yugoslavia*, Federal People's Republic of Yugoslavia Federal Statistical Institute, Belgrade, August 1961. Calculated from: Table 202–23—Contracted Marriages by School Qualifications of Bridegroom and Bride in 1959 (preliminary data), p. 83; Table 202–27—Divorces by School Qualifications of Husband and Wife in 1959 (preliminary data), p. 85.

However, the ratios by occupation are puzzling. Here the technical problem of the ratio itself is important: if the ratio used is actual divorces and marriages in one given year, the result may be an anomaly: e.g., a high divorce-marriage ratio among pensioners because they do experience some divorces, but very few marriages on account of their age. However, this result is a function of age level rather than of a high propensity to divorce.

In any event, with this warning, the following table presents data comparable in part to the previous tables.

Ratio of Divorces to Marriages by Occupation of Husband[a]

Occupation of Husband	Number of Divorces per 1,000 Marriages	Occupation of Husband	Number of Divorces per 1,000 Marriages
Unskilled Workers in manufacturing industries, arts, crafts	144 140	Administrative and managing personnel Professional and technical occupations and artists	256 132

[a] Calculated from: *Statistical Yearbook of the Federal People's Republic of Yugoslavia*, Federal Statistical Institute, Belgrade, August 1961. Data calculated from: Table 202–21—Contracted Marriages by Occupation of Bridegroom and Bride in 1959 (preliminary data), p. 83; Table 202–28—Divorces by Occupation of Husband and Wife in 1959 (preliminary data), p. 85.

These figures are also somewhat different from those which Milic has calculated, apparently from the same sources.[23]

Egypt. Egyptian data on such a matter raires the problem, common to all countries in which divorce has been a limited concern of the State, of how adequate the coverage of divorces is, and whether the more literate or better educated couples who divorce are more likely to record their divorces. As can be seen in the succeeding table, the divorce/married ratio predicted holds good primarily for the distinction between employers on the one hand and all other occupations on the other.

Ratio of Divorces to Marriages by Occupation of Husband
(Excluding Agriculture, Fishing and Hunting)[a]

Categories	Number of Divorces per 1,000 Marriages	Categories	Number of Divorces per 1,000 Marriages
Employers	9	Employees	11
On own account	18	Labourers and	
Directors and sub-		artisans	18
directors	12	Unemployed	117

[a] Calculated from: *Population Census of Egypt*, 1947, General Tables, Ministry of Finance and Economy, Statistical and Census Department, Government Press, Cairo, 1954. Table XXIX (concluded)— Working Status for Persons Engaged in Industries by Sex, Age Group and Civil Status (excluding children below 5 years). Table refers to males and excludes occupations in agriculture, fishing, and hunting, pp. 362–3.

However, one comparison of illiteracy and divorce shows no difference in the literacy of bridegrooms and divorced males in 1956 (47 and 45 per cent).[24]

Ratios calculated for those engaged in agriculture, fishing and hunting in Egypt follow the pattern presented above for occupations outside these categories.[25]

Jordan. Corresponding data do not exist for Jordan, but it is at least possible to calculate that in 1959, 75 per cent of the males who married were literate, but only 59 per cent of those who divorced; and 25 per cent of the females who married were literate, but only 5 per cent of the divorcees.[26] Therefore we can conclude that the better educated divorced less than the less educated. This general conclusion also emerges from many nonquantitative analyses of divorce in Arabic Islam. Specifically, it is sometimes asserted that divorce and remarriage are the "poor man's polygyny."[27]

Finland. Allardt found that in 1947 the divorce rate per 100,000 of the main supporters of the family was higher toward the upper strata, which would fit our first hypothesis. Using these three classes, labouring, middle, and upper, he found rates of 527, 543, and 1022.

However, most of the *élite* are to be found in Helsinki, where the divorce rates are higher than elsewhere in Finland and a comparison of the divorce applications in different classes in 1945–46 showed no statistically significant differences among them, i.e., in the more industrialized areas, the older class pattern had already changed. Allardt notes that the differences among the classes were greater at the beginning of the century but that there is now very little difference (second hypothesis).

Hungary. As a newly industrializing nation, Hungary would be expected to have a somewhat lower divorce rate toward the lower strata. Our data suggest caution but do conform.

Ratio of Divorces to Marriages, 1958

Occupation	Number of Divorces	Number of Marriages	Number of Divorces per 1,000
Agricultural workers	1,827	25,154	72
Manual workers	9,133	51,017	179
Intellectuals	3,481	15,156	223

SOURCE: *Statisztikai Evkonyv, 1958*, Kozponti Statisztikai Hivatal, Budapest, 1960. Table 20—Marriages by the Professional Status of Husband and Wife, p. 20; Table 26—Divorces by Professional Status of Husband and Wife, p. 22.

India. The Indian pattern is, of course, very well known though no quantitative data exist. Divorce has been impossible for Brahmans until very recently (1955). On the other hand, the lower castes and the outcasts, as well as tribal groups, have long permitted divorce. As a consequence there is no doubt that the general relationship presented earlier fits at least the observed differences among the strata—though in this instance it is perhaps not possible to make a strong case for differential strain.[28]

China. The case of China is similar to that of Japan. Though China has permitted divorce from at least the T'ang period, divorce has not been a respectable step in Chinese culture and thus would tend to be more common towards the lower strata. Indeed among the *élite*, other solutions were open to the dissatisfied husband.[29]

Japan. The divorce rate in Japan has been dropping over the past half century, though at the same time divorce has been much more completely recorded than formerly. Again, our hypothesis is confirmed.

The Ratio of Divorce per 1,000 Married Male Workers
15 Years and Over, Japan, July 1957[a]

Occupation	Number Divorced per 1,000 Male Workers
Technicians and engineers	7
Professors and teachers	3
Medical and public health technicians	5
Managers and officials	4
Clerical and related workers	8
Farmers, lumbermen, fishermen and related workers	10
Workers in mining and quarrying	18
Craftsmen, production process workers, and labourers not elsewhere included	18
Domestic	238

[a] Calculated from: Japan, Bureau of Statistics, Office of the Prime Minister, 1955 *Population Census of Japan*, Vol. II: *One Percent Sample Tabulation*, Part III, "Occupation, July 1957," Table 3— Occupation (Intermediate Group) of Employed Persons 15 Years Old and Over by Marital Status and Sex, for all Japan, all *Shi* and all *Gun*, pp. 136–7 (Males only).

THE "EASY DIVORCE" PHASE: FURTHER INFERENCES

Fully to resolve all of these irregularities would require an institutional analysis of each country. Our earlier analysis seems to be correct, that there is likely to be more marital instability towards the lower strata than towards the upper. But whether this set of forces is exhibited in actual divorce proceedings depends on the extent to which divorce itself has become easy, that is, has come to "cost" little—these costs being calculated necessarily by reference to the available resources of the family, and including both monetary and social costs. We also noted that in a country with "easy" divorce (Japan, Arab Islam), industrialization would reduce the divorce rate of the lower strata relative to the upper. In a country moving toward the easy divorce phase, the upper strata begin to furnish a smaller proportion of total divorces. Let us consider the further implications of these notions.

First, where divorce costs little, there will be a high divorce rate. This is a reciprocal and reinforcing relationship. Easy divorce means in effect that there are fewer strong factors to maintain the boundaries of the family unit. Moreover, in that type of situation, the peers of any individual are likely to have had similar experiences, that is, divorce, and therefore have less basis on which to chide or deprecate anyone who gets a divorce. And the ubiquitous strains in all marriage systems will ensure a high number of individuals who seek this way out and who are also available as potential mates.

Where divorce is difficult and costly, it is primarily an upper-class privilege. There are rarely special laws for the lower classes, other than those which prevent the lower classes from attacking the privileges of the *élite*. On the other hand, if and when there are upper-class family difficulties that have to be solved in a social structure posing barriers against divorce, there must be at least a few mechanisms for handling them, such as annulment and migratory divorce. The property stakes and problems of lineage are too important to permit the merely informal solutions which the lower classes may enjoy.

In a family system permitting easy divorce and thus having a high divorce rate, there will also be a very high rate of remarriage.[30] In the United States, this rate of eventual remarriage among divorcés is roughly as high as that for the unmarried population, about nine in ten. No such figures exist for Arab Islam, but the few data available, including observations made in specific studies, suggest that there is an extremely high rate of marital turnover. The percentage married in the upper age groups in Japan has been over 95 per cent for decades, while the divorce rate was extremely high, thus showing that the rate of remarriage was high. Irene Taeuber has in addition used demographic techniques to show that the divorced as well as the widowed "disappear" in successive age groups.[31] In such a high-divorce system, divorce creates no social stigma, there are many available divorcees to marry, and divorce is no longer likely to be deviant in many psychological or social respects.

Indeed the divorce system then becomes in effect part of the courtship and marriage system: that is, it is part of the "sifting out" process, analogous to the adolescent dating pattern. Individuals marry, but there is a free market both in getting a first spouse, and in getting a second spouse should the individuals not be able to create a harmonious life with the first one. Indeed, to the extent that marriage becomes a

personal bond between husband and wife, and they marry
after they are formed psychologically, there would seem to
be at least some ideological arguments for their being free
to shift about in order to find someone who fits better.

Finally, as such a system becomes established, heavy investments in bride-price or dowry will decline. These are
never individual investments in any family system, but represent the commitment of an extended family network to the
marriage. Where the likelihood is great that the marriage
will be unstable, and undoing it expensive, then neither side
is likely to be willing to make a large, long-term investment
in it.

Some but not all of these hypotheses can be tested by
available data, and in some of my current research I am
attempting to assemble such materials from many countries—a formidable task! The present paper has aimed at
presenting a small theoretical perspective, developing hypotheses from that theoretical position and then testing them.

TOWARD A THEORY FOR THERAPEUTIC
INTERVENTION IN FAMILIES

Roland G. Tharp and Gerald D. Otis[1]

THE STUDY of family therapy and the study of family interaction patterns have proceeded apace. Several patterns of
family interrelationship have been discovered to covary with
the development of particular disorders, notably schizophrenia.[2] Problems in family communication and interpersonal understanding have received the primary focus of investigation, but there are rumblings through the literature
which suggest that all symptoms can be viewed as functioning elements in the family system. Thus, behavior—including

Reprinted with permission of the authors and publisher from *Journal
of Consulting Psychology*, vol. 30, no. 5, pp. 426–434.

the pathological—requires examination along the entire continuum of family action, not only in the bedroom but in the living room, not only in terms of communication, but in terms of taking out the garbage. Change in one element of family action will necessitate other accommodating changes; and changes in behavior can well bring about changes in feeling-states. If this be so, the following hypothesis should be explored: adjustment of the family interaction pattern may render a symptom dysfunctional, and thus cause its disappearance.

This report covers the first, or clinical, phase of investigation of this hypothesis. We have attempted to reduce psychopathology by assisting in the reorganization of family role functioning. Our general position, both at the beginning of the study and now, is this: identifiable psychopathology occurs only when the absence of satisfying role-reciprocations produces conflict. The remainder of this paper is an elaboration of that position. First, the conceptual units in which we view behavior will be presented; second, a theoretical view of psychopathology; third, three brief therapeutic case studies; and, in conclusion, there will be listed several principles for therapeutic intervention.

THE CONCEPTUAL UNITS FOR FAMILY ROLE ANALYSIS

Individuals, by virtue of occupying particular social positions, have expectations and values concerning behavior appropriate to that position. A woman, when wife, values actions which may be quite different from those which she endorses when she is mother, or lover, or tennis partner. Also, the particular role performance requires particular reciprocations. She can only meet her expectations when others —husband, child, lover, tennis partner—act in ways which allow her to perform her role according to her desires. The same considerations apply for all individuals in all social positions.

The difficulty with role theory, of course, is the plethora of discrete roles, positions, expectations, reciprocations, etc., which make for a staggering complexity of analysis. Previously, we have suggested simplifying schemata, which allow for the grouping of role items into major categories.[3] We continue to find it useful to employ these five functional classes of family behavior, and to analyze families in terms of these units.

Any group which does not disintegrate must have elements of cohesiveness: thus, *solidarity.* The separate components of this function have been labeled *intimacy, social* and *emotional integration, togetherness, understanding,* and *companionship.* A minimum of solidarity must be available for any viable group, obviously; the marriage without it has ceased to function. . . .

The second function is that of *sexuality.* For the spouses the sexual is an obvious area. Our current knowledge of infantile and childhood sexuality also allows us to see that the regulation of sexual expression in children is part of the family task.

External relations, third on the list, refers to the negotiations carried on by the marriage and family with extrafamilial individuals and institutions: the school, the butcher, friends, relations, the tax collector.

Next is *internal instrumentality,* the function of work-accomplishment within the household: housework, yardwork, maintenance, cooking, budgeting, etc.

The fifth function, *division of responsibility,* is of a different logical base, because it refers to arrangements *within the other four.* Whether we are discussing the family or some other social group, the responsibility and authority for originating, maintaining, and terminating any activity is differentially delegated to one or more members; this is the case also for the four primary functions of family life. . . . It is no longer feasible to maintain that "relative influence" or "dominance" or "power" *in the abstract* are useful descriptions of marriage relationships. Division of responsibility always occurs over something, not in toto. For instance, in the so-called "traditional" family arrangement, the husband has primary responsibility in the areas of sexuality and external relations; the wife in solidarity. Responsibility is shared for various areas of internal instrumentality. In the "companionate" modern family responsibility may be equally divided within all four areas and is flexibly shifted according to changing circumstances—illness; wife's employment, etc.[4]

We see this position as continuous with the structural-functional analyses of Bell and Vogel.[5] That our functional divisions are somewhat different is to be expected, since ours are based on a factor-analytic reduction of discrete action units followed by further rational groupings.[6] We also find it useful to consider values as applying to specific role performances, and thus subsumed under the general functional groupings.

Family Roles and the Development of Psychopathology

Family functions. Five functional requirements are placed on the family unit: Solidarity, Sexuality, External Relations, Internal Instrumentality, and Division of Responsibility. Role performances may be classified usefully into one (or more) of these five categories.

Role definitions. In the family, modal role definitions exist which are sex and age differentiated. A degree of idiosyncrasy is usually present, however, and the particular role definitions of the individuals involved are crucial.[7] An individual's role in the family is defined in terms of the behavior he is expected to execute in the family group and reflects the (often implicit) differentiation of performances involved in carrying out the functions of the family.

Differences in role definitions. The members of the family may differ in the expectations they hold concerning the role performances of any given member, including those which pertain to the self. Such differences may arise independently in the areas of Solidarity or Sexuality, but more often arise in Division of Responsibility, Internal Instrumentality, and External Relations. When the latter occurs, the family members will usually experience the discord as residing primarily in Solidarity and/or Sexuality areas, even though role conflict in the other areas preceded the experienced conflict.

Roles and evaluations. For the individual, both self-evaluation and other-evaluation depend upon the satisfactory execution of a reciprocal role. Thus, a wife's self-evaluation depends upon her husband's performance of the role she expects of him, since most interpersonal roles require a reciprocal for completion. Similarly, her evaluation of her husband depends upon her performance of the role she expects of herself. All people are highly motivated to maintain a positive evaluation of self and others within the family. If evaluation is not positive, on balance, role revision will be attempted.

Role revisions. A number of different strategies for role revision have been identified. Speigel[8] has discussed several:

coercing (which he considers primary; see our discussion of negative sanctions below), coaxing, evaluating, masking, postponing, reversing, joking, exploring, compromising, and consolidating. Speigel suggests that these may be steps in the typical progress of the establishment of role reequilibration. Having examined our data with this view in mind, it now appears that the "steps" may be outcomes of a particular therapeutic technique. As we have modified our strategies, the patients have modified their own. We suggest that such processes can be grouped into the following general classes: (a) Revision, (b) Coercion, and (c) Transference.

Revision. A strategy for peaceful resolution of family role conflict may or may not exist in the minds of the participants. This may be very general, as in seeking some form of external assistance. It may also be relatively specific, as in family discussion programs, plans for arbitration, or the allocation of judicial functions to a particular member. In long-lived groups such as the family, which necessarily changes its structure over time, the absence of mutually accepted procedures for role revision leads to conflict, dysfunction, lowered evaluation, and (among other vicissitudes) individual "psychopathology."

Coercion. A negative evaluation is frequently the occasion for application of sanctions such as threats, nonperformance of role functions (in the case of another member), or guilt (in the case of one's self). The sanctions which a person can apply seem to be ordered as to perceived severity for the target individual to which they will be applied. The greater the expectation-perceived enactment discrepancy, the greater becomes the severity of applied sanctions. The ultimate sanction is termination of the relationship.

1. Application of sanctions which are not sufficiently powerful to induce the desired reciprocities has the unfortunate effect of escalating the conflicts.

2. Sanctions which are threatened but not applied have the effect of perpetuating the conflict.

3. Applications of sanctions which are sufficiently powerful to induce the desired reciprocities (frequently threat of divorce, running away, etc.) can serve temporarily as a means of reestablishing positive evaluation, but since they disrupt Solidarity, cannot serve as a permanent basis for

maintaining desired role enactments. However, their use is an effective strategy if the revised role performances provide enough positive evaluation so that they are maintained independent of the sanctions.

Transference. One method by which self-evaluation can be increased is to cast another family member into the role originally designed for someone occupying another position. For example, a child may be manipulated into playing the role of "confidant" when the husband does not, thus allowing the wife to play her (expected) reciprocal role vis-a-vis her child and as a result increasing her self-evaluation. Typically, this does not work well since a child does not have the requisite skills to adequately play "adult" roles.

The overchallenge of inappropriate role demands is deleterious for a child's emotional and social development. This, of course, occurs most often when the strategy of Role Transference is employed. In this way, a disturbance between husband and wife increases the probability that the disturbance in that function will spread to include the children.

Acquisition of roles. Role expectations are learned largely in the family of origin. Within a disturbed function, role learning is likely to be highly idiosyncratic. Thus, as an individual who learns these unusual role expectations moves to his own family of procreation, he is less likely to find a spouse with matching expectations than if he learned "standard" or modal roles. Thus within a new family, idiosyncratic roles are more likely to produce conflict. The functional disturbance has then spread from family of origin to family of procreation, within the same area, but not necessarily in identical behavioral units. As the individual reproduces, his marital-functional disturbance is likely to spread to his own children. Disturbances in role functioning may be transmitted through generations by this form of "social heredity."

Pathology. For the individual afflicted with highly idiosyncratic role definitions as a result of dysfunction within the family of origin, the probability of establishing satisfying reciprocities in the family of procreation is reduced. This will lead to lowered self-evaluation, and thus to intrapsychic distress with its vicissitudes. Thus is role dysfunction transmuted into psychopathology.

At this time, we have no scheme which will account for

the particular pathology selected. Some relate directly to a disturbed role area, others do not. We agree entirely with Speigel[9] that many consequences of role readjustment and of symptom development are unintended; undesired; and, by the family itself, unbelievable. Role analysis only describes the processes leading to devaluation, stress, and conflict. It focuses on the patterns of contingency by which the behavior of one family member is followed by a particular consequence from another member.

But for the purposes of therapeutic amelioration, we are attempting to test the limits of the position that role dysfunction analysis may be sufficient to the task. If a patient, while still carrying about his proclivity for some symptom, can maintain sufficient functional balance in his primary social unit so that he will never suffer from disabling self-devaluation, then he will never again manifest symptoms. This achievement, though perhaps modest, may be sufficient.

CASE STUDIES

Mr. and Mrs. I.I.

The first case to be discussed is of extraordinary complexity, when viewed psychiatrically. However, when seen in family-function terms, and in terms of therapeutic intervention, it is our simplest to date. It illustrates disturbance in Internal Instrumentality.

Mr. and Mrs. I.I. had been married less than a year. Now 22, Mr. I.I. was suffering from depression, obsessive rumination, night terrors, and severe guilt and anxiety. He had been diagnosed variously as chronic undifferentiated schizophrenic and passive-dependent personality. At the time of referral, his pregnant wife was diagnosed as depressive reaction, neurotic, severe. Their relationship was in turmoil. His possessive parents were constantly urging him to divorce and "come back home." Mrs. I.I. was fighting with every weapon at her disposal to hold her marriage together. Mr. I.I. was unsure of anything and flung himself dependently upon the therapists for a decision.

The Solidarity of the marriage was minimal and threatened to give way entirely. On analysis, it quickly appeared that most of their arguments were over money. No system of management for their extremely limited funds existed. They both literally grabbed for a share of his cashed pay check each week and resented whatever the other got. The imprecations of the parents were effective because no adequate counter-valence was available from the Solidarity of their new marriage. Division of Responsibility was unclear in the Internal Instrumentality function, leading to conflict and, epiphenomenally, disturbance in Solidarity. The couple was seen conjointly in one interview. They were instructed to come for their next interview only when they had prepared a detail financial budget, one which they would both be willing to sign and abide by. They left, confused and disappointed by this peculiar psychotherapy.

After 1 week, they returned as instructed, both radiantly happy over the resolution of their financial conflicts and over the new-found feelings of Solidarity and warmth which their joint decisions had produced. We told them then that their problems were solved, congratulated them, and said good-bye. Again, they were—though still pleased—astonished. We told them that we believed their symptoms would disappear within a month, and that we anticipated the need for no further treatment; however, if symptoms had not disappeared, they were to call us, and we would set another appointment.

After 10 months, they remain asymptomatic.

Mr. and Mrs. E.R.

The second case, that of Mr. and Mrs. E.R., illustrates a primary disturbance in External Relations. Prior to referral to us, Mrs. E.R. had been under intermittent but frequent psychiatric care for 18 years. Her original symptom of frigidity had been alleviated many years ago, and replaced by a vigorous and satisfactory marital-sexual adjustment. However, other symptoms of anxiety, psychophysiological reactions, and depression tormented her. On referral, the psychiatrist stated that her symptoms were direct reactions to severe marital conflict, and that psychotherapy had been ineffective in that the precipitating stress was unrelenting. A tall, cool, handsome woman, Mrs. E.R. was well matched with a brilliant, charming attorney, diagnosed during a year's psychotherapy of his own as a passive-aggressive personality.

At the time of our first contact, their family was near

explosion. A dramatic love affair of Mr. E.R.'s had ended, the several children were alienated from the father, Mrs. E.R. was threatening divorce (although both preferred to remain together, for family and financial reasons), and both professed to hate one another. Violent vituperation and physical abuse abounded. After 3 months of joint therapy, their relationship became what is reasonable to a marriage of 20 years: feelings of affection and sometimes warmth, infrequent and well-controlled spats, and a general pattern of family solidarity.

A narrative account of circularized causes-and-effects cannot accurately portray the complexities of a conflicted human relationship. The bare details presented below are those selected for the focus on intervention. Mr. E.R. was unpleasant to his wife "because" she gave him no nurturance. She hated him "because" he humiliated her, particularly in public (almost exclusively while drinking), through flirtatiousness, vulgarity, and coarseness. Thus, she restricted the social life which they both craved, and he "retaliated" by passively refusing to go out with her alone or in small groups. When sober, she reported, his conduct was quite satisfactory. He was not alcoholic, and only rarely drank at home.

The conflict culminated in his love affair. Because of this, and due to the therapist's insistence that either divorce, or status quo, or effective problem solving represented their only choices, Mrs. E.R. (after 1 month of treatment) issued an ultimatum: stop drinking, or a divorce. He tested this limit, and she called her lawyer. Reluctantly, he agreed not to drink again, and she cancelled her instructions to the attorney. Although another 2 months were spent in a therapeutic working out of the specifics of some of the marriage-role behaviors, and in increasing the strength of the Solidarity, in effect the case was solved when the limit was tested, and it held.

His drunken "offenses" disappeared, she became more nurturant, he responded by entertaining her socially, they reappeared in social circles, and with this solution of their External Relations problem, the marriage conflict reduced to a minimum. She has been psychiatrically asymptomatic since. She now occasionally allows him a couple of cocktails; they both smile over this Division of Responsibility.

The D.A. Family

The following case illustrates the transmission of an authority disturbance through three generations. In the first generation, the disturbance was manifested by partial reversal of the typical marital roles. In the second generation, the disturbance appeared in the form of arthritis and divorce. In the third generation, the disturbance takes the form of a "school phobia" and predelinquent behavior.

Kay D., a 13-year-old girl, was brought to us because of a school phobia. Previous treatment at a child guidance center had not alleviated her condition.

She lived with her mother, her 15-year-old sister, and her maternal grandmother and grandfather. Mrs. D., Kay's mother, was a wheelchair-bound arthritic who had been divorced by her husband several years previously. After her husband left her, she "gave up and went down"—became disabled by her arthritis. She and her children resumed living with her parents.

Mrs. A., the maternal grandmother, was the main source of family finances, and in addition, Mrs. D. had delegated all responsibility for the children to her. However, Mrs. A. was indulgent and overprotective toward the girls. She could not effectively discipline them and would often execute their duties when they refused or made excuses. Mrs. A. had assumed primary responsibility for family Solidarity, however. She was the one most likely to accommodate others, to provide understanding and companionship.

Mr. A. was an acute coronary case who was unable to perform any family duties. However, even befcre his heart condition, he had not participated actively in family life. A petulant and irrascible old man, he had lost his only area of responsibility in the family (i.e., as breadwinner). He attended only one family therapy session, then refused to participate further, thus demonstrating his preferred family role.

Rita, Kay's older sister, was a rebellious teenager, continuously testing limits and looking for some external control over her behavior. Like Kay, she looked to her mother for this control but did not find it.

Kay, the "patient," could not clearly identify the situations which elicited her phobic reaction, although fear of criticism by teachers and classmates was a frequent theme. She seemed to be preoccupied with thoughts of not being loved, being "left all alone," and losing loved ones. Kay was terribly afraid that the family would break apart: all, she felt, were going their separate ways. At home, Kay had assumed primary responsibility for most of the Internal Instrumentality functions (cooking, cleaning, etc.) and for controlling Rita's mode of representing the family. (Rita, of course, would resent Kay's attempts at control and would "tease" her in retribution.)

The family was "diagnosed" as having a disorder of the Division of Responsibility function, primarily in the areas of Internal Instrumentality and External Relations. This was seen as intimately related to Kay's perception of family instability and feelings of insecurity, her sometimes rather violent tactics at home, and her school phobia.

More precisely, Mrs. D.'s role enactments in the area of External Relations, as perceived by Kay (failure to exercise discipline, failure to "counsel" and train Kay in the ways of interpersonal relations, refusal to accompany the children to social functions) conflicted with the expectations about "mothers" that Kay had acquired outside the family. For example, Kay recalled instances where she received no disciplinary action for wrongdoings while her childhood accomplices did. The result, for Kay, was self-devaluation: she wondered if her mother really cared about her and she wondered what it was about her actions that did not elicit the expected reciprocities in her mother. Kay's grandmother could not adequately perform these functions, since the expectations Kay had developed specifically concerned her mother.

Kay assumed responsibility for Internal Instrumentality functions largely by default; no one else would take the responsibility in this area, and the other members could manufacture excuses that would satisfy a naive young girl. For a time, Kay was able to secure her place in the family by executing these household tasks. In order to maintain the role relationships, the other family members had to act in ways that would maintain Kay's motivation to meet their expectations, that is, they would have to meet her expectations for "gratitude" and the like by reciprocal enactments.

Soon, however, this system began to crumble. Kay, not really being prepared for this role, did not altogether meet family expectations. Grandfather was the first to complain about Kay's cooking skills and the least diplomatic in expressing his views. Other members began to slacken their role reciprocities. Frustrated in maintaining her positive self-evaluation, Kay tried to establish the former role relationships. Lacking mature skill, she used abrupt and sometimes violent techniques: barring doors; wrestling and slugging her sister; and, when her wheelchair-bound mother "misbehaved," Kay would roll her into a corner, facing the wall. Needless to say, the effects of these actions were opposite to that which was desired.

Contributing to the further breakdown of reciprocal actions was Kay's growing dissatisfaction with the division of responsibility in Internal Instrumentality functions. She wanted more time to devote to herself, to peer relationships and to social activities. But she was hampered by her many household duties and the unwillingness of other family members to share any of the responsibility in this area: her mother claimed inability because of her arthritis; her grandmother had to work; her grandfather was "too old to change his ways"; Rita simply disclaimed any obligation to the family. Kay had neither the power nor the tact to induce changes in the role performance of other family members (although she tried various coercive measures). If she tried to refer a conflict to a third member for resolution, either a coalition would exist (e.g., between mother and grandfather) or the third party would not accept the role of "mediator" expected of her (e.g., Mrs. D.'s refusal to mediate disputes between Kay and Rita). Nor did there exist any kind of mutually acceptable plan for the resolution of role conflict by bargaining. Thus, Kay was left with virtually no possibility of achieving her desired pattern of relationships within the family complex. Her self-evaluation was abysmal.

At this point, once-a-week conjoint family psychotherapy began. The therapeutic program focused on the disturbed functional area—Division of Responsibility.

All family members (except Mr. A.) were seen simultaneously for 1 hour per week. The first few hours were spent in specifying the expectations and perceived enactments of the family members. Although this continued throughout treatment, it was less prominent in the later hours. In the next "stage" the family members were urged to bargain for changes in role relationships that would be satisfactory to the participants. Here, the therapist attempted to reduce the effects of coercive devices and coalitions while focusing attention on the consequences of proposed role revisions. Finally, a number of strategies were employed to effect some commitment to agreed-upon role revisions. The family would, for example, be assigned the tasks of making out a work schedule or planning meals for a week in advance. Another tactic used was the development of a Family Reconciliation Agreement. This legal-looking document specified the agreed-upon division of responsibility for Internal Instrumentality functions (and part of External Relations) and required each member to acknowledge, in writing, her specific responsibilities.

Therapy lasted 5 months. After 2, phobic affect vis-a-vis school markedly decreased, and is now only rarely manifested and well under control. At the end of treatment, school absences and tardiness were more than halved. Her academic performance rose from D's and F's to B's and C's. Her weight dropped from 180 to 155. The frequency of hostile outbursts decreased to a minimum.

PRINCIPLES FOR THERAPEUTIC INTERVENTION

The primary area of role dysfunction should be identified and focused upon immediately. We have found the Kelly-Tharp Marriage Role Questionnaire useful for this purpose,[10] but the therapeutic interviews themselves quickly reveal this data if the therapist is active in asking the family members for clarification of their various role expectations.

Ordinarily, it is more profitable to select External Relations, Internal Instrumentality, and/or Division of Responsibility than Solidarity or Sexuality for original focus, even though the most salient presenting complaint of families is nearly always that of a disorder in Solidarity. Solidarity conflicts cannot be ameliorated until the "sandpaper" of other dysfunction is removed. Thus, we concentrate initially upon the other functional areas, treating Solidarity (and also Sexuality) dysfunctions as epiphenomena.

The aim of treatment is the negotiation of role allocation which will allow for the maximum role satisfaction within each individual.

The first technique to be attempted is family bargaining and compromise, arbitrated by the therapist. This involves a quid pro quo system of "I'll change this, if you change that." This is often sufficient; sometimes it is not.

The second technique to be attempted is inducing the family members to change their role behavior by the application of negative sanctions against one another. In most cases severely enough disturbed to request treatment, current role performances are clung to with desperation. It is necessary for the family members to squarely face their existential choices: live as you are or change. One or more will choose the former, one or more the latter. Those most dissatisfied must then increase the sanctions steadily until the others agree to modify. Those who have failed in bargaining, and thus require the sanction stage, also require powerful sanctions. Sanctions which have been effective include threat of divorce, running away, court commitment, taking a lover. Threats of suicide or murder are rarely effective, since they can be countered with the more powerful legal sanctions of incarceration (in jail or hospital).

Many times, of course, these threats are made mildly, subtly. The therapist must clarify them, and restate them on a quid pro quo basis. Needless to say, this is a crucial point and is accompanied by a high level of anxiety among all participants. The therapist, in order to maintain the dignity of all parties, emphasizes the choice: all present have the option of accepting the change or accepting the sanction. He must also emphasize that if A threatens B with X unless he does Y, A is also offering to give Z to B if he does comply with Y. If Mr. E.R. *does* stop drinking, Mrs. E.R. is offering him continued stability at home, and her efforts to re-establish Solidarity. This is necessary to prevent individuals from reacting to sanctions solely as threats and to enable them to respond as to a compromise.

Although the most crucial stage, this is by no means the final one.

Role modification, achieved by sanction or bargaining, must often be followed by therapeutic purgation of the excess role meaning attached to the new acts. This can frequently be the vehicle for the discussion of Solidarity issues as well.

During this stage, Mr. E.R. rather shyly requested that Mrs. E.R. polish his boots for him, as a good wife should. She exploded: mothers polish boots, wives do not. He despaired: what was the use of it all, if she would not behave as a wife. Rather than focus on their respective histories of mothering, the therapist insisted that the only substantive issue was boots. By thus illustrating the excess meaning attached to many disputed acts, the patients were freed to decide this (and many other role performances) on the merits of the particular issue, without gambling their entire role identities on the outcome of each petty dispute. As explained above, Solidarity ordinarily reestablishes itself "automatically" with the resolution of these issues.

The final aim is the creation of a strategy for the negotiation of role revision, which will be independent of therapy. Even upon the most successful termination, the solutions are only here-and-now. As life unfolds, role revisions must follow. Probably as a function of our middle-class, urban population of patients, the typical strategy adopted has been a semidemocratic one, involving careful discussion and compromise, but with a tacit assumption that parental authority allows for veto.

But these strategies are highly idiosyncratic. In another case (a first generation Austrian couple), the wife relaxed into an agreement that the husband's decisions would be final (after she had had her say). It appears that no strategy is ultimately better than any other, provided there is agreement among the family members as to the appropriate Division of Responsibility in renegotiating within all five areas.

We conclude with two final remarks. Of course, role-oriented therapy is no more a panacea than any other. The development of some disorders appears to produce such fundamental changes in individuals as to appear structural. Schizophrenia may be such an instance. Another notable limitation of this technique appeared in a case of severe sexual aversion: after 1 year of marital relations, and widespread role dysfunction, a young wife developed acute phobic reactions to sexual intercourse. Conjoint role therapy succeded in ameliorating all the multitudinous secondary manifestations, in Solidarity, Internal Instrumentality, etc. Yet the sexual disorder did not yield, since the sexual dysfunction triggered devaluation processes which had been original to a childhood trauma. For solution of this problem, we are relying on traditional individual psychotherapy. It is totally clear, however, that psychotherapy could not be efficacious but for the restored security system and heightened self-evaluation which the prior family treatment provided.

Thus, limits exist for the application of role-oriented therapy, although we do not know the precise boundaries.

One final statement concerning Solidarity, which also applies to values, the nuances of feeling and perception, and the inner experiential lives of our patients, is that our presentation here has largely ignored these facets of life, as does indeed our family role therapy. This is not because we do not value and respect them; on the contrary, we find this technique allows for greater respect. Bargains are driven, decisions are made on the basis of personal feelings, perceptions, tastes, aesthetics, style, and sometimes deep wellings-up such as dreams, hopes, and secret fears. The therapist need not know all this; he need know only the action into which it is summed. For in this treatment, different from all schools of psychotherapy, the significant healing relationship is not with the therapist, but, for the family, it is with one another. Our aim is to remove the abrasive role conflicts which wound individuals; once this is done, the natural relationships allow for healing and for growth. Sometimes, then, they come to share their secrets with one another. The therapist's curiosity need not be satisfied.

TOKEN REINFORCEMENT IN
MARITAL TREATMENT

Richard B. Stuart

HUSBANDS and wives seeking treatment for marital discord typically complain of a lack of understanding and love shown by the other mate. If "understanding" is used to mean an emotion reflecting acceptance of and tolerance for the behavior of the spouse, the therapist is powerless to promote change. On the other hand, if "understanding" is used to mean an awareness of the events which stimulate and consequate the partner's behavior, the therapist can do much to aid in promoting changes. If "love" is viewed as a deeply personal emotional state with highly individual meaning, it must be clearly beyond the control of the therapist. On the other hand, if "loving" behavior is sought, such behavior can clearly be brought under therapist and spouse control in much the same manner as any other response can be controlled. Used in this sense, "loving" refers to ". . . an increased tendency to aid, favor, be with, and caress and a lowered tendency to injure in any way."[1] The tasks of the marriage therapist are accordingly set as, first, to identify the desired ("loving") behaviors sought by each spouse from the other; second, to identify the contingencies which can be used to accelerate and maintain these behaviors; and third, to increase the probability that each of these behaviors will occur.

COMMUNICATIONAL PROBLEMS IN
DISORDERED MARRIAGES

Most parties to disordered marriages complain of an oppressive "lack of communication." At face value, this complaint would seem to have validity as recent research has

Reprinted with permission of the author and publisher from Richard Rubin and Cyril Franks, eds., *Advances in Behavior Therapy, 1968,* New York: Academic Press, Inc., 1969.

shown that silence is far more prevalent in disordered as compared to "normal" families.[2] Closer analysis, however, would suggest that this complaint merely masks a persistent tendency to engage in negative communication. This analysis proceeds from the dictum of the interpersonal school which suggests that: "One cannot not communicate."[3] In disordered marriages, the husband might ask his wife what is bothering her. She might respond with a grimace. Her grimace is not noncommunication; it says rather pointedly, first, that her husband should not ask for he alone is responsible for her distress and, second, that he is powerless to be of assistance to her. Therefore it would be more correct to say that while couples in marital conflict experience the same frequency of communications along the same range of communicational modes as their happier counterparts, their communication is more confined to a negative assortment of topics.

The emotional effect of this reliance upon negative or indirect communication is the feeling of despair expressed by so many prisoners of disturbed marriages. The functional effect is even more pernicious, however. When couples rely upon negative communication they express their wishes obliquely at best. To the extent that they fail to express their wishes directly, they reduce the probability that their wishes will be granted. For example, one recent study concluded that

. . . the more family members explicitly tell each other about their likes and dislikes, the greater their likelihood of arriving at family decisions which better represent and fulfill the wishes of everyone concerned.[4]

One major therapeutic goal must therefore stress the clear and unambiguous statement of the wishes and expectations of each partner.

INTERACTIONAL PATTERNS IN "NORMAL" AND DISORDERED MARRIAGES

Most persons entering marriage expect to enjoy reciprocal patterns of positive reinforcement. Reciprocity has the general sociological connotation that "each party has rights and duties"[5] and the specific behavioral connotation that each party should dispense social reinforcement to the other at an equitable rate.[6] When spouses elect to positively reward each other, this behavior can be understood to represent the best means available to each of maximizing individual rewards while maintaining minimal costs.[7] When spouses elect to reduce the rate of positive reinforcement, this too can be understood in terms of the reward/cost balance. In such situations, each spouse has learned from past experience that his rewards dispensed to the other will not be reciprocated and each seeks to conserve his resources. Thus, whether or not one partner positively reinforces the other will be a function of his past experience with the other,[8] while the presence of a reciprocal interaction suggests that: "Each individual has something to offer by way of reinforcing the other, and once established, the interaction sustains itself."[9]

Normal marriages can be characterized by reliance upon reciprocal relationships. Each partner has learned that if he positively reinforces the other, he will be compensated in the same magnitude. In effect, each partner seeks to raise the rate at which he reinforces the other with the assurance that the rate at which he is reinforced will rise a like amount. In contrast, the partners in disordered marriages seek to minimize individual costs as they have little hope of receiving compensatory rewards. Two broad patterns are available. First, the partners may retreat entirely into patterns of withdrawal. Such patterns can be explained in functional terms as the failure of the social environment to maintain high rates of behavior. Second, the partners may rely heavily upon the use of negative reinforcement (the removal of an aversive event following the emission of a designated response). For example, while the wife in a successful marriage might tell her husband that she will put his favorite dessert on the table while he takes out the garbage, the wife in an unsuccessful marriage might nag him about having not taken out the garbage until he finally does so (if he does at all). He is unlikely to do so, however, as taking out the garbage would reinforce his wife's nagging at the same time that it would be yielding to her coercion.

TOKEN REINFORCEMENT IN MARITAL TREATMENT

A token reinforcement system has proven useful in restoring functional communication and reciprocity in severely disordered marriages. In designing a token system, each partner is asked to specify exactly what responses he would like to see accelerated in the other. In specifying three such responses, each partner identifies the way in which he would like to be rewarded by the other. When a means is developed for the exchange of these responses, the partners can be assisted in recapturing reciprocity in their interaction. Token reinforcement can be used to "develop behaviors which lead to social reinforcement from others and to enhance the skills necessary for the individual to take a responsible social role. . . ."[10] Tokens have the following advantages: (a) they are tangible and unambiguously positive; (b) they permit the recipient to choose his reinforcement, thereby assuring the salience of the reinforcers which are proffered; (c) they are given immediately following a desired behavior; (d) they are typically given in association with some positive behavior; and (e) they may be retained and exchanged for actual reinforcement at a later time.

In establishing a token system with husbands and wives who are in conflict, it is typically necessary to overcome three myths. First, the myth that personality change must precede behavioral change must be overcome. This is done by indicating: (a) one knows "personality" through behavior; (b) it has been shown that changes may be brought about in behavior through rearrangement of the environment; and therefore, (c) "personality" can be changed through changing behavior through environmental control. Second, the myth that history is immutable must be overcome. Every event in every marriage, good or bad, has a history. While this history may contribute to an explanation of the conditions under which certain choices were made, the negative history does not preclude the possibility of positive choices in the present. Third, the myth that people in love "know without asking" the other's wishes must be refuted. This is a definitional matter and it is essential to designate effective participation in any relationship as both clearly stating one's wishes (stimulating the other to act) and rewarding his efforts (contingency management). Therefore, waiting for the other to anticipate one's wishes can be defined as low-level social behavior.

PROCEDURE

The characteristics of the five couples who underwent behavior therapy for intense marital conflict are presented in Table 1. All couples sought treatment as a "last ditch" effort to work out solutions to marriage problems of long standing, and none of the couples indicated an expectation that treatment would succeed. In each instance the wife complained that her husband neglected her conversational needs while the husband complained that his wife refused any and all sexual advances.

TABLE 1. *Characteristics of Five Couples Who Underwent Operant Marital Therapy*

	Couple	Age	Years Married	Number Children	Years Education
1	Husband	38	3	0	Ph.D
	Wife	31			B.S.
2	Husband	27	3	1	Ph.D
	Wife	24			Ph.D
3	Husband	52	23	1	M.S.
	Wife	47			M.A.
4	Husband	41	17	2	High school
	Wife	42			2 yrs. college
5	Husband	36	11	2	M.S.
	Wife	35			M.S.

Following a discussion of the logic of the treatment and rejection of the interfering myths (where necessary), the wife was pressed for details about what "acceptable" conversation meant to her. Behavioral rehearsal during treatment sessions was often needed as a means of specifying the wife's expectations with precision. The wife was then instructed to purchase a kitchen timer which she could carry about the house. She was instructed to set the timer as soon as her husband entered and to give him one token when the bell sounded, if he met her conversational needs at her criterion level during that period. If he failed to behave at the criterion level by the end of the first 30 minutes, she was required to notify him of this and to offer constructive suggestions, cuing him as to how his performance could be improved upon. If she failed to do this, she was required to give her husband a token despite his failure to meet her conversational needs. At his request, at the half-hour cuing time the timer could be reset so that he could earn a token within 60 minutes (rather than having to wait 90 minutes).

The criterion level for conversation was negotiable, with no husband being expected to engage in unending chatter with his wife. The criterion levels ranged from intense conversation to the wife's freedom to ask a casual question of her husband, with each couple employing a range of criteria as fit their changing situations.

The tokens were exchangeable by husbands for sexual favors from their wives. A different menu was constructed for each couple, taking into account their baseline level of sexual activity, the desired level of sexual activity and the number of hours available for nonsexual (in this instance conversational) activity. Each of these couples had sex less than once per week (ranging from once in the year prior to treatment to once in the week prior to treatment), each desired sex an average of three times per week, and each had approximately five hours together on weeknights and 14 hours on weekends, making a total of approximately 52–54 hours per week. Accordingly, husbands were charged three tokens for kissing and "lightly petting" with their wives, five tokens for "heavy petting," and 15 tokens for intercourse.

With each of these couples, all therapeutic sessions were held jointly. Sessions were held during the first four, the sixth, eighth and tenth weeks, for a total of seven sessions. When it is considered that these couples were each on the brink of filing for divorce, this could be considered relatively inexpensive treatment. Follow-up contacts were held by phone or by mail and all data, including that collected during sessions, were based upon self-report.

RESULTS

The number of tokens earned and spent was recorded on a monitoring sheet on a daily basis. This sheet provided each spouse with visual feedback of his own performance. The data recorded for the five couples is presented in Table 2. It will be seen that each couple recorded a steady increase in the rate of conversational and sexual interaction.

Following the start of treatment with the third couple, the husband collected a fortune of 30 tokens. He then precipitated a major conflict with his wife and in the heat of battle threw 15 chips on the table and demanded intercourse. Following this, tokens were given a life of three days and became valueless unless spent within that time. In addition to reducing the likelihood of such abuses of the system, this modification increased the probability that husbands and wives would enjoy the maximum number of sexual encounters.

TABLE 2. *Average Daily Hours of Conversation and Weekly Rate of Sex of Five Couples—Before, at Last Session and at Follow-up of Operant Marital Therapy*

Couple		Baseline	After Ten Weeks of Treatment	At Follow-up
1	Sex	0	2	3
	Conversation	1	5	5.25[a]
2	Sex	.3	3	5
	Conversation	1.25	4.75	4.50[a]
3	Sex	0	2	2
	Conversation	.25	3	4[a]
4	Sex	.25	2	3
	Conversation	1	5	6[b]
5	Sex	0	4	3
	Conversation	.50	4.25	5[c]

[a] 52 weeks.
[b] 28 weeks.
[c] 24 weeks.

In addition to monitoring the rate of token and reinforcement exchange, each couple completed a brief attitude inventory adapted from the work of Farber.[11] The results of this inventory are presented in Table 3, which shows that husbands and wives both reported increased satisfaction in and commitment to their marriage following treatment.

Audio-tape recordings were made of all treatment sessions held with two couples (numbers 4 and 5). These tapes were analyzed to determine the number of clearly positive and clearly negative statements made by each partner about the other, whether directed to the therapist or spouse. The results of this analysis are presented in Table 4. (A full account of the procedure and findings for all couples will be published at a later date.) It will be seen that the verbal behavior of clients during interviews became markedly more positive over time, paralleling the reported increase in approach behaviors outside of treatment.

TABLE 3. *Marital Satisfaction Assessment Inventory Scores of
Five Couples—Before, at Last Session and at
Follow-up of Operant Marital Treatment*

	SOURCE		PERIOD		
Couple	Spouse	Rating Self or Other Spouse	Before	After	Follow-up[a][b]
	Husband	Self	5	14	14
	Husband	Wife	2	8	12
1	Wife	Husband	4	8	14[a]
	Wife	Self	4	8	14
	Total		15	38	52
	Husband	Self	3	15	15
	Husband	Wife	2	5	13
2	Wife	Husband	3	14	15[a]
	Wife	Self	2	7	13
	Total		10	41	54
	Husband	Self	4	8	10
	Husband	Wife	0	7	10
3	Wife	Husband	5	9	8[a]
	Wife	Self	4	8	8
	Total		13	32	32
	Husband	Self	5	10	10
	Husband	Wife	2	4	10
4	Wife	Husband	4	8	10[b]
	Wife	Self	4	7	10
	Total		15	29	40
	Husband	Self	2	10	12
	Husband	Wife	4	10	12
5	Wife	Husband	0	8	8[c]
	Wife	Self	10	15	15
	Total		16	43	47

[a] 52 weeks.
[b] 28 weeks.
[c] 24 weeks.

TABLE 4. *Number of Positive and Negative Statements Made by
Each Spouse about the Other During
Operant Marital Treatment*

Couple		FIRST WEEK		FOURTH WEEK		TENTH WEEK	
		Pos	Neg	Pos	Neg	Pos	Neg
4	Husband	8	11	14	2	14	3
	Wife	1	23	10	0	12	1
5	Husband	5	5	10	4	10	0
	Wife	0	3	3	0	8	0

DISCUSSION

Each spouse was directed to make specific modifications
of his own behavior in an effort to modify the behavioral
environment in which his partner's behavior occurred. The
antecedents for changed behavior were probably twofold:
therapeutic recommendations exercised some S^D control as
did the expectation of changes in the behavior of the spouse.
The therapist suggested that each party engage in behavior
which had doubtless been requested, cajoled and demanded
by each party countless times before. As therapeutic directives, these new requests were differentiated from the old in
four important respects. First, they were made more specific.
Second, they were removed from the context of coercive
demands in which granting the request would have amounted
to reinforcing unpleasant patterns of negative reinforcement.
Third, it was possible to receive reciprocation immediately
so that each partner had greater assurance that he would, in
fact, receive his due. Finally, treatment was characterized as
a "game" in which each partner could utilize strategies which
would have greater payoff than he had experienced in the
past.

It is difficult to assess the importance of any specific therapeutic technique. Every marriage therapist must be cognizant
of the fact that his patients are torn between the actual distress of the present union and the imagined reward of future
unions. When it is recognized that at best the subjects of one
study treated "strangers more gently, and generally more
nicely than they do their spouses,"[12] one cannot overestimate
the importance of increasing the rate and salience of posi-

tive reinforcements exchanged in a marriage. The use of token reinforcement is designed specifically to achieve this goal, and its effectiveness appears to have been indicated by changes in both the behavior (within and outside treatment) and attitude of patients who underwent this treatment.

The results of this study must, however, be qualified. The data concerning the rate of conversational and sexual behavior is the product of self-report. While it is impossible to assess the truth of such data, both partners concurred in the report. The data concerning attitude was taken from a crude attitude scale which may be more closely tied to hope than reality. Finally, the data concerning verbal behavior in the interview might have been influenced in important ways by differential responses of the therapist, despite the fact that care was taken to eliminate such influence.

WHITHER FAMILY THERAPY

Jay Haley

THE TREATMENT of an entire family, interviewed together regularly as a group, is a new procedure in psychiatry. Just when Family Therapy originated is difficult to estimate because the movement has been largely a secret one. Until recently, therapists who treat whole families have not published on their methods, and their papers are still quite rare—although we may soon expect a deluge. The secrecy about Family Therapy has two sources: those using this method

Reprinted with permission of the author and publisher from *Family Process*, vol. 1, no. 1 (March 1962), pp. 69–100.

Project for the Study of Schizophrenic Communication, directed by Gregory Bateson. The staff consists of Jay Haley and John Weakland, Research Associates; Dr. Don D. Jackson, Consultant; and Dr. William F. Fry, Consultant. The research is financed by Grant OM–324 from the National Institute of Mental Health, which is administered by the Palo Alto Medical Research Foundation. The project is part of the research program of the Veterans Administration Hospital, Palo Alto, California.

have been too uncertain about their techniques and results to commit themselves to print (therapists of individuals have not let this dissuade them), and there has apparently been a fear of charges of heresy because the influence of family members has been considered irrelevant to the nature and cure of psychopathology in a patient. As a result, since the late 1940's one could attend psychiatric meetings and hear nothing about Family Therapy unless, in a quiet hotel room, one happened to confess that he treated whole families. Then another therapist would put down his drink and reveal that he too had attempted this type of therapy. These furtive conversations ultimately led to an underground movement of therapists devoted to this most challenging of all types of psychotherapy and this movement is now appearing on the surface.

There are three general arguments offered for treating the family as a whole rather than the individual with symptoms: (a) often individual therapy has failed with a type of patient, or a particular patient, and it is argued that his family environment is preventing change and should be treated, (b) when individual treatment is slow, difficult, and subject to frequent relapses, it is similarly argued that the environment of the patient is inhibiting change, and (c) the appearance of distress and symptoms in other family members when the patient improves raises questions about the responsibility of a therapist to other family members.

Granted these assumptions, a clinical portrait appears which is different from the portrait of psychopathology which has been sketched by psychiatric theoreticians in the past. The family therapist would seem to be arguing this: psychopathology in the individual is a product of the way he deals with intimate relations, the way they deal with him, and the way other family members involve him in their relations with each other. Further, the appearance of symptomatic behavior in an individual is necessary for the continued functioning of a particular family system. Therefore changes in the individual can only occur if the family system changes, and resistance to change in an individual centers in the influence of the family as a group. Most techniques of Family Therapy center in shifting the focus from the identified patient to the family and then resolving the problems in family relationships. At that point the individuals in the family undergo change.

This clinical portrait presented by the family therapist is revolutionary when contrasted with the traditional psychiatric portrait. The past point of view, which reached an extreme in psychoanalysis, assumes that symptoms, and resistance to change, center in the internal processes of the individual. The function of symptoms is to maintain an intrapsychic balance. From this point of view, family relations are secondary, if not peripheral, to the problems psychotherapy must resolve. The argument that the symptoms of an individual maintain the balance of his family system rather than maintaining a balance of intrapsychic forces is a request for a major change in psychiatric thinking. The difference in theory is so great that it is no wonder therapists who attempted Family Therapy worried about heresy and operated underground.

It is possible to have the broad, flexible viewpoint and say that both the individual and the family points of view are true, but such tolerance confuses the theoretical and descriptive problems. Those therapists who attempt such tolerance might find themselves talking about unconscious forces in the family system and family relations inside the individual. Only by stating the extremes clearly is it possible to raise a fundamental problem: if the point of view of the individual therapist is valid, Family Therapy should be superficial and unsuccessful (unless it focuses upon releasing repressed ideation), and if the Family Therapy point of view is valid, individual therapy should be superficial and unsuccessful (unless it provokes a change in the family system which permits the individual patient to change).

It is possible that what makes both forms of treatment successful is what they have in common, and some of these similarities will be discussed here. First there must be a description of types of Family Therapy. Over the years a variety of groups and individuals have been experimenting with different techniques for treating whole families, and their work has begun to solidify into schools of Family Therapy. Some of these schools will be described, but since few of the practitioners have published on their methods the schools will be given fictional names here so they can continue in their anonymity. After this somewhat facetious, but accurate, description of various schools, there will be a more serious discussion of the problems of family therapy and similarities with individual psychotherapy.

The Dignified School

Established by one of the early pioneers, the *Dignified School of Family Therapy* assumes that a child's problem is really a family problem. This school confines itself largely to families who have such problems as wetting the bed, stealing, failing in school, exhibiting themselves, and other mild difficulties. It also specializes in families where the disturbance centers in a child who must suffer the consequences of being too young to leave home.

The therapist of this school, a kindly, but firm, gentleman, first interviews the parents without the child. Routinely the parents point out that their only difficulty is one of their children who is such a problem. Their marriage is a happy one, the family close, the other children delightful, and they seek therapy only for the sake of their problem child. The therapist does not scoff at such statements or point out that the child is merely a scab on a family problem, he lets the parents make this discovery themselves. Accepting what they say with kindly understanding, he intervenes in a way which distinguishes this school from all others. His intervention takes the form of agreeing wholeheartedly that their child is the problem in the family and therefore the family must be in some way not quite right for the child. While the parents are attempting to absorb this twist of what they have said, the therapist makes a few suggestions. He asks them to bring all the family in with them next time and remain silent while he encourages the disturbed child to express his feelings. He will also ask the boy to suggest some minor change in his family arrangements, and it would be nice if the parents would cooperate in such a change. Faced with this benevolent gentleman who is only asking them to remain silent while he talks to their child and to make a small change if the boy requests one, the parents find themselves agreeing and even looking forward to the next interview.

When the parents bring in the child he is typically sullen, indifferent, and sure that he will be proven to be the cause of all the family and world troubles since the beginning of time. He discovers, after some good-natured encouragement from the therapist, that he can say two whole sentences without being interrupted by his parents. Further, he finds that they remain silent, though with rather strained smiles, when he makes some comments about how everyone in the family seems unhappy and his parents quarrel so often. When encouraged to, he asks for some minor change that would benefit him, and by the next interview he is being even more reckless. After an interview or two, when the child is reporting that things are going well for him now, the therapist releases the parents from the restraint of silence. By this time they have built up within themselves a desire to speak quite frankly. In fact, like two hounds who have flushed a rabbit, they pursue the child up one side of his weak protests and down the other. They point out that he has no right to be unhappy since everything in the family centers on him, that he shouldn't dare suggest that anyone else in the family is unhappy, and his mother screams at him that she and father never fight or even raise their voices. When the floodgates open and the parents get carried away in giving the boy his lumps, they also go too far in discussing the problems in the family and their coalition begins to break down as they turn on each other. For example, father may say that it is none of the boy's business if he drinks, and mother will step in and disagree, pointing out that his drinking upsets the whole family. Father will then reply that if she ever got dinner on time he wouldn't drink half as much. and mother will say that if he ever showed her the slightest consideration dinner might be on time, and so on. Usually the boy's symptoms dissipate at about the time the parents are openly fighting each other instead of him. Somewhat later the emphasis shifts to the problems with the siblings, if need be.

By agreeing with the parents that the child is the problem and also requiring them to be silent while the boy expresses his side of the story, the therapist manages to side with both parents and child simultaneously. As the family members struggle with each other more openly, he continues to attempt to be scrupulously fair and not take sides no matter how much he admires the skill of one family member in cutting down another.

Taking sides in family rows is dealt with by different

schools of Family Therapy in different ways, but all are in agreement that the therapist should not side consistently with one family member against another. Some therapists merely try not to take sides, and others take sides and shift at opportune moments to take the family unaware. Some therapists will dicuss the situation with the family, as does the therapist of the *Dynamic Psychodynamic School of Family Diagnosis*. He points out to the family that he may at any time be siding with one of them, but five minutes later he may side with another. This keeps family members uncertain just whose camp he will be in during the family campaigns. This therapist also manages an informal atmosphere, calling the parents by their first names as he says such things as, "Now look here, Sam, I'm not a judge and this isn't a courtroom. We're just trying to get some understanding of this." Therapists of all schools argue they are trying to bring about understanding, usually because they are trying to keep their feet in a slippery morass of accusations and counter-accusations.

The strain on the therapist as he is pulled in several directions at once in Family Therapy is compounded by the determination of family members to prove their innocence to the therapist. He may suggest that they should defend themselves to each other rather than him, since they must live together, but still family members continually attempt to use him to bring down one another. Therapists often wish they could flee the room, and a school of Family Therapy has been devised to let them do just that.

The Chuck It and Run School

The setting for this school is an office of two rooms with a one-way observation screen between them. A tape recorder is installed in the observation room. The therapist introduces the family to this setting and points out that their problem child represents a problem in the family which they can solve by talking to each other, expressing their feelings, opening the channels of communication, and all that. Advising them that they know more about each other than any outsider ever could, he tells them they are the best therapists for each other. He will provide them the opportunity to deal with each other by leaving them alone together a good part of the time. However, he will also help them by often entering the room and probing and pushing and encouraging them to talk about the sensitive subjects they have been avoiding so they can get closer to one another, which is clearly the goal of every right thinking person. He then flees the room, with a parting suggestion that someone bring up something, no matter how small. The family members sit and stare at each other uncomfortably for awhile, and usually the parents turn to the child, the family-agreed-upon patient, expecting him to come up with something they can object to. The child delivers something, the parents object, and soon everyone is talking. When the argument gets too hot, or when one member gets mad and shuts up, or when someone is being gored too fiercely, the therapist will enter the room and draw the fire for awhile. The first few times he enters, the family ceases and listens to him, but they may ultimately continue whether he is in the room or not and he must put out some effort to be heard above the din.

Being out of the room not only permits the therapist some relief from strain and a peaceful cigarette, but he also can observe the family struggle in a more detached way since it does not center on him. By not floundering in the morass with them, he can note the more subtle maneuvers in the family. At some point the family may call for him to come into the room and he does not, making it clear that he does not necessarily respond on their terms but on his own.

The family members in this situation are in a peculiar position. They are unable to use their more devastating man-euvers on the therapist because they may hardly begin when he vanishes from the room and leaves them feeling undone. They are forced to turn on each other. Yet they cannot even turn on each other with full freedom, since they are being observed by a therapist who may enter at any time and actively give someone the business.

In this type of therapy the family is further shaken by being forced to listen to themselves. If the therapist makes an interpretation which they will not accept, he may play back the tape recording of the last few minutes to demon-strate his point. The family discovers that their words may be flung into their faces from their own mouths at any moment by that dastardly machine, and so they tend to be inhibited in their usual maneuvers and forced to develop new ones.

Besides leaving the room and playing back the words of the families, this school of therapy is differentiated from others by the enthusiasm with which the therapist thumps the father in the family. It is the therapist's idea that if father would treat mother better she would stop gaining her emotional satisfaction by a sticky nurturing of the child's symptoms. Therefore the therapist rousts father into treating his wife better. The father, who usually has attempted many times to treat his wife better only to be met by distrust, denial, and derogation, is usually reluctant. Often the involvement of therapist and father on this issue is intense, but seldom does it come to blows. This approach by the therapist encourages mother to continue in therapy because she can have her point of view supported and watch her husband get his lumps. In many families father *does* finally give in and try again to treat his wife better, and such an issue has been made of the matter that mother is more receptive, thus astounding the father and child and pleasing the therapist.

This school was developed in work with delinquent families. When applied to more severe cases, such as schizophrenic families, the therapist can go out less often since he must shore up the family members enough that they will stay in the same room and talk to each other.

THE REALLY DISTURBED FAMILY

Family Therapy owes part of its origin to schizophrenia, as do many other psychiatric triumphs. It became apparent that it was not entirely reasonable to have a child driven mad by his family and then hospitalize him and get him on his feet and send him right back into his family to be driven mad again. Attempts were made to re-arrange the situation at home, and then came attempts to therapeut the whole family. The greatest challenge to any family therapist is the psychotic family. Whatever difficulties there are in neurotic families, they are exaggerated to the point of parody in the family of the schizophrenic. Various approaches have been used and schools established to deal with these families, from valiant therapists singly assaulting the schizophrenic family citadel to expeditions in twos and threes. An attempt was even made to surround the whole family with a hospital.

The severely disturbed, or psychotic, family is like a ship

with no rudder, floundering about in a sea of despond. The family members cannot get together nor can they separate, and so the psychotic "child" may be forty years of age and still struggling gamely to keep the ship afloat and floundering. The determination of each family member to avoid taking responsibility for anything requires the family therapist to be willing to be a steersman. All Family Therapy requires a therapist to be responsible, but with the severely disturbed family the therapist must be ready, willing, and stable enough to take direction of the family while benevolently dealing with their persistent sabotage of his efforts.

The Stonewall School

Just as a fat man is often called Skinny, the *Stonewall School of Family Therapy* derives its name from the activities of a slippery therapist who takes charge of the family in such a way that no one can come to grips with him. A characteristic of this school is the way it sprains the brain of family members. Often they leave a session batting themselves alongside the head to clear it. The therapist insists that all family members are absolutely right and absolutely wrong and that love is hate, criticism is complimentary, disloyalty is undying affection, and leaving home is really staying. Whatever direction the family members are going, in their aimless way, is accepted by the therapist but re-labeled as actually some other direction, so that the family must become less aimless to find out what the devil is really going on.

The members of the really disturbed family refuse to do whatever anyone asks of them, and the therapist of the Stonewall School offers suggestions so prettily packaged that it does not appear the family is being asked to do anything not already being done. For example, the mother in this type of family insists on being in charge of whatever happens and is reluctant to acknowledge this. The therapist typically directs mother to take charge of something that is to happen in the family. She cannot be in charge if someone is directing her, and so to take charge of the therapist she must rebel in the direction of letting others take charge of what happens at home.

The father in the really disturbed family is usually a man who is never home, and when at home he makes no attempt to put his wife in her place. In fact he avoids a struggle with

her as if he feels like an ant attempting to wrestle an ele-
phant. Because his wife incapacitates him, this type of man
becomes a philosopher. He adopts tactics of non-aggression
and passive resistance, except for occasional tantrums. The
wife inevitably has no respect for a philosopher and feels
that he is secretly disloyal to her and waiting to blow on
the flames if someone else roasts her. The therapist of the
Stonewall School agrees wholeheartedly with the wife that
her husband is disloyal. He points out that he must be since
he never criticizes her and any loyal husband would help his
wife by commenting on her bad points as well as her good
ones since he would accept her as she is. The wife finds herself supported by an ally who is encouraging her husband
to be critical of her, and the husband finds himself forced to
insult his wife to prove his loyalty. In the ensuing battles,
their confusion can resolve into mutually participant aggression on more equal terms. Such aggression is cheered on by
the therapist, who passes out the weapons as he points out
that if they cannot feel intensely enough about each other
to hate each other then they cannot really love each other.

The problem for the husband or child in the really disturbed family rests on mother's threats to leave them, or col-
lapse, if they oppose her. She also makes opposition difficult
by pointing out that she is always doing the right thing. She
bravely carries the burdens of the family, seeks help for
them, wants cleanliness, truth, clean thoughts, and stands
on the side of God and country at all times. If anything is
wrong in the family, only an idiot could consider it her fault.
If she does housework at four in the morning, it is not that
she is odd but merely that she is concerned about keeping
a clean house. If she is a lush, she drinks only to make
herself more cheerful for the family's sake. If she applauds
when the child behaves in a psychotic way, it is not that
she wants such behavior, but merely that she feels he should
have *someone* on his side, and father is never home. Because
of mother's righteousness and helpfulness, schizophrenia is
sometimes called the disease of Christianity. The early Christians could not be easily opposed since they insisted that
whatever they did was for your sake and if you wished to
harm them they would only turn the other cheek and make
you feel guilty. Just as the Romans could only deal with these
tactics by throwing Christians to the lions, so father and

child in this type of family can only fantasy what a good meal mother would make in the lion house at the local zoo. Their attitude makes her feel not wanted. She also feels indignant and bewildered because she has sacrificed herself all her life to help the family. The therapist of the Stonewall School commiserates with mother for depriving herself and for never having the opportunity to be irresponsible and unburdened of the family's problems. He suggests that she might let father share her burdens and perhaps take care of the budget or even take over some of the disciplining of the children. Unsettled by the idea that she might be really depriving herself, and determined to prove that her idiot of a husband could not write a check or speak firmly to the children, mother relinquishes her burdens and begins to lose her grip.

Of course the crisis comes in the disturbed family when father does begin to behave like he has testicles and so deals with his wife in the way she has insisted he should for the last twenty years. With encouragement from the therapist he may risk taking on a few burdens. When his wife inevitably interferes with his budgeting or disciplining, pointing out that he is doing them badly and will irresponsibly stop doing them at any moment, he may even suggest to her that she keep out of his new domain. The wife then erupts like a gored whale and furiously condemns him, insisting that he is only putting on an act, he's not really asserting himself but merely trying to please the therapist, he's behaving like a child and getting angry over the silliest things, and so on. Just in time to prevent father collapsing and proving his wife right, the therapist intervenes by raising the question whether the wife is loyal enough, true blue enough, and ready yet to tolerate her husband dealing with her in a more straight-forward way, thus hanging the wife on her perfectionistic tendencies. The psychotic family member, meanwhile, is usually trying to provoke the parents to return to their previous floundering arrangement, since this is the one he has always known. Typically, when the parents begin to get angry with each other they turn on the child, but if they do not, the child will intrude and draw the anger on himself, thereby preventing them from working out their problems. However, when the child finds that he cannot get a rise out of his parents by psychotic behavior because they are too involved in fighting with each other, he begins to give up his symptoms and return to reality. If this doesn't happen too rapidly, his parents will not develop symptoms of their own to maintain the floundering family system.

Usually the child can cease being psychotic when the parents have stopped devoting their lives to helping him and when they have ceased using him to avoid dealing with each other. He can also improve when mother learns she can survive without being perfect. Since the mother must insist she is the good and perfect mother, the child can bring her down merely by being ill and unhappy, like a woodsman brings down a giant redwood tree. When the child suffers the dread disease schizophrenia, the mother is in a particularly trying position because she can never be sure whether the child has something severely wrong, which is an indictment of her as a mother, or is a trickster making a fool of her, which is an indictment of her as a mother. For example, a schizophrenic daughter spent her time pulling at her hair and muttering to herself, thus damning the mother for having raised such an unfortunate creature, but the same girl at other times would threaten to call the police and tell them that her mother's house was dirty, thus making her mother unsure whether the whole business was not merely a farcical comedy to make her appear an idiot. In this situation the mother prefers to feel sad because schizophrenia is an organic difficulty, or sad because the child's father is a villain and the schizophrenia results from his weakness of character and sadistic inclinations.

The general task of the family therapist is to persuade mother to give up her perfection and acknowledge she influences others, persuade the child to give up the illness which is the one weapon he has developed, and persuade father to oppose them both and raise enough hell so they will believe he cares what happens at home. The difficulty with this type of family is based on their individual and joint efforts to desecrate any improvement which occurs. As a learned social scientist once said, "If one put all the most difficult people in the world on a train and put the least difficult up near the engine, all psychotic families would be piled up into the caboose."

One of the major tasks with the schizophrenic family is to persuade the psychotic child that he could find life just as hard outside the family, so that he will leave home. However, it would seem that only when the child is sure that he is wanted at home is he willing to leave. Therefore it is necessary to create a more amiable family if the child is ever to go off on his own.

The Great Mother School

The tactics for creating a more amiable family in this school are based upon defining whatever happens in the family, no matter how malignant, as essentially amiable. The therapist begins by seeing family members alone and establishing a positive relationship with them, leading them out on all their secrets. She learns their histories, hopes, disappointments, and points of view on family controversies. She then brings the family together and is a friend to all. She also knows a good deal about each of them that they haven't told each other, and none of them knows how much the other has squealed the family secrets. From this position of power, the therapist emanates a benevolent concern about resolving misunderstandings in the family.

The *Great Mother School of Family Therapy* emphasizes what good intentions all family members have and how unfortunate it is that accidental misunderstandings arise. Should the child threaten to set the house on fire, the therapist interprets this as an attempt to gain a positive response from his parents. Should mother detach father from his genitalia by her pity and by the ways she analyzes his character, his past, and his future, the therapist points out that Mumsy is trying to reach Daddy and overcome her fears that he will disappoint her. Should Daddy get drunk and lose his job, this act is defined as an expression of unconscious desire to seek a new position to better the family financial condition. A gold star was given this therapist in a case where father took an axe after mother and almost caught her. The therapist managed to persuade the family that father was really attempting to provoke a more affectionate response from his wife and a closer relationship between them.

With the Great Mother approach, the family system of strategies is inevitably undermined. Family members, who have spent years sharpening their weapons so they could cut each other down with adroit skill, are told that they are really reaching out for affection and understanding. Disconcerted, they become uncertain whether to knife each other in the usual manner for fear it will be interpreted as an affectionate gesture. Into this uncertainty charges the therapist with suggestions for positive behavior between them.

Since each family member likes to have the therapist on his side, they behave more positively to show her that it is hopeless to demonstrate any affection toward these other recalcitrant characters. However, to please her each must show that he is capable of receiving affection although the others are not. As a result of the competition to show her how positive they can be, the family is soon roasting popcorn instead of each other. They are cheered on by the therapist who asks regularly, "Have you had joy and pleasure this week?"

The Great Mother School is based upon the theory that family members in severely disturbed families grow older but never up, and so everyone in the family must be treated like a child. All aggression is taken dead seriously but re-defined as if it were occurring between little people. Murderous attempts become childish mischievousness, lustful incestuous assaults become affectionate teasing, and raving psychotic behavior may be labeled as involuntary naughtiness with good intentions behind it. Since these family members respond to the parental approach and do have positive feelings for each other underneath the destructiveness, the therapist is on sure ground.

In this school the therapist also puts great emphasis upon factual details. How the couple met, what they expected from each other, who proposed to whom, and so on, are the subject of careful inquiry called "getting the facts straight." By calling every re-phrasing of a situation by the therapist a fact, the therapist's interpretations are given the massive weight of scientific authority. If there is any uproar, the details of the context are thoroughly discussed. For example, should the parents have an argument in the car on the way downtown, the situation is thoroughly clarified, including the make of automobile and where it was purchased. The culmination of clarifying the facts is the discovery that the uproar and the black eye were really the result of an attempt to achieve affectionate understanding, and that is a fact.

The danger in this school is the possible competition between the Great Mother and the perfect mother. As the therapist shows how the mad child should really be treated, the perfect mother feels at a disadvantage. However, the more she feels at a disadvantage the more insecure she is, and so she welcomes the compliments which exude toward her from the therapist. Her desires to sabotage are undermined by her desires to please, and the delicate balance can be tipped by the skillful therapist saying at a timely moment that the perfect mother is a better mother than she is.

The Multiplication Schools

Just as many swimmers who are uneasy about drowning will associate with a life preserver, so do many family therapists prefer company when they dive into a family. An early pioneer established the *Eyebrows School of Family Therapy* in England with two therapists in the room with the family. The assault by twos has merits because the family is more disconcerted when forced to deal with two psychiatrists rather than one. Should both psychiatrists agree on something, even a six member family feels outnumbered. However, the difficulty with this approach rests on the inability of any two psychiatrists to agree on anything. To rationalize this fact, proponents of the Multiplication Schools argue that it is good for the family to hear therapists disagree and resolve their differences because it sets them a good example. Occasionally the psychiatrists can resolve a difference, if the situation puts sufficient professional pressure on them. But usually the assault by twos results in both therapists warily remaining silent and letting the family go about its business of self-destruction, or they become active and parallel the family fights with fights with each other. The noise from some rooms where dual therapy takes place can be deafening. Often family members huddle together and make peace with each other to prevent the therapists fighting to the death. Various combinations are used with this method: a male and female therapist may pretend they are parents for the whole family, two therapists may agree that one is the chief therapist and the other the subordinate (usually a temporary arrangement), or the therapists may decide in advance that one will side with the mother and one with the father, and away they go. Each of these variations has its advantages and disasters.

A variation of the multiplication school is the *Brotherly Love School*, where dual therapists meet the family on its home ground by holding the sessions in the family house. Most therapists prefer to struggle with a family in their offices, where the family is inevitably at a disadvantage. The *Brotherly Love School* risks the family living room. In this situation the family members can conduct their usual household procedures while talking to the therapist. That is, mother can go in and out of the kitchen whenever she gets nervous, son can flee to his bedroom if the argument goes the wrong way, and father can reach for his drink. The effect of the therapist's visit tends to persist since they remain as ghosts in the house after a session is over.

A further extension of the multiple assault on the family is the *Total Push in the Tall Country School*, where not only father and mother each are given a therapist, but all the kiddies too. The family is brought to an institution after agreeing to be assaulted for several days. Each family member is assigned a therapist, and the therapists and family coagulate together until the continuing debate begins to be too sticky. Each therapist then goes off with his patient and commiserates with him about his family. When their mutual strength is regenerated and their coalition established, all come together again for a continuation of the tournament. After two or three eight hour days, the family is sent home again, presumably changed for the better, while all the therapists stand on the steps and cheer them off.

A still further extension of the need for support when dealing with the maelstrom of the really disturbed family is a school which grew out of desperation and research interest. It was called the *Hospitalize the Whole Damn Maelstrom School*. Not only was the psychotic patient hospitalized, but so were his parents, brothers and sisters, and the family cat. With all family members flung into the hospital together, the families were seen individually and with all other families in one large group therapy. It was thought that the assault of many therapists, supported by nurses, aides, and hospital janitors, as well as the horrible examples of other families like themselves before them, would provoke these families to change their ways. It is a tribute to the tenacity of the really disturbed family system that it was the hospital staff which disintegrated rather than the family system and the project was abandoned.

FAMILY AND INDIVIDUAL THERAPY: SIMILARITIES

If individual and family therapy are examined in terms of theory, they are decidedly different. If they are looked upon in terms of practice, the differences are few. In the past there has been little description of practice—what the therapist of an individual actually does with a patient—and a great deal of emphasis upon the theory of what he does. For example, descriptions of the psychoanalytic method are typically about a theoretical process rather than descriptions of what therapist and patient do. Particular emphasis is put upon transference and the uncovering of repressed ideas. From the theory point of view, it is important that the transference relationship not be disturbed by the intrusion of other people; certainly not by relatives of the patient. The careful handling of defenses is another way of looking at individual therapy through the theroetical telescope. The process of interaction between therapist and patient is seen as a careful uncovering of ideas within the patient in the face of the patient's resistance to these ideas. Assuming that transference and dealing with internal resistance are crucial to change in individual therapy, the various ways of treating whole families which have been presented here are not only different but could be called anti-therapeutic. The transference relationship is thoroughly confused by the presence of other family members, and defenses cannot be dealt with in an orderly fashion when family members are flinging accusations, including accusations about incestuous desires and acts.

However, individual therapy need not be seen only through the narrow focus of past theories, particularly theories which are not based upon a description of what happens but upon conjecture about what happens. After all, one cannot observe the transference phenomenon; one can only observe certain behavior by a patient and therapist and *infer* that transference distortions are taking place. Similarly, one observes a patient responding to a therapist in certain ways and *conjectures* that he is defending himself against inferred repressed ideas.

If we merely note the obvious fact that individual therapy is a conversation between two people, similarities with types of family therapy begin to appear. At the descriptive level, the difference between the two methods centers largely in the presence of other family members in the room. Other differences are difficult to find, and apparent differences become similarities upon closer examination. For example, ostensibly individual therapy could be described as a two-person system and Family Therapy as a three or more person system. Related to this difference is the way the family therapist becomes a part of the family system as he is included in the family group and used by members in their dealings with each other. Yet individual therapy is not essentially a two person system, even if the therapist attempts such a restriction physically. The patient's family is in the room in his discussions, his wife is inquiring at home what he says in therapy, and he reports to his family ideas he gains in therapy and so uses the therapist at home. The therapist rapidly becomes included in the family group, although the other family members have all information about him funneled through the patient. The difference, again, resides in the physical absence of other family members during interviews, even though they may be present in the discourse or as indirect supervisors of what is to be said in the room.

It would be possible to argue that individual and Family Therapy are similar because some therapists in both situations encourage patients to understand themselves better and express their feelings. An implicit premise exists in psychiatry that self-understanding and the expression of affect are the source of therapeutic change. Yet even if one accepted this assumption, there is considerable confusion about what sort of self-understanding does the trick and under what circumstances it must occur, and it is unclear by what magic the expression of feelings leads to change. An additional problem is the embarrassing fact, often noted, that patients may exhibit all sorts of self-understanding and express their feelings in subtle detail, but they still continue in distress.

So much emphasis is put upon self-awareness and affect expression that apparently some important therapeutic tactic is involved. However, it would seem apparent that self-understanding and the expression of feelings in individual therapy is going to be rather different from the same behavior with other family members present. If a husband expresses his feelings while alone with an individual therapist, the therapist might not take his statements personally. Yet a wife will have a certain response when she is present in the interview, because she will think herself responsible for how her husband feels (as a therapist might after some years with the patient).

Now that the many methods of Family Therapy are being added to the many existing methods of individual therapy, an opportunity arises for examining what the various methods have in common in the hope that we can thereby discover the common factors or "causes" of therapeutic change. To make such an examination, it is necessary to step outside the framework of any particular school of therapy and take a more broad and formal look at patterns in all of them. The general argument will be offered here that all methods of therapy have in common an educational factor to help people behave differently and a paradoxical relationship to force them to do so.

Training in Metacommunication

It is the point of view of most dedicated Family Therapists that an individual cannot change unless his family system changes. Logically then, individual therapy must somehow provoke the patient to effect changes in his family system which permit him to undergo psychiatric change. We do not have sufficient data to discover the effects on a family system when a member improves in individual therapy. However, let us examine a typical case. A woman enters therapy suffering from psychogenic headaches. She is encouraged to talk about her past, her present, and her responses to the therapist. She reports a series of circumstances in her life with her husband which occurred at the time of a headache, and the therapist encourages her to discuss her feelings at that time. (The therapist is usually assuming that her problem centers in her guilts, fears, and repressed ideation and that she is turning her hostility on herself in the form of headaches.) At a certain point in the course of her therapy, the woman reports that she asserted herself with her husband in some way. For example, she told him that she would no longer put up with certain behavior she had objected to. At this point the therapist assumes that the woman has undergone an intrapsychic change and her assertive behavior is a product of that change (for example, a lessening of internal guilts). After reporting fewer headaches in conjunction with this self-assertive behavior, it is not uncommon for such a woman to relapse, perhaps protesting that her headaches are worse than ever. She is encouraged to verbalize about her feelings and about similarities between her current situation with her husband and her past dealings with her parents. She may even discover that she is "protecting" her husband because he became upset when she asserted herself, and she may relate this to past patterns of protection with her parents. The next step forward will be again manifested by an interaction with her husband which is different—more assertive and less helpless. In general, whenever the individual therapist would announce that a patient has changed, *it is when the patient manifests a different type of interaction with his intimates (including the therapist).*

Although the theoretical emphasis of the individual therapist may be upon the woman's repressed ideation, the success of her therapy appears with a change in the relationship—the family system—she had established with her husband. As she deals with him differently, he must respond to her differently, and the consequence is a change in the family and so a change in her. From the Family Therapy point of view, individual therapy uses the individual as a lever to produce a change in the family. An important question is what the patient learns in therapy that can be used to influence the family system.

If one looks for an understanding of what occurs in individual therapy, and how this is comparable to Family Therapy, an obvious fact appears. Both methods emphasize intensive training in verbalizing about one's relations with other people. The constant emphasis in individual therapy is upon talking—particularly talking rather than acting out or somatizing. Inevitably the individual patient will carry into into his family a newly learned way of commenting upon what is going on. At the moment a headache case comments on her husband's behavior, instead of exhibiting distress and withdrawing, she is requiring him to deal with her differently. Both of them must then change their behavior as a consequence.

The encouragement of verbal metacommunication is a common factor in various types of individual therapy, and the basic procedure in Family Therapy is to sit family members down together and have them talk about their relationships with each other. If mother offers the "hurt" look which provoked the others in the past, it becomes only a signal for the therapist to ask her to express her feeling verbally. Similarly, other family members may be asked to comment upon how they feel about mother's hurt look. Requiring family members to make verbal comments rather than use their previous tactics encourages the family system of behavior to undergo change.

The Therapist as a Model

In all types of therapy the therapist behaves differently from the people the patient is accustomed to. An important factor in change would seem to reside in the nature of this difference. In Family Therapy, the therapist is behaving differently from family members when he proceeds in the usual Family Therapy style of encouraging the democratic virtues: each person is to have a fair turn, minority views are to be expressed, and everyone is encouraged to make compromises for the good of the group. Therapists of all schools particularly emphasize being fair and not taking sides consistently with any one family member. Ideally he sides with all at once by finding a level where differences are reconcilable. By not joining the family members in their insistence that one member is the problem, the therapist sets a model for them to look at the entire family for the source of problem behavior.

The therapist also provides the family a model, either implicitly or explicitly, for handling disciplinary problems. Typically the disturbed family is an inconsistent family. Extreme behavior is permitted and opposed and permitted again. Both overprotection and harsh punishment occur, and the problem member usually has few consistent constraints put upon him by the family. In advice, and in the way he handles the family in the room, the therapist exhibits a way for family members to deal with each other consistently.

Related to both restraints and metacommunicative training, the therapist also sets a model by not letting himself be provoked by family members. Symptomatic behavior, or distress in a family member, does not set the terms for his behavior as it does other family members. For example, the father in the family might always be provoked to exaspera-

tion by pained looks or weeping from the wife, but the therapist does not let her distress engineer a particular response
from him. Similarly, a husband who can provoke condemnation from his wife by behaving irresponsibly finds that the
therapist does not condemn him as expected. Regularly the
therapist may set an example of metacommunication by
commenting on the way he is being handled rather than
merely responding on the other person's terms.

Whether the individual therapist is largely silent, as in
psychoanalysis, or directive with patients, he does not respond to provocation and so does not behave on the patient's
terms. By not responding on the patient's terms when the
patient is exhibiting symptomatic or distressful behavior, the
therapist requires the patient to deal with him in other ways
in both family and individual treatment. A difference lies
in the fact that in Family Therapy the other family members
can observe, and utilize for themselves, the ways the therapist handles provocation. In individual therapy only the patient can do this by observing how he himself is handled.
He might then carry the therapist's techniques into his
family, as people report who have lived with a family member undergoing psychoanalysis.

The Control Aspect of Family Therapy

If a Family Therapist is to induce change in a family
system, he must influence and control what happens in the
therapy. If the family members gain control of what happens,
they will perpetuate their system and their distress. One
way therapists gain control of what happens is by posing
paradoxical situations to families so that family members
cannot deal with them in their usual ways. The Family
Therapist poses a paradox when he accepts the position of
an expert adviser and then does not offer advice. Typically
a therapist takes charge by placing the family in charge of
what is to happen, emphasizing how the initiative for solving problems must come from the family. The family is
thereby placed in a position where their usual attempts to
take charge of a relationship are encouraged by the person
in charge. This situation is particularly obvious when the
Family Therapist uses passive silence as a way of dealing
with the family. The paradox faced by the family is essentially the one faced by the individual in the psychoanalytic

procedure. More active therapists set up a framework of taking charge, and within this framework they proceed to constantly disinvolve themselves from responsibility and to encourage the family members to be in charge. For example, if mother asks what she shall do with a recalcitrant daughter, the therapist does not tell her: he might ask her what she feels like doing, he might suggest more discussion to clarify the situation, he might suggest she feels helpless in this situation, he might raise a question why it is such a problem to her, he might turn to other family members for suggestions, and so on. As he shifts the responsibility for what to do with the daughter to her, the mother is being placed in charge by the therapist and so cannot take charge of him.

One typical problem of control centers in attempts by family members to engineer coalitions with the therapist. Usually the therapist frustrates these attempts or arranges that coalitions only occur on his own terms. Such attempts by family members can be active or passive: mother might say, "Don't you think my husband should go to work?" thus inviting a coalition against husband. Or she might appear helpless and anxious at particular times, inviting a coalition with the therapist against the family members who are distressing her. If the therapist does accept the coalition, he manages not to side with one against the others. For example, he might say, "Naturally you would want your husband to go to work, but perhaps he doesn't feel ready to yet." In this way he sides with the wife, but also with the husband by indicating the husband has rights about going to work. Similarly, faced with helplessness or distress as an invitation to join mother in coalition against the others, the therapist might say, "Have you noticed how the rest of the family becomes anxious when you're upset?" Or he might in some other way shift to a level of coalition with the group as a whole.

A major control problem is the power given to the identified patient by his symptomatic behavior as well as his function as a scapegoat. A major problem in Family Therapy is to shift the emphasis from the ostensible patient to the family as a group or the parental conflict. A child who refuses to talk, such as a mute schizophrenic, can carry more weight in a family conversation than the most loquacious parent. Typically such a child is only mute verbally: if the conversation goes in directions he dislikes, he usually moves restlessly, thereby suddenly calling the attention of the whole family to him. Similarly, a child can set off in psychotic verbiage at certain times, or he can casually threaten some act which arouses the parents, or in some other way exhibit his symptomatic behavior at those moments a change is threatened in other relationships in the family. If the therapist is provoked by the symptomatic behavior, then the child is gaining control of the situation.

If the child does not respond in a provoking way when change is threatened almost invariably the parents choose that moment to turn upon the child or to refer to him. For example, if mother and father begin to exhibit more open conflict with each other, one or both will choose that moment to say, "Well, if it wasn't for our son's difficulties everything would be all right."

Although a therapist usually handles the emphasis upon the child by commenting upon it when it occurs, such comments do not necessarily produce a change if the family problem is a severe one. Ways to deal with this problem have by no means been solved, but the tendency of family therapists is to take charge by encouraging the emphasis on the problem person as well as by making this emphasis explicit. When the parents are talking about their problems with each other and the mute patient moves restlessly, there is a tendency for everyone to half listen and half notice the patient. Partly because the distraction is welcome, the parents often comment on the movement, thus dropping their discussion. Various family therapists handle the problem differently, but often they will take charge by stopping the discussion themselves when the situation has become a problem. The therapist may then use one of several tactics: he might say that something is distressing the child and suggest examining what has been said to see if a sensitive family problem is being touched upon, he might go further and say to the child that it would be helpful in the future if he exhibited some distress whenever the parents are talking about something that is too sensitive for them (thus defining the patient as a thermometer of family tensions), or he might merely stop the conversation and deal with the interruption and then return precisely to the point where the conversation left off so that the interruption loses its function. Some therapists will define the child's behavior as an attempt to divide the parents, and so encourage them to form a coalition against the child's intrusion. Other therapists will occasionally see the parents without the child so that they are not distracted from sensitive subjects by him.

The behavior of the problem member of a family, usually a child in Family Therapy, is gross enough to observe a reaction when there is a shift in relationship in other members of the family. However, similar reactions occur in father and mother. If father and child threaten a change in their relationship with each other, mother will react in such a way that change is inhibited, and if mother and child are shifting their relationship, the father will respond. It is the activation of each member of the family when a change occurs which both creates therapeutic problems and makes evident a possible theoretical model for describing families.

THE FAMILY MODEL

When one begins to conceptualize the family as a group of people who respond to change in each other in an "error-activated" way, it becomes possible to view the family as a homeostatic system. Such a system contains within itself self-corrective processes which permit it to continue to function in habitual ways. It is these points of self-correction which must be changed if a change in the family system is to occur.

A homeostatic system is like the heating system of a house which is connected with a thermostat; the system governs itself. If the room becomes too cold, the thermostat signals the furnace to turn on, the furnace heats the room until a warmer temperature is reached and the heater turns off. If the room is too hot, one cannot say it is the fault of any element in the system. It is not the fault of the heater because that is controlled by the thermostat, and yet the thermostat is not to blame because it is controlled by the heat produced by the heater. If one wishes to change the system when the room is too hot, it is not sufficient merely to open the windows and try to influence the room. The introduction of cold air lowers the temperature, but it also impels the thermostat to cause the heater to burn more fiercely to raise the temperature of the room. The only way to make a change in any element of the system is to change the "setting," the correction point which regulates the range of all the elements in the system.

Past attempts to discuss families have concentrated upon a single element. It was first argued that if a family with a schizophrenic member had problems, it was the "fault" of the schizophrenic, who must be changed by individual therapy. Then it was argued that there was a "schizophrenogenic" mother who was causing schizophrenia in the child, and she should be changed. Later it was suggested that the *real* cause was an inadequate father, and if he were influenced to change, the system would change. The latest point of view of the problem is that the total system must be influenced if any of the elements are to change.

The simple model of a homeostatic system, such as a household heating system, is obviously not adequate to describe a family, for although the elements influence each other, the range or "setting" of the system is set by an outsider. A human being in the house sets the thermostat at, for example, 70 degrees and the system fluctuates around that setting. In the family, no outsider sets the limits of family behavior, although the culture may be said to partially function in that way. The range of behavior of family members is set largely by the other family members. Two sorts of governing processes occur in the family: the family members behave in an error-activated way if one member exceeds a certain established limit, but individual family members also attempt to be the one who sets or establishes that limit. It is at this second level the control problem enters the picture in the disturbed family.

At this second level, the problem is this: who is going to tell whom what to do and so govern the limits of behavior. All activity in a disturbed family centers in a struggle at this level. If father suggests going to a movie, the merits of the movie are not the issue as they might be in a more normal family; the issue is whether or not to do what father says. Similarly, if the child asks mother to tie his shoes, this request is not received as a simple one; it is received as an attempt by the child to govern mother's behavior and so be in control of what sort of relationship there will be.

When a child is raised in a disturbed family, all of his actions become exaggeratedly significant because they are received at this governing level. If the child merely takes a walk, his action might be received as a comment on, or a criticism of, the home rather than a desire to take a walk. Because what he does is given such significance, the child is given power in a disturbed home—particularly being in distress gives him power—which other children do not have. A particular sort of power he has is to divide his parents and set them against each other. For the parents to induce a change and set the limits of the child's behavior, they must work out the problem of who is to set the limits of each other. Insofar as the child's behavior is a part of their struggle with each other, his actions are necessary to continue that particular system of struggle.

When a group of people are interrelated in this sort of self-corrective network, a change in one of them will have repercussions throughout the system. For example, one might encourage a rebellious child to accept being told what to do by his parents and follow their direction. However, if the child is to accept such a relationship with them, they must also be willing to accept it—they must be willing to direct him. Further, the parents must create a relationship with each other where they can agree on directing the child rather than being divided by the attempt. Additionally, they might have to shift their relationship with siblings if they are to treat this child in a different way. Therefore, to effect a change in one element of the system, adjustments are necessary in those self-corrective processes which have maintained the system unchanged.

Resistance to Change: Conflict of Levels

It can be argued that the reason a family system resists change without therapeutic intervention is because the attempt by a family member to induce a change provokes the self-corrective processes in other family members which oppose it. For example, if a wife in a disturbed family attempts to "reform" her husband, her attempts are not likely to lead to change and in fact could be said to maintain the system as it is. Each of her attempts will be the provocation which requires her husband to refuse to reform, and so the system remains stable. At times it appears that the husband's indication he is about to change sets off the wife to encourage him to reform, which returns them to the previous system. Since the struggle is at the level of who is to control whose behavior, the attempt to change will provoke a response at that level.

A more elaborate example illustrates the complications which occur because people communicate with one another at several levels. Suppose a rebellious child is blamed for family difficulties because he does not do what he is told but busily tells his parents what to do. His parents respond with angry helplessness to his directives, irritated with him but unable to force him to do as they say. They indicate they wish he would accept a relationship where they tell him to behave and he does, but they do not consistently require him to accept such a relationship. Let us suppose further that the child attempts to change; he asks his parents to tell him what to do because he is now willing to do it. Although he has apparently "changed," his parents can respond as if he has not. They can find themselves in a paradox which, put in crude terms, is this: if the child says, "All right, tell me what to do and I'll do it," he is offering to accept direction from them at one level, but at another level he is directing them. He is telling them what to do. If they comply with his demand, they are not directing him because at a higher level they are following his directions, and so no change has taken place.

When someone *orders* someone else to take charge, he is posing a "double bind" or paradox, defined as two levels of message which conflict in a paradoxical way. It is this problem a husband faces if his wife orders him to be more manly and take charge of her. If he does so, he is taking charge at one level but conceding that she is in charge at another, since he is doing what she ordered.

If parents receive a rebellious child's attempts to be more compliant as demanding, the child will naturally enough respond to their continued angry helplessness by reverting to his previous rebellious behavior. (A naive therapist might then blame the parents for not accepting the child's willingness to be directed without seeing that if they direct him they are following his directions as they always have.) From this point of view, each attempt by a family member to induce change will be a reinforcement of the previous system so the family continues in its circular pattern.

Often parents will attempt to treat a child as an equal

while also attempting to treat him as someone who should do what he is told. When they treat him in both of these ways simultaneously, they are posing him two conflicting levels of message and he cannot respond to one level without being wrong at the other. For example, parents will sometimes ask a child's permission—thus defining the relationship as one between equals—to tell him what to do—thus defining the relationship as one where they are in charge. If the child simply does as he is told, he is not responding to their request for equality; if he does not do what he is told, he is not accepting direction. This sort of situation occurs whenever parents seek to make either directives or punishment agreeable to the child; they are asking an equal to be treated as an unequal. As one mother put it, "It's simple to get a child to do something. You say, 'Do you want to do it? Do it.'" The fact that the problem in her family was a disturbed child who did not do what she said could be related to the paradoxical nature of her requests.

Often mothers who are unable to be directive with a child exhibit this helplessness because if they assume an "authoritarian" position with the child, there are repercussions in their relationships with their husbands. Some mothers will behave helplessly in order to encourage the father in the family to take charge more. But at the same time they cannot cope with the children if they behave helplessly, and so the attempt to establish conflicting types of relationship poses paradoxical situations for the persons attempting to deal with them.

Although it is difficult for a family member to induce change because of the repercussions and the conflicts of levels which occur, the introduction of a therapist can make change possible. For example, if a shift in a child's behavior is labeled as instigated by the therapist, the child is then not directing his parents on his own initiative but following the direction of the therapist. The parents can more easily accept the child's being the one who defines the type of relationship if it is labeled as actually the therapist doing so. However, if the child is labeled as "merely" following the directions of the therapist, change has not occurred because he is not initiating new behavior himself. Therefore direction by the therapist for a change in behavior is typically given in such a way that the therapist is indicating he isn't directing the change. At some point the therapist emphasizes that the change is occurring independently of him. When he indicates this, the therapist is following a rule typical of many kinds of psychotherapy: he is indicating the paradox, "I am influencing you to change, but the change which occurs is spontaneous."

Resistance to Change: Resisting the Therapist

If there were no control problem in human relations, a therapist could direct family members to behave more sensibly and reasonably with each other, they would do so, and the system would change. However, family members in disturbed families do not respond in this way. In fact they respond to him as if he has been included in the family system and so is subject to the same struggle they have with each other over the problem of who is to "set" or circumscribe their range of behavior. Should he offer them advice to behave more sensibly, they could not do so without conceding that he is governing them. It is their unwillingness to have their behavior governed by others that causes the struggle in these families. If the family members can provoke the therapist to offer good advice, then frustrate him and provoke him to offer more, they have succeeded in governing him rather than the reverse, and when the family members set the terms for the system it will continue unchanged.

The tactics used by therapists to gain control, or become the governor, of a family system are various. Some of them have been presented in the description of schools of Family Therapy. One therapist will influence a family by not being in the room with them a good part of the time; they cannot resist his governing them because he is often not there, and when he is there he is so on his own terms. Another therapist will be so slippery in his terminology and directives that the family cannot resist him because they cannot pin him. Some other therapist will define everything done as being for the good of each family member and therefore so benevolent that they cannot resist him without appearing recalcitrant malcontents. Another way is to offer the family two therapists so that although they might be able to govern one, they will find it difficult to govern two (unless they can pit them against each other and so deal with both simultaneously).

An additional tactic becomes apparent if one thinks of the peculiar way therapists of all methods avoid telling patients what to do. They do not openly and directly govern the behavior of a patient or family. If, in disturbed families, the problem is a resistance to being governed, then it would follow that directing family members to behave differently would not be successful (unless the weight of massive authority is exerted). Such a directive would provoke the self-corrective activity which would maintain the system. However, it would also follow that a tactic to deal with this resistance to change would be to govern at a higher level by encouraging the family members to continue to behave in their usual ways. The only way the family faced with this approach could resist having their behavior governed would be to behave differently. If one permits, or encourages, a person to resist him, the person cannot resist without conceding that his behavior is being governed. The idea that one should encourage a patient to behave in his usual ways is implicit in most psychotherapy because a major characteristic of therapists is their permissiveness. They do not oppose patients; they accept what they are doing, rarely telling them to behave differently. If one assumes that permissiveness is synonymous with encouragement, it can be argued that therapists usually encourage typical patient behavior. Certainly if a therapist observes parents permitting temper tantrums in a child, he will point out that they are encouraging such behavior. If a therapist permits temper tantrums in his office by a family, he is also encouraging this situation. Sometimes a therapist will explicitly encourage a patient to continue as he is behaving; for example, when a therapist asks mother to take charge in the family when she is already the group leader, he is encouraging her to do what she is already doing. If her problem is resisting being governed, she can only prevent this, if the therapist has directed her in this way, by permitting other family members to govern her. The encouragement of usual behavior is also implicit in many of the instructions by therapists about ways to gain understanding. A Family Therapist will say, "I want you to talk together now so we can discover what the problems are." He is asking them to demonstrate their system and so asking them to continue it, just as the silent therapist is tacitly permitting the family to continue with its usual procedures.

An important point for those therapists who seek a source of new techniques is this: when Family Therapy is described in this way, the tactics of therapists are astonishingly similar to the tactics members of disturbed families use in dealing with each other. Such members often withdraw and enter on their own terms, are slippery in their directives, do not take responsibility for telling people what to do, attempt to form coalitions (usually unstable ones) of two against the others, and typically define what they do as benevolent and protective. In addition, the mothers in disturbed families often take charge by encouraging the others toward self-understanding, particularly of their faults. Such mothers will also encourage other family members to continue in their usual ways, particularly when those members are resisting mother. As one mother of a schizophrenic said to her schizophrenic child when he was about to criticize her, "Go right ahead and criticize me, dear, I'm perfectly willing to be hurt if it will help you."

The problems of the Family Therapist are multiplied by the additional relationships he must deal with, in contrast to individual therapy. The therapist may begin to influence one member's range of behavior only to have other family members intrude and rock that relationship. The presence of other family members also makes it difficult to use some of the tactics of individual therapy. For example, one can control a single patient largely by the use of silent permissiveness. The individual patient faced with an unresponsive therapist must deal with him no matter how frustrating this might be. A family, however, can ignore a silent therapist and go about its business of mutual destruction without feeling at all frustrated. Although silence as a tactic does not appear to work with families, it is sometimes necessary and is useful if it is interspersed with occasional comments. What the therapist says after long silence becomes powerful because he speaks so rarely. But more than in individual therapy the Family Therapist must be responsive and must intervene in the patient's life. With the resulting interaction comes all the complications which center upon a struggle over who is to define what types of relationships there will be.

The resistance of families to being governed by a therapist provides problems when the identified patient begins to improve. If the parents assume that improvement in the child is because of the therapist's influence, they may take this improvement as a condemnation of themselves. After all, their child was disturbed when they were dealing with him but is not when the therapist intervenes. The parents may also use this opportunity to turn against each other; one or the other will use improvement of the child to indicate that the other was always inadequate. If he or she had dealt with the child as the therapist has, all would have been happier. Therefore improvement in the identified patient may provoke considerable disturbance in the marital relationship, whether in Family Therapy or when the child is seen by an individual therapist. Rather typically, therapists handle this problem by indicating that the improvement is the result of parental activity or cooperation from the child and not their own influence. When credit is given to family members for producing change, the change is more acceptable.

SUMMARY

A variety of treatment methods are being developed to deal with families containing a member suffering from some form of psychopathology. These methods are based upon the assumption that symptoms in a family member are the product of a disturbed family system. The problem in Family Therapy is to shift the focus of treatment from the member identified as the patient to the family as a whole, and then to produce change in the system of family relationships so the member with symptoms can improve. From this point of view, individual therapy is an attempt to change a family system by using only one member, with the problem that improvement in that member error-activates the other members to negate that improvement and maintain the previous system.

Since both individual and Family Therapy appear to bring about change, an important question is what the methods have in common. There are diverse styles of individual therapy and equally diverse schools of Family Therapy. One difference between the two methods is the physical presence of all family members in the interview. One similarity is the attempt in both methods to help the patient to better self-understanding. However, the type of understanding varies considerably to the point where comparisons are difficult to make. One question raised in this paper has been whether it is the achieving of more self-understanding which causes a patient to change, or whether bringing about self-understanding can be seen as a tactic by therapists with the "cause" of change residing in the attempt by patients to deal with this tactic.

If one attempts to examine the actual practice in various methods of individual and Family Therapy, certain formal similarities appear. Including both therapists and patients in the description reveals a peculiar type of relationship imposed upon patients by the therapeutic milieu in all forms of psychotherapy. It can be argued that patients are caught in a situation where they face unresolvable paradoxes as long as they continue disturbed behavior. Some of the obvious paradoxes of the therapeutic situation which have been suggested in this paper can be summarized with the emphasis upon their appearance in both individual and Family Therapy.

First of all, the family comes to a therapist expecting an expert who will take charge and tell them what to do to recover from their distress. While taking charge as an expert, the therapist puts the family in charge; he indicates that conduct of family affairs rests with them and he will not advise them how to behave differently or what to do to solve their problem; his function is to help them understand their difficulties. Similarly, in individual therapy the therapist assumes the posture of an expert while declining to offer the advice and direction one would expect of an expert.

When the family enters treatment, they identify one member as the problem they wish cured. The Family Therapist indicates that their choice is not the problem, the entire family is the problem. The family is faced with a situation where their habitual ways of dealing with other people through a problem child are frustrated: what they consider the problem is said not to be the problem. Similarly, in individual therapy the patient indicates his problem is his symptom, but the therapist says the problem is what is behind the symptom and so the patient cannot deal with him in symptomatic ways. However, while saying the child is not the problem, the therapist will make regular interpretations which point out the reasons why the child (or the symptom) is a problem.

Blame is also handled in a paradoxical way in psychotherapy. Patients are typically skillful in arranging that people blame them, but therapists do not cooperate in this endeavor. In individual therapy, the patient is not blamed for his actions because he is said to be driven by forces beyond him, such as repressed ideas and unconscious drives, while it is also made clear to him that he is responsible for his actions since he arranges his life to perpetuate his distress. In Family Therapy, the parents are told they are not to blame for the child's difficulties, because they cannot help themselves, and yet it is indicated that they should behave differently so the child will not have difficulties. The patients cannot get a clear accusation of blame or a release from it: they get both, paradoxically presented.

All types of psychotherapy are defined as benevolent and helpful, while at the same time therapists put patients through a considerable ordeal. In family work, the family must expose all the unsavory aspects of their family life to someone who apparently has a successful family. Similarly, the individual patient must expose all his unsavory thoughts and desires to a therapist who apparently has none. Patients find it difficult to oppose therapists because the setting is one of benevolent help; yet they cannot merely accept the benevolence because it takes the form of a punishing experience which will continue until there are no more problems to present. If the patient attempts to escape the ordeal, he finds his attempt interpreted as a resistance to the change he seeks.

Related to the therapeutic ordeal is the peculiar unwillingness of therapists to tell families to change; typically the therapist accepts and permits the family members to continue their usual behavior because he says his task is to help them understand it. In fact the therapist will, directly or indirectly, imply encouragement of a family's usual behavior when he is permissive and indicates they should demonstrate how they usually interact so this can be studied.

In any examination of why therapeutic change occurs with a family, it should be noted that the family is placed in an almost impossible situation in therapy. The therapist de-

fines the situation as one where (a) they are being benevolently helped to change, while within that framework they
are (b) permitted, or encouraged, to continue in their usual
ways and not opposed or told to behave differently, while (c)
simultaneously they must go through the ordeal of the therapeutic process—as long as they continue to behave in their
usual ways and do not change.

Finally, the family is paying money to a therapist to influence them to change, and typically the Family Therapist—
and the individual therapist—indicates that he is not attempting to influence them but trying to help them understand their difficulties. When they do change, the therapist
points out that the change has occurred as a result of their
own efforts, while pocketing the fee for changing them.

Whether a patient encounters a therapist alone or in company with his family, he finds himself involved in a relationship which educates him by teaching him new tactics
and providing a model for new behavior. Simultaneously, he
is faced with a relationship containing multiple paradoxes
which force him to abandon his old behavior since he can
only deal with this relationship, or escape from it amiably,
by undergoing change.

Part IV

Illness and
Disability

Preliminary Comments

THIS VOLUME attempts to provide a variety of theoretical orientations to an understanding of and solutions to problems in family functioning. The section on poverty emphasized the interpenetration of the family with the social and physical environment that surrounds this social unit. The next section focused more on the internal dynamics of family life, revealing the close relationship between this nuclear group and the interpersonal and psychological difficulties of its members expressed in culturally conditioned ways. This section indicates the ties between physical and mental health and illness in the context of family life and the social milieu that surrounds the members of this group. The book ends with an article that attempts to pull together these complexly interwoven factors of family performance as a means of giving direction to future efforts in research, treatment, and social policy.

Although the first selection was published almost twenty-five years ago, the author's insights and generalizations about hospital bureaucracy and treatment of the poor remain essentially true today. This is so despite the advent of Medicare and Medicaid. The issue is not the amount of medical services available but the ways in which they are delivered, particularly how they are integrated with one another and other services in the hospital and in the community. The author clearly demonstrates that unless the physical, psychological, and social functioning of each family member are viewed with respect to one another, the diagnosis may be incorrect and the recommended treatment either inappropriate or not carried out. Dr. Richardson's pioneer study would be very useful required reading for medical students and their mentors right now.

The first article is a documentary; the second is a more systematic analysis of how the prevention, diagnosis, and treatment of physical illness are closely related to family

functioning patterns. Through a review of research it identifies major problematic areas, which can be used by families
as a guide in their attempt to maintain the physical health
of their members.

The selection by Thomas is a broad discussion of the interpersonal problems of the disabled person from the perspective of role theory. Although the author's orientation is more
general than that of Mabry, through example Thomas points
out that the family, as the most important primary group
in the handicapped person's life, has the greatest influence
on how he views himself and, in turn, whether this results
in social functioning appropriate to the disability. Illness
must be seen in the context of the social experience the
patient has encountered in the past and faces in the present.

Kaplan begins by comparing nosology in physical and
mental disorders. He notes that much attention has been
given to acute physical illness, with many beneficial results,
but until recently, almost all mental disorders have been
defined as chronic. He then goes on to trace the development of stress (crisis) theory in psychiatry and to indicate
its utility in the treatment of mental problems. Of particular
interest is his review of Lindemann's characteristics of acute
stress disorders, which helped to lay the foundation for much
of the work that followed.

In the second half of the article the author illustrates the
use of crisis theory through a summary of the study of the
stress of premature birth on the family group. He reveals
how one might predict good or poor family adjustment on
the basis of parental behavior just prior to and immediately
following the birth of the premature child. Finally, he illustrates how poor family reactions to stress can be helped
through therapeutic intervention.

The next two articles go together. Although published
separately, each is a different part of the same study, which
attempts to describe family breakdown and recovery processes from an integrated social and behavioral science point
of view.

The first in the set summarizes and illustrates criteria for
satisfactory family functioning. Stress or crisis is again seen
as a precipitating event in a downward spiral of interaction
among the members of the family group. In addition, the relationship between the physical conditions and the social and

psychological processes of family members is made evident in a way somewhat different from that in previous material.

The second article uses the same families as examples as the prior one. Here the focus is on the interaction effects between individual psychoanalytic psychotherapy and family functioning. Each process has significant effects on the other. Changes in the family at different stages in treatment are described, and some practice implications are discussed.

Clark Vincent's article is a fit ending to this volume since it encompasses almost all the great variety of orientations found among the selections. After briefly tracing the history of the mental health movement, he indicates how the family as a whole and the marital pair in particular are required to constantly adapt to new and changing circumstances. This includes adaptation to the physical and psychological states of others within the family, but more importantly, to the subsystems of the society that impinge upon the family. While the demands of Western culture require all systems to be in a constant state of change, the author contends that in our individualistically oriented society, the family must change more rapidly and adapt more quickly.

Thus, the family has not lost its functions but rather, these have changed. The requirement that the family have great flexibility so that it can change often in response to the society around it may actually be increasing its importance. On the other hand, we may be expecting too much of the family. We may be expecting too many changes too soon and overloading it with more tasks than it can handle. This may be responsible for the high rate of breakdown of this social unit as well as the constant threat of impairment of the physical and mental health of its members.

But the family cannot easily fight back against the other systems in society. It is the smallest and least organized institution. As a result it is not carefully considered in treatment or well represented in social policy. This is especially true for the marital pair. The threat of family disintegration means we must give it considerably more attention in the future, particularly in the formulation of government policy. Professor Vincent finishes by providing us with some direction in the achievement of this goal.

A FAMILY AS SEEN IN THE HOSPITAL

Henry B. Richardson

PATIENTS have families: hospitals have patients: therefore the hospital has something to do with the family. This syllogism would appear to be self-evident; but in any large metropolitan hospital, at any ordinary time of the day, very little tangible evidence can be found to support it. You might see perhaps a baby-carriage parked outside an entrance, or a relative or friend accompanying an apprehensive patient to the ambulatory clinic; but unless you followed the baby and its mother into the department of pediatrics, this is about all. Only at one hour in the twenty-four is there any substantial evidence that friends and relatives of the patient really do exist, and this is during the time which is allotted to visitors.

When the visiting hour approaches the buses begin to discharge their heavy loads and automobiles crowd every available parking space. The relatives come early to conserve every minute of the precious hour allotted to them. They form a line, like a great passive worm, which yields slightly to the passer-by but displays no will of its own, and moves only in fragments. These crowd the elevators and clutter up the wards, preventing all activities with the exception of emergencies. The drab suits of the men and the bright colors of the women seem out of place in the hospital atmosphere, with its white uniforms and geometrical array of beds.

These relatives are not very welcome to the young house physician, who perhaps feels that he had enough of quizzing as a medical student. Of course they may give him information which will help him in his treatment, but they interrupt

Reprinted with permission of the publisher from *Patients Have Families*, New York: The Commonwealth Fund, 1945, chap. 1, pp. 13–23.

his work and, worse still, they divert his thinking. (Should that cardiac have more digitalis, or less? Has the pneumonia received about enough sulfa drug? What's the matter with that student that he didn't report the blood count? Hard enough to keep all these things in mind, especially if you've been up half the night with a case of diabetic coma.) Yes, Mrs. Jones, Jenny has rheumatic fever. Yes, I know it's hard for her to be away from her mother so long. Quite right, her joints don't pain her any more. I'm not worried about her joints, it's the heart. No, there is very little damage now, perhaps none at all. I wouldn't like her to get heart trouble. If she's bright at school she will catch up. Her health is more important now. Yes, six weeks at least; depends on how it goes. Maybe we can get her into a convalescent home later if we're lucky. No, Mrs. Smith, we can't tell yet what the trouble is; no, the x-ray doesn't show everything. . . . And so on. (Time to examine donors for that transfusion. Hope I get through in time to read up for the conference.)

Other visitors come at will to see the patients who are "on the serious list." They come brightly and leave quickly, or they sit for hours in silence by the sick-bed. (Hadn't you better go home and get some rest? The nurse has your phone number, she will call you if anything happens.) Or they form disconsolate groups, conversing in low tones.

The young doctor may not know it, but this is his first experience of the process by which the patient and the family sit like a jury in trial of his qualities and defects, his achievements or failures. On the sum of such judgments depends his future career.

These visitors represent the families of some quarter of a million people who come as patients to a large hospital in a period of ten years. Some of the patients have emerged in good health, some better able to carry on, some afflicted with a progressive disease. Some come to give birth; others to die. This is an enormous responsibility for which the hospital allows itself to be called into account for one hour each day; not to boards of trustees through its administrative staff, but to the public through its doctors. Reports are made, not in terms of funds, maintenance, or budget, but of health, sickness, and human understanding; in short, of professional capacity and a knowledge of the stuff of which life is made.

Visiting hour is also the time when the hospital admits that the patient has a family. The doctors do not go quite so far as this admission would imply; they think not so much of families as of relatives of patients and how they affect the sick. It is the patient and not the family who becomes ill; it was John who got pneumonia and Fred who had that accident to his hand in the factory. In a busy service there is no time to consider that John's pneumonia followed a week of cold in the head; too bad he had to go on changing tires in a snowstorm, but what else could he do in a new job? Maybe Fred wouldn't have had the accident if he hadn't been thinking about "aggravation" at home. The doctor in the wards has all he can do to meet the urgent problems of the repair of the human machine without concerning himself with the intricate problems of keeping it in running order. The human machine continues, however, to function, and not as an individual unit but geared to other machines which are more or less similar. One of them is Mrs. Martin Q—.

A tour of the hospital during visiting hours thus shows us relatives of patients, rather than families. Little could be expected, however, of a search for the family in person, for the obvious reason that the stay in the hospital is an interruption of the family life. It would be fairer, as well as more rational, to conduct the inquiry by means of the written records. For this purpose we can select a family at random and follow its fortunes as a family in its contacts with the out-patient department of the hospital.

THE FAMILY AS SEEN IN THE RECORDS

Catherine

Mrs. Q— might have been seen on a May morning on her way to the hospital with her younger daughter, Catherine, whose slimness contrasts with her own short, dumpy figure. Occasionally she brushes back a straggling wisp of hair from her eyes. Mrs. Martin Q— is no stranger to hospitals, but this is nothing like the one to which she had taken her first-born daughter Laura to consult the eminent specialist on heart disease. Mrs Q— is familiar with illness. She, too, knows the long line of waiting visitors, and before Laura died she had joined one of those disconsolate groups at the bedside.

Sickness is not news in her family; her parents died at an early age, and of several brothers and sisters only one sister is living. Last week the sister visited a clinic for her ulcer. Maybe the doctor will give Mrs. Q— some of that medicine for the pain which is gnawing in on her. Laura would be eighteen years old now if she had lived. Agnes, too—the doctor had said that she had a heart murmur. He spoke of rheumatism. And now Catherine! The doctor at the other hospital said she had chorea. He shook his head a bit when he explained that chorea was a rheumatic ailment. At least it had passed away quickly. What will the doctor in this new hospital say? Anyhow it's not hard to find the hospital. When you're there you're not much nearer. Maybe the policeman can help. "Second entrance on the right, lady."

The heavy door yields to an energetic pull, and then the storm door inside, opening into a sudden wail of protesting babies. A mother with a baby is talking to a young doctor in a white suit . . . "Next. What's the matter with the child; sore throat?" (Yes, she . . .) "Let me see her throat. Now her chest. That's all. Go across the hall to the small window."

The registrar now questions Mrs Q—. "Yes, madam. Name of child?" (Catherine Q—.) "Address? . . . Ground floor?" (You see I'm a . . .) "Number of rooms?" (Four.) "Rent?" ($6.25 a week.) "Age?" (Twelve.) "Occupation?" (Public school.) "Father?" (Martin, mechanic, born in the city.) "Mother?" (Catherine Q—, housewife.) "Who referred her? The school doctor?" . . . "Adults in family?" (Two.) "Children in family?" (Two.) "Number working?" (One.) . . . "Fifty cents, please. Go up one flight of stairs to your right."

(So there's the nurse.) "You can leave your daughter here while I weigh her. The doctor will be ready when he gets through with this patient . . ." (The doctor isn't as young as I expected.) "Will you sit here, Mrs. Q—, and tell me about your daughter? Sore throat and fever for a week? Father and mother are well, are they? Daughter at home has heart trouble? First daughter died of heart trouble? At what age?" (She would be eighteen years old this year.) "No serious illnesses?"

Thus we can reconstruct from the hospital records the first visit of the Q— family to the private general hospital.

Reading the report of the physical examination we find nothing much the matter with the throat, but a loud heart murmur, without enlargement of the heart. Opinion: quesionable heart disease of congenital origin. Recommendations appear under the *Recipe* sign for a prescription (℞). "X-ray of chest for the heart. Return in one week." . . . "Report on x-ray not ready. Skin test for tuberculosis started. Return in four days." . . . "Tuberculin test negative. X-ray negative. Case referred for cardiac appointment." Note in pencil: "Dr. X (of the cardiac clinic) not taking any more appointments."

There is no further visit until two years later, this time in the adult medical clinic, because in the meantime Catherine had passed the maximum age for treatment in the pediatrics clinic. We find: "Patient was sent from school for examination of the heart. One year ago [actually two] seen in the pediatrics clinic, where a diagnosis of possible congenital heart disease was made. Since then has been up and around, active and well. One year ago while trying to do two years of school work in one she grew irritable, 'nervous' and jumpy, and her doctor advised that she be kept out of school for six months."

Examination: "Slender, intelligent, somewhat overactive, slightly undernourished." The heart was found to be rapid and regular. The same murmur was found as before, but louder. *Impression:* "Overactive heart in an adolescent girl. Question of rheumatic heart disease, mitral insufficiency." *Recommendations:* "Electrocardiogram; x-ray of chest; basal metabolism." None of these recommendations was carried out, and the next visit was another two years later.

The medical history of this patient records one catastrophe, the death of her oldest sister Laura from rheumatic heart disease. At Catherine's first visit the doctor detects the murmur, and he sets in motion the machinery for the further diagnosis and the ultimate recommendations for treatment, by referring the patient to the cardiac clinic. But the machinery gets stuck, because there are no vacancies in the clinic, and the problem remains at the stage of an unsolved diagnosis. This does not prevent the fixation of the diagnosis in subsequent records.

Two years later the patient comes in, not with cardiac symptoms, but with definite evidences of maladjustment showing in her school work. Again the murmur is heard, and again attention is concentrated on the heart, in spite of the fact that there are no symptoms referable to this organ. Once more action is deferred awaiting the results of laboratory work, and the problem remains in the same state of unsolved diagnosis, this time because the recommendations are not carried out by the mother, Ms. Q—. The presence of the murmur is enough to divert the doctor from the consideration of the pressing problem, which is in the psychiatric or social field, and to make him order laboratory tests instead of social service interviews or psychiatric consultations.

Mrs. Martin Q—

Meanwhile Mrs. Martin Q— has felt the need of medical attention for herself and she appears in the general medical out-patient clinic of the hospital. She has just turned forty as shown under "Age" in the "Record for Admission"; address changed, now the top floor; birthplace, U.S.; religion, Roman Catholic. Father deceased, born in the United States; mother likewise. Husband, Martin, mechanic. Occupation, housewife. Referred by private doctor. Two children, sex not stated, ages sixteen and thirteen. Number working, one. Average family income per week, $18. The medical record was set down in great detail by a student, and countersigned by a doctor. Mrs. Q— complained of pain in the stomach (epigastrium), and belching. The family history records the fact, already alluded to, that her father died of pneumonia, and her mother of pneumonia following childbirth. The patient's age at the time is not recorded; actually it was the occasion of her own birth. Under the marital history are recorded four pregnancies, the last of which was a "miscarriage"; also the ages of the children, and the diagnoses: "Girl, sixteen, 'chronic heart disease,' rheumatic fever. Girl, thirteen, 'possible heart disease.' Heart disease also diagnosed at school."

There is a detailed record of the menstrual history of Mrs. Q—, with hot flushes, delayed menstrual periods, and headaches of the past two or three years. Mrs. Q—'s occupation is recorded as "Housewife, superintendent, shovels coal. Husband does WPA work for $78 a month. She has worked very hard. Trouble in past seven years. Husband earned $50 a week before the economic depression." Under "present illness" is recorded the statement by a doctor that when she was between eighteen and twenty-one years of age she had high blood pressure. She was suffering from "gas" at the time, and this has continued ever since. About a year ago she missed two successive menstrual periods and began to feel melancholy, nervous, and irritable. Also she began to have an occasional lump in her throat. Details are given of the pain in her abdomen. Physical examination reveals obesity, but nothing else of importance. Teeth, which were later found to play an important part in the family life, are described as bad, with many missing and many bad cavities, but no treatment is recommended. The blood pressure, although presumably measured, is not recorded. The impression (provisional diagnosis) is: (1) Moderate hypertension, (2) menopausal syndrome (i.e., symptoms of menopause), (3) hypothyroidism (thyroid insufficiency), (4) indigestion, etiology? (i.e., indigestion of unknown cause). Laboratory work was recommended, but did not include an x-ray of the stomach. All the reports showed normal results. Examination in the gynecological clinic revealed nothing of importance, except that under "abortions" is recorded: "One at a month, fell down stairs." Treatment: Sedatives and a mild alkaline cathartic. None of the subsequent blood pressure readings showed a high blood pressure. Mrs. Q— was seen in the thyroid-endocrine ("gland") clinic, and injections were recommended later for her menopausal symptoms.

The medical records in the case of Mrs. Q— revealed obesity and the symptoms of the menopause, neither of which gave a complete account of her illness. Treatment recommended for these conditions was not carried into effect by the patient. The nervous symptoms were recognized only in the prescription for a sedative. The indigestion "of unknown cause" was not investigated until much later, and even then repeated x-rays were required to demonstrate a gastric (duodenal) ulcer.

Agnes

A third member of the family, the elder daughter Agnes, was admitted to the medical out-patient department two years later than her sister. The record for admission adds little to our previous information about the family, except that under income we find "$3.50 from church." There is also a cross-reference to the history number of her mother; the only instance of this in the whole series of records. Agnes was then sixteen years of age. The sources of history were the patient and the patient's mother. Her complaint was weakness and tremor of the legs for two weeks. The family history contains the definite statement, derived from the mother, that Mrs. Q— has high blood pressure. As we have seen, this was not the fact. The statement that the younger daughter has heart trouble has likewise crystallized in the records, and the question marks are omitted.

The past history of Agnes reveals the usual list of diseases, and includes headaches with dizzy spells, and "gas" pains along the margin of the ribs. It notes also the late onset of menstruation at the age of fifteen. Present illness: Has always been sluggish and lazy (here one who knows Mrs. Q— recognizes that it is she who is talking) but recently has become cranky (again a mother's phrase), drowsy, and more sluggish. Summary: A sixteen-year-old girl who has been increasingly lazy and sluggish and who complains of weakness and tremor of the legs on descending the stairs. Constipated, and inadequate diet intake because of finances. Physical examination reveals nothing abnormal, except that she is slighly undernourished. *Impression:* Malnutrition, slight. Inadequate intake due to poverty. *Treatment:* Encouragement that the child has no heart disease and is well. *Medication:* Cod-liver oil tablets. *Signed:* Student's name, O.K., doctor's signature. *Directions:* Return in one week for report on the routine Wassermann test. . . . Revisit, Wassermann negative. . . . Two months later, dermatophytosis of hands and feet (athlete's foot).

At these visits items begin to appear which are new in the hospital records of the family. For the first time mention is made of a possible connection between illness and economic stress. The fact that the skin trouble on her hands cost Agnes her job does not, however, appear at this time. Also the medical picture of illness is beginning to change; although heart trouble and high blood pressure have crystallized into definite form in the family records, gastrointestinal symptoms begin to replace those of cardiac trouble.

Two years elapse before Agnes makes another visit to the medical out-patient department. She had improved with the treatment. Her weight had risen to 106 pounds, but she stopped taking the vitamins after a few months and began to lose weight, and at present she weighs only 89 pounds. She has had an increase in the frequency and severity of the "gas" pain, which is felt under the left rib margin, and which she has had for many years. She is still constipated. She is not working or going to school, but stays at home most of the time. She does not eat regularly, but picks here and there all day long. She has had no menstrual period for four months. Physical examination shows a young undernourished girl of nineteen who looks fifteen or sixteen years old, pale conjunctivae (whites of eyes); undeveloped breasts; slight increase of body hair; small infantile uterus (womb). The impression is: (1) endocrine hypofunction (insufficiency of glands) probably anterior pituitary with ovarian insufficiency; (2) malnutrition with hypovitaminosis (not enough vitamins); (3) gastric ulcer to be "ruled out." The laboratory work which was recommended was negative, including x-ray of the stomach and intestines.

A month later, "the patient is probably suffering from an endocrine disturbance and added dietary deficiency caused by fear of eating." Basal metabolism was minus 17. She was referred to the thyroid-endocrine clinic. Treatment was vitamin supplement, thyroid tablets, and tincture of belladonna for the gas pains. She was referred to the dietician for a high-calory, high-vitamin diet. "The patient wishes a letter to Home Relief as to why she cannot work. At present I think it is advisable for her not to work until her condition has improved."

At this visit for the first time we have an explicit statement of the relationship between emotion and illness, the "fear of eating." Also the economic situation has to be taken into account in the treatment, and for this purpose a letter was written to the Home Relief authorities.

Mr. Martin Q—

Mr. Martin Q—, the fourth and last member of the family, visits the out-patient department in July three years after his wife's first visit. They are both in their middle forties. Mr. Martin Q— is a little man with a pinched expression and a furtive look, who sits quietly but with an air of restlessness, like a bird perched for flight. He has an ingratiating manner which betrays his desire for approval. The record for admission adds the fact that both his parents were of Irish stock, but were born in the United States. The occupation is repeated and the employer is given as WPA. Weekly income of the family, $25. Rent free for service as janitor. A note on the record, dated a few days later: "Patient insists he cannot pay x-ray fees." A year later the record was to show instead of WPA the statement "unemployed for a year," coupled with the statement "Home Relief $22.80 a week."

Mr. Q— has been troubled with hemorrhoids for eighteen years, and at one time, as we find out later, he expressed the fear of cancer in connection with them. We can imagine his sensations when the admitting doctor in the out-patient clinic refers him to the surgical out-patient clinic, instead of the medical clinic to which he went at the city hospital four years previously. For over ten years he had been having trouble with his stomach. (Let's see, ten years. Wonder what happened then. Oh, yes, the industrial depression.) Family history: mother died of tuberculosis, no date given. Father died of a heart attack, no date. Review of parts of the body includes pyorrhea, toothaches, slight spitting of blood six months previously, "nervous heart." "Has practiced withdrawal for fifteen years, marital relationship otherwise satisfactory" (seems like a large qualification). *Present illness:* Stomach trouble, fullness, belching, for approximately ten years, increasing in frequency and severity, not relieved by treatment. This is worse when he is lying down at night, and he vomits nearly all night, as many as twenty-five times, being repeatedly awakened. *Physical examination:* Slightly undernourished. No evidence of recent weight loss. No positive physical findings, except slight pyorrhea, with many teeth missing and many bad cavities. *Impression:* Cancer of the stomach. This is qualified by the highly important question mark. Recommendations for laboratory work include extensive x-rays of the gastrointestinal tract, but these are negative. The case was then closed in surgery and referred to the gastrointestinal clinic, where it was noted that the only food which makes his vomiting worse is milk. X-rays of the gallbladder were also negative. The patient was given belladonna to relieve spasms of the stomach. Shortly after this, he came to see me at my request, as one of the Martin Q— family.

The extensive investigations in the case of Martin Q—

were in the same category as those for the rest of the family. Although undertaken for good reasons, they added nothing to the understanding of the case. This was also true of the medical examinations in the wards of the hospital a year later, at which time minor conditions were found: chronic inflammation of the stomach and duodenum, a diverticulum (pocket) the size of a finger branching off the esophagus (gullet), external hemorrhoids (piles). None of these singly, or in combination, was sufficient to explain the symptoms. On the basis of psychiatric examinations in the interval, the diagnosis of "mixed psychoneurosis with anxiety and conversion symptoms" was added; in other words, his nervous state was recognized as having something to do with vomiting.

Two years after the first admission of a member of this family to the out-patient department of a leading teaching hospital comes the first statement that there might be a connection between the financial status of the family and their symptoms. This is in the rudimentary form of: "Inadequate intake of food due to poverty." Glimpses of emotional problems can be seen in the records by this time: Mrs. Q—'s symptoms of anxiety, Catherine's difficulties at school, and Agnes' crankiness. But no connection is made between these and the complaints of the patients, nor is there any further mention of them.

It is only after four years that a definite statement is made of the relationship between the symptoms and emotional stress. The notation of WPA on the record for admission is used only for administrative purposes, not as anything of medical value. The doctor who saw Agnes was the first to take action along social or economic lines, and this action took two forms. The first was the writing of a letter to Home Relief, to explain his opinion that Agnes was not fit to work. The second was referring her to me, because of my interest in the field in question and in emotional problems in general. Prior to this time there was no referral to the social service department of the hospital.

Some picture of the family can be formed from the hospital histories, but chiefly from the administrative portions, where the rough outlines of the family picture can be discerned. This is an American family of Irish extraction which has been in this country for three or four generations. The family is Roman Catholic, and receives a small sum monthly from the church. Mrs. Q— appears first as a housewife and later as janitor in addition. This shows a fall in the family fortunes, which is reflected in the notes as to the husband's occupation: first mechanic, then the same with the initials "WPA" added, then "unemployed for a year," with the notation of Home Relief, No. RH1AB2345. The couple are both in their middle forties, and comparison of their age with the ages of their children shows that they married young. The significant items, that Mr. Q— was on WPA, that he used to earn good wages before the economic depression, that the family has had "trouble" in the past several years, and that Mrs. Q— has had to work very hard, even having to shovel coal, are mentioned in an inconspicuous part of the medical record at Mrs. Q—'s first visit to the out-patient department; but these items are not given any particular consideration in the treatment recommended.

The professional records in the hospital are oriented, and quite properly so, to the search for the diagnosis in each case. Yet, in spite of the care and skill which were exercised, the medical labels prove to be misleading, and at best they provide very little understanding of the disease, and correspondingly little as to the proper treatment. The medical records do, however, supply certain clues to the family situation, which was a vital factor in the respective illnesses. From them we learn, in addition to Mrs. Q—'s statement at her first visit, that the family had had "trouble" for several years, that at the beginning of this period she had a "miscarriage" which she said was the result of a fall. The parents used withdrawal as a contraceptive measure. Agnes had malnutrition and amenorrhea[1] and her x-rays were negative. The doctor stated that she was afraid of eating. She was not doing well at school. The younger daughter, Catherine, had to be taken out of school for six months because of nervousness and crying spells. Mr. Q— vomited, but his x-rays were negative. In fact, none of the special tests had revealed any cause for the symptoms in any member of the family. The teeth were very bad, but there was no medical reason for supposing that they affected the family relationships. Mrs. Q— accompanied her nineteen-year-old daughter to the hospital out-patient department, and did most of the talking for her.

When the medical social service department was finally consulted, it "cleared" the family through a central office and found that they had been in contact with a number of organizations, only one or two of which had been listed on the hospital records. These included a family agency which reported a wealth of information about the family. Particularly illuminating was the description of the intra-family relationships and tensions. It comprised also the "identifying data," the historical development of the family-social situation, a list of medical contacts in the form of the official diagnoses, and descriptions in each case of the symptoms of illness as viewed by the patient. This information was vital to the understanding of the family and to the adjustment of the family situation, but it had not been sought by the hospital. The family asked for aid on the basis of economic considerations. The interviews were monopolized by Mrs. Q—, and it was felt that no progress was made. "The possibility of any constructive help being given Mrs. Q— by this agency seems limited in view of her rather rigid personality pattern, as well as her long-standing conception of the agency only as a source of financial assistance." The contact was therefore allowed to lapse. This happened about the time when Agnes' maladjustment was beginning to take the serious form of malnutrition and amenorrhea. No opportunity had been found to work through the presenting problem of economic stress toward a general family adjustment.

Thus for three years the family had been in contact not only with the hospital but also with a family agency in the community, with so little coordination that the hospital was not even aware of the work which was being done outside. Neither of these parallel approaches had been successful, and in spite of them the family showed the strain at its weakest point by the development of an alarming neurosis in the elder daughter Agnes.

THE FAMILY AS DESCRIBED BY THE PATIENT

The search for the family in the medical records has thus produced very meagre results. Even the individuals do not appear as personalities, but rather as shadowy figures which function chiefly to bring a potential medical diagnosis to the out-patient department of the hospital. This was not from any lack of picturesqueness in their appearance, speech, or action.

Catherine

Catherine Q— later was described by the psychiatrist as "of small build, light brown hair and hazel eyes, pretty face." When I first saw her, she said: "I think I feel all right. Lately since I went back to school I used to get pains under my heart. They used to annoy me. They'd come suddenly and go just as suddenly. Just about a minute or so, in school or at home. Doing nothing, standing, working at blackboard. We stand up to correct homework. Sometimes the pain comes after fooling around with my sister, sometimes I annoy my sister. She gets after me. Sometimes after coming upstairs to apartment, I feel funny just where the pain is. Whole class write their homework on blackboard at once. The pain started only lately about a week or so ago. (What happened?) Nothing happened. Might fail in examination. This might come any day (i.e., not announced in advance). Bound to get by if I stay well. (Exercise?) Monday, basket-ball, Tuesday, skating. Sometimes movies. (Basket-ball?) Feel better than ever after playing, especially if we win. (Stairs?) I fly up and I fly down. The first time I had pain I was scared myself, I didn't know what to do. It occurred at 10 A.M. at school. Had French that period. Excited about homework, wanted to get a mark of 100 per cent. French much better than Latin. Pain bothers me for a minute when it comes. Very sharp. Slightly to right of breastbone." Lately complaining of eyes; is studying a lot. If she lies on her stomach, her eyes water. Same with reading. This trouble began about third week of school. She can read any print, for example, small type in newspaper. Appetite fine. Eats "as good as my sister." "You should see her eat now." Sister now weighs more than Catherine does, formerly less. Catherine is able to eat things she likes, no indigestion. Doesn't like apple-sauce, clams, oysters. "I think it's because my mother has been making it [apple-sauce] for my father." Father is up every night. Daughter hears him vomiting. He has short intermissions of about three days, then gets sick again. Bowels "fine."

Catherine's conversation makes it abundantly clear that her complaints are not related to physical exertion, but to her rivalry with her elder sister, and to her determination to get perfect marks at school. She also brings out her loss of appetite for foods which her father eats, and the fact that she hears him at night vomiting. The murmurs in the heart noted on previous examination have disappeared. *Impression:* Pain of psychogenic (nervous) origin, associated with examinations at school.

After this visit Catherine disappeared from the medical clinic until she made another biennial visit, at which time she had pain suggesting increase in the motor activity of the gastrointestinal tract above and below the stomach, associated with her activities in connection with graduation at school. These attacks alarmed her. She had been getting very nervous and would like to scream, especially about her sister. Physical examination was negative, also the examination of the chest by x-ray.

Mrs. Martin Q—

Mrs. Martin Q— was a "fat, jolly woman, given to bursts of spontaneous laughter." She connects her flushes with nervousness and worry over "conditions." "Flushes wake me up at night terribly. So nervous I can't seem to rest. Of course, I'm worried. That has a lot to do with conditions. I have a lot on my mind. I sleep alone by myself; no particular reason for not sleeping." She has had flushes for the past seven years. They began early, at the age of thirty-seven, which she attributes to hard work. "I get very warm sometimes, head like pins and needles, I have to get air and am like burning up. They make me feel very weak and I perspire. They only last a few minutes but I get several in the day." At night she moves around to get a cool place in the bed and is always throwing the covers off. That is why she has slept alone for the last few years.

Past history: She used to be like Agnes. She was raised in an institution without a mother's affection, "but that doesn't make any difference. I suffered like Agnes, always very thin and delicate and had pain." "I suffered terribly having my children," both in labor and with nausea during the whole nine months, unable to keep anything on her stomach. She is often melancholy and wants to cry. "If I hear anybody sing, I want to cry." Both daughters are fond of singing. Weight: fat since the children were born, nursed the two younger children but not the first. This was the one who died later of heart disease. She also says that her sister is very sick with ulcers in "tubing" (points to pit of stomach). Her bottom teeth are out and she is trying to get the others out. "I seem to bloat up terribly when I eat."

When I saw her a month later she said she had had indigestion, a terrible pain which crawls up her back, to heart and left breast. When upset, "the first thing which affects me is my digestion. I have to keep eating to keep the pain away." The pain makes her "nauseous" when it is "real bad." She has been upset the past few months. Mr. Q— is not working, and there is some hitch about Home Relief because of Agnes' application for work. The medical social worker saw Agnes on Saturday.

A few days later Mrs. Q— comes in sighing, saying it is due to a heavy feeling. She still has pain in the epigastrium and tosses all night. It is not severe, she does not let it worry her. She feels as if she has lost weight (not so). Her pain is only gas. It comes only once in a while. . . . She had breakfast at 8 A.M. "Now it is eating in on me and I have to eat." "When I break [belch?] the gas, I feel O.K. It's because I'm upset, things aren't going right." "It wouldn't be an ulcer by any chance?" (Answer: no, it is gas. How does she know about ulcers?) Her sister has had them for four years and she is on a very strict diet . . . "If you don't have one thing, you have another. If I don't have flushes, I have something else to bother me."

Three weeks later, her stomach is "O.K." "I'm having trouble with breathing; I smother. I don't know whether it's the steam heat. I can't get my breath. I sort of smother" (illustrates by taking a deep breath). It comes at any time of the day. "I'm not doing anything in particular when it comes on." She may be sitting, or in bed. Sometimes when talking she loses her breath; the subject of conversation doesn't matter. She has to keep the apartment at 80 degrees to give the tenants heat.

Besides the symptoms of the menopause, already noted, and the stomach complaints which are later found to be associated in her mind with an ulcer, Mrs. Q— has trouble with her breathing. Details of her account of this show that it is a symptom of anxiety, and she herself is aware that much of her trouble is due to home and financial "conditions." Almost with her first words, and entirely impromptu, she finds it necessary to explain to a strange doctor the reason why she is not sleeping with her husband. She states also her identification with Agnes, the fact that her husband is not working, and that they are having some technical difficulty with Home Relief.

Agnes

Agnes came to me for examination at the age of nineteen, with her mother, who did the greater part of the talking. She was dressed according to the current style for her age, with a moderate degree of make-up, but without much care. Her hair was rather unkempt. Whenever I saw one of the sisters sitting on the bench, I could not be sure which one it was; as in physical resemblance, they seemed to be intellectually on a par. On this occasion the combined conversation of Agnes and her mother is recorded as follows:

Complaints: "Supposed to get injections this morning," says Agnes. She has pains around "here" (upper abdomen) like gas, and has had them ever since she first started going to school, all kinds of pains. "I can't understand it myself, if I eat I get them and also if I don't. Food doesn't agree with me," for example, soft-boiled eggs and cold cuts. The mother says the patient takes no fruit or green vegetables.

Past history: Menstruation started at fifteen, never on time, flow five days, not abnormal in amount; she sometimes skips a month, and at the present time has had no period for five months. Concerning her weight she says: "I just went down, that's all." "My appetite is fine when I feel right, but I don't eat everything." "Sometimes I don't eat at all. When I have pain I have no appetite for eating." Present weight 90 pounds, but 106 a few months ago. She is sluggish and feels like sleeping all the time. She has always had trouble with her bowels, and takes laxatives. She says again that she is supposed to get injections today. The mother then takes up the account of Agnes' complaints, saying that the minute she eats she has pain in her stomach (upper abdomen) and shoulder blades. Agnes is afraid to eat, or to go to bed, because of the pain. Reference to the record shows that she weighs 28 pounds less than the average. One hundred and six pounds is the most that she ever weighed, and she has lost weight all summer. She has had the pain and gas for a long time and it might be hereditary, as the mother was much like her as a young girl. The patient was very slow to develop, and had no "stomach" teeth until three years old. She did not make any headway at school. She was never fat. When she became "more of a woman" at fifteen years of age, she began to complain more. When she was seventeen she lost weight and her appetite was very poor.

Social: Her mother says that she has no friends, no "boy friends," is a "real little home girl," goes to the movies with her younger sister, but to no dances. She "hangs out with her little sister who is sixteen, all right, and a smart little girl." According to the mother, the patient is very lacking; mother could not make her out; she has had no interest in school, "is backward in coming forward," her mind does not seem to grasp things. She is a very good girl, no trouble at home where she tidies up, cooks supper and prepares lunch. The mother is teaching her how to cook.

Physical examination: Uncommunicative, replies briefly to questions in a somewhat antagonistic manner, and volunteers nothing. She concentrates on pain and makes no mention of loss of weight or deficient diet. Her figure is markedly linear. Hands and feet are blue and she has defective sexual development. Infantile uterus reported.

Impression: Anorexia nervosa;[2] hypogonadism.[3]

A month later, Agnes speaks of gaining little weight. She has had very little pain; once after eating a sandwich hurriedly. She says her mother tells her to eat; if she doesn't she will go back to her previous state; will be "put in a box," that is, will lie in it and have the dirt put over her (says this in response to query about "box").

The family relationship, as exhibited by the reaction between the mother and daughter, comes out with great clarity at the first interview. Although the daughter is nineteen, the mother comes into the examining room as a matter of course, and monopolizes most of the conversation. This in itself is enough to suggest undue domination by the mother. Agnes wishes, not unnaturally, to put her complaints on a physical basis. The medical details include the fact that she has no appetite when she has the pain. Her mother was much like her as a young girl. In the presence of the daughter the mother expresses her favoritism for the other daughter and her open depreciation of Agnes, coupling this with her statement of Agnes' backwardness in many ways. Later we hear that the mother has threatened her with a coffin if she does not eat.

Mr. Martin Q—

Mr. Martin Q—'s first visit had yielded little information that was new. Everyone who commented on his appearance mentioned his short stature. At his second visit, a month later, details were obtained which indicated the nature of the illness. Weight, 107 pounds. "Still strong with me" (i.e., symptoms). After the teeth were out he seemed to be worse. Recently has had attacks during the day at odd times, with a lump; unable to swallow, has a distressed feeling, "can't talk, like a convulsion inside; just like a choked sensation . . . griping feeling . . . odd sensation." Has had attacks during the day only lately. Nothing he eats seems to bother him. Last night helped a "feller" mopping a building, couldn't talk; the man did not know what was the matter with him. Mr. Q— does not know himself. "If I didn't have that I'd feel good." It starts when he is doing anything, sitting or walking around. It does not remind him of any experience. "You'd think it was like a ball of gas trying to break, like something needed to be swallowed." "It is just a reaction." Something is stuck, he tries to force it down. "It feels down in the stomach but the way you act it's up in the throat . . . it kind of takes the pep out of you for a second." He got it a couple of times from the exercise of mopping.

Four months later: His stomach has been bothering him for about fifteen years; it began when he was still employed. He was making "good money" at the time. It began as indigestion, like sort of a choking feeling (points to breastbone). It was as if he had taken too much food. On question, he says that his youngest child, Catherine, was born seven years after his marriage. His symptoms began a year after her birth.

Mr. Q— gives a description of complaints which suggest increased motor activity in the region of the inlet and outlet of the stomach. His troubles began when he was making "good money" as a mechanic. They began after the birth of the youngest child, that is, at the time when he and his wife began to use withdrawal as a contraceptive measure. Like his wife, he recognizes that his symptoms are a "reaction to family troubles."

From the conversation of the individual members of the family much light is thrown on their illnesses. All of the previous impressions as to heart disease, in three of the members of the family, had to be reversed. It became abundantly clear that in each member of the family the illness had a strong neurotic component. In the case of Agnes this took an unusually clear-cut form which is known as anorexia nervosa. Fortunately her case was incipient and relatively mild, but she had the beginnings of a crippling and sometimes fatal illness. In each member the spontaneous conversation revealed the connection between the illness and the individual lack of security as affected by the family situation.

In our search for the family in the hospital we were not, of course, able to discover the family in person, nor should we expect to do so. When we leave the search to the doctors who have seen the Martin Q— family and let the records speak for themselves, we find that they speak only the language of individual diagnoses, and therefore say nothing about the family. Although the two propositions mentioned at the beginning of this chapter still hold, that hospitals have patients, and patients have families, the conclusion that the hospital has something to do with the Martin Q—s as a family could not be established.

MEDICINE AND THE FAMILY

John H. Mabrey

SINCE WORLD WAR II, medical educators and practitioners have become increasingly concerned over the relationship between the family and medicine.[1] During this period, social scientists have continued their accumulation of data and

Reprinted with permission of the author and publisher from *Marriage and the Family*, vol. 26, no. 2 (May 1964), pp. 160–165.

This research was supported in part by a grant to the University of Kentucky from the Commonwealth Fund of New York City and in part by a grant from the University of Kentucky Research Fund.

development of theory concerning family structure, functions, and behavior. Therefore, it is not surprising that somewhat different approaches to the family have emerged. This paper discusses points of relevance between medical and sociological images of home and family life.

The need to consider home and family relationships in the promotion of health and in the etiology, treatment, and prevention of disease has long been recognized by some members of thé medical, nursing, and social welfare professions.[2] Implications of the home environment have been suggested with respect to mental illness,[3] infectious disease,[4] skin reactions,[5] rehabilitation,[6] nutrition,[7] and many other health problems. Family members influence the perception and interpretation of symptoms.[8] The family may perpetuate a heritage of cabinet medicines,[9] it may encourage or discourage patterns of consultation with physicians,[10] and it often provides help.[11]

When Robert Frost's irresponsible, peripatetic hired man returned to die, the disgruntled farmer remarked: "Home is the place where, when you have to go there/They have to take you in." The farmer's more sympathetic wife replied: "I should have called it/Something you somehow haven't to deserve."[12] "The Death of the Hired Man" dramatizes the vicissitudes of family obligation and questions whether one has to deserve or earn membership in a family.

Family life has been characterized as an arena of interacting personalities, each of whom has a history.[13] The family is the most intense emotional unit of society. Each family has high and low emotional points which result from the pleasures and vicissitudes of living together. Thus, the emotional atmosphere of the home reflects how well each person is able to do his part in helping the family to function as a unit. The capacity for doing one's part is influenced by the balance between satisfactions and dissatisfactions which arise in social interaction within the family.

The family is also a genetic unit. Personality development occurs largely as the result of familial and childrearing practices which act upon, and within the limits and potentialities posed by, the inherited and constitutional characteristics of the newborn.[14] Indeed, an unsung component of courtship and marriage is the sorting of personality characteristics and, often unconsciously, of such inherited characteristics as eye color, curliness of hair and blood type.

But there is evidence that home is not only an arena of interacting personalities, each with a history. The American dwelling is also an arena of interacting hosts, disease vectors, and such invisible life forms as viruses and bacteria.[15] In addition, one result of technological progress has been to enlarge the home's environmental spectrum of exposure to health problems associated with cosmetics, insecticides, herbicides, plastics, food additives, and patent medicines.[16]

Behavior patterns and attitudes in the home often interfere with efforts to treat illness or to promote good health. Not infrequently, there are difficulties in coordinating the goals of medicine with those of the family. Family patterns may not function effectively with treatment regimens, giving rise to the paradox that treatment is often thwarted by those for whom it is intended.

CHANGING STRUCTURE OF THE FAMILY

Those living at home make up a *dramatis personae* for family love, life, and work in sickness and in health. Family members, and the roles that they play, set the stage for conversations about symptoms of illness and are a potential reservoir of help in time of need.[17] Thus, the family has health and medical roles. But like other social roles and their concomitant social structures, these roles continually change. Changes in the American family have been described in existing literature[18] and need not be elaborated here.

Dramatic accretions in medical knowledge and arts have accompanied changes in the American family. As medical knowledge became more comprehensive and yet more detailed, the tendency to specialize in subareas of medicine, nursing, and social work became more pronounced. Specialization has meant that the patient and his family have increasing opportunities for taking advantage of new and specialized medical knowledge. Yet, in the medical professions there is increasing concern with how to integrate the various facets of this knowledge into a comprehensive approach to patients and their families.

That there is often difficulty in establishing therapeutic practices within the family is testimony to the need for integrating the arts and knowledge of the helping professions with current knowledge of the family. Some families appear to be indifferent or uncooperative because treatment and personal care regimens have not taken an effective place among interlocking family functions, values, and habit patterns. Rarely does a family become so dominated by illness that all other activities cease; therefore, the health, socio-economic, and emotional needs of other family members must be met along with the needs of the patient. Although much more research is needed,[19] integration of existing knowledge is furthered by a consideration of points of relevance between medicine and family functioning.

MEDICINE AND FAMILY FUNCTIONING

In all world cultures there are basic functions which the family must perform. These functions are important to the individual and to society as well. The manner in which families perform these social functions varies in different cultures.[20] However, it is customary to consider six family functions: physical well-being and health maintenance, biological reproduction, emotional development,[21] socialization,[22] organization of statuses and roles, and relations between the family and the community.[23] Specific discussion of the functions of health maintenance and biological reproduction is appropriate.

Physical well-being and health maintenance are necessary if family members are to have the energy and personal resources for meeting the everyday demands of life and work. The maintenance of energy levels and necessary personal resources is influenced by familial and cultural learnings of health behaviors, attitudes toward symptoms of illness, and what, if anything, is done about them. For example, personal hygiene practices and differences with respect to the sick role[24] are transmitted parts of familial and cultural heritages.

The family function of health maintenance has other dimensions. First, any human meeting place involves not only social interaction but also a setting for the transmission of infectious disease. Home may be a man's castle, but it also may be a rooming house for numerous microorganisms, some of which may produce antibodies if not disease. Even "man's best friend," the dog, may occupy both affectional and disease vector niches in the home.[25] Second, exposure to the risk of home accidents is related to home architecture, maintenance, and the extent to which safe practices are a part of the family habit system.[26] Third, a recent room-by-room survey of the American home suggests numerous exposure risks for those who are susceptible to skin allergies.[27] Fourth, economically deprived homes and neighborhoods have long been known to have more than their share of health problems.[28]

Most people are oblivious to the relationship between their health and the microscopic animals and plants in their homes. For most people, exposure to potentially noxious agents like detergents and lipsticks normally has no noticeable effect. However, if an allergic skin rash appears, the costly time-consuming process of medical detection may be necessary if trial-and-error omissions of soap and other potential allergens do not help the condition.

In addition to providing *biological reproduction,* the family perpetuates a culture or way of life by transmitting to new members of society its customs and values. Attitudes toward sexual behavior and practices, concepts of "ideal" family size, and the place of children in the hierarchy of family values all have an influence upon conception and birth.[29] Recurrent controversy over the dissemination of knowledge about birth control methods exemplifies great social conflict over these matters.

While social custom and law set kinship limits to the selection of marriage partners, the reproduction of society's new members is also influenced by genetics, microorganisms, and other environmental influences. For example, the effects of blood type incompatibilities (Rh blood factor) and of inborn errors in metabolism (from which some types of mental retardation may result) are well known. Furthermore, injuries to the fetus may result from infectious diseases, exposure to radioactivity, or severe malnutrition. If parent-child interaction is accompanied by the transmission of rubeola to a susceptible mother during the first trimester of pregnancy, congenital malformations in the newborn may appear.

In summary, the production of new members of society who will be future bearers of the cultural heritage results from (a) the fecundity of the parents and such influences upon fertility as (b) attitudes toward sex and the value placed upon children, (c) genetics, (d) the "familial epidemiology" of infectious diseases, and (e) maternal nutrition.

Family solidarity. Through assuring that family members have the energy and personal resources for meeting the everyday demands of life and work, the health and welfare professions contribute to the solidarity of family life. Some of the ingredients of family solidarity are: first, sound physical well-being and health maintenance, including a minimum of irreversible or untreatable genetic defects; second, meeting the social and emotional needs of family members so that there are loyalties, affections, and hopes that the family group will continue; third, the development of behaviors and values which are socially acceptable to the reference groups and to the community in which the family participates; and fourth, sufficient income and resources for an adequate level of living.[30]

THE FAMILY AS A UNIT IN MEDICAL CARE

Having mentioned several examples of the interaction between the family and medicine and of the impact which family values and behavior can have on professional efforts to help, attention is now focused on the home as a unit in medical care. Among others, important influences upon maintaining physical and emotional well-being are family diagnosis, treatment, and nursing patterns.

Diagnosis

The decision to consult a physician often comes after discussion within the family of bumps, swelling, bloody or liquid discharges, or "feeling bad." More often than not, there are vague thoughts and misapprehensions about the diagnosis. Home medical reference books, newspaper reports of illness and death, various folk explanations of symptoms may all contribute to discussion and interpretation within the family.

The patient tries to incorporate the medical diagnosis into his own way of viewing illness. His wife, older children, and other relatives may serve as a reference group. The success of this incorporative attempt depends upon the extent to which the patient and his family have attitudes and beliefs that are consistent with scientific medicine. When patients report the physician's diagnosis, the result often bears little resemblance to the original communication. For example, a patient with moderately severe heart damage reported his doctor's explanation: "Your trouble is, your stomach is on fire and the flames reach out and grab hold of your heart." In this patient's family and other reference groups, the scientific explanation of heart disease was less dramatic and less a conversational *piece de resistance* than was a flaming stomach.

Patient and family reactions to diagnoses vary according to their private, often nonscientific concepts of disease. Some families view all illness as lasting a relatively short time. Like folk treatment of the common cold, immediate results are often expected. There may be very limited concepts of inborn biochemical error or other chronic illness which requires treatment for a very long period, perhaps for life.

Emotional problems are frequently somaticized or "explained" in physical and environmental terms rather than considered within a psychological frame of reference.[31] Dreads and misapprehensions which impair family functioning or work may be "explained" by such ideas as "trying to do too much" and "just being run down." Often one hears that the trouble is a case of "nerves" or a "nervous breakdown." This lay understanding seems vaguely to envision some changes in or wearing down of nerve tissues rather than the person's concept of himself and his relation to others.

Treatment

If the recommended treatment is followed, the patient's own personal diagnosis may not be of great concern. For example, if the heart patient takes his digitalis as prescribed, it may not matter whether the patient explains it scientifically or whether he feels that the medicine is putting the fire out in his stomach. However, if the patient feels better after several weeks on his medicine, he and his family may decide that this "spell" of illness has run its course and that the fire must be out. Thus, familial concepts of treatment are often intertwined with ideas about causation. Since the concept of chronic disease is limited in many families, there may be no awareness that father must always take his medicine or, in their own terms, that father will always have a smoldering fire which will leap into flames if the medicine is not taken.

There are other ways in which family members may mis-

understand treatment regimens. Without knowledge of
scientific similarities and differences in diagnosis, family
members may "try out" one another's medicine. The details
of directions, such as medication before meals, may be vio-
lated with subsequent nausea and the feeling that the medicine is contributing toward sickness rather than curing it.
The two pills four times a day may become four pills two
times daily with resultant discomfort. Or, if it is really good
medicine, some may ask, why not take four pills four times
per day? These misunderstandings about dosage may lead
a physician to ask his patients to bring their medicine with
them during subsequent office visits so that he can determine
the extent of their consumption. In the treatment of tuberculosis, active pharmacologic ingredients may be compounded with an inert chemical which can be traced in
subsequent urinalysis.[32] Sometimes it is necessary to help
the family organize household routines in such a way as to
ensure adherence to the treatment regimen.

When an ailing father is home from work, or when illness
involves a mother's limitation of her activity, dislocation in
the spatial arrangement of the home may occur. In a study
in Syracuse, New York, several years ago, it was found that
medium-priced homes were often deficient in space and facilities for caring for the ill, the elderly, and infants.[33] Bed-
rooms located far from the madding crowd of family noise
may imply isolation for ill persons at a time when support
and companionship are desired. Furthermore, isolation of the
ill person may involve extra steps for mother in her nursing
role. The "meaning" of the home, the arrangement and tidi-
ness of rooms, may be important. In some homes, the entire
house appears to be one big family room with much evidence
of the human tendency to clutter. Other homes may have a
living room that scarcely looks lived in, a dining room that
suggests a daily formal dinner, and play space for children
in the basement.

Nursing

The capacity of family members to care for one another
in a nursing role is influenced by their personal history, past
experience, arrangement of the home, and the physical and
emotional needs of the patient. In most illness, the home is
the first element in nursing care. The nursing role involves

emotional support in addition to providing liquids and preparing food. If the patient is glum and sorrowful in appearance, some family members may find it difficult to relate to him even if the demands for nursing are minimal. Others may find an hyperactive, "can't-stay-in-bed" patient even more difficult to accept.

There are greater demands in incapacitating illness, and there is often increased difficulty in the assumption of the nursing role by family members. Home arrangements for wheel chair patients may ideally require widened doorways, special bathroom facilities, or a ramp over the front steps. Deficiencies in these home arrangements may so confine a patient that his nursing needs increase. Furthermore, family members may need to learn techniques of injection, bathing in bed, simple urinalysis and stool inspection, maintenance of a temperature chart, helping in home exercises, and close supervision of the patient. And these nursing roles may be required simultaneously with continuing other household roles and meeting the needs of other members of the family.

CONCLUSION

When illness strikes, most families are supportive and helpful or at least "muddle through" without drastically compromising efforts to make the person and his family well. This is particularly so in a high proportion of so-called minor complaints. Even with severely disruptive illness, the heights of adaptation to which many families rise are examples of courage and fortitude.

But families vary in the amount and nature of their strengths and in their capacity to adapt to illness. Often there is inadequate attention to the treatment regimen. Since Hippocrates, if not since Aesculapius, the medical professions have recognized the importance of enlisting the cooperation not only of the patient but also of the family and others who are intimately associated with him.[34] The medical and nursing functions of the family are interwoven with various social functions of the family and the changing social structure of the American home. Being aware of the possible relevance of family living is much like being aware of the possible conditions of which headache may be a symptom. Not every headache will require detailed knowledge of the anat-

omy of the neck and not every treatment will require attention to the entire family. But, just as some headaches do
require consideration of anatomy, effective medical treatment often requires an assessment of the diagnostic, treatment, and nursing patterns of the patient's family.

PROBLEMS OF DISABILITY FROM THE
PERSPECTIVE OF ROLE THEORY

Edwin J. Thomas

INTRODUCTION

The disabled are a mixed lot; all sorts of conditions—psychological, sociological and economic—are to be found
among them, and the impairments that medically define
these individuals as disabled are also remarkably diverse.[1]
In her concluding comments concerning an assessment of
the field of somatopsychology, Beatrice Wright has captured
what is perhaps the heart of the matter for the case of the
disabled. She said ". . . *somatic abnormality as a physical fact
is not linked in a direct or simple way to psychological behavior.*"[2] In support of this is the sobering fact that the scholars who have reviewed the scientifically reputable studies
concerning the effects of disability upon adjustment have
not found that there is presently any known, general, deleterious effect upon adjustment attending disablement.[3] That
is, there is no evidence that an impaired physique results in
any general maladjustment or that there is an association between types of physical disability and particular personality
characteristics, such as tolerance for frustration or feelings
of inferiority. Future research, of course, may force a revision of these observations. In any case, these results do not
deny another equally important generalization, one that is
based upon personal accounts of disabled persons, the ob-

Reprinted with permission of the author and publisher from *Journal
of Health and Human Behavior*, vol. 7, no. 1 (Spring 1966), pp. 2–13.

servations of practitioners who work with the disabled, and the rehabilitation literature in general. This conclusion is that there are significant behavioral correlates of disability for given impairments and for given individuals, and that disability often profoundly affects the person's life.[4]

One must therefore turn to the underlying psychological and social conditions responsible for these different reactions in order to gain a richer understanding of the problems of disability. It is here that role theory is useful. Its concepts make possible a consistent, general description of the behaviors of the disabled and of those with whom he relates, and this perspective helps predict and explain the strains and adjustmental difficulties that may attend disablement.[5]

This paper focuses upon problems of role that are linked to the behavioral changes associated with disability or to the behavioral changes deriving from the reactions of others to the disabled. The problems of role that disabled individuals share with the nondisabled and that do not, therefore, distinguish their condition particularly, will not be discussed here. Because of this emphasis upon the disability-linked factors, only portions of role theory will be employed.[6] Also, the problems of role associated with an individual's disability may not always create severe adjustmental difficulties. The disability-related role problem may contribute little or much to an individual's overall adjustment, depending upon the entire complex of personal and environmental pressures in his life. This is true despite the fact that role difficulties to be treated here generally have undesirable adjustmental consequences, assuming all other factors are equal.

THE ROLES OF THE DISABLED

Because of the great diversity of impairments characterizing persons designated as disabled, and because of their almost infinite conditions of psyche and environment, is it meaningful at all to talk about the *roles* of the disabled? Are the behavioral repertoires, or roles, of the disabled and the repertoires of those with whom they interact sufficiently distinct to be singled out, analyzed, and labelled? The answer is decidedly affirmative. Whether he is disabled from birth or suffers the disability later in life, the disabled person has some segment of his behavioral repertoire that is different from that of his normal fellow humans. The difference may derive from any or all of the following: some responses may be lost, some regained, some may be substitutes, or some simply different or new.

Five disability-related roles have been singled out for analysis: disabled patient, handicapped performer, helped person, disability comanager, and public relations man. The names are but convenient designations for particular aspects of the disabled persons behavioral repertoire or for the behaviors of others with whom he interacts. The behavioral repertoires so labelled are really complx clusters of conceptions, rules, and performances. The behaviors associated with each role, however, are descriptively similar and are different from, and independent of, the behaviors grouped as belonging with another role. Although these roles, hopefully, capture the essential differences between the behavioral repertoires of the disabled and of those with whom they interact, all five roles are not necessarily applicable to every disabled individual. One or more of the roles, however, should apply to every disabled person.

Disabled Patient

At the onset of the impairment—and later, too—the disabled individual is typically a patient, and is thereby exposed to a characteristic set of expectations. To quote from Parsons' seminal discussion of the sick role:

The first of these is the exemption of the sick person from the performance of certain of his normal social obligations. Thus, to take a very simple case, "Johnny has a fever, he ought not to go to school today."

. . . Secondly, the sick person is, in a very specific sense, also exempted from a certain type of responsibility for his own state. . . . He will either have to get well spontaneously or to "be cured" by having something done to him. He cannot reasonably be expected to "pull himself together" by a mere act of will, and thus decide to be all right. . . . The third aspect of the sick role is the partial character of its legitimation, hence the deprivation of a claim to full legitimacy. To be sick . . . is to be in a state which is socially defined as undesirable, to be gotten out of as expeditiously as possible. . . .

Finally, fourth, being sick is also defined, except for the mildest cases, as being "in need of help.". . . He . . . incurs certain obligations, especially that of "co-operating" with his physician—or other therapist—on the process of trying to get well.[7]

In addition, most disabled persons are also hospitalized at some point. The expectations placed upon hospital patients are partly those relating to the sick role and partly those attending the particular subculture of the hospital. King has described this particular set of expectations for the hospitalized as follows:

The first general expectation is that of *dependence,* of compliance by the patient to hospital rules and regulations, to the daily routine, to the decisions that are made for him by physicians or nurses. The compliant patient is therefore likely to be perceived as the good patient by hospital staff, whereas the patient who tries to exert authority will be perceived negatively. . . .

In line with dependence, the patient is expected *not to fulfill his normal role responsibilities.* This is one of the prerequisites of the sick role . . . and a factor that receives strong support from hospital expectations. The patient is encouraged not to worry about cares of family or job and to concentrate on the process of getting well. . . .

A third expectation concerns the *de-emphasis on external power and prestige* which the patient carries in his life outside the hospital. The taking away of patients' clothes is a symbol of this loss, all patients being rendered as naked as the day they came into the world, and supposedly as innocent. Indeed, there is nothing quite so deflating to an individual's sense of prestige as his own nakedness in public. A positive function is also served by this action and expectation, that of emotional neutrality and fairness. . . .

Suffering and pain are to be expected and should be borne with as much grace as possible under the circumstances, so goes the general expectation. Hospital personnel know that rarely do patients come without pain or malaise and often the suffering is intense. Furthermore, the procedures involved in curing sickness in themselves often produce pain. . . .

Finally, *the patient should want to get well* and do all he can to aid the process. Again, this expectation grows out of the definition of the sick role and is an aspect of the role that is subject to rewards and punishments. The faintest hint of malingering can be picked up quickly by nurse or physician and is a sign that the patient is not living up to his obligations. If malingering can be clearly established, it acts to release the hospital from its obligations and brings about attempts to get rid of the patients as quickly as possible. . . .[8]

We add to these the expectation that there be tolerance for prognostic uncertainty. With most medical problems there is a period between the recognition that there may be something wrong medically and the time following a diagnosis when there is relative certainty concerning the prognosis for the individual. During this period the illness or disability must be followed to see how it develops, and time is required to gather the information and to make decisions about the case. In addition to this time required to reach a medically sound prognostication, there are other factors that prolong the period of uncertainty. This is well illustrated in Davis' analysis of this problem for polio victims.

> . . . As we have seen, medically there is a pronounced shift from prognostic uncertainty to certainty after the first six weeks to three months following the onset of the disease. Yet nothing approximating a commensurate gain in the patients' knowledge of outcome probabilities occurred then or for a considerable period thereafter. Thus, "uncertainty," a real factor at the beginning of polio convalescence, came more and more to serve social-managerial ends for treatment personnel. Instead of openly confronting the parents with the prognosis—by then a virtual certainty—that the child would be left with a disability, treatment personnel sought to cushion its impact by hedging, evading questions, and acting as if the outcome were still uncertain. Thus they tried to spare themselves the emotional scenes that outright utterances of the prognosis would probably have entailed. . . .
>
> . . . we must . . . not lose sight of the possibility that in many illnesses, especially those of a chronic or permanently incapacitating nature, "uncertainty" is to some extent feigned by the doctor for the purpose of gradually—to use Goffman's very descriptive analogy—"cooling the mark out," i.e., getting the patient ultimately to accept and put up with a state-of-being that initially is intolerable to him.[9]

One consequence of this prognostic limbo is that the patient and those closest to him lack authoritative opinion with respect to which realistic levels of performance may be set. Without the moorings of definite expert opinion, the patient and others may easily entertain unrealistically high or low expectations.

Another expectation held for patients is that they define themselves as sick. This requires that the individual acknowledge the unalterable fact that he is ill, injured, or otherwise impaired, and that his assumptive world and actions be structured accordingly.[10] For the disabled, this, of course, is represented by beliefs and behavior commensurate with the premise that the individual in fact has a disability. The hospitalized and nonhospitalized patient alike are expected to conceive of themselves as sick, although the entry into a hospital is likely to impress this fact more emphatically upon patients.

There will be wide variations in the forms that the patient role takes for given disabled persons, depending upon the specific nature of the disability. But to the degree that the impairment is permanent, most of the elements of the patient role are extended or made enduring. The exemption from responsibility for the impairment may be granted for the duration of the disablement; the period of prognostic uncertainty, rather than being a matter of days or weeks, may be months or even years; the exemption from ordinary social responsibilities, as it takes form for the particular person and disability, may be permanent.

The expectation that the patient should want to get well, however, is not merely extended for many disabled. Rather, it is elaborated in complex detail, as is revealed in present-day rehabilitation practice and philosophy. Thus, the disabled is encouraged to make the most of his capacities, within the restrictions set by the impairment. Motivation is the key word and has reference to a major theme in much of the rehabilitation literature. The expectation that the disabled realize his potentialities is manifested in numerous services, these variously providing counsel, therapy, training and education, prosthetic devices, employment opportunities, and money.

This philosophy also informs us that the disabled must accept his impairment, the acceptance being nearly a necessary condition, one gathers, to the proper realization of his capabilities. Acceptance of one's disability typically requires at least that the disabled conceive his limitations and promise realistically, and that rules for performance be made commensurate with his true degree of handicap, his capabilities, and the environmental opportunities. The rationale attending the idea that acceptance is important for the disabled is a specification, in the context of disability, of the expectation mentioned earlier that patients conceive of themselves as "sick."

Handicapped Performer

Because of the disablement there will very probably be an attending handicapping of performance. The impairment, of course, may range from complete loss of function, at one extreme, to a very minimal loss, at the other. As a consequence, some portion—large or small—of the normal individual's behavioral repertoire is somehow circumscribed, limited, or eliminated. All this is well known, of course.

But there are important ramifications deriving from having this more limited behavioral repertoire. First, the disabled person may be less able to care for himself physically: he may not be able to feed himself, dress, or move around, to select common instances. Second, the impaired function may be one which is requisite to the performance of normal social roles. For all adults there are at least three key roles or role clusters: one is the individual's sex role, either as a female or male; another is one's occupational role; and the third is the individual's family roles, as son, daughter, father, mother, or spouse. The disability may reduce the level of performance for these roles or make it variable and unpredictable. In the extreme case, of course, repertoires required for all these roles may be essentially lost, resulting in the removal of the person from the main avenues society provides for accomplishment, reward, and a sense of personal identity. A third and related point is that the disablement may preclude the fulfillment of normal responsibilities to others. Thus, if disabled, the father may no longer be able to be the breadwinner or the mother may have to relinquish homemaking and child-care activities. And fourth, the disabled may simply hinder others; for example, the family members of the disabled may be constrained to forfeit vacations, educational advancement, social and recreational opportunities—all because of the added drain on the family resources of time, money, and effort consequent to the impairment.

The behavioral repertoire of the disabled person is not merely less complete than that of his nondisabled counterpart, it is also a partial collection of behaviors that are substitutes for those lost because of the impairment or for those which the person never had in the first place. The blind learns to read and write with braille, the deaf comes to read lips and use a sign language, the extensively crippled find devices to aid their physical locomotion, to mention common illustrations of essentially substitute behaviors with which disabled individuals may embellish their repertoires and thereby increase their effective functioning.

It is in all of these ways that the individual with an impairment may be said to be a handicapped performer.

Helped Person

All persons receive help from others from the beginning of life to its end, and the amount of aid is generally much more than is usually realized or acknowledged. The person with an impairment usually receives more help than does his normal counterpart, of course. His physical needs may have to be ministered to and the responsibilities he ordinarily shouldered may have to be taken on by others. The disabled is thus on the receiving end of helping acts, and he must adjust, accommodate, and respond to being an object of aid; he is thus a helped person. The help received may be relatively small or large but it is nonetheless sufficient generally to constitute a deviation from cultural standards of self-reliance and independence so esteemed and revered even now in the United States. The implications of this will be discussed further at a later point.

Disability Comanager

The disabled person often becomes an active participant in the decisions and regimen of living attending his impairment and rehabilitation. He may participate in the selection of an artificial limb, may assume responsibility for giving himself injections, taking medication, following a diet, taking exercises, or following a schedule of rest and activity. In all these ways, he may thus be said to be a disability comanager, following Beatrice Wright's terms.[11]

Public Relations Man

Nondisabled persons conduct a large share of the business of living in institutionalized roles and in the context of widely shared understanding relating to expected behaviors. As a consequence, it is not common that a person has to explain his role to others. How often does a man, for instance, have to explain his role to a woman, or vice versa? The disabled, in contrast, typically has a particular impairment, the understanding of which is not provided for others by such a widely held, common store of knowledge. The relative uniqueness of the particular person's impaired condition and the associated ignorance of others place a burden of explanation and interpretation upon the disabled over and above that which the nondisabled carries. The necessities to educate others are of at least two sorts. The first is mainly unsolicited in which another person behaves toward the disabled so as literally to force him to account for his problem. Thus the blind individual is asked what it is like to be blind or his arm is grasped by the well-intentioned sighted person who believes that he needs to be led across the street. The other set of occasions necessitating explanation, in contrast to the gratuitous, may be regarded as the relevant and legitimate. Consider these: the blind job applicant is called upon to indicate how he would perform with this handicap; the potential mate requests information about how the marital relationship will be affected by the other's disability; the prospective student is asked how his impairment will affect his ability to perform academically.

The information conveyed ranges over many themes: explanations of the nature of the disease, injury, or birth condition; the extent of disability and handicap; the regimen of rehabilitation and disability management. All these pertain to the disability itself. There are also those features relating to the individual's attitudes, beliefs, and life philosophy developed in relationship to his condition. Rich examples are provided in the rehabilitation literature of the diverse ways in which disabled persons handle these themes of public relations. At one extreme there is the educator, the one who dispassionately conveys the facts pertaining to his particular disability; and at a different extreme are those people who perform the function more as propagandists, apologists, defeatists, or deceivers. Erving Goffman has described a particular variant of explanation in his notion of apologia. In this respect he says:

> First, in many total institutions a peculiar kind and level of self-concern is engendered. The low position of inmates relative to their station on the outside, established initially through the stripping processes, creates a milieu of personal failure in which one's fall from grace is continuously pressed home. In response, the inmate tends to develop a story, a line, a sad tale—a kind of lamentation and apologia—which he constantly tells to his fellows as a means of accounting for his present low estate.[12]

The fact that the person's disability is particular, if not unique, for him, and because of the absence of a uniform corpus of common knowledge pertaining to that disability, great latitude is provided for personal differences to shape the explanations given to others

Patterns of Disability Roles for Individuals

As observed earlier, a given impairment does not necessitate all of the behavioral changes identified with these five roles, but most disabilities implicate most if not all of them. A given person will characteristically display his particular pattern or profile, through time. Some roles may be engaged in for longer periods than others. At any moment, some persons may manifest two, three, four, or all five of the roles; and the sequence of going from one role to the others may also vary from person to person.

Beyond these individual differences is the question of when the disablement occurs in the person's lifetime. If the person has an impairment from birth or one acquired early in life, he must learn the behavioral patterns associated with these five roles in the course of growing up, where these behavioral patterns—with the possible exception of portions of the patient role—are not common with those of the population at large. The socialization of such a disabled person is, therefore, partially deviant. The person disabled later in life also has to learn these new behaviors, but in addition he must unlearn other behaviors no longer possible or appropriate. For these persons the task is that of resocialization into a deviant social category and, of course, this may be gradual or rapid. A large proportion of disabilities occur relatively suddenly and this therefore poses the occasion for rapid resocialization.

PROBLEMS OF ROLE

We turn now to the problems of role which attend disability. These difficulties arise partly because of the role changes just described and partly because of general societal conditions, to be referred to shortly.

Role Discontinuity

Ruth Benedict introduced the concept of role discontinuity to characterize the lack of order and smooth sequence in the cultural role training of the life cycle.[13] She documented how various primitive cultures provided for more continuity in the training for responsibility, dominance, and sexuality than was characteristic in the United States. The storm and stress of adolescence so often attributed only to physiological changes, she concluded, was in fact caused by the particular discontinuities resulting from prior role training.

This seminal conception is sufficiently important to merit elaboration and extension. First, although Benedict used the term in connection with age-graded transitions universal for all mankind, it is but a simple step to realize that discontinuities may occur also for specific groups and individuals whenever there is a transition from one position to another in which the role behaviors associated with each are different. Such is the case with large numbers of the disabled.

Second, the elements requisite to continuous role training need specification. There are at least these five: (1) There should be congruence of the expected behaviors between the new and the old positions. (2) The person should have the capacity to acquire the new behaviors. (3) He should be properly motivated for the transition. (4) He should have been socialized in anticipation of the impending transition through prior rehearsal—either imaginative or actual—of the new behaviors. (5) The rate of change in moving from one position to the next should not be too rapid.

On most of these counts a disability that occurs later in life involves discontinuity. An abrupt, sudden change probably serves to exacerbate the effects of the other factors. Even a gradual, progressive change may never eliminate a basic incongruence of expected behaviors, rectify the possible absence of capacity to perform the new and different behaviors, or achieve proper motivation to change. A gradual rate may (but will not necessarily) make possible anticipatory socialization. Thus, even disabilities that involve gradual deterioration are mainly discontinuous role transitions, considering all of the requisites of role continuity here proposed.

Role discontinuity may result in confusion, anxiety and stress for the individual, and we assume that these effects will be more probable to the extent that there are many rather than few discontinuous junctures.[14]

Role Conflict

Whether or not the person's disability is attended by role discontinuity, there are various conflicts of expectations that are disability related. An expectation is a statement that defines given behavior as obligatory, forbidden, or permitted. Role conflict exists when there are two opposing expectations held for the behavior of an individual such that he cannot perform consistently with both at the same time. Role conflict may take many forms. Others may hold different expectations for you as compared with those which you hold for yourself; thus the child with a heart disorder may hold expectations for himself as if he were normal, whereas his parents may hold expectations requiring restriction of activity and rest. Another variant of role conflict occurs when others who prescribe behavior for the individual disagree between themselves; for instance, a parent, in attempting to deny a child's disability, may prescribe expectations for his behavior which do not take into account the disability, whereas the child's physician may advocate expectations more commensurate with the degree of impairment. A more subtle variant of role conflict occurs when the two conflicting expectations reside within the same skin, that is, are held by the same person for his own behavior; consider the father who has had a heart attack and who experiences conflict between his understanding of the doctor's orders that he care for himself properly and the expectations he has learned as a middle-class male that he be achieving, hard working, and successful in his work. Conflicts of role may result in stress for the individual, particularly to the extent that the conflicts are strong, enduring, or numerous.

Conflict of Role Definitions

Role definitions are in conflict when contradictory role conceptions are held for the same person. In the case of disability, the conceptions most likely to be conflicting pertain to ideas that the disabled person is normal or disabled. Thus the person may view himself appropriately as disabled in a given area, whereas selected others may view him as normal. More specifically, conceptions that the disabled hold for themselves may disagree with the conceptions others hold for them in any or all of the five disability-related roles described earlier. Consider, for instance, the youth with a serious heart condition, the visibility and significance of which is not apparent to the casual acquaintance. When meeting such a person for the first time it is not likely that others will conceive of him as disabled. The parallel problem involving the possible conflict of conceptions for the individual with a highly visible disability, such as blindness, is that the casual acquaintance is likely to conceive of him as more handicapped than he in fact may be. Conflicts of role definitions, at the very least, result in confusion and asynchronous behaviors of individuals vis-à-vis one another; more seriously, such conflicts may result in anxiety and stress, again to the extent that they are strong, recurring, or numerous.

Nonfacilitative Interdependence

Because of the impairment and the resulting inability to care for himself, the disabled person is usually less able to help others, yet others are constrained to act helpfully toward him. This helplessness and nonfacilitative relationship with others departs from the dominant cultural emphasis upon self-reliance and independence. The person may have been well trained to be self-reliant, autonomous, and independent in the course of his social learning prior to the advent of the disability. Robin Williams, in his perceptive analysis of the values and beliefs in American society, has described achievement (success) and activity (work) as major value orientations in America,[15] and he has noted further that Americans esteem active mastery more than passive acceptance. The psychological needs for achievement and autonomy may be regarded as individual dispositions which derive in part from these highly esteemed cultural values.[16] The disabled may depart from this cultural standard of self-reliance and independence on many counts, and, as a consequence, there may be various psychological effects. First, the individual may experience what Bertha Reynolds called the poignant "hurt" associated with the receipt of assistance when he is unable to repay others for the help received.[17] Second, the individual may experience a drop in his self esteem.[18] Third, the help offered is likely to be apprehended ambivalently or even negatively.[19]

Role Strain

All these role problems—role discontinuity, role conflict, conflict of role definitions, and nonfacilitatively interdependent relationships—conspire, either singly or in complex combinations, to create role strain, i.e., to affect the experienced difficulty that an individual has in performing his role.[20] This strain differs from anxiety and stress in general only by virtue of its particular association with the problems attending one's social role.

SPECIAL PROBLEMS OF ROLE SYNCHRONY

In addition to the role difficulties already discussed, there is a special set of problems relating to the synchronization or meshing of the behavior of the disabled with that of others with whom he interacts. Because the problems of role synchrony are subtle and complex, they deserve more extended comments.[21] Let us begin with an example.

Consider the blind person about to catch a train in a subway. Through practice and the use of the cane he has become proficient at navigating steps and turnstiles and knows the correct moves required to get on and off subway trains and, as a consequence, he is able to locomote relatively independently from one section of the city to another. In only one respect is this person unable to be totally self-reliant in his travels: he must inquire of others concerning whether the forthcoming train is the one he wishes to board. As he hears the distant roar of a forthcoming train, he asks this question: "Pardon me, is this an E train?" "Oh, yes!" comes the startled reply, "I've got you—" and the man to his left takes a firm grasp on his arm. In attempting to free himself, the blind person says, "That's all right, I can make it. . . ." "It's no trouble at all," he protests, and then taking the blind man's arm, the other says "This way," and the train is boarded. Although the blind man is now able to fend for himself, his guide announces that there don't seem to be any seats, in a distinctly audible voice, whereupon one of the passengers looks up and says "Here, he can have my seat." After the blind man is seated the guide inquires shortly after, in a voice louder than is required by the roar of the train, "Where are you going?" Pausing briefly, the blind man replies, "I'm getting off at Forty-second." "Oh," says the guide, "Well, I get off here. Good luck. Maybe someone else will help you."[22]

All that the blind individual needed was information regarding which train was coming, yet by virtue of the unsolicited help provided by the guide, he was treated as more handicapped than he was. The excessive handicap that was presumed was thus invalid. Furthermore, the blind person went along with the guide, this presumably being the course of least resistance, and he thereby fictitiously feigned a handicap that he did not have. The role behaviors of each were synchronic, however; the behavior of each meshed with that of the other, both sets of behaviors apparently being based upon the same behavioral assumptions. Thus, in this example we have *role synchrony* between the disabled and the other, but it was essentially invalid because the behavior of both presumed a handicap that in fact was not present— a *fictitious handicap,* as it were.

Now for another example. Fred is a ten-year-old boy with a mildly handicapping heart disorder. He does not choose to recognize his disability, however, and consequently he does not rest appropriately and, when he plays with others, he participates altogether too vigorously. Fred does all of this in spite of the admonitions and advice of doctors, parents, and even his friends.

In this example, Fred has ignored his disability and consequently he behaves essentially as if he were not handicapped. His behavior is thus invalid with respect to the true degree of handicap. Others behave toward him much more realistically, however, in that their behavior is commensurate with the true degree of handicap that exists. Because Fred's behavior does not mesh with that of others in respect to the degree of handicap, we may say that there is *role asynchrony* between him and others. The source of the asynchrony is *self originated,* for Fred has chosen essentially invalid behavioral options. This particular variety of role asynchrony, in the context of disability, might be termed *autistic normalcy.*

Valid Role Synchronies

The significance of role asynchrony and of invalidity is highlighted by considering the typical role relationship characterizing the interactions of most persons, namely, that of valid role synchronies. The nondisabled person typically behaves in a normal fashion with others, and he thus may be said to be performing validly; and others relate to him on the assumption that he is normal, and their behaviors vis-a-vis him are appropriately complementary. This might be called *true normalcy* and is a valid role synchrony which characterizes the large majority of the normal interaction encounters of nondisabled persons and, of course, it is characteristic for nondisabled persons prior to their disability (see Table 1). The problem posed by the advent of disability is that the valid role synchrony of true normalcy becomes less common and, in certain cases, is virtually ruled out.

TABLE 1. *Varieties of Synchrony of Repertoires of Role Behavior for Self and Others*

	Behavioral Options of Others	
Behavioral Options of Self	Behaviors Appropriate for a Handicapped Self	Behaviors Appropriate for a Normal Self
Handicapped Behaviors		
Correct for self	I. True handicap	II. Imposed normalcy
Incorrect for self	III. Fictionalized handicap	IV. Autistic handicap
Nonhandicapped Behaviors		
Correct for self	V. Imposed handicap	VI. True normalcy
Incorrect for self	VII. Autistic normalcy	VIII. Fictionalized normalcy

The ideal interaction encounter, from the perspective of role theory, is the valid role synchrony. Because the synchrony we have called true normalcy is generally precluded for the disabled person, the appropriate valid role synchrony for the disabled is therefore that which might be called *true handicap*. This is defined by behavior on the part of the disabled person commensurate with the true degree of handicap, and by related behavior of others also commensurate with the actual degree of the disabled person's handicap (see Table 1).[23] Interaction contexts in which this form of valid role synchrony is most likely to occur are the hospital, where the disabled person is on a ward with similarly disabled individuals cared for by a perceptive and competent staff, and in the disabled person's own family, assuming of course that he and his family members behave realistically. Interaction encounters outside of these more protected contexts have a greatly increased likelihood of being either asynchronous or invalid synchronies.

Invalid Role Synchronies

There are two varieties of invalid role synchrony to which the disabled are peculiarly subject. The first is characterized by a form of mutual denial of the disability in which the disabled performs in a manner implying or indicating less handicap than truly exists, coupled with the behavior of others toward him which analogously is appropriate for the absence of the handicap (see Table 1). This might be called *fictitious normalcy*. In his analysis of polio victims and their families, Davis has described an extreme case of what he termed normalization.[24] This was the case of six-year-old Laura Paulus, the most handicapped child in his group of nine study participants. Laura wore full-length braces on both legs, a pelvic band, high orthopedic shoes and had to use crutches. From a purely physical standpoint, she was extremely limited in what she could do. Her energetic mother was determined, however, to make Laura "normal." She was registered in the school that she attended before her illness, and took a regular city bus to school; parties, games and other festivities were held for her and she was enrolled in a Brownie troop. By joining willingly with her mother in this normalization, Laura was entering into fictitious normalcy. If the situation of fictitious normalcy is enduring and his health and rehabilitation depends upon how well he cares for himself, the disabled may of course expose himself to unnecessary hazards. The excessive striving, in any case, may greatly increase role strain.

The second invalid role synchrony is the *fictitious handicap*. This, too, involves a pluralistic deception, for the disabled and others jointly adopt invalid behaviors in terms of the disabled person's true degree of handicap; but fictitious handicap also involves behavior on the part of the disabled and others that exaggerates the actual degree of handicap. Many of the examples of so-called overprotection cited in the literature on disability would be illustrative here (see Table 1).

LD was a 40-year-old insurance salesman married to an aggressive, strong-willed woman at the time of his first heart attack. The attack proved to be a mildly disabling condition which left the patient with shortness of breath when performing physical labor over an extended period of time. Thorough medical examination revealed he was able to continue with his work on a reduced schedule. Mrs. D, however, was fearful that continued work of any nature would result in further attacks, or even death, in spite of medical reassurance to the contrary. She earned an adequate income to support both herself and her husband, and convinced him without difficulty that he should not return to work. Both refused repeated offers to help.[25]

The difficulty with fictitious handicap, clearly, is that as long as such a situation exists the disabled person will perform at a lower level than is necessitated by his disability.

Role Asynchronies

Role asynchronies occur when either the disabled person or the other adopts invalid behavior with respect to the true degree of the disabled person's handicap. We have already made reference to autistic normalcy in our example of Fred. Another self-originating asynchrony is *autistic handicap*. Here the individual displays more handicapped behavior than the disability actually warrants while others behave toward him in a fashion commensurate with the true degree of handicap (see Table 1). This is a variety of hypochondriasis for the disabled, as it were.

HB, a 35-year-old married Southern Missouri sharecropper with five children, had a brain infection five years prior to being referred for social casework help. The infection left him with a mild shuffling gait and general slowed ability to move hands and arms. Formerly an unskilled laborer, he quickly settled into apathy and developed a passive attitude toward various rehabilitative efforts which were attempted with him. His wife was unable to convince her husband that he should take more responsibility in helping himself since he believed he had a more serious and incapacitating illness than the doctors advised. The patient and his wife went on public assistance, and subsequent efforts toward re-employment became feebler with the patient finding numerous reasons why he could not work.[26]

Both autistic handicap and autistic normalcy are self originating, i.e., they derive from invalid behaviors and assumptions on the part of the disabled person himself. All kinds of personal and environmental conditions may generate these particular autisms, as the clinical examples in the rehabilitation literature amply demonstrate. Emotional difficulties are most patently likely to be operative in such cases.

In contrast to these asynchronies, there are two others that arise from the invalid behaviors of others. For this reason these have been called the imposed role asynchronies. The first, an *imposed handicap,* occurs when others behave toward the disabled person as if he were more handicapped than he actually is, while the disabled behaves validly (see Table 1).

> Joe was a 19-year-old plumber's apprentice when he was critically injured in an automobile accident resulting in what was at first considered severe brain damage. Gradually and unexpectedly, he improved to the point where he was considered medically capable of continuing in his previous occupation in spite of some clumsiness and a slight tendency to lose balance. Although both the patient and his employer were eager for him to resume work, his parents vigorously resisted and successfully interrupted his return to work. They had nursed him back from a critical illness, "protected" him to the extent of doing for him needlessly, and were fearful he would "get hurt" on the job and that it would be their "fault" if anything further should happen to him.[27]

An enduring imposed handicap may clearly eventuate in a fictitious handicap. In response to the extreme solicitousness, in other words, the disabled individual may succumb, lowering his performance to a level less than that of his true handicap.

The second asynchrony is that of *imposed normalcy.* Here the others who relate to the disabled person behave toward him as if he were less handicapped than he truly is, while the disabled maintains valid behavior (see Table 1). The case of Laura Paulus cited earlier would illustrate imposed normalcy had Mrs. Paulus foisted the normalization on Laura against her wishes. An imposed normalcy probably exists early in the development of fictitious normalcy, especially when the disabled are children. One apparent difficulty with imposed normalcy is that the disabled person is constrained to perform above the level appropriate to the true degree of his handicap.

These are the eight varieties of role synchrony for the disabled. The details of their exposition should not obscure the two basic points. The first is that disability generally restricts the possibilities for valid role-synchronic encounters, and the second is that the particular problems of role synchrony characteristic of the disabled appear either as an invalid role synchrony or as a role asynchrony. The particular problems of synchrony may be complexly patterned in the life of any given disabled person. The more enduring contexts of human encounter—such as home, school, and work—may involve one or more varieties of synchronic difficulty, and the more fleeting, casual encounters may involve different and possibly highly diverse confrontations.

Underlying Conditions

A basic condition that gives rise to these problems of role synchrony is that society has not provided a social niche for the disabled that is as clear, predictable, and as guiding as that which the nondisabled enjoys. There simply are not uniform, clear rules for disabled persons in the same way that there are rules for the performance of nondisabled persons, and the rules and conceptions that are held for these persons are generally diverse and lacking in agreement. Furthermore, an uncommon ignorance pervades the situation for the disabled. There is a widespread lack of public knowledge concerning the various types of disabilities, and there are many stereotypes concerning the disabled that substitute for genuine knowledge and operate along with ignorance. Contributing to the uncertainty is the disabled person himself; unless he is known rather well, he presents an ambiguous stimulus, as it were, in human form. The individual encounter with a disabled person is fraught with uncertainty about the conditions of his particular impairment, combined with ignorance of the individual personality and of how he has coped with his disability.

This lack of tradition, consensus, and knowledge—of institutionalization in general—surrounding the social niche of the disabled, has a singular consequence: the customary social moorings that control the choice of behavior in human encounters are weakened. The disabled and those who behave toward them consequently have more choices of behavioral alternatives. Speaking more generally, there is *role optionality,* a condition that is defined by the existence of two or more behavioral repertoires, each of which (1) attaches to a different social position, (2) has different implications for the person behaving and for the others with whom he interacts, and (3) lacks definition by the society and culture as preferred over other alternatives.

The main axis with respect to which the optionality exists for the disabled concerns that of normalcy versus disability, these being the central, opposing behavior repertoires. The disabled may behave so as to imply a greater or lesser handicap than he has, or he may behave consistently with the true degree of handicap. If he behaves consistently with the true degree of handicap, he may be said to be performing validly, as we have observed. And the other person (or persons) who interact with him may behave in analogous terms; i.e., they may perform so as to imply a greater or lesser degree of handicap than actually exists, or they may behave consistently with the actual degree of handicap. If the other (or others) behave toward the disabled commensurate with the actual degree of his handicap, then the performance may be said to be valid. Without a condition of role optionality for the disabled or for those with whom he interacts, problems of role synchrony would not exist.

Now, given these behavioral options the question is what factors determine which choices will be made. In short, what conditions determine whether the disabled will choose valid or invalid options and analogously, what affects the selection of options when others behave with a disabled person? There are a few conditions that immediately come to mind.

The first is the very degree of disablement. The nondisabled person obviously has little occasion to perform as if he were handicapped, and others are most unlikely to relate to him as if he were handicapped. Also, the person who is nearly totally handicapped in all areas of functioning is going to have little role optionality with respect to performing as a nondisabled person. Others, however, may or may not perform toward him as if he were as severely handicapped and thus even the totally disabled may face problems of role synchrony. Thus we see that occasions for invalid role options—and the consequent difficulties of synchrony—are more likely to be posed for persons who are partially, rather than more extensively, disabled.

Visibility of the disability also affects the behavioral options, especially those of the others who relate to the disabled person. The casual encounter with an individual with a visible impairment may cause others to behave toward him as if he were more disabled than he actually is, thus creating the occasion for what we have called an imposed handicap and possibly fictitious handicap as well. The situation is different for the disabled with an essentially nonvisible impairment, for cues are generally not present to signify disablement and, for that reason, others frequently behave toward him as if he were normal. Under these conditions, for the nonvisibly disabled, we would therefore anticipate that there would be problems of role synchrony involving either fictitious or imposed normalcy.

The disabled person's acceptance of his disabled condition is still another factor which influences behavioral options. If he fails to acknowledge his impairment and behaves accordingly, his denial clearly increases the probability that his encounters with others will involve the particular asynchrony called autistic normalcy. Analogously, if the person accepts his disability with resignation and denigration his behavioral options may well be biased toward excessive handicapping. This creates the conditions for the particular asynchrony called autistic handicap. Only when acceptance involves a realistic appraisal of one's impairment along with behavior commensurate with this viewpoint on the part of the disabled person are the conditions established for averting asynchronies that derive from invalid, self-originated behaviors. Although the proper acceptance of the disability by the disabled person does not guarantee, of course, that others will adopt valid options in their encounters with him, the disabled person's genuine acceptance of his impairment, when communicated to others, may greatly increase the chances that they will similarly adopt valid behaviors when interacting with him.

The society and culture also shape the choice of options, directing them mainly toward normalization. The design of society is based on the premise that its members are not disabled. As many writers have observed, the society has been created and is run for the benefit of the normal person. Also, the cultural values in the United States—stressing self-reliance, independence, and autonomy as they do—bias choice toward behaviors that would be designated as normal.

Independence is esteemed, and there is still some stigma, generally covert and subtle, which attaches to most every disability.

These pressures toward the normalization of behavior are to be pitted against essentially countervailing conditions that constrain the disabled to select the invalid options of excessive handicapping. I am thinking particularly of the factors that give rise to self pity, to secondary gains from disability, and to the solicitude of others in general. Humanitarian mores constrain others to err generously rather than niggardly in the public treatment of the disabled, and the pain and stress of disablement conspire, along with various personality factors, to make the disabled accept and sometimes to exploit these opportunities for attention, love, and care.

SUMMARY

The perspective of role theory was employed in this analysis of the disabled. Two general topics were discussed, the first being that of the roles of the disabled. Five disability-related roles were described: the disabled patient, handicapped performer, helped person, disability comanager, and public relations man.

The second topic concerned the problems of role that may attend disablement. These problems were those of role discontinuity, role conflict, conflict of role definition, nonfacilitative interdependence, role strain, and the special difficulties of role synchrony. In addition to the synchronies of true normalcy (precluded for the disabled by virtue of the impairment) and true handicap (an ideal and sometimes uncommon encounter), the asynchronies of imposed normalcy and imposed handicap and of autistic normalcy and autistic handicap were discussed, as were the invalid synchronies of fictionalized handicap and fictionalized normalcy. Defining conditions and clinical examples were elaborated.

The conditions underlying the various problems of role synchrony were discussed, among these being role optionality, the extent of disablement, the visibility of the impairment, the acceptance of the disability, and selected societal and personal factors.

PROBLEM CONCEPTION AND
PLANNED INTERVENTION

David M. Kaplan

THE GOAL of rehabilitation is the restoration to effective functioning of individuals who have been disabled by disease or other causes.

In a comprehensive health strategy, rehabilitation represents the terminal process in a continuum of intervention beginning with prevention and including treatment as the intermediate phase. The aims of these three related processes are:

1. The maintenance of health by preventive measures in individuals who are free from disease;
2. The limitation of disability in those who become ill, through treatment; and
3. The restoration of those individuals disabled by disease, through rehabilitation.

The effectiveness of this health strategy is dependent upon how well we understand the nature and varieties of the diseases and problems that beset human beings. Our nosology, the system by which we classify and conceptualize diseases and problems, profoundly influences the focus, strategy, and logistics of our planned intervention. Our conception of the nature and varieties of human problems prescribes what we think needs to be prevented, treated, or rehabilitated and how we should proceed with these tasks.

The nosology of somatic medicine includes two major disease conceptions. One category encompasses chronic diseases such as cancer, arthritis, heart disease, and other ailments. The other category refers to acute infectious diseases, includ-

Reprinted with permission of the author and publisher from *Health and Disability Concepts in Social Work Education,* Minneapolis Minn., United States Department of Health, Education, and Welfare, Vocational Rehabilitation Administration (April 1964), pp. 5–15.

ing a host of illnesses precipitated by bacteriologic and viral agents, such as polio, measles, diphtheria, small pox, etc. These two disease conceptions have separate and unique etiologies.

Psychiatric disease classification, in contrast, contains only one disease conception, that of chronic disorders.

Because a good deal is known about the etiology of the acute infectious diseases, much progress in disease control has been made at all health levels. The success of medicine in preventing and treating acute somatic disorders has substantially reduced infant mortality, increased the human life span by many years, and reduced drastically the prevalence of chronic somatic disorders which would otherwise occur as a residue of acute somatic diseases. The reduced incidence of rheumatic heart disease cases which results from successful prevention or treatment of septic sore throat is one example of disease control inherent in this classificatory system.

As a direct consequence of this two-field classification of somatic diseases, there is a smaller pool of the chronic physically disabled to rehabilitate. Moreover, an important segment of the rehabilitation effort can be addressed to those individuals who have been disabled by acute disorders. Rehabilitation experience indicates a considerably greater success is achieved with patients who are disabled by acute illness. The acutely-disabled patient does not ordinarily have to contend with a long history of illness, disability of prolonged absence from effective functioning. This syndrome, found with much greater frequency among those disabled by chronic disorders, constitutes a rehabilitation problem of considerable proportions.[1]

In recent years social work has been urged to devote more of its efforts to those problems which are a result of the current interaction between the individual and his environment. Boehm, for example, suggests that we view the individual and his environment not as two separate entities, but as a continuous process of interaction. In this formulation social work places its primary focus on the *process of current psychosocial interaction:*

More and more it appears that social work is essential at that point in the interaction between the individual and his social environment where, either through limitations within the individual or because of his situation and the nature of his environment, effective functioning is hampered or has broken down.[2]

This recommended focus on problems of current interaction provides an opportunity to develop a new theory with which to diagnose, study, and treat this important group of human problems—a theory which may place us in a favorable position comparable to that of somatic medicine with its dual system of disease classification.

Problems of current psycho-social interaction have been appropriately conceived of as situations involving individuals reacting to different types of stress. Those problems, a result of acute environmental pressures, constitute the particular focus of this presentation.

In psychiatric theory, reaction to stress and stress outcome has traditionally been accounted for by the "stress-personality" formulation in which it is assumed that individual behavior in stress situations is determined basically by pre-stress personality.[3] Put in simple terms, the theory assumes that an individual with a healthy personality will have a good chance of mastering a given stress situation; conversely, that an unhealthy personality will have trouble in coping with stress.

During World War II and the Korean Conflict, several attempts were made by psychiatrists to predict the performance of soldiers who might later experience military stress.

These predictions, made on reasonably large samples of soldiers, were based upon psychiatric personality assessments. The predictive studies serve as an empirical test of the "stress-personality" theory. Results of these studies in both World War II and the Korean Conflict were substantially alike—in both studies a surprisingly large number of those soldiers who had been expected to do poorly did well. Only twenty-five per cent (25%) of the psychiatrists' predictions of unsatisfactory service proved to be correct; whereas their estimates of satisfactory service proved ninety per cent (90%) accurate.[4]

In subsequent evaluations of these predictions, psychiatrists attributed the satisfactory military performance of those from whom poor results had been anticipated to the influence of situational factors such as group unity, good leadership, quality of communication, etc.[5] In the military stress situation, current psychological factors apparently had the power to affect significant personality deficiencies.

In a more recent attempt to screen volunteers for the Peace Corps, Dr. Israel Zwerling, a psychiatrist, described the experiment as follows:

My training and experience have provided me with knowledge about mental illness and some competence in its recognition, diagnosis, and treatment. Setting aside for awhile the question of what mental health is, it is at this point only relevant that it certainly is not solely the absence of mental illness; and one may reasonably question whether psychiatry has any special contribution to make to a discussion of mental health beyond this single dimension of the absence of illness. I had a very recent and very pointed reminder of this limitation. I was in charge of a team of eight psychiatrists for the screening of Peace Corps volunteers gathered for training for a project in South America. The psychiatrists interviewed each volunteer upon his arrival at the training site. They then summarized their findings in a traditional psychiatric history and on a rating scale devised for this purpose, and offered two prognoses, one as to the amount and kind of psycho-pathology which was likely to appear under the conditions of life in the overseas assignment, and one as to the level of effectiveness of functioning which could be expected. At the end of a very rigorous training period the men were evaluated and the selection of the required number made from the larger number who completed training. A careful correlation of the training evaluations with the psychiatric predictions revealed two facts:

1. When the psychiatrists found substantial amounts of illness and judged that there would be serious interference with effective functioning, their predictions were most impressively accurate.

2. When the psychiatrists did not find substantial amounts of illness and made judgments purely on the basis of ego strengths, the quality of object relationships, the motivational system, and the cognitive capacities of the volunteers, their predictions about effective functioning were barely better than chance.

Psychiatrists, then, are competent assessors of illness, but are doubtful assessors of wellness or of health. (Parenthetically, I have here implicitly sneaked in one of my criteria for mental health—i.e., effective functioning.)[6]

The result of these predictive studies of military performance as well as the findings of other predictive studies based on personality assessment[7] suggest an important modification of "stress-personality" theory to account more adequately for stress outcome, i.e., the "stress-personality" formula required modification so as to include situational factors as a major additional theoretical component.

What are the implications for treatment of the "stress-personality" theory modified so as to include situational factors? Under the original formulation the treatment attitude in stress situations is one of pessimism. Little can be done to improve the outcome if the response to stress is thought to be determined by pre-stress personality. Col. A. J. Glass, who was Chief Psychiatrist Consultant for the United States Army, describes the early military psychiatric experience in World War II as follows:

The difficulties encountered in recovering patients for combat duty . . . influenced many of the psychiatrists, including the writer, to place undue emphasis upon predisposition or personality as a major etiologic agent in the war neuroses. The well known formula, "stress plus personality equals reactions," was seized upon to provide a simple rational basis for explaining the cause of psychological break-down in battle . . . Unfortunately, the stress personality concept tended to produce a defeatist and fatalistic approach to the problem of war neuroses. From a practical standpoint neither the amount of external trauma nor the strength of various personality constituents can be measured with the accuracy required for the operation of the stress personality formula . . . But even more important are the many imponderable elements of battle, such as an inspiring leader, a strong buddy, group unity, and the quality of communication and physiological status. . . .[8]

The revised stress formulation which includes current situational factors as an important theoretical component provides a more optimistic basis for intervention in individual stress reactions. *Under this theory treatment which takes place in the period immediately following the stress event, that is based upon greater knowledge of stress situations and the appropriate use of current situational factors, can influence response and outcome for the better.*

In the last twenty (20) years a number of studies of acute stress situations have been made which support the modified stress theory and also lend credence to the conceptualization of a new category of psychiatric disorders.[9]

These studies suggest that responses to acute stress may appropriately be conceived of as psychological phenomena with their own special structure and dynamics. The evidence from these stress studies suggests that acute stress response represents a discrete and distinct form of emotional disorder whose essential form is more comparable to the acute infectious disease model than to the structure of the chronic mental disorder under which category acute emotional responses are currently subsumed. Leopold and Dillon, in their analysis of reactions to trauma, state:

. . . the psychiatric community as a whole has failed to recognize the significance of the nature of the trauma itself, and particularly its suddenness, in the development of the post-traumatic states. For reasons not entirely clear it appears more usual to regard the pre-trauma personality as a major factor, and to relegate the trauma itself to the role of a mere triggering circumstance which sets off an illness considered almost certain to have occurred in any case. This approach discards the tremendous potential, from both the treatment and the research standpoint, which is available if one instead regards the post-traumatic psychological states as diagnostic categories in themselves. . . . These categories are unique in the cognizance they give to the role of the trauma itself in producing a discrete illness, which, in all likelihood, would not have occurred had there been no trauma.

The important question here, from the psychiatric standpoint, is why the normal coping techniques are inoperative. The psychiatric community will not find out by dismissing the trauma as merely an incidental factor. Nor can it adequately treat the post-traumatic psychiatric casualty unless it finds out first what this trauma in itself meant to this individual; unless it regards the post-traumatic psychological state as a separate entity which represents the failure of this individual's mechanisms for defending himself.[10]

Erich Lindemann's study of bereavement was the first study of acute stress to make use, at least implicitly, of this new theoretical formulation of acute emotional disorders.[11] His work suggests that acute stress disorders have the following characteristics:

1. These reactions are typically acute in nature with a specifiable onset and relatively brief period of duration regardless of whether outcome is adaptive or maladaptive.

2. These reactions follow a limited number of adaptive and maladaptive courses.

3. These courses of response are clinically identifiable and predictive of outcome.

4. The observable symptoms of stress response are not always signs of chronic mental illness, as we have long thought, but such symptoms are often *transitory* aspects of the struggle to master the stress situation.

5. The essence of the struggle for stress mastery can be specified by characteristic psychological tasks which each stress situation poses for the individual. It is possible to specify clearly what the individual must do, psychologically and behaviorally, to achieve mastery of each stress problem.

Jahoda, in discussing criteria for defining mental health, suggests that there are two different but equally important standards for such measurement.[12] She points out that mental health can be defined as *a function of personality* alone; this method of assessment leads to a *classification of individuals as more or less healthy*. In the second method, mental health is defined as a *function of personality and situation*, which leads to a *classification of individual actions as being healthy or unhealthy*. In the acute emotional disorder conception, mental health is measured by the second method, by classifying healthy and unhealthy actions. The actions of the individual under stress reflect the adequacy of his coping with the psychological tasks posed by a stress situation.[6] Clinical intervention in stress situations can help a large proportion of those having difficulty mastering the problem, primarily, by focusing on the successful accomplishment of the stress tasks. Such therapy is generally brief, but it may be intensive and limited to the period of acute disturbance.

In one of the studies of reactions to premature birth which the author conducted as a member of Gerald Caplan's group at the Harvard School of Public Health, the primary objective was to test the nosological assumptions derived from Lindemann's bereavement.[13] Specifically, the aims of this study were:

1. To determine the psychological tasks whose successful completion are required for mastery of the premature birth crises

2. To identify clinically the adaptive and maladaptive responses to premature birth
3. To predict outcome from this stress situation on the basis of whether the early maternal response was adaptive or maladaptive

This study excluded any planned clinical intervention. It was reasoned that if the study attained these objectives, it would lend support to the concept of acute emotional disorders as a discrete disease entity.

Detailed case records of family reactions to premature birth were studied in order to identify typical patterns of mothers who apparently mastered the problems posed by premature birth and a contrasting group of cases in which the problems were not mastered. In the first group the outcome seemed good, in that the mother developed a healthy relationship to the baby in the first two months of home care. She gave the infant realistic care in relation to its needs; she took pride and satisfaction in handling the baby; and she saw the child as potentially normal.

The cases also included mothers who did not follow the above pattern. Some mothers handled the hazard to the life of the baby and their own maternal failure by denial. Other mothers failed to respond with hope to the indications of survival and satisfactory development of the infant. In these cases it appeared that the baby continued to symbolize the mother's failure, despite its progress, and she continued to perceive the infant in a distorted way, as though impending death or abnormality were assured. This perception seriously impeded the mother's sensitivity to the baby's real needs. Other mothers either took insufficient precautions in sheltering the baby—that is, treated it "like a normal infant," or they continued to coddle and over-protect it after such special care was no longer realistically necessary.

In these cases, the problems posed by prematurity were not adequately accomplished or not in the optimal time period; and the mother's handling as well as her attitude towards the baby at the end of the study period seemed less healthy than in the other group. Such mothers did not seem perceptive of the needs of their babies. They overprotected or underprotected them. They overfed or underfed them. They showed a lack of pride in them, and there were varied signs of tension in the mother-child relationship.

The study focused upon the mother's experience with premature birth and upon the successive problems with which she was confronted by this crisis. On the basis of clinical study, five major psychological tasks were identified which appeared to be characteristic of this experience for most mothers. The adequate accomplishment of these tasks appeared to be essential for successful mastery of the premie crisis situation and for a healthy mother-child relationship in early stages. The following were postulated as the five tasks posed by premature birth:

1. The first task confronts the mother at the time of delivery. It is the preparation for the possible loss of the infant whose life is in jeopardy. This "anticipatory grief" for possible object loss involves a withdrawal from the relationship already begun during pregnancy with the expected child. The mother immediately after the premature delivery hopes the infant will survive, but simultaneously and realistically she prepares herself for its possible death.

2. At approximately the same time the mother must face and accept her feelings of failure which result from not having delivered a normal, full-term baby. The mother struggles with both of these tasks until the infant's chances for survival seem secure.

3. According to its weight and physical condition, the baby may continue to remain in the hospital for a further period of one to ten weeks. During this period the third and fourth tasks need to be accomplished. The third task involves the resumption of the process of relating to the infant as a forthcoming member of the family and an immediate care responsibility of the mother. The mother has lost the normal opportunity provided by a full-time pregnancy for the development of readiness for the mothering role. She had to prepare herself earlier for the infant's death, but as its chances for survival improve, she must respond with hope and anticipation. She must realize that she will, after all, be able to retrieve a good measure of her hopes from what earlier had appeared to be a tragic situation. Characteristically, there is a point at which the mother really begins to

believe that her baby will survive. The event which stimulates activity on her third task may be the infant's gain in weight, a new feeding pattern, a change in its activity or appearance, or an encouraging optimism in the nurse's or physician's attitude.

4. The fourth task faces the mother with the challenge of understanding how a premature baby differs from a normal baby in terms of its special needs and growth patterns. This task is in preparation for her imminent job of caring for the infant when it comes home. The accomplishment of the fourth task takes place while she is visiting the nursery, observing the baby's appearance and behavior, talking with the doctors and nurses, reading infant books, or discussing baby care with other mothers of prematures.

5. In order to provide the baby with the necessary extra care and protection, the mother must see the infant as a premature with special needs and characteristics. But it is equally important for her to see that these special needs are temporary and will yield in time to more normal patterns. Her task is to take necessary precautions without depriving herself and the child of enjoyable interactions.

Following the identification of the psychological tasks and of the characteristic adaptive and maladaptive responses to premature birth, the second phase of the study was initiated. In this phase a quantitative study was conducted to test the hypothesis that premie task accomplishment was associated with outcome—that is, successful task accomplishment was predictive of good outcome in the premature birth crisis, while failure to complete these tasks led to poor outcome.

Thirty (30) longitudinal case studies of families in which premature birth had occurred were selected for the test. These families had been studied intensively from the period shortly after birth of their premature infants until two months of home care had elapsed. Each case study consisted of at least ten home visits. Each carefully-recorded home visit included interview and observational data on both maternal and family reactions to premature birth and the premature infant.

The data of each of the thirty case studies were divided into two consecutive sections, and these two sections were rated independently by separate sets of evaluators who had access only to records of one section of the case being rated. The first rating was of the maternal coping pattern manifested after birth until the infant's discharge from the hospital to home. The second rating was of the maternal care pattern manifested during the first two months of home care.

On the basis of the rating of maternal coping pattern, a prediction of outcome was made in each of the thirty cases. Using a three-category classification of good, poor, and very poor outcome, these predictions proved accurate in twenty-four (24) out of thirty (30) cases or eighty per cent (80%) successful.[14]

Predicting Outcome on Basis of
Maternal Coping Patterns

	Outcome		
	Good (N=18)	Poor (N=10)	Very Poor (N=2)
14 cases— Good outcome predicted	13	1	0
14 cases— Poor outcome predicted	5	9	0
2 cases— Very poor outcome predicted	0	0	2
	60%	33%	7%

.01>P>.001.

One variable—the mother's pattern of visiting her infant while the infant was cared for in the hospital premie nursery —was most closely associated with outcome. In twenty-seven (27) out of thirty (30) cases the visiting pattern was predictive of outcome—that is, visiting pattern was an accurate predictor in nine (9) out of ten (10) instances. The mother who visited her infant once a week or more appeared, by the last two weeks of the infant's stay in the nursery, to have successfully worked through the premie tasks—good outcome was virtually assured in such instances.[15]

Relationship Between Maternal
Nursery Visiting and Outcome

| | Outcome | |
| | Good | Poor |
	(N=18)	(N=12)
Active nursery visiting	17	2
Inactive nursery visiting	1	10

.02>P>.01.

The predictive test in these thirty cases indicated:

1. That premature birth outcome is closely associated with the ability to resolve the tasks posed by premature birth.
2. That there are clinically observable, behavioral indications of the maternal ability to master the premature birth crisis specified in consistent courses in the medical sense of this term

In other words, we discovered that it was possible to differentiate those families in which the mother was handling the stress of premature birth successfully from those in which the mother was having difficulty in mastering this stress and headed for trouble in her early relation with the infant. With this ability to differentiate healthy from unhealthy coping in the premature birth situation, some preliminary attempts were made to treat mothers having clear difficulty in handling premature birth, based on knowledge gained of this stress situation and the tasks posed for the mother by premature birth.

For this presentation, a case involving treatment attempts will be described briefly. The case came into treatment because of early maternal difficulty in handling a premie.

THE CASE

The V. family was one of those in the Boston premie study. Family members included father, age 28; mother 27; and three boys, 3, 1½ and the newborn premie: The infant was about three or four weeks premature and weighed four pounds, fourteen ounces at birth. Family contact began shortly after the premature birth.

Relationships in the family between the parents and children were very positive prior to the premature birth. Father was affectionate with his wife and close to his older children. He was disappointed in his vocational hope to become a musician, but he had a good work history and steady employment as a mechanic and television repairman. Prior to the premature birth, the family had been slowly acquiring new furniture. The father had bought a recent-model used car shortly before the birth of the premie. He was strongly supported by his wife, who did much to build up his ego when he expressed self doubts. The mother was devoted to her family. Her children, the two older boys, were healthy, bright, attractive, loved, but not over-indulged by their parents. Of the parents, the mother appeared to be the stronger person, although she was careful not to make her strength obvious; she deferred to her husband as the leader of the family.

There was a history of mental illness in the families of both parents. The maternal grandmother had been hospitalized since mother was eight years old. Mother visited grandmother regularly all her life. The father's spinster sister, who lived with the paternal grandparents, had suffered an acute breakdown as an adult and was hospitalized once for several months. Mother also had Cooley's anemia, a hereditary disease. This condition was kept under control by regular iron intake. None of her children inherited the anemia.

The birth of the premie was a cause of considerable disruption in the family—the two older children had been born normally at term. The father was not supportive at all to the wife with respect to the premature birth. He blamed her anemia for the premature delivery and was convinced that the infant was seriously damaged. This perception was augmented by an intestinal block which required surgery, before the infant was released to the home. The family had allowed hospitalization insurance to lapse and consequently had to contend with a large medical bill. For this expense the father also blamed the mother.

In the hospital the mother controlled her feelings and did not appear to be disturbed. She did not cry or protest being in a room with another mother whose normal baby was brought in regularly for feeding. Actually, the premature birth was a great concern for the mother, but she repressed it at first. Later she revealed her feeling of having let the father down. For a woman who valued her family so much, her failure to deliver normally was a great burden and disappointment. Both parents were concerned about the infant's inheriting physical and mental defects. The father's attitude to the premie was especially difficult for the mother, whose normal response was to support the father. In this situation she badly needed his support and approval of the premie, but was in serious conflict about defending herself and the child while she recognized the father's concern about the infant and the money problems created by surgery and prolonged hospitalization of the infant.

The mother visited the hospital nursery once per week at the outset but seemed to get little satisfaction from these visits. The frequency of the visits dropped shortly before discharge of the infant. The pediatrician urged the mother to visit the nursery to become familiar with the care of the infant, but she made only one such visit although she was invited to come to the nursery as often as possible. The family delayed the infant's discharge from the hospital, expressing concern about possible defects in the infant, despite encouraging pediatric reports.

When the infant finally was brought home, the father at first refused to care for the child in any way. He developed G.I. trouble which interfered with his working. The mother, under great pressure, had difficulty in managing her household chores, which previously presented no problem. She felt responsible for the complete care of the premie and the two older boys without help from the father. She did not recover well from the delivery, slept poorly, felt continually fatigued, and soon developed "headaches" that turned out to be acute depersonalization experiences lasting ten to fifteen minutes each. During these periods no one could communicate with her.

Both parents began to describe the infant as a "nervous" baby and became concerned when the older boys made any noise or commotion in the house. The infant's normal startle reaction was cited as evidence of "nervousness." The observation of the infant by the pediatrician and research interviewer did not confirm parents' view of infant's nervousness. The infant gained weight slowly but progressed satisfactorily.

At the end of the study visits the father asked how the family compared with other study families in the handling of the premie crisis. The interviewer took the opportunity provided by this question to try to improve the situation. Part of the report follows:

In response to the father's question, I said that, compared with other families, they had shown a considerable amount of concern about their infant. I referred to their reaction specifically as "over concern." At this point the mother looked very keenly at the father and gratefully at me for my remarks, but made no comment of her own to the father. The father said that he did not feel that he was overly concerned.

These remarks were followed by an argument between the parents, with the mother complaining and the father on the defensive. He was not helpful enough with the children; he resented her leaving the children even briefly to go out; he didn't give her enough say over money management. The father countered by saying her place was with the children and he had given her say over money, but she had handled it poorly. They argued over whether to repair the old car or buy a new one; the father blamed the mother's "blood condition" for high medical bills in connection with the premie birth.

I left the home with the father walking me to the car. He again referred to the family's response to the premie. I pointed out that the pediatrician was pleased with the infant's progress. The father said he was still not sure how the infant would develop. I asked when he would feel more comfortable, and he ruefully replied, "When the baby will be 21."

On the next visit, the mother talked more cheerfully about the premie's progress. The pediatrician said the child did not have anemia. The infant had been eating some solids and sleeping through the night. The father had not been working steadily but was returning to work. The mother referred to my last visit, saying she had had no "headache" since then. She could now believe the doctor, who felt good about the premie's progress. The care of the infant and the home was improving. She said the father was feeling better too; he had less G.I. difficulty. He had for the first time fed the infant. She described this with a big smile. The mother had much less concern about the baby's future development; she felt he would be okay.

I referred to the concern I had observed that the mother had in relation to illness and children. She said she thought this went back to her childhood. She recalled as a child a fight she had had with her father when she told him, "I wish I were like mother in the hospital."

The mother recalled her reactions to the premature birth. She did not cry in the hospital but let her feelings build up. She thought this was the reason for her "headaches." In the hospital she slept and ate well. She remembered missing the baby, but she was not aware of a feeling of sadness. She recalled that when the baby was moved out of her hospital [room], she played that she was visiting the baby and imagined what he was like. The other mothers, particularly the one with whom she roomed, were quite free to talk about their own babies because Mrs. V. did not seem upset about not having her baby with her. She thought that her own response to the baby's difficulties—of not being upset—related to the fact that she had had a lot of experience with illness. She said she didn't become weepy until she returned home. She was in the hospital in a semi-private room in the obstetrics ward, and she recalled that when they told her the baby needed an operation, she became tremulous and nervous, but her husband was very matter-of-fact. He told her that the doctors were confident they could handle the situation. He held off telling her any bad news. The fact that she knew her husband was not upset and seemed to be in control of his feelings gave her comfort.

The improvement in the mother's outlook and in the relationship between the parents and the premie was maintained during the next several weeks without any indication of the earlier problem.

This case material can be discussed from several different points of view. I would like to make some observations about the material which are related to the theme of this paper.

The focus of treatment was the disruption in the family balance and in parental roles which was precipitated by the premature birth. The treatment plan grew out of special knowledge of the acute problems posed by premature birth and was deliberately limited to improving relations between: (1) parents and child and (2) between the parents themselves in relation to the problem that premature birth posed for them. Such crisis-focused treatment does not preclude the use of relevant, historical, dynamic information derived from the parents' own histories, but it does preclude any plan to change the basic personalities of the patient, which is often the goal of traditional psychotherapy. Perhaps, the most significant contribution of crisis therapy is in its preventive potential. When crisis therapy is successful, it precludes the internalization of traumatic experiences. Crisis intervention can effectively reduce thereby the formation of chronic emotional disorders.

I believe the case material illustrates a number of important principles in the treatment of acute crisis problems:

1. The importance of identifying the many and varied forms of acute problems which commonly occur in the lives of people. As Perlman suggests, these are problems that occur in addition to the chronic personality problems.

2. The value of studying each of these situational crises in depth in order to determine specific treatment measures. Intervention in situational crises must be based upon specific knowledge of each stress situation, for, while the reactions to different stresses appear to be similar in many respects, the treatment of any situational crisis must be based upon knowledge of each crisis rather than formulated in general terms. Information about personality history as well as knowledge of the individual's previous stress responses may be helpful in formulating crisis therapy. But neither personality evaluations nor history of previous stress response is enough knowledge on which to base crisis intervention without detailed knowledge of each crisis and the specific tasks posed by each crisis.

3. The need to provide the earliest possible treatment during the period of acute difficulty and not later on if we are to achieve treatment success.

4. The new theoretical concept that individual response to specific acute stress is treatable, based upon understanding of the psychological tasks specific to each crisis and upon appropriate use of current situational factors as well as individual historical material.

5. In general, recent research in acute stress situations suggests that as in the field of general medicine, psychiatric nosology does in fact include both acute and chronic disorders. Each category of disease has its own unique structure, etiology, and specific type of treatment. The general medical practitioner experiences professional satisfaction from the successful treatment of septic sore throat even when he realizes that the same patient suffers from a lung disorder which may or may not be treatable. He does not think of septic sore throat as a "superficial" problem, since he knows that if these infections go unattended, they may lead to rheumatic fever.

There is increasing evidence which suggests that the same

relation between acute and chronic conditions holds true for emotional as well as for somatic disorders. The mother with an acute problem such as premature birth who is not helped when she is having difficulty resolving this problem is more likely to contribute to the later development of chronic emotional disorders in her child.

ADEQUATE FAMILY FUNCTIONING

Paul H. Glasser and Lois N. Glasser

INTRODUCTION

Recent emphasis on family diagnosis and treatment of the family as a unit has led to new conceptions of the psychiatric patient and his family. Often associated with psychiatric illness is family disorganization. This maladaption of the group must be related to previous methods of organization, which in at least some respects were satisfactory, and which provide leads for successful organization in the future. Thus, family breakdown cannot be understood and dealt with without a concurrent understanding of adequate family functioning.

This report summarizes one section of a larger study of families in which at least one member of the primary group is undergoing psychotherapy. It was done with the cooperation of the staff of the Psychiatric Service at North Carolina Memorial Hospital. As an exploratory project, three families were studied in depth over a long period of time.[1] This paper focuses on the group problems families must solve to maintain adequate functioning.

Reprinted with permission of the publisher from *Family Structure Dynamics and Therapy, Psychiatric Research Report #20*, Irvin M. Cohen (ed.), (Washington, D.C.: American Psychiatric Association, 1966), pp. 8–17.

This investigation was partially supported by a National Institute of Mental Health Training Grant through the University of North Carolina Institute for Research in Social Science. The authors are especially indebted to Professors Harvey L. Smith, Reuben Hill, and Charles Bowerman, who served as advisors during the project.

FIVE CRITERIA OF ADEQUATE FAMILY FUNCTIONING

1. Internal role consistency among family members.
2. Consistency of family roles and norms and actual role performance.
3. Compatibility of family roles and norms with community norms.
4. Meeting the psychological needs of family members.
5. The ability of the family group to respond to change.

The ways in which each study family dealt with these social-psychological problems will be reviewed and illustrated, and the causes for the disruption of these patterns will be suggested. Implications for practice will be evident.

An adequately functioning family is defined as one engaged in the creation and preservation of the emotional well-being of its members.[2] This visualizes "emotional well-being" or personal adjustment as the dependent variable, the independent or antecedent variables being those patterns of family functioning which characterize an adequately functioning or competent family.

Internal Role Consistency

One basic requirement for adequate family functioning seems to be consistency of individual role expectations for oneself and others within the group. In order to behave appropriately in a way which contributes to the solution of family problems, each member must understand what is expected of himself and others. Each individual within the family must see himself in a way which is consistent with the way others see him.[3] In general, this was true for the members of each of the study families prior to the psychiatric illness of the patient and the beginning of family disorganization.

The O's were a couple in their early forties. Mr. O was a prominent minister in the community. Mr. O was seen by himself, his wife, and twelve year old daughter as primarily the family provider. In addition, his occupation as minister brought to the family a certain status in the community of which his wife and child were quite proud. As long as he was able to maintain this role in his own eyes and in the eyes of his family, the threat of family disorganization was minimized. Similarly, Mrs. O saw herself as the person who controlled the internal aspects of family life in a way which expedited the performance of her husband's role and led to the healthy development of her child. In this Mr. O agreed. These consistent expectations minimized conflict and contributed to smooth family functioning.

Despite socio-economic differences, a similar situation existed in the A family. The A's were a couple in their early forties who had been married twenty years, and had three children. Mr. A spent most of his occupational life as a mechanic in one of the largest mills in the Piedmont section of North Carolina. He was the consistent provider of physical needs, that is, food, clothing, and shelter. Mrs. A cared for the home and children. Mrs. A had been in a tuberculosis sanitarium for eight years and was able to resume her place in the family only five years before the study began. When Mrs. A was ill, her extended family took on her roles for her, but Mr. A continued to see himself in the same image. When Mr. A became physically ill with rheumatic heart disease, this image began to break down for himself and others, and the process of family disorganization was accelerated.

In the U family the situation was somewhat different. The U's were a couple in their late twenties who had married young, and each spouse had achieved little autonomy from his parents. What kept this family together was the consistency in expectations of the two families of orientation which the U's shared, and the emotional affection the spouses had for one another. When the two parental families began to openly disagree, after eight years of marriage, the U family became disorganized and the affectional bond between spouses became more precarious.

The criterion of internal role consistency is closely related to the concept of role integration. It implies a close fit among the roles of each family member; that is, high role complementarity and many shared norms within the group. However, consistency in expectations among the members of the family is only one step toward adequate family functioning.

Consistency of Family Roles and Norms and Actual Role Performance

To maintain consistent expectations and norms within the group, it is necessary that the members carry out their roles in the ways anticipated. Member behavior will tend either to reinforce previous expectations and norms, or require new definitions. In the adequately functioning family consistent patterns of behavior tend to persist, and new roles and norms tend to evolve over a considerable period of time. There are fewer abrupt changes in behavior which require new roles and norms than in families that are in the process of disorganization or reorganization.

These generalizations were confirmed in each of the families prior to the patient's initial signs of disturbance. All the husbands consistently provided for their families in the ways expected of them by their spouses and children. Mrs. O and Mrs. U handled the care of the home and the children in a manner which was acceptable to their husbands. When Mrs. A was unable to perform the expected roles, a second pattern evolved which continued while she was ill.

Internal role consistency, and consistency in member roles and actual behavior are indications of a minimum of role conflict and role confusion. Under these circumstances, however, it is still possible for there to be a great deal of role dissatisfaction. Families which appear to be functioning adequately may have the seeds of disorganization implanted within them. This will be discussed in greater detail below.

Compatibility of Family Roles and Norms with Societal Norms

The nature of the internal organization of the family must be carried out in behavior acceptable to the external system or environment surrounding it. Within the community other groups and organizations must perceive the family as functioning adequately. While there is considerable variation permitted in modern American society, the limits of such variation are narrowed a great deal for any particular family. Expectations placed upon the nuclear family by the extended family, neighbors, the school system, *etc.*, define in much greater detail how any one family should function within the community. If the family does not meet these expectations of the wider community, pressures will be put upon it to conform.

Before disorganization became apparent, all three families met these expectations well. Mr. O was a prominent minister; Mr. U inherited a third interest and control in his father's large and profitable business. These two families held rather high status positions within the community, and others thought them to be particularly happy and well adjusted. This was equally as true for the A family within their working class environment. Mr. A was admired for handling the difficult situation of his wife's long illness and hospitalization so well. His children were well cared for and he worked many extra hours to support them and pay the hospital bills. In general, the picture each family presented to the world immediately surrounding them tended to be a good one.

Meeting the Psychological Needs of Family Members

The experiences of the study families lends strength to the theory that family breakdown can be attributed to no single cause. Roles and norms may be defined within the family in such a way that they meet the requirements for group maintenance but do not meet the long-run psychological, social, and/or emotional needs of its members. A member may perform roles which are consistent with his own expectations and the expectations of other group members but frustrate his socio-emotional needs. He may or may not be aware of the causes for this sense of frustration. Such families are not preserving the "emotional well-being" of all their members, and may even encourage personal maladjustment despite the group's ability to handle reality problems. For this reason, they cannot be considered to be functioning adequately although they present a picture of at least stability, if not happiness, to the community. When additional pressures are placed upon these families, frustrations are likely to come to the surface in the form of family disagreement and role conflict, and they are more likely to become disorganized. Data from the therapeutic and research interviews indicate that the three families all showed signs of an unhealthy emotional climate before disorganization became apparent.[4] A few examples will serve to clarify this phenomenon.

That the psychological and emotional needs of Mrs. O were unmet in the sexual-affectional area seems quite obvious from the case study material. For more than five years after marriage she did not have sexual intercourse. Following this Mr. O performed the sexual act but without spontaneity and affection, and then only at infrequent intervals. In general he was not very affectionate towards his wife, and as their marriage continued, Mrs. O became more and more dissatisfied with her husband's sexual and affectional responses. Later, this dissatisfaction erupted into role conflict for both spouses and open disagreement. Another sign of an unhealthy climate was the behavior of the O's twelve year old daughter Ann. The case study states, "She had few friends, felt awkward and unpopular, and had little confidence in her abilities and talents." With a father that was hardly aware of his daughter's presence except when she disrupted his work and routines, it seems obvious she would show signs of insecurity and disturbance. Further, there are indications that Mrs. O resented her husband's inactivity in this area. Thus, the emotional climate in the O family was unhealthy in at least some respects.

Mrs. U also craved attention and affection but preferred its expressions in ways other than through the sexual act. Mr. U preferred sexual intercourse. While Mr. U showered attention and affection upon his wife during courtship and early in their marriage, this diminished considerably as time went on. After the birth of their first child Mrs. U became frigid. Thus, each spouse created frustrations for the other. In cyclical fashion, as Mrs. U received less attention and affection from her husband she became less willing to have intercourse, and he gave her less attention and affection. The emotional needs of both spouses were met less successfully as time went on. These problems reached a climax during the period of Mrs. U's psychiatric treatment.

Mr. A experienced many frustrations during his wife's long illness. Not only was his wife not available as a sexual partner and for companionship, but he found himself unable to exert authority with his own children who were under the care of his wife's relatives. When his wife became ill again with similar symptoms, after she had made an almost complete recovery from her tubercular condition, the threat of the loss of these satisfactions once more became a personal threat to him, and may have accelerated the family disorganization that had begun.

Rapoport and Rosow point out that the fit among personalities of family members is an important factor in determining psychiatric illness and family breakdown. "The function of any pattern of fit can only be judged against the respective self-images, the personality systems, and the organization of the relationship itself" (among family members).[5] The normative structure of the group and the personality fit among its members are related in ways which have not yet been determined. Both of these create, however, an emotional climate within the family, which can encourage personal growth and development or psychiatric illness among its members. A poor fit among personalities may thus hasten family disorganization.

The Ability of the Family Group to Respond to Change

The four criteria just described are necessary but not sufficient conditions for adequate family functioning. Successful handling of these system problems enables a family to achieve some stability. Such families can be considered to be in a state of static equilibrium. However, all families are required to respond to demands for change, brought about by both pressures within the system itself as well as pressures from the external environment. To maintain itself the family must be in a state of dynamic equilibrium, responding appropriately to these ever present demands for change. Families must find a means by which patterns of expectations and behavior can be altered to meet newly emerging needs and the problems they create. The ability of system members to meet this challenge is sometimes referred to as role flexibility.[6] The material below classifies many of the types of pressures the study families faced.

Family developmental pressures. At different points in the life history of a family, the group and its members must deal with different types of problems. As children are born, grow up, go to school, marry and leave home, and have children of their own, new demands are continuously being made upon the parents. This involves sometimes gradual and sometimes more abrupt changes in the organization of all members' roles and the evolvement of new norms for behavior. The developmental task concept implies that success in meeting previous tasks leads to success with later tasks.[7] Nonetheless, these tasks cannot be easily avoided. For example, children change physically, emotionally, and socially with chronological age and our culture demands new expectations from them as they do so. Thus, new demands are placed upon their parents. This is one reason why the family as a group must develop methods and procedures for change.

The study families, like other families, were subject to the pressures for such internal change. Unlike many other families, however, lack of complete success at previous family developmental tasks and other pressures toward disequilibrium which were occurring simultaneously were often too great for them to handle successfully.

The A family was getting ready to launch their children into the community as autonomous adults when family disorganization began to occur. This developmental problem seems to have been particularly difficult for the group to handle. Following Mrs. A's stay in the tuberculosis sanitarium, the A family had been re-united in their home less than six years when two children left the home almost within one month's time. Each left because of major disagreements with the parents over a long period of time. These difficulties during the launching stage served as concrete expressions to Mr. and Mrs. A of their failure as parents during earlier stages of development.

Thus, Mr. and Mrs. A had to begin to face making a life for themselves alone after having felt a sense of failure with two of their three children, and expecting the third to leave within a few years. Although relatively young, after such failure, they felt that they had little useful purpose left for them in life. They were having great difficulty in restructuring family life in response to this almost inevitable change. The psychiatric staff recognized this in indicating the involutional characteristics of both of their illnesses.

The U's were at a much earlier family developmental stage than A's. Mrs. U was able to handle her passive dependent in-fants, but when the two children became more autonomous she experienced great difficulty. As they became physically mobile and verbally expressive, and interactive with each other and their parents with greater frequency, she felt she was losing con-trol of the situation. Since neither she nor her husband had achieved real independence for themselves, they seemed to be at a loss as to how to channel and limit the striving in this direction by their children. Having had no acceptable role models for themselves, especially Mrs. U, they were unable to re-organize their roles as parents to meet these new demands successfully. Mrs. U tried to escape from her children and it was at this point that the process of family disorganization was accelerated.

A similar problem existed in the O family although at a some-what later stage in family development. Mrs. O had effectively limited Ann's behavior so that she would not interrupt her father's work and routines. In this way it was hardly ever necessary for him to involve himself in child care. However, as she moved through the latency period to pre-adolescence, she became more independent and more active. She invited friends over to the house, played more active games, used the phonograph, *etc.* Mr. O found himself forced to recognize the existence of the third mem-ber of the family. Further, he recognized Ann as a rival for his wife's attention. He found it extremely difficult to learn the ap-propriate father role, and it was only after therapeutic intervention that he made improvements in this area. Ann's growth was also a problem for Mrs. O, but in a somewhat different way. Ann became less and less dependent upon her mother as she entered early adolescence, finding friends among her peer group and interests away from home. Mrs. O had spent much time with her only child and she found these new developments difficult to handle.

Unanticipated situational changes within the family. The types of pressures described above grow out of inadequate interpersonal relationships. Roles were not structured in a way which enabled the group to handle new problems and at the same time satisfy the personal needs of all its members. All of the study families also experienced pressures which neither they nor the observer could have easily anticipated, but which required changes in the content and structure of role relationships. It seems interesting to note that in each case the psychiatrist and/or the patient associated the onset of symptoms with the beginning of this type of pressure.

Mr. O's drinking began at about the time his wife had her first serious illness, a blockage of the intestinal system, requiring an operation during hospitalization and a long period of convalescence. A second similar but less serious operation followed a year later. The role gaps created by Mrs. O's illness at this time required Mr. O to assume new responsibilities. It became necessary for him to pitch in on household tasks and take responsibility for Ann. The old mode of adjustment would no longer work, and a new method for handling family problems had to be worked out, at least until she became well. It seems to have upset the equilibrium balance, serving as a trigger mechanism which released other pressures which lay close to the surface.

A similar situation occurred in the A family. The psychiatrist associated the onset of Mrs. A's symptoms with Mr. A's first hospitalization, required for a hernia operation. Ten months later he was hospitalized again, this time for pneumonia, and it was discovered that he had a heart condition. Mr. A's hospitalization and knowledge of his serious illness forced him and other family members to alter their expectations of his role and position in the family. No longer was Mr. A the healthy, strong, independent person he once was. He and his wife agreed that there was even a drastic change in his physical build. The family had adapted an alternate mode of adjustment to handle Mrs. A's illness, but they had never experienced handling the problem of the serious illness of Mr. A. The old methods for handling family problems were no longer effective.

In the U family the situation seemed to have been more complex. Both spouses were highly dependent upon their extended families. When Mr. U was out of town frequently on business, Mrs. U felt uncomfortable, but surrounded by sympathetic family and friends in their apartment in the center of the city, she managed satisfactorily. When she moved to the sparsely settled suburbs, circumstances had changed. Both families were less sympathetic, friends were separated by a much greater distance, and there were no close neighbors. Mrs. U was expected to be less dependent and more autonomous. Unable to live up to these new expectations, she put pressure upon her husband to move back to town. He responded by demanding even greater autonomy. Mrs. U was unable to change although she was motivated to do so. With differing opinions among extended family members, she underwent a great deal of role conflict. These added pressures seemed to turn the tide in upsetting the precariously balanced equilibrium that had been present. The move into the new home required a new mode of family adjustment, but Mrs. U was unable to make this adaptation. This helped push the family into a period of disorganization. The family dates the onset of Mrs. U's symptoms to the time when they had moved into their new home. This had not been an expected pressure.

Environmental pressures for change. All families have pressures placed upon them by the social environment surrounding them. The family system should be organized in a way which enables the group to not only handle internal pressures but such external pressures as well. In the study families it seems that there was a heightening of such pressures prior to and early in the process of family disorganization. While unexpected internal pressures were associated with the onset of symptoms, external pressures were often focused upon by the patient and the family during the therapeutic period.

These pressures were most clearly delineated in the U family. Pressures arising out of inconsistent expectations among extended family members and placed upon these very dependent spouses seem to have been an important aspect of family disorganization. Mr. and Mrs. U first became aware of this pressure when they were about to move into their new home. Both of the spouses found themselves in almost continual role conflict. As Mrs. U implied, no matter what she did someone would think it was wrong. Until the couple was able to become more autonomous this pressure continued to disrupt their family life.

In the O family, Mr. O's job was a persistent pressure. The church congregation was split into two sub-groups, one of which was asking for his resignation. Mr. O was under constant stress, to which his wife and daughter also reacted. Mrs. O had to be a source of continuous support to her husband to keep him going. Problems within the church consumed a great deal of family time and energy, and the couple tended to project these problems as the source of Mr. O's illness.

In the A family work was again a source of pressure, but in a different way. Mr. A had been the sole and stable family wage earner for many years. Low wages and the cost of his wife's medical and hospital bills had permitted few savings. However, steady work and a good deal of overtime had permitted him to pay off most of his debts. His own illness had incurred more debts. It was at this time that mill work slowed down for the first time in many years. Some weeks he did not work a full five days although he had worked six days a week before; a few weeks the men were required to take vacations without pay. Thus, as never before, the family was in much financial debt which added to the pressures already present.

FAMILY ORGANIZATION

These five criteria are meant to serve as diagnostic indicators of whether families are functioning adequately. The relationship system used to solve these small group problems characterizes the organization of the family, and varies from one family to another, and at different points in time in the same family. While there are innumerable ways in which expectations, roles, and behavior can be organized, ideal types can be described which provide greater depth of understanding for a large number of families.[8] These descriptions of family organization may include summaries of the structural arrangements of members of the group along with such dimensions as power, affection, communication, tasks, etc.

The authors believe that no one organizational type is better than another for all families. Rather, specified types may be better for particular personality types in a particular sub-culture, and for family groups facing particular types of system problems. An indication of this is that the families in this study changed their organization radically during the course of the psychotherapy of one family member.

Our job as researchers and practitioners is to develop typologies of family organization relevant to differences in the characteristics of family members and differences in the problems facing family groups, and seek out means or techniques by which we can help families achieve such ideal states of organization. This is a large order, but only then will we achieve our goal of "emotional well-being" through adequate family functioning for the great majority of those who seek our help today.

CONCLUSION

Traditional psychoanalytic theory focused attention on intrapsychic variables, often at the expense of the social, psychological, and situational components. This is not to say that the latter were completely neglected, but rather, in general, cause was attributed to the former and effect to the latter. Today we have greater appreciation of the complexity of associations between these three levels of variables, and realize that any number of factors at any and all levels may be antecedents to any particular behavior pattern. We can return to Freud's admonition that no effect has a single cause with greater depth of understanding. This paper, in describing criteria for adequate family functioning, focused on the social and psychological problems family groups must handle, and in so doing, attempted to remind us of this premise.

CHANGES IN FAMILY EQUILIBRIUM
DURING PSYCHOTHERAPY

Paul H. Glasser

THIS REPORT summarizes one section of a larger study of the
ways in which role changes occur in a family when a parent
is mentally ill and undergoes psychotherapy. A large number
of case records from the Psychiatric Clinic at North Carolina
Memorial Hospital were examined following a review of the
literature on family-crisis studies,[1] marital-adjustment studies.[2] family-development theory,[3] role theory,[4] and social psychiatry.[5] Out of this survey and from beginning contacts
with study families, an investigation emerged which focused
upon the equilibrium of the family as a small group[6] in the
following areas: How internal stresses within the family
arise, what changes take place in the behavior of family
members, and what changes take place in group methods for
handling problems. This paper discusses primarily the intrafamilial processes which accompany the psychotherapy of
one member of the family group.

During the psychotherapeutic process, three stages of family equilibrium were delineated: (1) re-equilibrium following
the patient's initial improvement, (2) disequilibrium (family
crisis) during intensive psychoanalytically oriented treatment, and (3) the emergence of a new equilibrium prior
to termination of treatment. Each stage is associated with a
series of factors related to (1) the therapeutic techniques
used and the depth of the transference relationship at different periods in the treatment process, (2) the reactions
of family members to the patient's new behavior patterns,

Reprinted with permission of the publisher from *Family Process*, vol.
2, no. 2 (Sept. 1963), pp. 245–264.

Reprinted by permission of the author and the journal. This investigation was partially supported by a National Institute of Mental
Health Training Grant through the University of North Carolina Institute for Research in Social Science.

his changing symptom picture, and his treatment, and (3) other situational factors (hospitalization, loss of income, etc.). At the second stage, these elements lead to inconsistent expectations between the patient and other members of the family; that is, a serious crisis. Changes in the patient's behavior and expectations require other members of the family to change also. This change process in the family group is described in detail in the body of the paper. A final section of the report discusses implications for social work practice, emphasizing particularly the need for family diagnosis even when the patient is receiving individual psychotherapy and the important part the worker can play in facilitating treatment and in keeping the group together by seeing other members of the patient's family.

RESEARCH METHOD

Since this was an exploratory study which attempted to shed at least some light on the ways in which families change and the causes for this change in order to generate new and insightful hypotheses, the decision was made to use the case-study method. Three families in which both spouses (one of them the patient) and at least one child under the age of eighteen were living at home were chosen for study. Each of the patients was either under, or expected to begin, intensive psychotherapy over a long period of time with a staff or resident physician. These families were followed carefully for a period of about thirteen months. Four types of data were collected in the study:

1. Interviews with individual family members, most often with the patient's spouse.
2. Observations and interviews with the family as a group during home visits.
3. Data collected in conferences with the psychiatrists treating the patients. These conferences were held at fairly regular intervals (two to four times a month for each case).
4. Psychiatric and social work records and identifying data sheets, which included information not found in the first three sources.

A total of at least 153 contacts concerning the families in

the study was made. More than 204 contacts with individuals either singly or in groups occurred. Thus, the researcher got to know these families and their methods of functioning extremely well.

Process records were written or dictated soon after each contact with one or more family members or the patient's psychiatrist. As the data were gathered, the records were read and reread for new insights into the material. These were set down in rudimentary form and in progress reports and checked again through another reading of the material and later interviews. At this point some insights were discarded, revised, or embellished.

Once all the data were collected, a role framework was used as the basis for a content analysis of all of the record material in order to check the earlier insights and find new understanding in a more rigorous manner. Each paragraph, sentence, or even phrase which related to one of the seven role areas was identified with a number and letter indicating in which of the six stages of family organization the behavior occurred, and to which of the seven role areas it applied.[7] In this way a description of the role of each family member in each of the seven role areas during each of the six stages was written. Role conflicts, role confusions, role gaps, and role dissatisfactions were more clearly discerned by reading through all of the material in each role area during each stage. The content which follows is based upon an analysis of the above material.

THE RETURN TO THE FAMILIAR

Following the patient's initial contact with the psychiatric clinic, there appear to have been vigorous attempts by each of the families to return to the old ways of doing things. Each family member tried to resume the roles used before the family disequilibrium which appeared during the stages of the patient's mental illness. There are numerous reasons why this seems to have occurred.

The onset of treatment in itself served to give the family some sense of relief. There was the hope that the intervention of a professional outsider would interrupt the downward spiral of family disequilibrium. Some family members felt that matters could not get much worse, so that with psychiatric aid they were bound to get better. Knowing no other method of family adjustment which had been satisfying to them, family members attempted to return to old patterns.

Hospitalization early in the treatment sequence tended to reinforce hopes and aid members in their return to old roles.[8] Familiar with the analogy of physical illness, family members believed that the patient would return from the hospital in a greatly improved state of health. Further, removal of the patient from the home had a number of positive consequences. It permitted the family some relief from the patient's symptoms and interpersonal difficulties. There was time to reorganize the family along the old lines with the patient absent, and members were able to assert their strengths in the adjustment process. Spouses and children tended to recall the patient's strengths and the once satisfying interpersonal relationships, repeating stories of the happy times they had had together. There is a chance to love the patient for what he once was like when the reality demands of his difficulties are removed. While the patient's absence from the home is not always easy to handle, the positives seemed to outweigh the negatives at this point in the family's history. Since the patient is expected home soon, the threat of continued absence and its consequences is minimized, and as the family members move into the old role structure, the patient's roles tend to be preserved for him until his return home.

Visits to the hospital tend to reinforce the expectation of re-equilibrium and the return to the old family pattern. The patient seems calmer, better behaved, easier to get along with, and more relaxed. For the first time in months or years, in the controlled environment of the hospital, spouses are able to discuss important matters together and even make some decisions without getting upset. Promises are made to behave in the same way when the patient returns home and to return to the old ways of handling problems, which seem much more satisfying in comparison with the turmoil that took place during family disequilibrium while the patient was acutely ill. There seems little awareness of the causes for family demoralization or mental illness.

A sense of relief is also expressed by the patient and his family when they know what is wrong, despite a diagnosis of psychiatric illness and the fear attached to this. The concreteness of the label seems to provide more security than uncertainty and the suspicion of mental illness. With the addition of a supportive and warm response from the psychiatrist, the social worker, and others, the patient and his family feel reassured that the group will be able to return to the former level of equilibrium.

Often there is an expectation by the patient, his family, and the therapist that the patient will respond positively to treatment and get well. In the eyes of the patient and his family this means that he will be as he was before the illness and so they can all assume their old ways. Many of the individuals in the study saw in psychiatry a magical component, believing that something the physician will do will change the patient's behavior and enable him to recover. It is only after the patient has been in treatment for some time that he is able to give up this belief. Until this occurs the family is encouraged to believe that there will be a return to the good old days.

When there is some improvement in the patient's behavior and symptoms—and there generally is in the protected environment of the hospital and/or when treatment first begins —these hopeful expectations about the patient and psychiatry are confirmed. There is the feeling that now the patient is almost his old self again, that members can pick up where they left off before his illness began. The self-fulfilling prophecy has been fulfilled. Neither the family nor the patient seem to understand that separation from the family, the sense of relief associated with diagnosis and treatment, the expectation that the patient will get well, and the therapeuic environment of the hospital, have all contributed to the patient's temporary relief of symptoms, and that in time these same or other symptoms are likely to return after the patient leaves the hospital.

This flight into health and the family process associated with it was particularly noticeable in two families. Mr. O gave up alcohol for some time after hospitalization. Mrs. U gave up many of her somatic complaints while at the hospital, and her behavior became somewhat more tolerable to the nuclear and extended family members for the first few months after discharge. Since the patients generally show improvement in the hospital, the family eagerly awaits the patient's return home.

When the patient does return home, family morale is high. There is less need to hide the patient's behavior since he has improved, and sometimes his hospitalization has made this impossible.[9] Thus, one source of pressure has been removed. The patient is better, which gives the family reason to rejoice. The family itself has reorganized somewhat during the patient's absence, enabling its members to better tolerate and handle the patient's deviant behavior, if some of this remains. The family has preserved the patient's roles in its structures, and his return home in an improved state leads them to believe that he will assume these roles in the very near future. This pushes the patient to conform to the pressure of these expectations. He does attempt to assume his old roles in the family. The husband returns to his job, takes his wife out socially, does repairs around the house, and resumes some responsibility for the children. The wife returns to cooking and cleaning, caring for the children, etc. This is reason for further rejoicing.

High morale contributes to the avoidance of arguments and the expression of discontent. Since the underlying causes for family disequilibrium and mental illness have not yet been handled, role dissatisfaction continues to exist, but it remains below the surface. There are persistent attempts by the spouses of the patients and other family members to avoid arguments and to conceal discontent with expected behavior in fear of encouraging the return of the patient's symptoms. The result is less effective communication than before the patient's illness began, while at the same time the family has the illusion that things are running smoothly. Mrs. O verbalized these fears to the researcher a number of times. For example she said that she was afraid to express any of her hostility. Mr. O seemed to remember weeks and months later what she might say in anger, and he would bring it up. This was one reason why she was afraid to express herself. Secondly, she was afraid he would react at the moment, and that this would upset him further. She didn't want to undo the work of the psychiatrist.

Finally, the process of psychotherapy also indirectly encourages this family process. Treatment at this early stage is primarily directed at catharsis, relief of guilt, and emotional support. The effect is to reduce the patient's anxiety, which results in the relief of some symptoms, with the consequences described earlier. The family appears to be functioning in the same manner as before the onset of family disequilibrium and the patient's symptoms.

A SECOND PERIOD OF DISEQUILIBRIUM

The previous method of family organization had not worked successfully in the past, either because it did not satisfy personal needs or was inadequate to handle problems facing the group, or for both of these reasons. Thus, after the initial rejoicing following hospitalization and/or the beginning of treatment, the process of family disequilibrium gradually began once again. The rapidity with which this process became apparent to members of the family depended upon many factors in the family and treatment situation. In each of the study families, however, there was a recurrence of symptoms in the patient concurrent with the second period of family disequilibrium.

There were many pressures towards disequilibrium in addition to the important ones stated above. First of all, the family and its members were not really the same after treatment began as before the onset of the patient's symptoms. Many events had occurred in the interval which made a difference in the reactions of family members to each other and the external system. The group had gone through one crisis, mental illness of the patient, during which interpersonal relationships had been markedly strained. One of the members of the family had become acutely ill. While some of the patient's symptoms had been removed after treatment had begun, sometimes the more prominent ones, other symptoms generally remained. The crisis had been a learning experience in itself so that individuals in the family were no longer the same as before the crisis, and they could no longer play the same roles as easily as before. Their psychosocial reactions to each other were different.

Family members were aware that these changes had taken place but found it difficult to be specific about them. These changes provided motivation for more change. If Mr. O could pick up his daughter Ann at the home of her girlfriend for the first time, why couldn't he do this more often, especially when Mrs. O most needed this kind of help? If Mrs. U could face up to her mother's anger once, why couldn't she do this consistently? Members of the family found it difficult to put these feelings into words, but they felt them nonetheless. The results seemed to be role confusion and ambiguous and unclear expectations. Behind this lay role dissatisfaction which gradually arose to the surface and began to get expressed.

Another cause for role dissatisfaction and role confusion was that the role gaps created by the patient had been filled by other family members during the crisis. It was not always clear to the family which roles were played by which members, and even if it was clear, some members were reluctant to give up some of these new tasks. Mrs. O, the wife of a minister, was not certain what responsibilities she had had in her husband's church before his illness, but she knew that she enjoyed many of her present responsibilities. When her husband pressured her to give up some of these responsibilities while he was in intensive psychotherapy, she became upset. When the onset of family disequilibrium and the patient's symptoms is more rapid than in the O family, this seems to be less of a problem.

Further, when there is a considerable period of time between the onset of symptoms and the beginning of psychiatric treatment, as in the O family, the group may face new developmental problems. Over a period of more than five years, from the beginning of illness to the end of treatment, Ann changed from a latency age child to an adolescent who had acquired dating patterns and other new interests. This caused a good deal of disruption in household routines and was the focus for discussion between Mr. and Mrs. O. The family faces new types of problems and has to find new ways of handling them.

Another cause for disequilibrium in the family at this period is related to the increased pressure on the patient to conform to family roles and tasks. The patient's ability to assume some of his old responsibilities, and his improvement after hospitalization and the beginning of treatment, lead the family to believe that the patient is fully recovered much before this is really so. If he can do some tasks then he should be able to do all is the reasoning of many spouses and children. Since the patient is not ready nor able to do so, he may become increasingly upset under this pressure and there will be a return of some or all of his symptoms. The secondary gain from such symptoms seems rather important in this situation.

Often, after the onset of treatment, the patient begins to perform his basic tasks in the family, as is expected of him. As stated above, the pressure to do so is great. In the past he may have expressed his frustration and anger by refusing to do so. Now, however, the family and his therapist keep him reality-oriented. The avoidance of such tasks is no longer considered as legitimate after hospitalization and the beginning of treatment as before. Frustration and anger may be expressed in new ways; new symptoms may become prominent. Mr. O, who never before had expressed his hostility except through drinking, exploded at his wife and child at the breakfast table over a burned piece of toast. Mrs. U no longer neglected the care of the home and her children and complained much less about somatic difficulties, but became much more argumentative with her husband over little things and blew up at the children a few times a day. To some family members, the old symptoms seemed easier to handle than the new ones. At least they had experience with the former. They may have even indirectly encouraged a return to these old symptoms in the attempt to help the patient give up the new ones.

Reality orientation had another important effect in increasing pressure towards disequilibrium. It seemed much more socially acceptable to act out within the confines of the nuclear family than in situations outside the family. Mrs. U exploded at her mother and grandmother, and in-laws much less often, but argued vigorously with her husband whenever they were alone together. In the confines of her home she also frequently exploded at the children. Aware of this, Mr. U attempted to get her and the children out of the house and in social relations with friends and family as much as possible. Similarly, Mr. O was much more effective as a minister following hospitalization and the beginning of therapy, especially since he was not drinking, but he exploded within the home much more often.

This type of pressure in itself is difficult for family members, and tends to be more so because there is less acting-out behavior outside the home at this period. To members of the extended family, friends, and neighbors, the patient appears to be normal and functioning well. Thus, difficulty within the family cannot be explained to others as easily. The spouse is less able to confide in others. She and the children tend to blame themselves more for interpersonal difficulties with the patient. This increases anxiety and tension in them, and the second downward spiral of disequilibrium continues.

Finally, the psychotherapeutic process itself indirectly encourages family disequilibrium. If the patient does not withdraw from treatment once the most prominent symptoms are removed, the therapist begins to focus upon the understanding of present behavior in terms of the past. Old wounds are reopened for the patient. Once more he becomes anxious and this may revive old symptoms or bring out new ones. The consequences for the family have been noted.

As intensive insight treatment begins, the patient may begin to test out new behavior within the nuclear family. This is not consistent with former expectations and becomes the focus of considerable stress for the group. Since the patient does not know what will be effective and what will not, this behavior is very variable. In Mrs. U's attempt to become more autonomous, she refused a vacation with her husband and children, often changed her mind suddenly after decisions and plans had been made, and sometimes refused to visit her parents and in-laws, but at other times visited them unexpectedly. Mr. O sometimes relied heavily upon his wife for aid in making social calls, as he had in the past, but occasionally he showed an ability to function well in this area independently. This situation was confusing and difficult for spouses and children. Thus, it seems necessary that there occur a breakdown in the old organization accompanied by family disequilibrium before and during the evolvement of a new equilibrium.

RE-EQUILIBRIUM

This new crisis during treatment may be more difficult for the family to cope with than the disequilibrium precipitated by mental illness. In some families the threat of divorce is persistent throughout this period despite many years of marriage. The personal needs of the family members can no longer be successfully met in the old ways. The old methods for handling family problems are no longer effective, and a new organization of the family is required. In addition, there are new needs and new problems. In their interaction together family members force changes upon each other during the development of a new role structure.

Role dissatisfactions become expressed during the crises, resulting in role expectations placed on an individual which are in opposition, or role conflict. This leads to many open disagreements and arguments in the family. While each of the families characterized this period as very difficult and unpleasant, there was a great deal of pressure to change. There was also an increase in communication over the preceding stage, as family members tended to have it out. This led to the acceptance of new patterns of behavior.

In this climate, there was a gradual clarification of those patterns of behavior which provided more personal satisfaction for the patient and for the other family members as well. Roles which enabled the group to handle its problems more effectively were also evolved. Through trial and error new behavior was tested out within the nuclear group. Some behavior was abandoned; other ways of acting developed into a successful and effective pattern. While the patient may have been the first to test out new behavior, encouraged by the therapeutic process, this in turn forced changes in behavior upon the other family members. Their response to the patient becomes different and old symptoms may be handled in new ways. In this atmosphere of experimentation, the upward cycle of new organization and reequilibrium begins.

For example, Mr. O learned that he enjoyed spending time with his daughter and participating in the purchase of a gift for her. At first, his wife resented her husband's interference in what she thought was an exclusive relationship between Ann and herself. However, she found that her husband provided her with new satisfactions. He bought her gifts for the first time also. She found that Mr. O could be quite helpful in handling Ann's sometimes difficult behavior. She thus came to expect him to take a much greater interest in their daughter. In a much oversimplified way, this illustrates the process that took place.

Similarly, in the U family, Mrs. U resented her husband's out-of-town business trips. These trips not only forced her to be alone but also seemed very exciting compared to her dull life at home. On the spur of the moment, Mr. U invited her to go along with him one day. At first fearful, she finally agreed. She enjoyed the trip so much that Mr. U was also pleased and gratified. He promised to take her along again. One source of role dissatisfaction is lessened through a new pattern of behavior.

As the incidents above indicate, these changes in the patient's behavior may place the spouse and children in a difficult position. While it may be inconsistent with their expectations, they cannot always define it as sick behavior. Some new behavior may be defined in this way, but it is discouraged. Some new behavior may be very pleasing to the family, and this is encouraged. Some new behavior which did not meet expectations may be confusing and result in role conflict for spouse and children.

Mr. O, a man known for his even temper, had explosive outbursts at his wife and child during this period. Mrs. O's negative reactions conveyed to him her dislike of this type of behavior. On the other hand, when he arranged for a special gift of flowers for her birthday, she was overwhelmed and pleased, although this too, was quite unexpected. However, when he arranged for her to give up her secretarial services at the church, she was confused and unhappy. This was not sick behavior, especially since she occasionally complained about the burden of work. Nonetheless, she enjoyed this responsibility and was reluctant to give it up, just as she was reluctant to give up many other church duties. She could either argue this decision with her husband, or conform to these new expectations. Sometimes she took the former choice, and often the result was clarification of the problem and compromise. Sometimes she took the latter choice, attempting to find substitute gratifications. Neither choice was easy for her to handle, but both led to changes in patterns of behavior and new role relationships.

This, in turn, encourages the spouse and children to try out new ways of handling the patient and his symptoms. It was during this same period that Mr. O made an obvious attempt at suicide, similar to the half dozen attempts which brought him to psychiatric treatment. Instead of indicating concern, sympathy, emotional support, and becoming upset, Mrs. O let her husband know that she did not consider this behavior appropriate and acceptable. He quickly got over his sulking and they were able to discuss the causes for his recent depression.

Many such critical incidents occurred in the families during this period. While they were sometimes very emotionally upsetting to family members, that behavior which seemed more effective than old ways of handling similar situations tended to be repeated. Thus, these new patterns were reinforced through time and tended to replace the old ways. Furthermore, success in one role area encouraged family members to try out new behavior in other areas. As negative contagion occurred during family disequilibrium, positive contagion occurred during re-equilibrium. It also led group members to expect more and more changes from each other, changes which would be more personally satisfying to them and enable the family to deal with their problems more effectively. If Mrs. U enjoyed the out of town business trip with her husband, she might also enjoy going along with her husband to sports events away from home. If Mr. O can respond more naturally and spontaneously to his wife during the sexual act while under the influence of alcohol, he ought to be able to do so while sober. Gradually, the content of roles changed and a new type of organization evolved. An upward cycle or re-equilibrium replaced the downward spiral of disequilibrium.

In addition, these new patterns were reinforced by members of the external system. Some changes were noted by extended family members, friends, and neighbors. This was especially true as role conflicts began to diminish and family disagreements occurred less often. Members became more satisfied with family life and the group became more cohesive. For example, parishioners commented about the improved job Mr. O was doing as minister of the church. Friends and family noted Mrs. U's new ability to handle her children. Members of the nuclear family were pleased about such comments, which reinforced their wishes to continue using these new patterns.

Once again, there is a close tie between this stage of family organization and the therapeutic process. Insight therapy helped the patient to understand better the causes for his own behavior, to perceive reality more clearly, and to behave in a manner more appropriate to this reality. New, more appropriate patterns of behavior became established, and the patient's interpersonal relationships and his social functioning in general improved. To the therapist, these were strong indications that the patient was getting well, and the need for therapy decreased. The therapist began to think of termination.

The final stage in therapy before termination involves the interpretation of the transference relationship between the therapist and the patient, and the consolidation of gains made by the patient through emotional support and the understanding of recent events in the light of current reality.

In less technical language, the therapist helped the patient to understand better the therapeutic relationship in the same way that he had helped him to understand his relationships with others. This allowed the patient to be less dependent upon the therapist. In addition, the therapist encouraged the continuation of newly established, more appropriate patterns of behavior, thus acting as another reinforcement agent. Thus, these new patterns tended to persist. As the focus on insight therapy diminished, the pressure for the patient to change his behavior diminished, enabling new behavior patterns and their concomitant expectations to become established.

As new roles are seen to provide greater psychosocial satisfactions for family members and to be more effective for handling family problems, there is internal pressure to reduce testing out and behavior change. The new role structure becomes clarified and the new equilibrium more firmly established. There is internal role consistency, consistency of family roles and norms and actual role performance, and compatibility of family roles and norms with societal norms. There continues to be change to meet new demands, but it occurs much more slowly. There is a new type of family organization, the crisis is over, and the family is in a period of equilibrium once again.

IMPLICATIONS FOR PRACTICE

This study has many complex implications for practice in the helping professions. Only a few of the more important ones will be discussed in this paper.

The need for, and the utility of, family diagnosis prior to the beginning of treatment for the patient and/or other members of his family is one of the more obvious and significant practice considerations that grows out of this research project.[10] This is necessary before the therapist can make two vital decisions regarding the patient and his family:

1. What is the treatment of choice for this patient? This becomes particularly vital if intensive insight therapy is considered as one method which might be helpful to this patient since it has significant effects upon the rest of the family group, effects which may well hinder the progress of therapy or result in family disequilibrium, separation, and even divorce. Are the efforts directed at one person worthwhile if it may have major detrimental effects upon other members of the family group?[11] This is partially a value decision, but also should be a decision based upon knowledge.

2. If the patient is to receive some form of individual psychotherapy, how much and what kind of help will the spouse and children require? As is implied above, this requires an evaluation of the effects of individual psychotherapy for the patient upon other family members and the family as a group. Included must be some anticipation of the degree of disturbance psychotherapy might cause for other family members. In addition, the therapist must evaluate the extent of disequilibrium and the type of disorganization in the family that may result from any treatment method.

These decisions require knowledge of the types and depth of interaction patterns (dyadic role relationships) between the patient and other members of his family. What are the strengths and limitations of other family members, and are role relationships interlocked in such a way that changes in behavior of the patient or his expectations for others will be resisted by them, tend to result in personality disorganization in others, etc.? Thus, family diagnosis requires an evaluation of the personality dimensions of each of the family members.

But further, family diagnosis requires a knowledge of the family as a group, particularly the ways in which it handles its problems as a social system.[12] Knowledge of the parts and their interaction should be supplemented by knowledge of the whole (the Gestalt). Finally disequilibrium need not be accompanied by personality breakdown. Psychotherapy may not lead to psychopathology in other family members but may lead to inefficient family functioning and even the breakdown of the family as a group. We have much more to learn about this aspect of the treatment process.

A second implication has to do with the role of the worker during the treatment process. Two periods of disequilibrium in the family were identified in the larger study: (1) during the acute phase of the patient's illness and (2) during the period in therapy when the patient is focusing on the development of insight through the recall of significant material in his life history, and he is testing out new patterns of behavior, primarily within the nuclear family group. It is at these times that the patient's spouse often needs and seeks help and a professional person can be especially helpful.

During this first diagnostic period the family tends to experience a sense of relief about getting the patient some help, which they often feel he desperately requires. For this reason they are often willing and anxious to cooperate in any way possible. However, they are also quite fearful about the meaning of mental illness and psychiatric treatment. It is an unknown to them which is confusing. In addition, these same reactions in extended-family members, friends, and neighbors may reinforce their own reactions, and many times these members external to the nuclear family will pressure spouse and children not to permit the patient to undergo psychiatric treatment. While the nuclear group tends to align itself with the patient against the external system, this causes internal conflict and anxiety for each member.

The fear of mental illness and psychiatry will diminish if the family has some contacts with the clinic, and if they have been informed of the diagnosis and treatment plan by a warm, friendly, supportive person. This concrete material, given in this manner, reinforces their hope that the patient will get better, and they are willing to make many sacrifices, financial and other, to see this goal accomplished.

The therapeutic stage in which the patient is developing insight into his problems is a very difficult period for the family group. Unfortunately, the optimism present in reequilibrium during the previous stage of family life leaves the family unprepared for the hardships and tasks they must face.

The return of the patient's symptoms and the development of new symptoms is a threatening experience to the spouse and children. Since the patient is continuing treatment, they find it difficult to understand. The magical component of psychiatric treatment is shattered, sometimes rather abruptly, and they don't know what to expect next. Further, they feel they have no way of finding out.

As the patient begins to test out new behavior inconsistent with the family's former expectations, some of which they may interpret quite negatively, the group members become confused and angry. They don't know where to place the blame for this as well as the recurrence of the patient's symptoms. They alternate in placing responsibility upon themselves (guilt), others outside the family, and the therapist. They find it difficult to handle the patient's new behavior, and even if they wish to change, they are confused as to how to behave. Further, they don't know where to turn. The patient's behavior outside the family often continues to show improvement, which makes the spouse feel that relatives and friends will not understand. Traditionally, the therapist has refused to see the spouse during this therapeutic stage in fear of damaging his relationship with the patient.

This situation is complicated by the deep transference relationship between the patient and the therapist. The patient tends to lean a great deal less upon his family for the gratification of a variety of psychological needs, and a great deal more upon the therapist. He often discusses serious problems and decisions with the therapist and not with his spouse. Further, he tends to see the therapist as an ideal spouse, one which a spouse in real life could not live up to. The result is that the relationship between spouses may grow more distant and cold, and meaningful communication between them may reach in all-time low. The spouse feels left out of the therapeutic system, which has become more meaningful to the patient at this point than any other experience in his life.

Family members may thus become envious, competitive, hostile, and frightened. It is then that there are threats by the patient and the spouse to break up the marriage. The spouse's inability to change and the disagreements between marital partners may confirm the patient's belief that his spouse is no longer for him. Neither patient nor spouse understands what is happening, but both tend to become bitter and angry. In the study families, there were two prominent reactions to this situation. The spouse may feel in need of

treatment for herself and make demands to see the therapist
or another staff person for help with her problems, for the
problems she is having with the patient, or for both reasons.
The second reaction is to put pressure on the patient to withdraw from therapy. Both of these reactions can sometimes
be handled if the spouse can be seen by another therapist. By
seeing the spouse, the worker can give her some opportunity
for catharsis which is badly needed at this point in the
family's history. It also brings the spouse into the therapeutic
system, if even indirectly, by enabling the spouse to better
understand the causes for her husband's reactions at home
and some of what he is going through in therapy. Further,
the worker can give the spouse reassurance and support,
pointing up that this is probably a temporary situation, and
the long history of marriage may well be built upon a firm
foundation which can stand this type of stress.

This exploratory study investigated one aspect of the social
situation in which the psychiatric patient finds himself, that
is, the family. As the most important primary group for children and adults in our society, the family seems to have a
significant influence on the patient, his illness, and his therapy. This paper presents some generalizations which we hope
will be meaningful for theory, practice and future research.

MENTAL HEALTH AND THE FAMILY

Clark E. Vincent

A COMPREHENSIVE review of mental health legislation and
funding programs at the national level would comprise several volumes, as would any comprehensive survey of the
impacts such legislation may have had or possibly will have
upon families. In the first section of this chapter, therefore,

Reprinted with permission of the author and publisher from *Marriage and the Family*, vol. 29, no. 1 (February 1967), pp. 18–39.

This article was prepared upon request for the *Journal of Marriage and the Family* and was supported by a grant from the Russell Sage Foundation.

only a highly selective review of a few broad developments and trends will be given to illustrate the very recent and rapid emergence of a predominant role of the federal government in the mental health field. This selective review provides a historical context for the second section, in which the broad relevance of the family to mental health is examined by means of an extensive discussion of the *adaptive* function of the family. Increased understanding of this function is postulated to be of crucial significance in discussions of social policy regarding the family and in considering the specific impacts upon the family of any given federal legislation and funding in the mental health field.

In the third section, "marital health" is proposed as a needed specialty and new health field in order to overcome some of the *a*family and *a*marital bias (a) in federal funding as noted in the first section and (b) in research and treatment as noted in the second and third sections. An explicit emphasis upon marital health is also posited as a fruitful means of addressing some of the unknowns and gaps in knowledge directly relevant to the impacts upon families of returning the mental patient to the home and community. The final section comprises a summary discussion of social policy concerning the family and suggestions for initiating marital health as a specialty health field in its own right.

Of central concern throughout the chapter is the fact that federal legislation and funding in the mental health field shows, at best, only indirect and minimal interest in families qua families. It would appear that the family is regarded as being either of only minor importance in mental health or of such primary importance as to be taken for granted and consequently overlooked. The multimillion-dollar funds authorized by federal legislation to support programs of training, research, treatment, and service in the field of mental health are specifically focused upon a wide variety of social and individual problems (narcotic addiction, alcoholism, delinquency, gerontology, mental illness, mental retardation, and suicide, among others) but bypass the family unit, within which many of these social and individual problems are thought to originate. The first session of the 89th Congress (1965) enacted 59 laws (involving 23 federal agencies or departments) which have some implications for funded programs in the mental health field;[1] "the family" is not included in any of the titles and subject areas of these 59 laws.

The omission of specific reference to the family qua family in federal legislation and funding is not peculiar to the field of mental health. In 1965 the Office of Economic Opportunity published a 393-page summary of "Government programs to help individuals and communities meet their own goals for economic and social development." The word "family" does not appear in its title (*Catalog of Federal Programs for Individual and Community Improvement*),[2] and the index contains only three indirect references to "the family" in its 262 topical headings and only 13 in its 563 subheadings.

THE GROWTH OF GOVERNMENT PARTICIPATION IN THE FIELD OF MENTAL HEALTH[3]

The Early Period: Federal Noninvolvement

The federal government's interest in the mental health field has developed so rapidly within the past decade that it is easy to forget how slowly and reluctantly the government assumed responsibility for the mental health of the nation's citizens. In Colonial times the mentally ill were "cared for" in the home (frequently an attic or garret of the house) and in the community (usually a jail or poorhouse). In the early 1800's state and federal involvement in mental health (or mental illness) was nonexistent. The deplorable conditions which existed at that time are described graphically in Deutsch's book, *The Mentally Ill in America*.[4] Dorothea Dix, a Massachusetts schoolteacher, started her great crusade on behalf of the mentally ill in the 1840's after visiting a number of jails and almshouses, where she found victims of mental illness chained and treated as if they were animals. Her subsequent writings and her speeches to nearly a score of state legislatures and before the U.S. Congress (in an era when women did not yet have the right to vote) became the major stimulus responsible for the establishment of state mental hospitals. Hence, she is frequently regarded as the founder of the state mental hospital system, although her intended goal was involvement of the federal government. This goal was almost realized in 1848, when both houses of Congress passed a bill which, had it not been vetoed by

President Pierce, would have provided large federal land grants to the states (comparable to those given for land-grant colleges) for the construction of facilities to care for the mentally ill.

Individual states continued the construction and management of mental hospitals throughout the latter part of the nineteenth century. Construction of new state mental hospitals had reached a virtual plateau at the turn of the century, however, and between 1900 and 1950 the average population in the existing hospitals increased from 450 to 2,500.

During the 1940's several factors combined to accelerate the nation's awareness that something had to be done besides simply increasing the population of already overcrowded and understaffed state mental hospitals. One major long-term factor was the prior development and ongoing influence of what today is a worldwide movement of voluntary citizens concerned with mental health, the National Association of Mental Health (NAMH). This organization had its beginning with a private citizen, a businessman named Clifford Beers, who had spent three years in locked wards of mental hospitals. His remarkable recovery and his classic autobiography, *A Mind That Found Itself*,[5] interjected into the mainstream of American thought an optimistic note concerning mental illness. A committee on mental hygiene which he founded became the State Mental Health Association of Connecticut, and in 1910 the leaders of this association helped form the National Committee on Mental Hygiene—the forerunner of the NAMH.

The World War II Era

The hope, optimism, and fervor permeating Beers' early work and that of his followers were such as to invite criticisms that mental hygiene was more akin to a religious movement than to a health field.[6] Such hope and optimism, however, had an increasingly receptive audience in the 1940's, when the rejection on neuropsychiatric grounds of nearly two million draftees during World War II and the soaring costs of maintaining bulging state mental hospitals accelerated public awareness that alternatives were needed.

Although many of the techniques developed during World War II for screening and treating psychiatric cases were similar to those discovered during the first world war, they had been forgotten and largely unused in the interim. The large number of neuropsychiatric rejections and the increased awareness of the critical shortage of personnel trained in the mental health professions encouraged the use of group therapy and short-term techniques of treatment. The reported success with such techniques gave rise to renewed optimism concerning the treatability of mental illness.

The Veterans Administration programs for dealing with the psychiatric casualties of World War II sought to demonstrate the value of treating the mentally ill with the objective of restoring their ability to cope with the demands of normal living. In pursuit of this objective, the VA developed outpatient clinics, part-time hospitalization, and various transitional facilities to help former hospital patients adjust to life outside an institution. A few hospitals also began experimenting with the development of transitional experiences between institutional living and full return to the community. At the same time, the findings from a number of studies began to suggest that the patient's recovery was hampered if he was permitted to make too complete an adjustment to institutional life.

In the 1950's the increasing use of tranquilizing and antidepressant drugs made possible the release of increasing numbers of hospitalized mental patients. Although the drugs were not regarded as curative, they often induced sufficient remission of symptoms to make it possible for many patients to live at home or in foster homes while continuing their treatment on an outpatient basis. This development stimulated further interest in community services for mentally ill persons who no longer were considered sick enough to be confined to an institution.

It is obviously impossible to describe here the many interlocking factors which combined and converged to stimulate the federal government's initial assumption of major responsibility for mental health. Some of the factors were the rejectees of World War II, the VA programs, the shortage of psychiatric manpower and hospital beds, drug research, and the spiraling costs of confining increasing numbers of patients in institutional facilities that were fast wearing out. These and other factors, combined with an interested and hopeful lay public organized into local, state, and national mental health associations, provided much of the impetus for federal action.

Meanwhile, optimism continued to be spread by local citizens working at community, state, and national levels. The NAMH was continuing its lobbying activities at the national levels. City, county, and state mental health associations were making use of townhall meetings and nationwide television programs to educate the public that mental illness (1) can happen to anyone, (2) is a socially acceptable "disease" that can be discussed openly, (3) can be cured, (4) needs to be recognized as a national problem requiring federal funding on a scale comparable to the size of the problem.

The National Mental Health Act of 1946

With the passage of the National Mental Health Act in 1946 (almost 100 years after President Pierce's veto of Dorothea Dix's effort), the federal government clearly began to assume what has become a major responsibility for the nation's mental health. The magnitude of increase in the responsibility assumed is evident when the original 1948 budget[7] of $4,000,000 for NIMH is compared with its 1967 budget request for $303,000,000. The National Mental Health Act authorized the existing Division on Mental Hygiene[8] to support training programs in the four basic mental-health disciplines: psychiatry, psychology, nursing, and social work. The first two years of support were focused exclusively on an effort to cope with the overwhelming demand for clinical specialists trained in these four disciplines.

In 1949 the Division of Mental Hygiene was abolished, and the National Institute of Mental Health, directed by Dr. Robert Felix,[9] was established as one of the National Institutes of Health. At the same time, there was initiated a new series of training grants supporting special programs designed to improve methods of teaching the basic or "core" mental-health disciplines and to develop programs for training specialists to deal with such urgent problems as alcoholism, gerontology, and mental retardation. Among the important program developments that took place during succeeding years was the provision of support for research training, an early objective that had been delayed because of the high priority given to the training of clinical personnel.

The most comprehensive mandate given by Congress to

the National Institute of Mental Health is that of improving the mental health of the nation. This mandate involves four basic funcions: (1) to conduct research in the etiology, diagnosis, treatment, and prevention of mental illness; (2) to support such research activities within universities, medical schools, and other public and private agencies; (3) to provide consultation, technical services, and grants to states and communities to aid in the development of comprehensive mental health programs; and (4) to support training programs to increase the quantity and quality of manpower available for research and service in the field of mental health.

During the first decade of the National Mental Health Act, however, the problem of the state mental hospital system only worsened. An average of about 8,000 patients were being added each year to already overcrowded and understaffed facilities. Recognizing that current research, training, and services were not even keeping up with the problem and not sure of future directions, Congress in 1955 passed the Mental Health Study Act. This act authorized $1,250,000 for "an objective, thorough nationwide analysis and reevaluation of the human and economic problems of mental illness." From 1955 to 1960 the Joint Commission on Mental Illness and Health studied the problem of mental illness in the United States, and in 1961 it sent its final report (*Action for Mental Health*)[10] back to Congress.

The Community Mental Health Centers Construction Act

In the fall of 1961, a cabinet-level committee was given the joint commission's report to study as a basis for proposed federal action. At the same time, President Kennedy's Panel on Retardation was hard at work. The President's message to Congress on February 5, 1963, concerning mental illness and mental retardation was based on the recommendations of the committee and of the panel, studied and put together by the White House staff in the winter of 1962–63. The result was the Community Mental Health Centers Construction Act (P.L. 88–164), signed into law by President Kennedy on October 31, 1963. With present staffing amendments, this act provides nearly half a billion dollars in federal matching grants for building and staffing comprehensive mental health centers.

The relative speed with which federal legislation and funding for the community mental health centers emerged in the early 1960's owed much to the joint commission's report and to the many developments that have been reviewed briefly in this chapter. An added incentive was a highly pragmatic one. In the early 1950's a number of states had initiated plans for developing new facilities to care for a part of the huge populations of state-supported mental hospitals, which were even then costing the taxpayers a billion dollars annually. With the growing interest in mental health, there was a very real possibility that many states would allocate huge sums for existing mental hospitals. Once made, such an investment would discourage the hoped-for trend from large mental institutions to smaller community-centered facilities for treatment.

Three factors, then, helped to spur the rather rapid emergence of federal legislation, plans, and funding for the comprehensive community mental health centers in the early 1960's: (1) community experiments showing the merits of such centers; (2) the results of research showing the need for helping psychiatric patients readjust to community and family life through day-care and night-care services and "half-way cottages"; and (3) the desire to avoid spending millions more on existing, outdated mental institutions.

The concept of community mental health centers, however, comprises much more than simply multiplying the number of existing local clinics and hospitals. Its intent is to provide every community with a wide variety of services related to mental health that will be at the disposal of anyone who has need of a particular service at any time. The five essential components of a comprehensive community mental health center are (1) inpatient care, (2) outpatient care, (3) some form of partial hospitalization such as day care or night care, (4) 24-hour emergency service, and (5) educational and consultative services to the community.

The Community Mental Health Centers Construction Act represents a pivotal juncture in the history of federal mental health legislation having direct relevance to the family. Looking back, one can see that this legislation embodied the fruition of many developments underway before, during, and after World War II. Looking forward, P.L. 88–164 obviously indicates that the federal government is willing to assume considerable responsibility for mental health research, training, and services by providing standards, criteria, and regulations for both bricks and brains. With the funding of almost half a billion dollars in matching funds as a potent reinforcement of regulations, this particular bit of legislation provides the ground rules, the ideological framework, and the points of departure for new directions and emphases that extend far into the foreseeable future of the mental health field.

Significant and comprehensive as it is, P.L. 88–164 represents only a part of current federal funding and legislation in the mental health field with potential impacts upon the family. It has already been noted that the first session of the 89th Congress passed 59 laws which have implications for programs in the mental health field. For example, the 1965 amendments and funding for the Economic Opportunity Act of 1964 (P.L. 88–452) provide $880,000,000 for the fiscal year 1966 under Title II: "Urban and Rural Community Action Programs." Under the broad definition given in this bill, a "community action program" includes programs to improve "human performance, motivation and productivity"—areas surely relevant to mental health. The Appalachian Regional Development Act of 1965 (P.L. 89–4) has a similar relevance for mental health.

A variety of programs involving all stages of the family life cycle is contained in current legislation relevant to mental health—from Project Headstart and the provisions of the Elementary and Secondary Education Act of 1965 (P.L. 89–10) to the Social Security Amendments of 1965 (P.L. 89–97, Medicare), which provide that psychiatric services for the elderly are covered as fully as the other services of a general hospital.

The foregoing highly abbreviated and selective review of federal involvement in the field of mental health reveals two obvious trends. One is the movement from the attitude that mental health is not a responsibility of government to the gradual assumption of more and more governmental responsibility in this field, first at the state level and subsequently at the national level. The second trend is the completion of a full circle in the treatment (custodial) setting—from the home and community to state mental institutions and now back to the community and home. This second trend and its implications will now be considered in some detail.

RELEVANCE OF THE FAMILY TO MENTAL HEALTH

An underlying premise of the community mental health center concept is that the family is crucial in the rehabilitation of the mentally ill person. In fact, there is a considerable body of research literature which emphasizes the significance of the family in the prevention, cause, and treatment of individual mental illness.

Prior to the mid-1950's, however, much of this literature reflected at least two major limitations. The first was the one-way focus upon the contribution of the family or family members to the emotional or mental illness of the individual. Few attempts were made to answer the question, "What does illness or the ill person do to the family?" A second major limitation was the lack of concern with families qua families. For example, the several hundred studies of childrearing patterns and parent-child relationships as causal factors in mental illness largely ignored the family unit by excluding the patient's siblings, the mother's relationships with her well children, and the impact of the ill child upon the whole family. Only within the past decade have researchers given sustained and systematic attention to the role of the total family in individual mental illness.[11]

The earlier emphasis upon study of the illness and the patient was consistent, of course, with the traditional focus of "problem research" upon the illness or disease to be eliminated and with humanitarian concern for the sick individual. This emphasis was also consistent with the earlier belief that the patient's relatives are anti-therapeutic—a belief reflected in the practice of institutional routines and treatment processes. Modifications of this belief and practice have been underway for at least two decades,[12] and undoubtedly will proceed quite rapidly within the context of community mental health centers.

Sick-Care Functions and the Modern Family

The emphasis upon returning the mentally or emotionally disturbed patient to the family has developed well ahead of knowledge concerning the effect of this practice upon the family and in spite of the widespread belief that the stability and harmony of the family are endangered by the presence in the home of retarded, sick, old, or handicapped family members. This belief, explicit in popular literature and implicit in many family textbooks, has received support from the writings of Parsons and Fox, among others. Starting with the welfare of the patient as their reference point, Parsons and Fox have postulated that the structural organization of the modern urban nuclear family makes it increasingly necessary for the family to surrender to the hospital its traditional functions of caring for the sick. They have noted that "the optimal balance between permissive-supportive and disciplinary facets of treating illness is peculiarly difficult to maintain in the kind of situation presented by the American Family."[13]

The conflict between this belief and the concept of the Community Mental Health Centers Construction Act, involving multi-millions of tax funds, points to the need for some social-policy guide lines, or perhaps a committee of scholars charged with examining in advance the potential implications which proposed federal legislation might have for the family.

In the absence of clear-cut information, it is possible that the conflict between (a) the current trend back toward treatment of mentally and emotionally disturbed persons within the setting of the community and the family and (b) the belief that sick-care functions are incompatible with the structure of the modern family is more apparent than real. Let us look for a moment at a blind spot fostered by some theoretical and methodological shortcomings in family theory —specifically, the heuristic use of paired concepts and ideal types such as rural-urban and nuclear-extended families.[14] These ideal types, existing nowhere in time or space, are often accepted all too readily as accurate portrayals of real-life families.

A case in point is the generally accepted belief that the current American family is predominantly an isolated, nuclear family, consisting of mother, father, and their immediate offspring. This idea has become so widespread in the literature that it is regarded as factual; yet data obtained by several investigators indicate that the "exended" family or a "modified nuclear" family is still very viable in this country. Sussman, for example, found that related kin provided a major form of assistance during illness. He found no significant differences between social classes in the amount of help given or received during an illness of a family member. He also reported such assistance was given in 92 percent of the reported illness occurring among kin-related families living in the neighborhood during the 12-month period preceding his study.[15] The work of Eugene Litwak has also suggested the viability of the extended family as related to help provided in educational and occupational upward mobility.[16]

One of the pitfalls involved in deriving theories from ideal types is suggested in the following quotation from Dennis Wrong: "Social theory must be seen primarily as a set of answers to questions we ask of social reality."[17] It is possible that the recent developments indicative of a trend back to the family, home, and community treatment setting may be consistent with a social reality which too many professionals in the family field have simply ignored—namely, the existence of a modified but very viable extended family system.

Unfortunately, however, many of the questions asked by researchers during the last two decades have dealt with the nuclear family. We now need to ask questions such as the following: How many elders choose not to live with their relatives because they have been indoctrinated with the belief that their presence in the home is harmful? What proportion of our citizens aged 65 or more *do* live with members of their extended family or receive help from them? Is it possible that this group represents a majority of older people outside of hospitals, nursing homes, and mental institutions and that in most cases this situation augments financial stability and family cohesion? What proportion of the chronically ill, handicapped, or incapacitated persons in this country are cared for partially or completely by some members of their extended families? Is the nearness of elderly parents with limited financial resources a factor restricting the mobility of families? How much support for the medicare legislation came from young couples with aged parents? What proportion of young wives depend upon help from their mothers or other female members of their extended families at the time of a baby's birth?

These are just a few of the questions that need to be asked of a social reality that may exist in the form of a very effectual, though modified, extended family. With our rapid means of transportation and communication, extended family members who today live 100 miles apart may be more accessible to each other than were extended family members who lived on adjacent farms several generations ago.

Another area wherein social reality regarding the family needs clarification concerns the loss, gain, and transfer of functions performed by the family as a social system in a changing society. If the family is to be required to provide increasingly the care-taking (custodial) and care-giving (therapeutic) settings for its emotionally disturbed or mentally ill members, we need to know more about the adaptability of the family system.

The External Adaptive Function of the Family[18]

A better understanding of the family's adaptive function is central to all arguments concerning national social policy regarding the family. This adaptive function is an all-important variable to be taken into account when examining the impacts upon the family of federal mental health legislation in general and of the community mental health center concept in particular. The family's adaptive function is also of considerable relevance to the growing use, at least implicitly, of family members as a partial solution to the man-power shortage in the mental health field.

The parameters of the following discussion are formed by a thesis: *The adaptive function is a vital but overlooked function of the family as a social system in all societies that are either highly industrialized or undergoing industrialization.* This thesis could also be stated as follows: The rapid and pervasive social changes associated with industrialization necessitate a family system that, both structurally and functionally, is highly adaptive to the demands of other social institutions externally and to the needs of its own members internally. Although my discussion is limited to the family system in the United States, the reader may wish to consider the thesis within the context of a country undergoing industrialization. In the case of South Africa, for example, Alan Paton (*Cry, the Beloved Country*) and Wulf Sachs (*Black Hamlet*) have provided highly sensitive and discerning descriptions of both eufunctional and dysfunctional adaptations of the family system to rapid industrialization.

This thesis does not imply that the family is *the* cause or prime mover in social change, nor does it imply that the adaptive function is performed exclusively by the family or that the family is essentially passive in relation to other institutions. Other social institutions are deeply involved in social change and on occasion do respond to the changing needs and demands of the family system. Moreover, the family system can be quite selective in its adaptations. But the family, to a greater degree and more frequently than any other major social institution, facilitates social change by adapting its structure and activities to the changing needs of society and of other social institutions. A major reason is that the family's strategic *socialization* function, that of preparing its members for adult roles in the larger society, is inseparable from its *mediation* function,[19] whereby the changing requirements (demands, goals) of the society and its other social institutions are translated and incorporated into the ongoing socialization of *all* members of the family, both children and adults. A second reason is that the family as a social institution lacks an organizational spokesman or representative voice through which it might resist change.

That the adaptive function has been and continues to be overlooked can best be illustrated by a highly selective review of some of the theories and historical junctures in the literature on "functions" of the family. We shall then consider very briefly the adaptive function of the family in relation to other social institutions and to its own individual members before considering the question of when adaptation becomes dysfunctional.

Theories regarding changing family functions. One of the most significant contributors to the literature on functions of the family was William F. Ogburn, whose major interest was in the processes of social change. His earlier writings, dealing with the impacts of technology, inventions, and ideologies upon the family, set the stage for the massive amount of empirical data he compiled in the late 1920's to emphasize the increasing transfer of economic, protective, recreational, educational, and religious activities from the family to outside agencies. His initial interpretation that these increases in outside-the-home activities reflected decreases in the *traditional* functions of the family gave way in his later writings to assertions that the family was losing its functions.[20]

Ogburn's stature as a sociologist, his considerable ability in compiling empirical data, and his delineation of broad categories of functions purportedly lost by the family all combined to make his writings an important juncture for the family literature of the past three decades. The issues involved are of long standing, however, and there exists a much earlier and voluminous literature in which changes in the structure and function of the family were interpreted to support quite different "theories" of social change. Space permits only passing reference to these earlier writers, some of whom subscribed to the optimistic premise of unilinear progress and made considerable use of the "voyage literature" and "social Darwinism" to try to demonstrate a progressive evolution of the family from "primitive" to "modern" forms and from promiscuity to monogamy.[21] Others, with a more pessimistic premise, attempted to show that changes from a previous form of social order represented decay, instability, or disorganization of the family.[22]

Since Ogburn's initial interpretation was rarely given critical examination in the literature of the 1930's and 1940's, his observations and impressive statistical data concerning the decrease in the *traditional* (forms of) functions of the family became the basis or reference point for two widely held beliefs: (1) The family has lost many of its functions, and (2) this loss of functions represents a decline (decay, disorganization) of the family. Sorokin wrote:

The family as a sacred union of husband and wife, of parents and children will continue to disintegrate. . . . The main sociocultural functions of the family will further decrease until the family becomes a mere overnight parking place mainly for sex relationship.[23]

John B. Watson in the field of psychology and Carle Zimmerman and Ruth Anshen in sociology were among the many other writers in the 1930's and 1940's, who not only assumed a decay or decline of the family but (a) attempted to explain how that decline had come about and (b) posited that the family was the prime mover or first cause of social change.[24]

Textbooks and journal articles published since the early 1930's have included a variety of data and illustrative materials interpreted as demonstrating the thesis that the family has lost many of its functions. Descriptions of a "typical" pioneer or rural family needing only a few dollars a year for supplies it could not produce were contrasted with census data regarding, for example, the number of women in the labor force or the increasing numbers of restaurants, laundries, stores, and so forth—all for the purpose of showing that the family was no longer a self-sustaining economic production unit. Loss of the educational function was illustrated with observations that sons were no longer apprenticed to their fathers, that daughters learned cooking in home economics courses rather than at home, and that the teaching hours and authority of the schools had increased constantly since the turn of the century. The loss of the protective function was illustrated by references to the duties of the policeman, truant officer, nurse and fireman, and to the use of nursing homes and mental institutions. Statistics showing that a decreasing proportion of families were having daily devotions, reading the Bible, and saying grace before meals were cited as evidence that the religious function was being transferred from the family. In regard to recreational activities, it was noted that the family no longer produced its own recreation in the form of quilting parties, cornhusking bees and parlor games, and figures were given to show the marked increase in attendance at movies and spectator sports.

Is the loss of functions a myth? It is interesting to speculate about what might have happened if students of the family (a) had kept in mind Ogburn's central interest in social change and (b) had emphasized that it was the *traditional content and form* of given functions, rather than functions qua functions, that were being performed decreasingly by the family.

Beginning with the latter possibility, one can argue that, in each case of a traditional function supposedly lost to the family as a social institution, the loss has in reality been but a *change in content and form*. While it is true, for example, that the family in the United States is no longer the *economic producing unit* that it was several generations ago, it is now an *economic consuming unit*. We need to ask, therefore, whether consumption by the family unit is any less important as an economic function in today's society than production by a family unit was in yesterday's society. To what degree does our current economy depend upon the family qua family to perform the economic function of "consuming" houses, cars, boats, cereals, furniture, vacations, sterling silver, china, and pet food? As our economy is based more and more on "planned obsolescence," society's dependence upon the economic-consumption function of the family unit becomes greater and greater.

One might argue further that society is currently quite dependent upon the family function of "consuming" recreation. It would be most difficult to measure the total time and money that today's family spends not only in consuming recreation but also in producing its own recreation. It is quite possible that today's family produces more of its own recreation than did the family of 50 or 100 years ago. Consider, for example, not only the multimillions of dollars spent annually for croquet, Ping-Pong and badminton sets, cameras and home movies, family games, and barbecue equipment, but also the family's expenditures for the use of such major recreational equipment as swimming pools, rumpus rooms, camping equipment, summer homes, boats, and television and hi-fi sets.

Similar arguments can be advanced concerning the purported loss of the educational, religious, and protective functions. That fewer families, for example, say grace and have daily Bible reading today than 100 years ago (assuming this to be the case) does not demonstrate the loss of a religious function. The very *omission* of grace before meals, nightly prayers, and daily Bible reading is one kind of religious instruction, albeit not the traditional kind. If the family has lost its educational and religious functions, why do the majority of children hold religious, political, and social-class beliefs similar to those of their parents? Why are the asocial attitudes and immoral practices of the delinquent and the criminal traced to the family and not to the school or church? Why is it that the family in general and the parents in particular are considered to be key variables in determining how well and how far the child progresses in school? Why does the family receive more blame for dropouts than the school system? Did parents 100, 50, or even 20 years ago spend as much time as today's parents do in helping their children with homework and prodding them to do it? Did the pioneer parents who withdrew their children from school to work on the farm perform more of an educational function than today's parents who save, borrow, and mortgage to provide 16 or more years of schooling for their children?

The foregoing arguments are grossly oversimplified, and many of them would be irrelevant if Ogburn and the writers of textbooks on the family, instead of emphasizing the *loss* of family functions, had emphasized change—for example, the change from an *economic production function* to an *economic consumption function*. By emphasizing the family's loss of its religious, educational, protective, and recreational functions, they precluded analysis of *changes* in form and content of the family's various functions and set the stage for the pessimists who equated a loss of functions with a decline of the family. The foregoing questions are intended to provoke critical examinations of the widely held belief in the family's loss of functions—a belief that may well prove to be a myth when attention is focused upon the structural changes, the sharing of functions among social institutions, and the changing content and form of the functions of the family.

If Ogburn's observations and data had not been taken out of the context of his general interest in social change and his specific interest in tracing the causes of changes in the family, would the predominant emphasis in the family literature of the past three decades still have been on the declining importance of the family? Probably! Since the family first became recognized as an institution subject to study, changes occurring in that institution have been interpreted to support either an optimistic or a pessimistic premise concerning social trends; but the pessimists have consistently outnumbered the optimists. And, as Goode[25] has noted, the misleading stereotype of the United States family of the past as "the classical family of Western nostalgia" has been accepted as the base line both by those who view subsequent changes as progress and by those who interpret them as retrogression of the family.

Optimistic views of changes in family functions.   In the late 1940's the more optimistic interpretations of changes in the family's functions began to assume increasing importance. One interpretation, largely attributable to Burgess and Locke,[26] was that changes in the family really represented progress from an "institutional" orientation toward a companionship orientation. In the late 1950's and early 1960's a number of writers, while accepting the premise of a loss of family functions, argued that the remaining functions had become more important. An increasing variety of conceptual labels have been used to convey this more optimistic view of the changing nature of the American family. As an alternative to Burgess and Locke's "companionship family," Miller and Swanson[27] have proposed the "colleague family" and Farber[28] has suggested the "permanent-availability model."

Notable among the writers emphasizing the greater importance of the remaining family functions is Parsons, whose current interpretations represent a much more optimistic position than he had taken earlier.[29] In his more recent writings, Parsons has emphasized that changes occurring in the family involve gains as well as losses and that a unit in society which loses some of its functions is then freer to concentrate upon other functions. "When two functions, previously imbedded in the same structure, are subsequently performed by two newly differentiated structures, they can *both* be fulfilled more intensively and with a greater degree of freedom."[30] Parsons has also emphasized increasingly that the contemporary American family is differentiated rather than disorganized. "The family is more specialized than before, but not in any general sense less important, because the society is dependent *more* exclusively on it for the performance of *certain* of its various functions."[31]

Goode[32] has also supported a more optimistic interpretation of changes in the family by emphasizing its *mediating* function. The idea that the family is a mediator (buffer, strainer, funnel) between the individual and the larger society has been both implicit and explicit in the family textbooks for several decades, but Goode is the first (to my knowledge) to base the strategic significance of the family specifically on its mediating function.

The adaptive function of the family in relation to society. The following discussion of the adaptive function of the family in relation to society and to other social systems in that society is within the framework of what Mannheim[33] called "relationism" and what Goode[34] and others have referred to as the "fit" between a given family system and the larger society. Thus, the discussion is not dependent on an "organic analogy" or on the idea that there is some inherent or ideal function that the family "ought to perform."[35]

Superficially, the adaptive function of the family has some sponge-like characteristics, evidenced by the family's absorption of blame for most social problems (mental illness, delinquency, dropouts, alcoholism, suicide, crime, illegitimacy, and so forth). Future studies of the scapegoat function within and among groups may have some applicability to the scapegoat function among social systems or institutions. The family's adaptive function, as it relates to the present discussion, may be illustrated with reference to the economic system.

The economic system of a highly industrialized society demands a mobile labor force as well as some professional, skilled, and semi-skilled personnel who will work on holidays, Sundays, and at night. When the company employing Father decrees that Father shall move to another city, furtherance of the company's objectives is made possible by the adaptiveness (willing or grudging) of the entire family; collectively and individually the family members uproot themselves, adapt to a new city and neighborhood, enter different schools, and make new friends.

The varieties of family adaptation required by particular occupations have been illustrated in a number of studies such as the early one by W. F. Cottrell, "Of Time and the Railroader."[36] The family of the railroad engineer, fireman, conductor, or porter might celebrate Christmas on December 23 or December 27, as directed by the railroad schedule. The reader can supply many examples of jobs in transportation, communication, entertainment, and various professional services which require considerable adaptiveness in the schedule and patterns of family life. The adaptations necessitated in both marital and parental roles as a concomitant of working during hours other than the day shift have been examined in some detail by Mott, et al.[37] Whyte,[38] among others, has described in some detail the degree to which the families, and particularly the wives, of executives are required to adapt to the large corporation.

Somewhat conversely, studies such as the one by Gouldner[39] have shown how becoming a husband and father can influence a man's performance on the job. That adaptation is not always one-sided becomes quite evident when the demand for personnel in any given profession or occupation sufficiently exceeds the supply so as to enable the worker to force changes in institutional hiring, exact benefits in the form of preferred working hours and family vacations, and so forth.

Another illustration of the family's adaptation to occupational demands and economic pressures is the pattern observed in the Appalachian area, where employment is more readily obtained by wives and where thousands of husbands have had to adapt to the role of homemaker. The same reversal of roles is often necessary in lower-class Negro families.

It is true that the family breadwinner has a choice and that the family can be somewhat selective in its adaptation. The breadwinner can change jobs, but unless his talents and skills are in high demand he rarely is able to refuse to adapt to the demands of the present job or position without some future adaptation of his family to a lesser degree of security and income.

The reproductive function and reciprocal adaptation. The adaptations involving the family and other social systems work both ways. Reciprocal adaptation of the educational, religious, and economic systems to the family is most often brought about by changes deriving from the reproductive function. Educational and religious institutions have had to expand their facilities considerably as a result of the "baby boom" that occurred in the middle and late 1940's. The business world has adapted its advertising and merchandising to the crest of the population wave—initially with a boom in infant foods, children's toys, and clothes; later by catering to teen-agers' tastes and influence upon family buying habits and by recognizing the increasing market in automobiles for newly licensed drivers; and most recently by "gearing up" for the increase in sales of diamond rings and sterling silver and anticipating an uptrend in housing for newlywed couples in the late 1960's.

The reciprocal and even circular adaptations associated with the reproductive function were evidenced when the rise in the birth rate and the shortage of classroom space resulted in double shifts in school which in turn meant modifications in family schedules. The rise in the birth rate also was associated with expansion of church buildings and occasionally double shifts for church services, as well as the movement of some churches to suburbia. Efforts of the religious system to influence the family's reproductive function are as old as history, but within the last decade a number of denominations have reversed the age-old injunction to "beget, be fruitful and multiply," as family planning and "wise fertility control" are being taught as Christian principles. The family retains, of course, its age-old modes of resistance to or pressure against church policy and personnel by smaller allocations for the church from the family budget and by sporadic attendance.

At least three crucial points may be hypothesized concerning the reciprocal adaptation among various social systems: (1) Social institutions or systems other than the family adapt only to the degree that such adaptation is in the interest of their respective goals. (2) If there is a conflict of interests or goals, it is most frequently the family which "gives in" and adapts. (3) The family usually adapts for lack of an alternative and in so doing serves the goals of other social systems and facilitates the survival of a society based on social change.

The plausibility of the first hypothesis is suggested by the fact that, although the reproductive function would appear to be one major function whereby the family "forces" adaptation from other social institutions, this is tolerated only to the degree that such adaptation furthers the ends or goals of the other institutions. The "baby boom" of the 1940's was initially interpreted to represent more profits for business and was equated with prosperity. Religious and educational institutions were pleased with the prospect of more potential converts for the churches and higher wages and better job security for teachers, school administrators, and professors. In the late 1950's and early 1960's, however, the baby boom was viewed in an entirely different light as the increasing number of teen-agers about to enter the labor market added to fears about the unemployment rate and as high schools and colleges faced building programs that necessitated sharp increases in tax monies. Of equal, if not greater, concern has been the worldwide depletion of natural resources and living space.

The subsequent and current attack upon the problem of

the "population explosion" is providing a fascinating illustration of the way the family, even in regard to its traditional function of reproduction, is expected to adapt to the goals and interests of the society and of its other major social systems.

That it is the family system which gives in or adapts whenever a conflict of interests or goals arises was shown earlier in the discussion of the demands of the economic system. The school system, the business world, and even church services are geared to time schedules that serve first the needs, interest, and efficiency of the school, the business, and the church; the family adapts its schedule accordingly. Even in times of armed conflict, the adaptations required of economic, educational, and religious institutions usually have some side effects beneficial to those social institutions; it is the family that sacrifices most in the interests of winning the war.

Adaptativeness and the protective-caretaker function. That the family lacks an alternative to adaptation (although it may select among several patterns of adaptation) may be illustrated further with reference to what Ogburn called the "protective function." There is little doubt that the family has shared this function increasingly with agencies or organizational units outside the home. For the family, however, this sharing has often meant less authority but more responsibility —at least financially. The family provides sons and husband-fathers to protect us in time of war, but the government decides at what age, where, and how the draftee will protect us. An invalid grandparent may come under the care and authority of a nursing home, but the family, if able, assumes financial responsibility. The authority of the county, state, and FBI to apprehend and incarcerate delinquents and criminals for the "protection of society" includes the regulation of family-prisoner contacts during imprisonment and supervisory authority over the individual when he is returned to the family on probation or parole.

And now, backed by multimillion dollars in federal funds, the comprehensive community health centers, with their emphasis upon out-patient, night-care, day-care, and "half-way cottage" services will transfer from mental institutions to the family an increased responsibility for the protective-caretaker function. The family will be expected to adapt to the return of its mentally ill or emotionally disturbed member, just as it was expected to adapt to the return of the parolee member several decades ago. The family will also be expected to adapt to the "intrusion" of the mental health personnel who will have implicit if not explicit authority for the rehabilitation and treatment of the patient, just as earlier it adapted to the "intrusion" of the parole and probation officers, the judge of the juvenile court, and the social worker.

Why must the family adapt in this way? Because it has no realistic alternative. Given the mores of our society, how could the family maintain its ideological image if it refused to accept one of its members convalescing from mental illness or in the process of rehabilitation from crime or delinquency?

More important, who would be the spokesman for the family's refusal? The National Association for Mental Health has a powerful and effective lobby; the family has none. Almost every segment of the religious, educational, professional, recreational, political, and occupational worlds has strong and powerful spokesmen at local, state, and national levels. Each group of 20 physicians, 30 ministers, 40 schoolteachers, five manufacturers, or three union men in a given city usually can exert more influence and pressure—directly or indirectly—than can 5,000 families living in that same city.

Thus, no authoritative spokesman asks prior to the passage of legislation: How will the family be affected by the return of the mentally ill member? What will double shifts at school do to the family? Will the regulations of the program of Aid to the Families of Dependent Children (AFDC) encourage husbands to desert their families? Will urban renewal disrupt the family and the network of extended family relationships? Would it be easier on the family to draft 45-year-old fathers for many service tasks before drafting 25-year-old fathers for those same tasks?

The inverse relation between adaptiveness and organization. Even if such questions were asked, who would answer? The family system has no collective representative, no lobbyist, no official spokesman. Therefore, to observe that the family is the most adaptive of the several social systems in a rapidly changing society is perhaps only to recognize that it is the least organized. The adaptiveness of a group appears to be inversely related to its degree of organization and to its size. The army furnishes a good example of a large, highly organized, and extremely rigid group. At the other extreme is the family system. The size or number involved in what we refer to as the family system tends to be the number in each individual family; and, because the family system is *un*organized beyond each individual family, it is easily divided and its resistance conquered. Thus, it is not surprising that in a given community the organization spokesmen for the teachers, the union, the clergy, or business can be and are heard and heeded much more clearly than are 5,000 *individual* families. To be sure, individual members of the family express their preferences in voting, but political campaigns are rarely directed toward the family as a political unit.

Adaptation Within the Family

The individual family's small numerical size and its lack of an organizational tie-in with all other families do serve a *use*ful purpose—that of facilitating the family's adaptation to the needs of its individual members. The highly individualized needs of each of 40 persons in a classroom, factory, office, or church cannot possibly be heard or met to the same degree as within the respective families of those 40 persons.

Much of the lament about the impersonalization, alienation, or dehumanization of human beings in the "multiversity," the factory, the corporation, the hospital, or the large urban church ignores the lack of an alternative. The same individuals who may bemoan the apersonal cashier in the supermarket, the tight-lipped teller in the bank, the hurried physician, the unavailable professor, or the uncommunicative dispenser of other professional services would strongly object to waiting in line for an extra hour while other customers and clients were being responded to warmly and personally on an individual basis. Like the Lilliputians who thought that Gulliver's timepiece must be a god to require such frequent consultations, a stranger on this planet would justifiably infer that the citizens of highly industrialized societies not only worship time but are governed and ruled by it. In such societies, the family becomes even more important as a flexible social unit wherein there is time and tolerance for expressing and acting out individual needs and wherein being a few minutes late does not disrupt the production line, board meetings, transportation schedules, and classroom lectures.

The time-scheduling demands that a technological society makes on the individual are perhaps minor in comparison with its demands for productive output, self-discipline, and emotional control. In combination, these demands increase the importance of what Goode has called the family's "task of restoring the input-output emotional balance of individualism."[40]

The church, the school, the office, and the marketplace cannot possibly provide sufficient freedom for the amount of emotional release and input apparently needed by the individual. In an elementary class of 30 to 50 students, Junior is no more a distinct individual than are the "two-legged numbers" protesting that fact on college campuses today. The teen-age peer group does provide a supportive audience for Daughter, but only within the confines of the immediate family is she able to express many of her individual foibles, anxieties, and doubts. And Father, who can rarely express his feelings of anger at a client, customer, or superior within the work situation, needs on occasion to ventilate such feelings within the privacy of the home and family.

Dysfunctional Adaptation

To return the aged, convalescing, or mentally disturbed patient to the family may well serve the goals of reducing the loads of nursing homes and state mental hospitals, save the taxpayers' money, and prove highly therapeutic for the patient. But what will be the effects on the family and on society? How much can the family take? Will it still be able to permit the emotional blowoffs and to provide the relaxation and the emotional input needed daily by its "well" members, whose output, tight schedules, and emotional control will continue to be expected in the office, factory, and schoolroom?

The foregoing paragraph is not intended as an argument against the gradual return of emotionally disturbed, aged, or infirm persons to their families. It is simply a further attempt to illustrate (a) that the adaptive function of the family system is crucial in any society characterized by rapid social change; (b) that the adaptive family system of our industrial era generally is *un*organized and unrepresented beyond each individual family; and (c) that it, therefore, is predisposed to being overloaded with or over-adaptive to the demands with which it is confronted internally and externally.[41]

This adaptiveness of the family will be interpreted by some as evidence of weakness and by others, as evidence of strength. Those who view it as weakness may point to the family's loss of power and authority; while those who interpret it as strength may recognize the dependence of the larger social system upon the flexibility of the family and see the family's adaptive function as crucial to its socialization and mediation functions. Certainly the family's internal adaptiveness may well prove to be a key variable in the socialization of the child for the flexibility needed in future adult roles within a rapidly changing society. At times, however, the adaptive function of the family may become dysfunctional rather than eufunctional.

One example of dysfunctional adaptation has been provided by the program of Aid to Families of Dependent Children (AFDC). In adapting to the early regulations of AFDC, an unknown proportion of fathers deserted their families or perhaps, in collusion with their wives, simply disappeared from public view, to enable their wives and children to qualify for AFDC funds. Subsequent awareness that the early regulations may have encouraged such desertions and the belief that an unemployed father in the home is better than no father, or a series of adult males, have resulted in much discussion and some revisions of the earlier regulations, to which the low-income parents may have adapted too well— to the detriment of the family unit. Similarly, the low-income family's adaptiveness (for lack of an alternative) to urban renewal may prove in some instances to have ill served the interests of either the families forced to move or the city planners and taxpayers.

These examples, both of which pertain to lower-income families, also serve to illustrate the fact that the degree and form of adaptive activities vary widely among the family systems of various socioeconomic and ethnic groups. In the United States, for example, it has been postulated that in the middle class the nuclear family system is more likely to manipulate the extended family, whereas in the lower and upper classes, nuclear family systems are more likely to be manipulated by or to adapt to the extended family.[42]

An illustration which cuts across class lines is to be found in the internal adaptiveness of the family to its teen-age members. When familial adaptation to the needs and wants of these members reaches the point where parental control is lost, it becomes dysfunctional and ceases to serve the social-ization function of the family. That parental control is fre-quently lost or, at best, tenuously held is not surprising when we consider that (a) a sizable proportion of the current gen-eration of teen-agers was reared by a permissive philosophy that equated wants with needs; (b) teen-agers are highly organized in their selective translations to parents about what other parents allow; and (c) parents are remarkably unorganized in their resistance to teen-agers' demands and expectations.

The reader will be able to supply many examples of both external and internal adaptations of the family which he regards as dysfunctional. A more difficult task, one involving a hierarchy of values, is to answer the explicit questions: dys-functional *for whom* and for *what goals?* The President's Commission on National Goals affirmed that "the family is at the heart of society,"[43] but the ethos of individualism over-shadows this affirmation. It is the value affixed to the in-dividual patient which earlier excluded the family from the treatment process and which now involves the family in both diagnosis and treatment of the ill individual. For per-spective on this switch, we need to consider briefly "family therapies" as an inadvertent by-product of earlier mental health research.

Mental Health Research and "Family Therapies"

Our earlier review of some of the stimuli for the current degree of federal involvement in the mental health field omitted the considerable role of federal funding for research, from which have come data to both stimulate and buttress the trend of the treatment setting back to the family and community. Space here is obviously inadequate to review a literature so voluminous that 162 pages are required for an annotated bibliography of articles published between 1960 and 1964 on psychiatry and the family.[44] There is space, however, to point out that the interest in family therapies which has developed so rapidly within the past decade was at first an inadvertent by-product of mental health research supported largely by federal funds, but is now the stimulus for concerted research and training activities carried on under the auspices of NIMH and elsewhere.

Several reviews of the development of family therapy (a term applied to a method of treatment as well as to an area of research) have been summarized by Zuk and Rubinstein.[45] In one of these reviews, Parloff[46] described the completion of a full circle in the treatment setting. Involvement of the family with its mentally ill member was minimal when orthodox psychoanalytic thinking held that even contact between the therapist and family members was anti-therapeutic, because it would disturb the patient-therapist transference and counter-transference processes. During the height of the orthodox psychoanalytic thinking, even the social workers and social agencies changed their traditional procedures and tended to substitute a one-to-one involvement with individual family members for their much older practice of relating to the total family.

Gradually, however, increasing awareness of some of the *negative* impacts of family members upon the patient led to interest in studying the "significant-other" members of the family. Thus, in the case of schizophrenia, theories have undergone a series of changes, recapitulated by Haley[47] as follows: (1) the causal agent is within the individual; (2) the causal agent may be within the mother-child relationship or in a pathogenic mother; (3) an inadequate father also is involved; and (4) at least three family members are involved in a "pathological system of interaction."

A review by Jackson and Satir,[48] in addition to citing some of the factors and trends noted by Parloff and by Haley, emphasizes the contributions of Sullivan, Horney, Fromm, Erikson, and others who gave increasing attention to the influence of culture and current life situations and stresses upon the individual. Jackson and Satir also point up the important contribution of sociological studies such as those by Hollingshead and Redlich[49] which showed that the prevalence of schizophrenia varies widely among different social, ethnic, and subcultural groups in the United States. Finally, some of the anxiety about the effect on transference and counter-transference of having more than two persons present in the psychotherapeutic situation was reduced as the techniques of psychodrama and sociodrama were developed and demonstrated publicly.

As increasing numbers of researchers gave systematic attention to the roles of several family members in contributing to individual mental illness,[50] the pattern of research results stimulated "family therapies." For example, the training program in family therapy currently supported by NIMH at the Mental Health Research Institute in Palo Alto had its roots in the earlier research of Gregory Bateson and others concerning the "double bind" theory. The hundreds of studies supported by federal funds in universities and medical schools, as well as the intramural research program at NIMH, are producing data which have intensified the attention given to family therapies and to the families of mentally ill persons.[51] For a long time to come, the study of family pathology as a significant factor in mental disturbance will undoubtedly continue to provide as many questions as answers relevant to the trend of returning the treatment setting to the home and community.[52]

The quasi-family orientation of "family" therapies. The vast majority of research projects dealing with the family and mental illness and the wide variety of family therapies being employed still are not, strictly speaking, family oriented. Rather, they are oriented to the pathological elements or members involved in the mental or emotional stress. As Spiegel and Bell[53] noted several years ago, the focus upon the "patient-in-the-family" is still fragmented by concern with the family members presumed to be involved in the pathology; and, as a result, the *total* familial relationships are ignored almost as if the family as a whole did not exist.

The *a*family bias of such research and treatment is perhaps most apparent in the fact that studies of the mother-child dyad and even of the father-mother-child triad in schizophrenia rarely use the other children within the same family as the control group of nonschizophrenics.[54] Thus, although federal funds have supported several hundred studies of patients with schizophrenic, psychosomatic, psychoneurotic, and certain organic illnesses, there are few data available concerning the proportion of the patients' siblings who are similarly afflicted. If the proportion were very small, then we would need to search for factors within the family unit or the total network of intrafamilial relationships to account for the fact that only one of several children fell victim to that particular illness.

The variety of techniques employed in family psychotherapy, which quite obviously are still in a highly preliminary phase of development, seldom reflect concern with the family qua family. Even studies of the way in which an individual's mental illness and subsequent recovery are perceived and handled within the family are generally limited to the marital dyad. Although the therapeutic developments and the research are providing considerable information pointing to further research and innovations in treatment techniques, most of the available information has been derived from studying (a) only selected aspects and dyadic relationships of the family and (b) only certain members of the family. Thus, few data are available concerning the effect of mental illness or a convalescing patient upon the total family unit. It seems unlikely that such data will be forthcoming in time to provide sound guide lines for policy regarding the operation of community mental health centers and for "before" measurements needed in evaluating treatment procedures which utilize community and family contexts.

MARITAL HEALTH: A NEEDED SPECIALTY

The frustrating search for theories adequate to explain the process involved in "family therapies"[55] and the data derived from studies of these therapies reflect some of the limitations imposed by the failure to distinguish between marriage and the family. Our understanding of marital dynamics has not been greatly furthered by borrowing in one direction from the individualistically oriented concepts of psychoanalysis and psychology and in the other direction from the institutionally oriented concepts of family sociologists. The transition from an institutional to a companionship orientation for the family has not been accompanied by the development of concepts for this companionship orientation.

"Marriage" needs to be divorced from "the family." The romantic and nostalgic image of "the family" has for too long postponed the specialization needed to develop concepts

and methods for studying marital health, marital roles, and dyadic dynamics as distinct from parental roles, parent-child dynamics, child development, and child socialization. Many if not most couples will admit that on occasion conflict arises between marital and parental roles. (For example, being a good father is frequently incompatible with being a good husband, and vice versa.)

The "family life cycle," or "developmental," approach represents one attempt to bridge this gap, but it is the weakest in the area of marital dynamics—just where it should be strongest. Even the concept of the "empty nest" reflects the implicit assumption that marital roles are secondary to parental roles; yet the marital dyad lasts longer and is more intimate than any other family relationship. Children come and go, but husband and wife remain. The roles, dynamics, and "health" of the marital dyad need to be given attention proportional to their significance. Even though the current NIMH intramural research activities of Goodrich, Ryder, and others[56] indicate that increasing attention is being given to the marital dyad, far more attention is needed; hence, the deliberately provocative spirit of the following argument that marital health should be recognized as a distinct specialty field and substantive area for research and training supported by federal funds.

The Field of Marital Health

Some justification is needed for the conceptual label of "marital health," as well as some clarification of what it might encompass as a health field. Some may argue that there already are too many "health" fields. Local, state, and national organizations already abound with personnel, moneys, and programs dedicated to the promotion of physical, dental, mental, school, environmental, community, family, child, maternal, and industrial health. My justification for adding marriage to the growing list of areas in which one is supposed to be "hale and sound" is based on at least four assumptions:

1. Marital health is no more amorphous and no less significant than most of the other health fields now in existence.

2. A positive conceptual label such as "marital health" is needed to facilitate multi-disciplinary and interprofessional

collaboration and to stimulate the provision of funds for programs of research, training, and treatment.

3. The explicit recognition of marital health as a specialty area will stimulate much-needed critiques concerning the reality, criteria, and scientific basis of what is slowly and implicitly emerging as a "marital health field."

4. The continued coupling of "marriage and the family" in courses and textbooks perpetuates an ideological lag which is at least partially responsible for the fact that concepts appropriate for studying the family with an institutional orientation have not been supplemented with concepts appropriate for studying the marital dyad of a companionship-oriented family. There should quite rightly remain a specialty for those interested in the family as a social system or institution, just as there is a specialty in child development for those interested in that subsystem of the family. Explication of the marital dyad as a subsystem of the family and a concerted focus upon it as a specialty field would show up some of the gaps in knowledge and make more obvious the mislabeling, for example, of many parent-child studies as family research.

The first three of these assumptions are derived from a number of superficial similarities in the historical development, the conceptual labeling, and the public acceptance of the various "health fields" now in existence:

1. A given health or social problem (mental illness, divorce, tooth decay, air pollution) may exist for a long time before public interest and concern are sufficient to stimulate efforts at prevention, treatment, and research on the part of personnel from a wide variety of disciplines and professions.

2. The initial phases of arousing public interest are usually accompanied by predominantly "negative" approaches which emphasize and publicize the "badness," "evilness," or economic costs of the particular disease or problem to be eliminated.

3. The early negative emphasis is gradually replaced by a more "positive" approach and the adoption of a conceptual label, such as "mental health," "school health," or "environmental health," which makes it easier for interested persons to organize and be *for* health rather than simply *against*

disease. "National Council Against Tooth Decay" is a far less appealing title than "National Council for Dental Health."

4. The positive label which designates a health field consisting of several related health problems, while providing a cohesive focus for multi-disciplinary collaboration, also leads to intermittent divisive concerns about "professional domain." In the field of mental health, for example, considerable interdisciplinary collaboration is accompanied by a wide range of opinions about which mental health discipline is "more equal" than the other mental health disciplines.

5. The gradual evolvement of community, state, and national organizational units in a given health field is accompanied by the creation or enlargement of state and federal agencies with funds to support programs of research, training, and public education in that particular field. The "area" or field may be identified with reference to age (child health, Medicare), location (school health, community health, industrial health), or specific diseases (mental health, dental health). The process of identifying and labeling a particular health field within the federal government and particularly the Public Health Service and the National Institutes of Health is perhaps best known as the "categorical approach to health problems."

6. The acceptance of positive labels and approaches is facilitated when the particular disease or ailment is regarded as being not primarily the fault of the individual affected. (For example, the specialty of environmental health has emerged very rapidly as a positive approach to the relatively recent and non-individual problems of air and water pollution; and "mental health" became more readily acceptable as a positive label when attention was focused on forces beyond the control of the individual as causal agents in mental illness. But "sexual health" has not yet replaced the negatively labeled approaches to the age-old problem of venereal disease —a disease for which the individual is held responsible.)

7. The emergence of a health field with a positive label is accompanied by much-needed critiques. These critiques question (a) the reality or existence of such an entity, (b) the criteria for "health" in that particular area, and (c) the "social movement" versus the scientific bases of the given field.

The specialty of marital health could encompass at least four major foci. Two of these are within the medical framework: (1) the impact of illness upon marital dynamics and (2) ways in which the marital relationship may contribute to mental illness, physical illness, accident-proneness, alcoholism, and so on. The third and forth foci of the marital health field move away from the medical context to the larger society. They are (3) marital health as the *dependent* variable influenced by the social and psychological demands of a technological society and (4) marital health as an *independent* variable influencing individual role performance in various social systems and relating to social problems relevant to mental health.

Impacts of Illness upon Marital Health

The first two foci are but two sides of the same coin, one of which—the impact of illness upon marital dynamics—has been almost totally neglected. Do the specific illnesses of one spouse influence the marital relationship or the state of marital health? The focus of this question, which reverses the one-way emphasis of much of the literature on psychosomatic illness, is the least developed of the four foci. It represents a field wide open for research at the present time.

It was noted earlier that Parsons and Fox[57] postulated sick-care functions as incompatible with the organization of the modern nuclear family. The disparity between this postulate and current developments leading to an earlier return of the mental patient to the home and community underscore the need for an understanding of the effect of illness, whether psychic or somatic, upon marital relations.

Most of the major illnesses, accidents, and handicaps are accompanied by psychological components. Some of these emotional components probably are present in all illnesses, while others are specifically associated with certain surgical operations and diseases. Diabetes, radical mastectomy, colostomy, cardiovascular ailments, paraplegia, and a broad range of physical illnesses must each have some highly unique emotional components about which we know very little. Replication research in this area is almost non-existent. The several hundred articles that have been published in this field contain predominantly impressionistic data. The predominant concern is with the disease or problem to be eliminated, and minimum attention has been given to what the illness does to the patient and to his marital health. Far more vigorous research and reliable data are needed in this area. In addition, the physician needs to be made aware of the importance of marital health and of the likelihood that the emotional components of physical illness will stimulate maladaptive responses and create marital stress.

If more knowledge were available concerning the psychological concomitants of specific illnesses and were communicated to both the patient and the spouse, they could undoubtedly cope with them much more constructively. For example, the general and sometimes marked depressive reactions associated with hepatitis and mononucleosis may make the victim of either of these diseases very difficult to live with for a period of several months. If the spouse is unaware that such a depression is "par for the course" and usually accompanies this particular illness, there is a good possibility that both patient and spouse will develop maladaptive responses to the depression. In cyclical fashion, these maladaptive responses may prolong the patient's depression and increase the probability of marital stress for the couple involved. Communicating the information about the emotional components of illness to the patient and the patient's spouse requires only a few minutes of the physician's time, yet could represent primary prevention of what might otherwise become the source of serious marital stress.

Another example is provided by the extreme irritability, hostility, and at times almost paranoid reactions of the severely burned patient during the period of prolonged treatment. These emotional components of convalescence from severe burns may impair the health of the marriage if maladaptive responses to them are developed by either partner.

Training will be as important as the search for reliable data, for the physician is not the only person who needs such knowledge. In the hospital the nurses, nurses' aides, and orderlies are usually given some orientation concerning the patient's physical needs as related to his illness. Rarely, however, are they oriented to the patient's emotional needs and reactions which may stem directly from the illness. Hospital personnel who know how to care for the cast on a broken leg and who recognize the significance of a temperature of

102°F are likely to regard marked depression in the patient with hepatitis as reflecting simply an unfriendly disposition or a cantankerous person.

The hospital stay, however, is a very small part of the patient's experience with illness; presumably it will become an even smaller part as hospitals become more and more crowded. As soon as possible the patient is returned home where, if it is the husband who is sick, the wife assumes the role of nurse. It is difficult to conceive of any physical illness, injury, or handicap that does not have some impact upon the marital relationship. It is equally difficult to conceive of any degree of marital stress which does not have some repercussions with reference to the physical and emotional states of the two people involved. What kinds of maladaptive responses to the emotional components of illnesses are developed when neither the ill nor the well spouse is aware that such components accompany the illness?

Parsons has suggested that "somatic illness may be defined in terms of incapacity for relevant task performance in a sense parallel to that in which mental illness is thought of as incapacity for role-performance."[58] He also has postulated that to be ill is to "be in a partially and conditionally *legitimated* state." This state is legitimate only as long as the sick person reaffirms the valuation of health by recognizing the undesirability of being sick and accepts the obligation to try to get well as soon as possible and to cooperate with others to that end. What then is the impact upon the marital relationship when the well spouse thinks the ill spouse is not trying to get well?

Marital Dynamics as a Factor in the Etiology of Illness

A second major focus of the marital health field is the reverse of the one just discussed and is concerned with the ways in which marital dynamics contribute to illness. The literature contains many books and articles to emphasize, if not document, the importance of the family in the prevention, cause, and treatment of individual illness. Much of this literature, however, may be seen upon closer inspection to have an *a*marital as well as an *a*family bias. Until quite recently, the emphasis has been only upon selected aspects of the total family—notably the parent-child system—which are thought to cause illness or contribute to it.

The concept of marital health suggests the possibility of "maritosomatic" illnesses. Are there maritosomatic ailments, real or imagined, that are accidentally or purposely developed to avoid some of the tasks and roles expected of a husband or of a wife? Maritosomatic or task-avoidance ailments of the wife in relation to coitus are myriad, but what of task-avoidance and role-avoidance ailments of the husband? Is alcoholism one such ailment? State and federal support of research, clinics, and treatment in the field of alcoholism has resulted in a considerable literature emphasizing the significant role of the spouse in the etiology, control, and treatment of alcoholism; but research in this area has been far more concerned with individual personality characteristics and with the alcoholic's relationship to his mother than with the alcoholic's marital health. Also, there are many unknowns surrounding the fact that the spouse, not the physician, is the initial diagnostician whose verbal and non-verbal responses to the partner's expression of symptoms may dangerously delay a needed visit to the physician or hospital.

Marital Health in Non-Medical Contexts

The two non-medical foci suggested for the marital health field are concerned with marital health as (1) a *dependent* variable influenced and affected by the considerable psychological pressures and economic demands of our modern technological society and (2) an *independent* variable contributing to various social problems, e.g., alcoholism, traffic accidents, dropouts, and delinquency.

Perhaps never before in the history of marriage has so much been expected and even demanded of the marital dyad. The emotional output and emotional discipline demanded in the school, office, factory, neighborhood, and church in a technological society call for a corresponding emotional input within the marriage. Such demands will increase rather than decrease. What is this entity called marital health? How can it be measured? What are its attributes? How does it remain viable, constantly providing emotional input for each spouse, when parental, occupational, and civic roles demand increasing emotional output and control?

In summary, recognition of marital health as a specialty area for research and training is long overdue. The critiques that will inevitably follow its emergence as a bona fide field for scientific inquiry, federal funding, and professional training are much needed and will be most welcome. Moreover, a specific and programmatic focus upon marital health would lead to increasing awareness of a variable—independent or dependent—that needs to be measured and taken into account as one of several base lines when the implications and impacts of federal programs in the mental health field are being assessed.

SOCIAL POLICY CONCERNING THE FAMILY

To hypothesize the existence of a statistically significant inverse relationship between marital health and problems related to mental health, such as alcoholism, juvenile delinquency, illegitimacy, suicide, and "negative parent-child relationships," is perhaps only to restate in modified form some time-honored beliefs concerning the importance of the family. If the hypothesis were made the subject of research, the results (a) might indicate the beliefs to be more sentimental than factual or (b) might demonstrate the merits of diverting some federal funds, research, and professional effort from social problems that are frequently presumed to originate within the family and directing them toward understanding and strengthening marital health.

The suggestion that marriage be divorced from the family for purposes of improved conceptualization and research methodologies affords belated recognition to the fact that the marital subsystem should be given attention equal to that given other subsystems of the family. The parent-child subsystem, for example, has already been singled out for study and treatment in the field of child development and in such professional specialties as child psychology and child psychiatry. In any consideration of social policy concerning the family, each of these subsystems, as well as the total family system as a social institution, needs to be made explicit as a separate but related part. Explication of each subsystem will help to point up the gaps in research knowledge that need to be filled in order to establish reliable guide lines for assessing the potential impacts of federal legislation. To point out the lack of specific focus upon the family qua family in federal legislation and funding in the field of mental health is perhaps but another way of indicating that there is no specific focus upon "wellness," only fragmented foci upon problematic aspects of the family and upon problems believed to have some of their origins in family life.

In many ways the absence of national policy concerning the family may be a blessing. In view of our thesis that the rapid social changes associated with industrialization necessitate at least one major social system or institution highly amenable to change, it may be fortunate that there are no official spokesmen, lobbying groups, or even Presidential advisory committees regarding the family. The adaptability of the family may well be its greatest and most significant contribution to modern society, and adaptability is seldom compatible with organization. Moreover, in a society where the primary goals are individualistic in orientation, the family's amenability to change and adaptation to the pressures and expectations of the larger society and of other social systems are consistent with its mediation and socialization functions of preparing individuals for adult life.

A group of social scientists called together during 1960 to advise the Commissioner of Social Security on "priorities for sustaining and enriching family life" dealt specifically with the question of whether they saw the family as an end in itself. The major premise and framework of the ensuing discussion was that the needs and interests of the individual were to be served within the context of the family.[59] However, as Alvin L. Schorr has noted,[60] attempts to formulate a national policy concerning the family quickly encounter a hierarchy of values which place individualism ahead of families—individualism not only in terms of the individual person but also in terms of individual families. As an example, legislation which supports the broken family may exclude or even inadvertently punish the intact family. Legislation which might assist the old person to live with his children may encroach upon the rights of the elderly parent who wants to live alone or upon the rights of couples who prefer not to have their parents live with them.

The ethos concerning the primacy of the individual has a long history prior to the legislation of the French Revolution, which sought to free the individual from the control of the church, the family, the guild, and the community. As Calhoun noted, it has become "the democratic disposition to deal with individuals, not families."[61] We are not likely to change this ethos, and few would want to.

Nor is it likely that any one organization or spokesman can really represent "the family," although many professional groups and lay organizations allegedly speak for the family. However, in view of the increasingly predominant role of federal funding and legislation in the mental health field, together with the established trend of moving the treatment setting back to the home and community and the increasing demands on the family to be all things to all people, it might be desirable to establish a national commission charged with some responsibilities comparable to those of the Royal Commission in England. One of the ongoing tasks of such a commission would be to point up gaps in research, to explicate what is known and draw attention to what is being neglected in efforts to understand the family systems of different social strata and the various subsystems within the family.

A more immediate objective of direct relevance to the projected research, training, consultation, and treatment activities of the comprehensive community mental health centers would be to establish an organizational unit within the Public Health Service to administer programmatic support for research and training in marital health. There is a Childrens Bureau, and the Bureau of Family Services was established in 1963 as a result of the Social Security Amendments. But again the predominant focus is on children and on those families needing aid and services.

A marital health unit—however small—could be created within the National Institute of Mental Health. The data and manpower resulting from the research and training programs that could be funded through such a unit are long overdue and sorely needed in relation to (a) ongoing evaluation and increased understanding of the impacts upon marital health of the explicit use of home and community contexts and of the implicit use of family members as manpower resources in the care and treatment of the mentally ill, (b) the projected treatment and educational services to be coordinated through or provided by the community mental health centers in a variety of areas relevant to marital health; (c) the emergence of marriage counseling as a multidisciplinary specialty; and (d) the increasing need for pre-

ventive psychiatry to have a concerted focus on research
and training in the primary prevention of mental and marital
stress originating in maladaptive responses to the emotional
components of physical illness, surgery, and physical handicaps.

Notes

INTRODUCTION

1 P. A. Sorokin, *Social and Cultural Dynamics*, New York: American Book Company, 1941, four volumes; and C. C. Zimmerman, *The Family and Civilization*, New York: Harper & Row, Publishers, 1947.

2 Ernest W. Burgess and Harvey J. Locke, *The Family: From Institution to Companionship*, New York: American Book Company, 1945.

3 Clark E. Vincent, "Mental Health and The Family," *Marriage and the Family*, vol. 29, no. 1, February, 1967, pp. 18–39. Included in this volume.

4 *Webster's New Collegiate Dictionary*, Springfield, Mass.: G. and C. Merriam Company, 1961, p. 197.

5 For a more technical discussion of this orientation, see Donald A. Hansen and Reuben Hill, "Families Under Stress," in *Handbook of Marriage and the Family*, Harold T. Christensen, ed., Chicago: Rand McNally and Company, 1964, pp. 787–792.

6 One of the first studies was Willard Waller, *The Old Love and the New: Divorce and Readjustment*, New York: Horace Liveright, 1930. A selection from this book is included in this volume.

7 T. D. Eliot, "Family Crises and Ways of Meeting Them," in *Marriage and the Family*, H. Becker and R. Hill, eds., Boston: Heath, 1942, pp. 489–536; and R. Hill, *Families Under Stress*, New York: Harper & Row, Publishers, 1949.

8 E. E. Le Masters, "Parenthood as Crisis," *Marriage and Family Living*, vol. 19, 1957, pp. 352–355.

9 Willard Waller and Reuben Hill, *The Family, A Dynamic Interpretation*, New York: The Dryden Press, 1951, p. 459.

10 L. L. Geismar and Beverly Ayres, *Patterns of Change in Problem Families*, St. Paul: Family Centered Project, 1959.

11 Hansen and Hill, *op. cit.*, pp. 798–801.

12 George Levinger, "Sources of Marital Dissatisfaction Among Applicants for Divorce," *American Journal of Orthopsychiatry*, vol. 36, no. 5, October, 1966, pp. 803–807. Included in this volume.

13 Jay Haley, "Whither Family Therapy," *Family Process*, vol. 1, no. 1, March, 1962, pp. 69–100. Included in this volume.

14 George P. Murdock, "Family Stability in Non-European Cultures," *Annals of the American Academy of Political and Social Science*, vol. 272, 1950, pp. 195–201; and W. J. Goode, *After Divorce*, Glencoe, Ill.: The Free Press, 1956.

LIVING POOR: PROVIDING THE BASIC NECESSITIES; PRIORITIES AND PROBLEMS

Camille Jeffers

1 This particular instance of "hunger" is probably best classified as an example of what is medically called *pica*.

2 It was this kind of experience that led me to be leery of the easy and sometimes automatic label, "maternal rejection," for a mother like Mrs. Todd.

3 I have often wondered whether Mrs. Todd was really saying to me, "I might have to use jelly glasses to drink out of in my house, but if you have salad plates in your house, then there is no reason to act as if you do not have any. I use what I've got, why don't you do the same thing?"

4 This was during a particularly harsh, snowy and cold winter during which building construction was at a standstill for prolonged periods.

5 On the way Mrs. Martin confided that she was closest to this sister, much closer than to her mother. Her sister was a warm, friendly person, the wife of a serviceman and the mother of five children.

UNEMPLOYMENT, FAMILY STRUCTURE, AND SOCIAL DISORGANIZATION

National Advisory Commission on Civil Disorders

1 Currently $3335 per year for an urban family of four.

2 Source: Social Security Administration. Based on 1964 data.

3 For the nation as a whole, the proportion of nonwhite families living in poverty dropped from 39 percent to 35 percent from 1964 to 1966 (defining "family" somewhat differently from the definition used in the data above). The number of such families declined from 1.9 million to 1.7 million. However, the number and proportion of all nonwhites living in central cities rose in the same period. As a result, the number of nonwhite families living in so-called "poverty areas" of large cities actually rose from 1,561,000 in 1960 to 1,588,000 in 1966.

4 Number of offenses per 1,000 persons 7–20 years (1965).

5 Number of cases per 100,000 persons under 21 years (1964).

6 Number of children in Aid to Dependent Children cases per 1,000 under 18 years, using 1960 population as base (1965).

7 Welfare Assistance recipients per 1,000 persons, using 1960 population as base (1965).

THE AMERICAN LOWER CLASSES: A TYPOLOGICAL APPROACH

S. M. Miller

1 Cf. Patricia Cayo Sexton, Education and Income: Inequalities in Our Public Schools, New York: Viking Press, 1961, pp. 10 ff. S. M. Miller, Carolyn Comings and Betty Saleem, The School Dropout Problem—Syracuse, Albany: New York State Division for Youth and the Syracuse University Youth Development Center, 1963. Herman P. Miller points out that the disadvantage of not having a college diploma grew from 1939 to 1958. See his "Money Value of an Education," Occupational Outlook Quarterly (September, 1961), p. 4.

2 Janet E. Weinandy, *Families Under Stress,* Syracuse: Syracuse University Youth Development Center, 1962.

3 Audrey Harvey, *Casualties of the Welfare State,* Fabian Tract 321, London: Fabian Society, 1959.

4 Michael Harrington, *The Other America: Poverty in the United States,* New York: The Macmillan Company, 1962; Conference on Economic Progress, *Poverty and Deprivation in the United States,* Washington: Conference on Economic Progress, 1961; the main author of this analysis is Leon Keyserling and it is known as the "Keyserling Report"; Gabriel Kolko, *Wealth and Power in the United States,* New York: Frederick Praeger, 1962; Robert J. Lampman, "The Low Income Population and Economic Growth," Study Paper No. 12, Joint Economic Committee, Congress of the United States, December 16, 1959, Washington: Government Printing Office, 1959; James N. Morgan et al., *Income and Welfare in the United States,* New York: McGraw-Hill Book Company, 1962. These books are reviewed in S. M. Miller, "Poverty and Inequality in America: Implications for the Social Services," *Child Welfare,* XLII (November, 1963), pp. 442–5 (republished in the Syracuse University Youth Development Center Reprint Series).

5 Brian Abel-Smith, "Whose Welfare State?" Norman MacKenzie, ed., *Conviction,* London: MacGibbon and Kee, 1958.

6 "The terms 'lower class' and 'middle class' are used here to refer to systems of behavior and concerns rather than groups defined in conventional economic terms." William C. Kvaraceus and Walter B. Miller, *Delinquent Behavior: Culture and the Individual,* Washington: National Education Association, 1959, p. 62.

7 S. M. Miller and Frank Riessman, "The Working-Class Subculture: A New View," *Social Problems,* IX (Summer, 1961), pp. 86–97.

8 Allison Davis, "The Motivation of the Underprivileged Worker," in William Foote Whyte, ed., *Industry and Society,* New York: McGraw-Hill Book Company, 1946, pp. 84–106.

9 August B. Hollingshead and Frederick C. Redlich, *Social Class and Mental Illness: A Community Study,* New York: John Wiley & Sons, 1958, pp. 387–97.

10 Walter B. Miller, "Lower Class Culture as a Generating Milieu of Gang Delinquency," *Journal of Social Issues,* XIV, no. 3 (1958), p. 6, footnote 3. In his penetrating analysis, Miller notes the existence of "subtypes of lower class culture" but does not pursue this point. While his emphasis is on cultural characteristics such as "female-based" household and "serial monogamy" mating patterns, he elsewhere employs educational, occupational and income variables to define the lower class. See his "Implications of Urban Lower-Class Culture for Social Work," *Social Service Review,* XXXIII (September, 1959), pp. 229 ff. His major stress is on cultural or status characteristics as defining the lower class culture.

11 *Ibid.*

12 Lee Rainwater assisted by Karol Kane Weinstein, *And the Poor Get Children,* Chicago: Quadrangle Books, 1960. See also the distinctions made within the lower-lower class by Martin Loeb, "Social Class and the American Social System," *Social Work,* 6 (April, 1961), p. 16.

13 Keyserling, *op cit.*, Lampman, *op. cit.*
14 See footnote 4.
15 Morgan, *op. cit.*, p. 3.
16 Not all families receiving welfare assistance should automatically
   be classified in the economically insecure category. For the aged,
   perhaps, welfare assistance does not constitute a lack of security.
   In general, however, the fact of welfare assistance would put a
   family in the economically insecure category.
17 Richard Cloward and Lloyd Ohlin, *Delinquency and Opportunity*,
   New York: The Free Press of Glencoe, 1960.
18 Dennis Wrong, in a personal communication, has influenced this
   and the following paragraph. "Skidding" is discussed in Harold
   Wilensky and Hugh Edwards, "The Skidder: Ideological Adjustments of Downward Mobile Workers," *American Sociological Review*, 24 (April, 1959), pp. 215–231.
19 Morgan, *op cit.*
20 S. M. Miller, "Comparative Social Mobility," *Current Sociology*,
   IX, no. 1 (1960), pp. 1–89.
21 *Ibid.*, pp. 32–33.
22 Hylan Lewis, "Child Rearing Among Low Income Families," Washington Center for Metropolitan Studies, June 8, 1961. This paper
   and others by Lewis are among the most stimulating on the
   problems of low-income patterns. Also see Hyman Rodman,
   "The Lower-Class Value Stretch," *Social Forces*, 42 (December,
   1963).
23 I have used the terms "dependent" and "dependence" here for want
   of a sharper term; I find the concept of dependence murky and frequently used to cover a variety of conditions which a writer does
   not like.
24 Raymond T. Smith, *The Negro Family in British Guiana*, London:
   Routledge & Kegan Paul, Ltd., 1956.
25 Edith Clarke, *My Mother Who Fathered Me*, New York: Humanities
   Press, 1957.
26 Peter Kunstadter, "A Survey of the Consanguine and Matrifocal
   Family," *American Anthropologist*, 65 (February, 1963), pp. 56–66.
27 A. H. Maslow, *Motivation and Personality*, New York: Harper &
   Row, pp. 80–106.
28 Carlsson has reintroduced the concept of elasticity into sociological
   thinking. Gosta Carlsson, "Okonomische Ungleichheit und Leben-
   schanchen," *Kolner Zeitschrift fur Soziologie*, 5 (1961), pp. 189–
   199.
29 Harrington, *op. cit.*
30 Richard Titmuss, *Essays on "The Welfare State,"* London: George
   Allen & Unwin, 1958, chapter 2, "The Social Division of Welfare,"
   and *Income Distribution and Social Change*, Toronto: University
   of Toronto Press, 1962. Although Titmuss is a seminal thinker in
   analyzing changes in the social structure of the modern society,
   he has been almost completely ignored by American sociologists.
31 Cf. S. M. Miller, "Poverty and Inequality in America," *op. cit.*
32 In his syndicated column which appeared in the *Syracuse Herald-
   Journal*, November 14, 1961.

33 Frank Riessman, *The Culturally Deprived Child*, New York: Harper & Row, 1962.

34 Harrington seems frequently to write and speak as though all low-income persons are bound in an immutable chain of apathy and ineffectiveness, characteristics of "the culture of poverty." He has obviously extended this term beyond the intent of Oscar Lewis who introduced it in his *Five Families*, New York: Basic Books, 1959, and in *The Children of Sanchez*, New York: Random House, 1961. Warren Haggstrom has countered this view in his "The Power of the Poor," Syracuse University Youth Development Center, 1963.

35 Helen Icken Safa, *From Shanty Town to Public Housing*, Syracuse University Youth Development Center, 1962. The peculiar stresses of public housing life may be functional equivalents of the economic conditions of matrifocality discussed by Kunstadter.

36 Cf. S. M. Miller and Frank Riessman, "Working Class Authoritarianism: A Critique of Lipset," *British Journal of Sociology* (September, 1961).

37 Peter Townsend, "Freedom and Equality," *New Statesman*, LXI, no. 1570 (April 14, 1961), p. 574.

38 Ralf Dahrendorf, "Unskilled Labour in British Industry," unpublished Ph.D. thesis in sociology, London School of Economics, 1956, pp. 429–30.

39 S. M. Miller, "Poverty, Race and Politics," in Irving Louis Horowitz, ed., *The New Sociology: Essays on Social Values and Social Theory in Honor of C. Wright Mills*, New York: Oxford University Press, 1964.

40 See Miller and Riessman, "The Working-Class Subculture," and Hylan Lewis, *op. cit.*

THE PROBLEMS OF FAMILIES IN THE AFDC PROGRAM

Paul H. Glasser and Elizabeth L. Navarre

1 *Poverty in the United States* (Washington, D.C.: House of Representatives, Committee on Education and Labor, 88th Congress, 2nd Session, April, 1964).

2 Cooperating with the project staff were Tom Cook, Ora Hinckley, Lynn Kellogg, Roger Lind, Frances McNeil, Winifred Quarton, Robert Rosema, June Thomas, Jeanne Walters, and Fred Wight.

3 Hans Gerth and C. Wright Mills, *Character and Social Structure; the Psychology of Social Institutions* (New York: Harcourt, Brace, 1953).

4 Allison Davis, *Social-Class Influences upon Learning* (Cambridge, Mass.: Harvard University Press, 1948).

5 W. Lloyd Warner, Robert J. Havighurst, Martin B. Loeb, *Who Shall Be Educated? The Challenge of Unequal Opportunities* (New York: Harper & Row, 1944).

6 David J. Kallen and Elizabeth L. Navarre, *Status and Ability* (Baltimore, Md.: Health and Welfare Council of the Metropolitan Area, 1962).

7 Urie Bronfenbrenner, "Socialization and Social Class Through Time and Space," in Eleanor E. Maccoby, Theodore M. Newcomb, and Eugene L. Hartley (eds.), *Readings in Social Psychology*, 3rd ed. (New York: Holt, Rinehart and Winston, 1958), pp. 400–425.

8 Earl Lomon Koos, *The Health of Regionville, What the People Thought and Did About It* (New York: Columbia University Press, 1954).

9 Joseph A. Kahl, *The American Class Structure* (New York: Rinehart, 1957).

10 Lee Rainwater, *And the Poor Get Children; Sex, Contraception, and Family Planning in the Working Class* (Chicago: Quadrangle Books, 1960).

11 Lee Rainwater, Richard P. Coleman, and Gerald Handel, *Workingman's Wife; Her Personality, World, and Life Style* (New York: Oceana, 1959).

12 *Ibid.*

13 Robert R. Sears, Eleanor E. Maccoby, and Harry Levin, *Patterns of Child Rearing* (Evanston, Ill.: Row, Peterson, 1957).

14 Mildred Buck, "Socialization Differences Between ADC Mothers and the Sears-Maccoby-Levin Norms" (University of Chicago, Master's research paper, 1963; mimeographed).

15 Edwin J. Thomas, "Effects of Facilitative Role Interdependence on Group Functioning," in Dorwin Cartwright and Alvin Zander (eds.), *Group Dynamics: Research and Theory*, 2nd ed., (Evanston, Ill.: Row, Peterson, 1960), pp. 449–471.

SOME IMPEDIMENTS TO THE EDUCATION
OF DISADVANTAGED CHILDREN

Norma L. Radin

1 Rosenthal, R.; Jacobson, L.: Self-fulfilling prophecies in the classroom. Paper presented at the 1967 meeting of the American Psychological Association, Washington, D.C. (Unpublished.)

2 Coleman, J. S., et al.: Equality of educational opportunity. U.S. Department of Health, Education, and Welfare, Office of Education, Washington, D.C. 1966.

3 Clark, K.: Dark ghetto. Harper & Row, New York, 1965.

4 Cloward, R.: Studies in tutoring. *Journal of Experimental Education*, Fall 1967.

5 Suppes, P.: Logical and mathematic concept formation in children. Paper presented at the 1966 meeting of the American Psychological Association, New York. (Unpublished.)

6 Karnes, M.: A research program to determine the effects of various preschool intervention programs on the development of disadvantaged children and the strategic age for such intervention. Paper presented at the 1968 convention of the American Educational Research Association, Chicago. (Unpublished.)

7 Schafer, W.: Student careers in two public high schools: a comparative cohort analysis. Unpublished doctoral dissertation, The University of Michigan, Ann Arbor, 1965.

8 Litwak, F.; Meyer, H. J.: A balance theory of coordination between bureaucratic organizations and community primary groups. *Administrative Science Quarterly*, June 1966.

9 McClelland, D. C.: Achieving society. The Free Press, New York. 1967.

10 Miller, W.: Lower class culture as a generating milieu of gang delinquency. *Journal of Social Issues*, vol. 14, no. 3, 1958.

11 Group for the Advancement of Psychiatry: Psychiatric aspects of school desegregation. New York. 1957.

12 Clark, K.; Clark, M.: Racial identification and preference in Negro children. *In* Readings in social psychology. (G. Swanson, T. Newcomb, and E. Hartley, eds.) Holt, Rinehart and Winston, New York. 1952.

13 Bernstein, B.: A socio-linguistic approach to social learning. *In* Penguin survey of the social sciences. (J. Gould, ed.) Penguin Books, Baltimore, Md.; 1965.

14 Radin, N.; Kamii, C.: The child-rearing attitudes of disadvantaged Negro mothers and some educational implications. *Journal of Negro Education*, Spring 1965.

15 Hunt, J. McV.: Inteligence and experience. Ronald Press Co., New York. 1961.

16 Hess, R.; Shipman, V.: Early blocks to children's learning. *Children*, September–October 1965.

17 Radin, N.; Weikart, D.: A home teaching program for disadvantaged children. *Journal of Special Education*, Winter 1967.

18 Piaget, J.: Six études de psychologie. Editions Gonthier, Geneva, Switzerland. 1964.

19 Rosenzweig, M., et. al.: Cerebral effects of environmental complexity and training effects among adult rats. *Journal of Comparative and Physiological Psychology*, June 1964.

20 Bloom, B.: Stability and change in human characteristics. John Wiley & Sons, New York. 1964.

21 Smilansky, S.: Promotion of preschool "culturally deprived" children through "dramatic play." Paper presented at the 1965 meeting of the American Orthopsychiatric Association, New York. (Unpublished.)

22 Piaget, J.: The construction of reality in the child. Basic Books, New York. 1954.

23 Cohen, H., et al.: Case I: an initial study of contingencies applicable to special education. Educational Facility Press, New York. 1967.

PROPOSED CHANGES IN AMERICAN SOCIAL WELFARE

Fedele F. Fauri

1 *United States Department of Commerce—Current Population Reports*—Series P-60, Number 55, August 5, 1968. The exact figure given is $8,017.

2 *United States Department of Health, Education, and Welfare, Social*

Security Bulletin, Volume 32, March, 1969. Statistic dated November 30, 1968.

3 *Ibid.* The lowest payment is in Mississippi; the highest payment is in Massachusetts.

4 *Ibid.* These are Arizona, Florida, Indiana, Mississippi, Rhode Island, South Carolina, and Utah.

5 *Report of the National Advisory Commission on Civil Disorders* (New York: Bantam Books, 1968).

6 *Having the Power, We Have the Duty,* Report of the Advisory Council on Public Welfare (Washington, D.C., U. S. Department of Health, Education, and Welfare, Welfare Administration, June 29, 1966).

THE OLD LOVE AND THE NEW:
DIVORCE AND READJUSTMENT
Willard Waller

1 This is a form of speech not infrequently employed. A Freudian interpretation suggests itself.

MARITAL COHESIVENESS AND DISSOLUTION:
AN INTEGRATIVE REVIEW
George Levinger

1 This state of affairs has not been uncommon in other areas of sociological investigation. See Hans L. Zetterberg, *On Theory and Verification in Sociology,* Totowa, N. J.: Bedminster, 1963.

2 William J. Goode, "Family Disorganization," in *Contemporary Social Problems,* ed. by Robert K. Merton and Robert A. Nisbet, New York: Harcourt, Brace, 1961, p. 425.

3 *Ibid.,* pp. 417–418.

4 Paul H. Jacobson, "Differentials in Divorce by Duration of Marriage and Size of Family," *American Sociological Review,* 15 (April 1950), pp. 235–244.

5 Harvey J. Locke, *Predicting Adjustment in Marriage,* New York: Holt, 1951, pp. 236–243.

6 Charles Ackerman, "Affiliations: Structural Determinants of Differential Divorce Rates," *American Journal of Sociology,* 69 (July 1963), pp. 13–20.

7 See also William J. Goode, *After Divorce,* Glencoe, Ill.: Free Press, 1956; Paul C. Glick, *American Families,* New York: Wiley, 1957; Hugh Carter and Alexander Plateris, "Trends in Divorce and Family Disruption," *HEW Indicators* (September 1963), pp. v–xiv.

8 Leon Festinger, Stanley Schachter, and Kurt Back, *Social Pressures in Informal Groups,* New York: Harper & Row, 1950, p. 164.

9 Goode, "Family Disorganization," *op. cit.,* pp. 441–442.

10 Glick, *op. cit.,* p. 156.

11 Paul H. Jacobson, *American Marriage and Divorce,* New York: Rinehart, 1959, p. 119.

12 Goode, *After Divorce, op. cit.*, has pointed out that in many divorce cases, the husband has precipitated the break by providing reasons for the wife's complaint. Nevertheless, the wife's *tolerance* for the husband's normative deviation is a crucial determinant of the decision to seek a divorce.

13 Numerals in parentheses in this review section pertain to the references in the footnote to Table 1.

14 A forthcoming paper by the author will report that income is also closely related to the outcome of *applications for divorce*, once such applications have actually been filed. This study avoids a criticism by Day, pertaining to some published studies of divorce. He points out that Census enumerations of persons currently occupying the status "divorced" have sometimes been erroneously taken to represent the *rate* of divorce itself. He suggests that ". . . socioeconomic differences in rates of remarriage or in the interval between divorce and re-marriage could seriously affect the relative sizes of these ratios." See Lincoln H. Day, "Patterns of Divorce in Australia and the United States," *American Sociological Review*, 29 (August 1964), p. 509. Day's reminder, published after this paper was written, is well to bear in mind in assessing findings reviewed here.

15 Unpublished data from the author's research indicate that homeowners are also more likely to dismiss an already filed divorce suit than are nonowners.

16 There are few good data to substantiate these predictions, because published divorce statistics do not generally reveal detailed occupational information. Possibly the best single source is a 1908 U. S. Census Bulletin (33), which relates occupation to divorce. Although its national returns were qualified as "incomplete and hardly acceptable," its New Jersey data for 1887–1906 covered 81.1 per cent of all husbands divorced. New Jersey husband occupied in agricultural, mechanical, and manufacturing pursuits showed lower than average divorce rates; those in professional or personal service or in trade and transportation had a higher rate. Particularly low were farmers, agricultural laborers, blacksmiths, carpenters, clergymen, engineers, and manufacturing officials. Clearly on the high side were actors, commercial travelers, musicians, bartenders, physicians and surgeons, sailors, and barbers and hairdressers, in that order. Husbands in the high-rate occupations seem to have been highly exposed to alternate attractions.

17 E.g., Alfred Cahen, *Statistical Analysis of American Divorce*, New York: Columbia U. Press, 1932; Walter F. Willcox, *Studies in American Demography*, Ithaca, N. Y.: Cornell U. Press, 1940.

18 William J. Goode (personal communication) has suggested that rural divorce rates in the United States may be low only for farmers, but higher for nonowners of farms.

19 William H. Whyte, Jr., *The Organization Man*, New York: Simon and Schuster, 1956, pp. 392–393.

20 In an unpublished study by the author, a comparison was made of two groups of divorce applicants, one set of whom later dismissed the action. It was found that husbands' complaints of "infidelity"

were more frequent in the divorcing group, while wives' complaints of the husband's "infidelity" were more frequent in the group of couples who dismissed their action and rejoined their marriage.

21 E. Lowell Kelly (personal communication) has reported anecdotal evidence from his own mariage research that substantiates this notion concerning mixed-religious marriages.

22 In an article based on assumptions similar to Goode's and the present author's, Heer has recently dealt with propositions about the wife's relative power in marriage. David M. Heer, "The Measurement and Bases of Family Power: An Overview," *Marriage and Family Living*, 25 (May 1963), pp. 133–139. Heer writes: ". . . the greater the difference between the value to the wife of the resources contributed by her husband and the value to the wife of the resources which she might earn outside the existing marriage, the greater the power of her husband, and vice-versa" (p. 138). We would propose that in cases of *low* difference, if the husband does not readily yield power within the marriage itself, the wife is inclined instead to dissolve the marriage.

23 Kurt Lewin, *Field Theory in Social Science*, New York: Harper & Row, 1951, p. 259.

24 *Ibid.*, p. 259.

25 For detailed discussions of conceptual and operational issues in research on group cohesiveness, see *Group Dynamics*, ed. by Dorwin Cartwright and Alvin Zander, Evanston, Ill.: Row Peterson, 1960, Chapter 3; Annie Van Bergen and J. Koekebakker, "Group Cohesiveness in Laboratory Experiments," *Acta Psychologica*, 16 (1959), pp. 81–98; Neal Gross and William Martin, "On Group Cohesiveness," *American Journal of Sociology*, 57 (May 1952), pp. 546–554.

26 Goode, "Family Disorganization," *op. cit.*, pp. 413–414.

SOURCES OF MARITAL DISSATISFACTION AMONG APPLICANTS FOR DIVORCE

George Levinger

1 Levinger, G. 1964. Task and social behavior in marriage. Sociometry. 27(4): 433–448.

2 Farber, B. 1957. An index of marital integration. Sociometry. 20(2): 117–134.

3 Hollingshead, A. B. 1957. Two factor index of social position. New Haven, Conn., multilithed.

4 Gurin, G., J. Veroff, and Sheila Feld. 1960. Americans View Their Mental Health. Basic Books, New York.

5 Komarovsky, Mirra, 1964. Blue-Collar Marriage. Random House, New York.

6 Galbraith, J. K. 1964. Economics and the quality of life. Science. 145(2): 117–123.

7 Maslow, A. H. 1954. Motivation and Personality. Harper & Row, Publishers, New York.

MARITAL SATISFACTION AND INSTABILITY: A CROSS-CULTURAL CLASS ANALYSIS OF DIVORCE RATES

William J. Goode

1 See the clear statement of this position by Robert K. Merton, "The Bearing of Sociological Theory on Empirical Research," in: *Social Theory and Social Structure*, 2nd edition, Glencoe, Ill., Free Press, 1957, pp. 85–101.

2 Three serious monograph attempts may be noted here: George P. Murdock, *Social Structure*, New York, Macmillan, 1949; Claude Levi-Strauss, *Les Structures Élémentaires de la Parenté*, Paris, Presses Universitaires de France, 1949; and William J. Goode, *After Divorce*, Glencoe, Ill., Free Press, 1956. Various reviews of the research over the past decade are now available: Robert F. Winch, "Marriage and the Family," in: Joseph B. Gittler (ed.), *Review of Sociology*, 1945–55, New York, Wiley, 1957; Reuben Hill and Richard L. Simpson, "Marriage and Family Sociology, 1945–55," in: Hans L. Zetterberg (ed.), *Sociology in the United States*, Paris, Unesco, 1956, pp. 93–101; and Nelson Foote and Leonard S. Cottrell, *Identity and Interpersonal Competence*, Chicago, University of Chicago Press, 1955. See also William J. Goode, "Horizons in Family Theory," in: Robert K. Merton, Leonard Broom and Leonard S. Cottrell (eds.), *Sociology Today*, New York, Basic Books, 1959.

3 Theorists of the rank of Talcott Parsons, Kingsley Davis, Robert K. Merton, and George C. Homans have all written theoretical papers on the family, however.

4 See Meyer Fortes, "Kinship and Marriage Among the Ashanti," in A. R. Radcliffe-Brown and Daryll Forde (eds.), *African Systems of Kinship and Marriage*, London, Oxford University Press, 1956, p. 282.

5 See Margaret Mead, "Sex and Temperament," in: *From The South Seas*, New York, Morrow, 1939.

6 "An Instrument for Measurement of Success in Marriage," *Publications of the American Sociological Society*, No. 27, 1933, pp. 94–106.

7 The major publications noted here are Ernest W. Burgess and Leonard S. Cottrell, *Predicting Success or Failure in Marriage*, New York, Prentice-Hall, 1939; Lewis M. Terman *et al.*, *Psychological Factors in Marital Happiness*, New York, McGraw-Hill, 1939; Harvey J. Locke, *Predicting Adjustments in Marriage*, New York, Henry Holt, 1951; Ernest W. Burgess and Paul W. Wallin, *Engagement and Marriage*, Philadelphia, Lippincott, 1953; and Georg Karlsson, *Adaptability and Communication in Marriage*, Uppsala, Sweden, Almqvist & Wiksells, 1951. For a convenient summary of the meaning of various parts of the instrument, see Ernest W. Burgess and Harvey J. Locke, *The Family*, 2nd edition, New York, American, 1953, Chapters 14, 15.

8 For a summary of the main findings, see: *ibid.*, pp. 408–29, and

Clifford Kirkpatrick, *What Science Says About Happiness in Marriage*, Minneapolis, Burgess Publishing Co., 1947.

9 Robert F. Winch, *Mate Selection*, New York, Harper & Row, 1958.

10 Several studies claim to have tested it, but they have not used the same measures for each important factor, or an appropriate population.

11 Burgess and Locke, *op. cit.*, p. 369; note that over one hundred studies exist to show that married couples are homogamous with respect to a wide variety of traits.

12 Winch developed his categories from the work of Henry A. Murray, *Explorations in Personality*, New York, Oxford University Press, 1938.

13 Personal communication, July 22, 1961.

14 Winch has commented on this point in *Mate Selection, op. cit.*, pp. 202–10, 300–3. For some of the consequences of such actions in general terms, see the author's two related papers, "Norm Commitment and Conformity to Role-Status Obligations," *American Journal of Sociology*, No. 65, November 1960, pp. 246–58; and "A Theory of Role Strain," *American Sociological Review*, No. 25, August 1960, pp. 483–96, as well as the use of this theory in "Illegitimacy in the Caribbean Social Structure," *American Sociological Review*, No. 25, February 1960, pp. 21–30.

15 This classification is developed and applied in my article, "Family Disorganization," in: Robert K. Merton and Robert A. Nisbet (eds.), *Contemporary Social Problems*, New York, Harcourt, Brace, 1961, pp. 390ff.

16 George P. Murdock notes that among the Crow a man might be ridiculed if he stayed too long with one woman ("Family Stability in Non-European Cultures," *Annals*, No. 272, November 1950, p. 198).

17 For example, I have been unable to locate in any Western country a monograph study comparable to my own *After Divorce*, dealing with the consequences of divorce in the lives of 425 young urban mothers.

18 See Sheldon and Eleanor Glueck, *Unraveling Juvenile Delinquency*, Cambridge, Mass., Harvard University Press, 1950, Table VIII-19, p. 91; Paul H. Landis, *The Broken Home in Teenage Adjustment*, Pullman, Washington, Institute of Agricultural Sciences, State College of Washington, 1953, p. 10 (*Rural Sociology Theories on The Family*, No. 4); and Raymond Ilsey and Barbara Thompson, "Women from Broken Homes," *Sociol. Rev.*, No. 9, March 1961, pp. 27–53.

19 Although in earlier drafts he does not deal systematically with the problem of divorce, David L. Schneider in his excellent analysis of matriliny shows some of the inherent strains in such a system. See "The Distinctive Features of Matrilineal Descent Groups," Chapter 1 of his larger book, *Matrilineal Descent Groups*, Palo Alto, Center for Advanced Study in the Social Sciences, 1959, mimeographed. See also his "A Note on Bridewealth and the Stability of Marriage," *Man*, No. 75, April 1953.

20 *Marriage and Divorce, 1867–1906*, Washington, Bureau of the

Census, 1909. See my critique of these items in *After Divorce,* pp. 52ff.

21 *After Divorce, op. cit.,* pp. 52 ff. *et passim.*
22 See the table on divorce and occupation in *Egskeiding in Suid-Afrika* by Hendrik Johannes Piek, Pretoria Ph.D., 1959, p. 262.
23 Vojin Milic, "Sklapanje I Razvod Braka Prema Zanimanju," *Statisticka Revija,* No. 7, March 1957, pp. 19–44, especially p. 38.
24 United Arab Republic (Egypt), Presidency of the Republic, Statistics and Census Department, *Vital Statistics, 1956,* Vol. II, Table XXIII, p. 340—Classification of Divorced Males by Locality According to Literacy for Year 1956; Table VI, pp. 274–5—Classification of Bridegrooms by Locality According to Literacy (and Marital Condition) for the Year 1956. Perhaps the literate are more likely to record their divorces officially.
25 Population Census of Egypt, 1947, General Tables, *op. cit.,* Table XXIX,—Working Status for Persons Engaged in Industries by Sex, Age Group and Civil Status (Excluding Children Under 5 Years). This table refers to those engaged in agriculture, fishing and hunting only.
26 *Statistical Yearbook,* 1959, Hashemite Kingdom of Jordan, Jerusalem, pp. 45–50.
27 Lester Mboria, *La Population de l'Égypte,* University of Paris Faculty of Law Thesis, Cairo, Procaccia, 1938, p. 68. Erik Allardt, *The Influence of Different Systems of Social Norms on Divorce Rates in Finland,* Columbia University, 1954, mimeographed. These data are taken from Allardt's *Milöbetingade differenser i skilsmässo-frekversen i Finland 1891–1950,* Helsingfors, Finska Vetenskaps-Societeten, 1953.
28 See *India: Sociological Background,* HRAF–44 Cornell 8, Vol. I (M. Opler, ed.), New Haven, Conn., Yale University Press, 1958, p. 25; P. V. Kane, *Hindu Custom and Modern Law,* Bombay, University of Bombay Press, 1950, p. 82; Mohindar Singh, *The Depressed Classes,* Bombay, Hind Kitebs, 1947, p. 168.
29 A good historical analysis of divorce in China is Wang Tse-Tsiu, *Le Divorce en Chine,* Paris, Lovitow, 1930.
30 Jesse Bernard, *Remarriage,* New York, Dryden, 1956, Chapters 2, 3.
31 Irene Taeuber, *The Population of Japan,* Princeton, N. J., Princeton University Press, 1958, pp. 226ff.

TOWARD A THEORY FOR THERAPEUTIC INTERVENTION IN FAMILIES

Ronald G. Tharp and Gerald D. Otis

1 Based on a version delivered at the 1965 meeting of the Western Psychological Association.
2 Jackson, D. D. (ed.) *The etiology of schizophrenia.* New York: Basic Books, 1960; Lidz, T., Cornelison, A. R., Fleck, S., and Terry, D. The intrafamilial environment of schizophrenic patients. II. Marital schism and marital skew. *American Journal of Psychiatry,* 1957, 94, 241–248; Wynne, L. D., Ryckoff, I. M., Day, J.,

and Hirsch, S. I. Pseudomutality in the family relations of schizophrenics. *Psychiatry*, 1958, 21, 205–220.

3 Tharp, R. G. Dimensions of marriage roles. *Marriage and Family Living*, 1963, 25, 389–404; Tharp, R. G. Marriage roles, child development and family treatment. *American Journal of Orthopsychiatry*, 1965, 35, 531–538.

4 *Ibid.*, 533–534.

5 Bell, N. W., and Vogel, E. F. Toward a framework for functional analysis of family behavior. In N. W. Bell & E. F. Vogel (eds.), *A modern introduction to the family*. Glencoe, Ill.: Free Press, 1960, pp. 1–36.

6 Tharp, 1963, *op. cit.*

7 Tharp, R. G. Psychological patterning in marriage. *Psychological Bulletin*, 1963, 60, 97–117; Tharp, R. G. Reply to Levinger's note. *Psychological Bulletin*, 1964, 61, 158–160.

8 Spiegel, J. P. The resolution of role conflict within the family. In N. W. Bell and E. F. Vogel (eds.), *A modern introduction to the family*. Glencoe, Ill.: Free Press, 1960, pp. 361–381.

9 *Ibid.*

10 Tharp, *Marriage and Family Living, op. cit.*

TOKEN REINFORCEMENT IN MARITAL TREATMENT

Richard B. Stuart

1 Skinner, B. F., *Science and human behavior* (New York: Free Press, 1953), p. 162.

2 Ferreira, A. J., and Winter, W. D., "Information exchange and silence in normal and abnormal families," *Family Process*, 1968, 7, p. 262.

3 Watzlawick, P., *An anthology of human communication* (Palo Alto, Calif.: Science and Behavior Books, 1964), p. 2.

4 Ferreira and Winter, *op. cit.*, pp. 260–261.

5 Gouldner, A. W., "The norm of reciprocity: A preliminary statement," *American Sociological Review*, 1960, 25, p. 169.

6 Patterson, G. R., and Reid, J., "Reciprocity and coercion: Two facets of social systems." Paper presented at the Ninth Annual Institute for Research in Clinical Psychology sponsored by the University of Kansas, Department of Psychology, Lawrence, April, 1967, p. 1.

7 Thibaut, J. W., and Kelley, H. H., *The social psychology of groups* (New York: Wiley, 1959), p. 7.

8 Homans, G. *Social behavior: Its elementary forms* (New York: Harcourt, Brace, 1961), pp. 53–59.

9 Skinner, *op. cit.*, p. 310.

10 Krasner, L., "Assessment of token economy programs in psychiatric hospitals." Paper presented at Ciba Symposium on "Learning and Psychotherapy," London, England, January 28, 1968, p. 2.

11 Farber, B., "An index of marital integration," *Sociometry*, 1957, 20, pp. 117–134.

12 Ryder, R. G., "Husband-wife dyads versus married strangers," *Family Process*, 1968, 7, p. 237.

A FAMILY AS SEEN IN THE HOSPITAL

Henry B. Richardson

1 Loss of menstruation.
2 Literally, loss of appetite, due to nervousness. Described in Chapter VI, pp. 131 ff.
3 Insufficient internal secretion of sex glands.

MEDICINE AND THE FAMILY

John H. Mabrey

1 Throughout this paper, the terms "medicine" and "medical" are used in the most general sense to include bodies of knowledge, techniques, and arts employed by physicians, nurses, social workers, and other personnel who recognize the importance of working with the patient and his family.
2 N. W. Sheahan, "The Family as a Unit for Public Health," in *The Family as the Unit of Health*, Milbank Memorial Fund, 1952.
3 Nathan W. Ackerman, *The Psychodynamics of Family Life*, New York: Basic Books, 1958; Jerome K. Myers and Bertram H. Roberts, *Family and Class Dynamics in Mental Illness*, New York: Wiley, 1959; Harold Sampson, Sheldon L. Messinger, and Robert D. Towne, "Family Processes and Becoming a Mental Patient," *American Journal of Sociology*, LXVIII (July 1962), pp. 88–96; Marian Radke Yarrow, Charlotte Green Schwartz, Harriet S. Murphy, and Leila Calhoun Deasy, "The Psychological Meaning of Mental Illness in the Family," *Journal of Social Issues*, XI (No. 4, 1955), pp. 12–24.
4 John H. Mabry, "Some Ecological Contributions to Epidemiology," in E. Gartley Jaco, ed., *Patients, Physicians and Illness*, Glencoe, Ill.: Free Press, 1958, pp. 49–54; Daniel M. Wilner *et al.*, *The Housing Environment and Family Life*, Baltimore: Johns Hopkins, 1962.
5 Rees B. Rees, ed., *Dermatoses Due to Environmental and Physical Factors*, Springfield, Ill.: Charles C. Thomas, 1962.
6 Howard A. Rusk, *Rehabilitation Medicine*, St. Louis: C. V. Mosby, 1958.
7 John Cassel, "Social and Cultural Implications of Food and Food Habits," in Jaco, *op. cit.*, pp. 134–143; H. D. Kruse, "The Place of Nutrition in the Relationship Between Environment and Health," in *Backgrounds of Social Medicine*, New York: Milbank Memorial Fund, 1949, pp. 138–155.
8 Lois Pratt *et al.*, "Physicians' Views on the Level of Medical Information Among Patients," in Jaco, *op. cit.*, pp. 222–229.
9 Earl Koos, *The Health of Regionville*, New York: Columbia University Press, 1954, pp. 86–92.

10 Robert Straus, "Sociological Determinants of Health Beliefs and Behavior," *American Journal of Public Health*, 51 (October 1961), pp. 1547–1552.

11 Halbert L. Dunn and Mort Gilbert, "Public Health Begins in the Family," *Public Health Reports*, LXXI (October 1956), pp. 1002–1010; Alfred McC. Lee and Elizabeth B. Lee, "Welfare Roles of the Family," in *Marriage and the Family*, New York: Barnes and Noble, 1961, pp. 54–68.

12 "The Death of the Hired Man," in *A Pocketbook of Robert Frost's Poems*, New York: Washington Square Press, 1961, pp. 165–166.

13 Ernest W. Burgess and Harvey J. Locke, *The Family: From Institution to Companionship*, 3rd ed., New York: American Book, 1960; Willard Waller, *The Family: A Dynamic Interpretation*, revised by Reuben Hill, New York: Dryden, 1951.

14 Barton Childs and James B. Sidbury, "A Survey of Genetics as It Applies to Problems in Medicine," *Pediatrics*, 20 (July 1957), pp. 177–218; J. W. Neel, "Applications of Genetics to Human Problems," in *Genetics and the Inheritance of Integrated Neurological and Psychiatric Patterns*, Research Publication of the Association for Research in Nervous and Mental Disease, 33 (1954), pp. 386–399.

15 Daniel M. Wilner, *op. cit.;* U. Christiansen, *Bolingforhold Og Brnesygelighed,* Copenhagen: Ejnar Muncksgaard, 1956 (English summary, pp. 188–205).

16 cf. Rees, *op. cit.*

17 Marvin B. Sussman, "The Help Pattern in the Middle-Class Family," in Sussman, ed., *Sourcebook in Marriage and the Family*, 2nd ed., Cambridge, Massachusetts: Houghton Mifflin, 1963, pp. 380–385. For a more pessimistic view of the capacity of the contemporary urban family for coping with illness, see Talcott Parsons and Renee Fox, "Illness, Therapy and the Modern American Family," in Jaco, *op. cit.*, pp. 234–245.

18 cf. any good text in this field. An easily available example is Lee and Lee, *op. cit.*

19 Clark L. Vincent, "The Family in Health and Illness: Some Neglected Areas," *Annals of the American Academy of Political and Social Sciences* (March, 1963), pp. 109–116.

20 Stuart A. Queen, Robert W. Habenstein, and John B. Adams, *The Family in Various Cultures*, New York: J. B. Lippincott, 1961.

21 Therese Benedek, "Personality Development," in Franz Alexander and Helen Ross, *Dynamic Psychiatry*, Chicago: University of Chicago Press, 1952, pp. 369–400; John Bowlby, *Child Care and the Growth of Love*, Baltimore: Penguin, 1957; Irene M. Josselyn, *Psychosocial Development of Children*, New York: Family Service Association, 1948; Erik H. Erikson, *Childhood and Society*, New York: Norton, 1950.

22 W. Allison Davis and Robert Havighurst, *Father of the Man*, Boston: Houghton Mifflin, 1947; Margaret Mead and Martha Wolfenstein, eds., *Childhood in Contemporary Cultures*, Chicago: University of Chicago Press, 1955.

23 Standard marriage and family texts discuss family structure and functions in more detail: cf. Burgess and Locke, *op. cit.;* Lee and Lee, *op. cit.;* Ruth S. Cavan, *American Marriage: A Way of Life,* New York: Crowell, 1959.

24 David Mechanic and Edward H. Volkart, "Stress, Illness Behavior and the Sick Role," *American Sociological Review,* 26 (February 1961), pp. 51–58; Talcott Parsons, "Definitions of Health and Illness in the Light of American Values and Social Structure," in Jaco, *op. cit.,* pp. 165–187.

25 H. A. Carothers, "Pets in the Home: Incidence and Significance," *Pediatrics,* 21 (May 1958), pp. 840–848.

26 Wilner, *op. cit.*

27 Rees, *op. cit.*

28 G. C. M. McGonigle, "Poverty, Nutrition and Public Health," *Proceedings of the Royal Society of Medicine,* 25 (February 1933), pp. 677–687.

29 Lee Rainwater, *And the Poor Get Children,* Chicago: Quadrangle Press, 1960; Charles F. Westoff, Robert G. Potter, Jr., Philip C. Sagi, and Elliott G. Mishler, *Family Growth in Metropolitan America,* Princeton: Princeton University Press, 1961.

30 Thomas Eliot, "Handling Family Strains and Shocks," in *Family, Marriage and Parenthood,* ed. by Howard Becker and Reuben Hill, Boston: D. C. Heath, 1948, pp. 616–640.

31 Normal G. Brill and Hugh A. Storrow, "Social Class and Psychiatric Treatment," *Archives of General Psychiatry,* 3 (October 1960), pp. 340–344; Gerald Gurin, Joseph Veroff, and Sheila Feld, *Americans View Their Mental Health,* New York: Basic Books, 1960, pp. 255–301.

32 Kurt W. Deuschle, Clarence Jardahl, and Gladys L. Hobby, "Clinical Usefulness of Riboflavin-Tagged Isoniazid for Self-Medication in Tuberculosis Patients," *American Review of Respiratory Diseases,* 82 (July 1960), pp. 1–10.

33 John H. Mabry, "Toward the Concept of Housing Adequacy," *Sociology and Social Research,* 44 (November–December 1959), pp. 86–92.

34 cf. Logan Clendening, *Sourcebook of Medical History,* New York: Dover, 1960, p. 15.

PROBLEMS OF DISABILITY FROM THE PERSPECTIVE OF ROLE THEORY

Edwin J. Thomas

1 Disability may be defined as ". . . a condition of impairment, physical or mental, having an objective aspect that can usually be described by a physician . . ."; in contrast, a handicap ". . . is the cumulative result of the obstacles which disability interposes between the individual and his maximum functional level." See G. W. Hamilton, *Counseling the Handicapped in the Rehabilitation Process* (New York: Ronald, 1950), p. 17, quoted in Beatrice A.

Wright, *Physical Disability—A Psychological Approach* (New York: Harper and Row, 1960), p. 9.

2 Beatrice A. Wright, *ibid.*, p. 373, as italicized by Wright.

3 For example, see Beatrice A. Wright, *ibid.*, pp. 373–377. Similar conclusions are supported by the analyses of the following writers: R. G. Barker, in collaboration with B. A. Wright, L. Meyerson, and M. R. Gonick, *Adjustment to Physical Handicap and Illness: A Survey of the Social Psychology of Physique and Disability* (Bulletin 55, revised 2nd ed.; New York: Social Science Research Council, 1953); L. Meyerson, "Special Disabilities," in P. R. Farnsworth and Q. McNemar (eds.), *Annual Review of Psychology*, 8 (Palo Alto, Calif.: Annual Reviews, Inc., 1957), pp. 437–457; E. L. Cowen, R. P. Underberg, R. T. Verrillo, and F. G. Benham, *Adjustment to Visual Disability in Adolescence* (New York: American Foundation for the Blind, 1961). An especially revealing study is that of T. F. Linde and C. N. Patterson, "Influence of Orthopedic Disability on Conformity Behavior," *Journal of Abnormal and Social Psychology*, 65 (1964), 115–118.

4 For example, see Beatrice A. Wright, *op. cit.*; Helen H. Perlman, "Family Diagnosis in Cases of Illness and Disability," in *Family-Centered Social Work in Illness and Disability: A Preventive Approach* (New York: National Association of Social Workers, 1961), pp. 7–21; Eileen Gambrill, "Post Hospitalized Disabled Children," *Journal of Health and Human Behavior*, 4 (1963), 206–10; F. Davis, *Passage Through Crisis: Polio Victims and Their Families* (Indianapolis: Bobbs-Merrill, 1963); A. G. Gowman, *The War Blind in American Social Structure* (New York: American Foundation for the Blind, 1957); and Jane Kamm, *A Study of Patients with Orthopedic Disabilities* (Ann Arbor, Mich.: The University of Michigan, School of Social Work, 1956, unpublished Master's thesis).

5 I know of no analysis of the behavioral problems of the disabled from the perspective of role theory, although there have been sociological analyses of specific disabilities (such as blindness) and descriptions of the patient role.

6 For a general treatment of role theory see B. J. Biddle and E. J. Thomas (eds.), *Role Theory: Concepts and Research* (New York: Wiley, 1966).

7 T. Parsons, "Illness and the Role of the Physicians: A Sociological Perspective," in C. Kluckhohn and H. A. Murray, with the collaboration of D. M. Schneider (eds.), *Personality in Nature, Society, and Culture* (2nd ed.; New York: Knopf, 1953), p. 613.

8 S. H. King, *Perceptions of Illness and Medical Practice* (New York: Russell Sage Foundation, 1962), pp. 355–357.

9 Davis, *op. cit.*, pp. 66–67.

10 F. Pine and D. J. Levinson, "A Sociopsychological Conception of Patienthood," *The International Journal of Social Psychiatry*, 7 (1961), 106–122.

11 Wright, *op. cit.*, pp. 345–364.

12 E. Goffman, *Asylums: Essays on the Social Situation of Mental*

Patients and Other Inmates (New York: Doubleday, 1961), pp. 66–67

13 Ruth Benedict, "Continuities and Discontinuities in Cultural Conditioning," *Psychiatry*, 1 (1938), 161–167.

14 Support for these conclusions may be documented with reference to studies on the effects of sudden change for animals, for humans in natural social situations, and in the psychological laboratory and clinic, but such evidence is far from conclusive. However plausible these effects may appear to be, their postulation must still be considered as hypothesized rather than as clearly demonstrated. The same conclusion pertains to the effects of role conflict, conception conflict and nonfacilitative interdependence, to be discussed.

15 R. M. Williams, *American Society: A Sociological Interpretation* (2nd ed.; New York: Knopf, 1960).

16 H. A. Murray, *Explorations and Personality* (New York: Oxford U., 1938).

17 Bertha Reynolds, *Social Work and Social Living* (New York: Citadel, 1951).

18 See D. Landy, "Problems of the Person Seeking Help in Our Culture," *Social Welfare Forum* (New York: National Conference on Social Welfare, 1960), pp. 127–45; and J. R. P. French, Jr., "The Social Environment and Mental Health," *The Journal of Social Issues*, 19 (1963), 39–56.

19 Beatrice A. Wright, *op. cit.*, pp. 224–229.

20 For an elaboration of this concept and of the conditions that may give rise to it in general, see W. J. Goode, "A Theory of Role Strain," *American Sociological Review*, 25 (1960), 483–496.

21 Problems of role synchrony have not been treated systematically in the literature, although related problems of marginality and so-called reciprocity and complementarity of role behavior have been discussed. For insightful discussions of the problem of marginality and of interaction problems of the disabled, see especially R. G. Barker, *op cit.*; Beatrice Wright, *op. cit.*; and A. G. Gowman, *op. cit.* For a discussion of reciprocity and complementarity see A. W. Gouldner, "The Norm of Reciprocity: A Preliminary Statement," *American Sociological Review*, 25 (1960), 161–178.

22 A. G. Gowman, *op. cit.*, quoted and paraphrased from pp. 120–121.

23 The "true" degree of handicap is difficult to assess because it requires judgments about the individual's impairment and his capabilities to perform with that impairment. The fact that professionals working with disability often have difficulty making these judgments is one of many factors conducive to generating either asynchronous or invalid role synchronies.

24 Fred Davis, *op. cit.*, pp. 149–152.

25 James Breedlove, "Casework and Rehabilitation," *Social Work*, 2 (1957), 35.

26 *Ibid.*, p. 34.

27 *Ibid.*, p. 35.

PROBLEM CONCEPTION AND PLANNED INTERVENTION

David M. Kaplan

1 Julius A. Roth and Elizabeth M. Eddy, "Rehabilitation for the Unwanted," Vocational Rehabilitation Adm. on Research, 1963.
2 Werner W. Boehm, "The Nature of Social Work," *Social Work,* 3:2 (April 1958), p. 16.
3 R. Grinker and J. Spiegel, *Men Under Stress* (Philadelphia: Blakiston, 1945), p. 248; O. Fenichel, *The Psychoanalytic Theory of Neurosis* (New York: Norton, 1945), p. 126.
4 John A. Aita, "Efficacy of the Brief Clinical Interview Method in Predicting Adjustments," *Archives of Neurology and Psychiatry,* 61:2 (February 1949), pp. 170–176; Albert J. Glass, et al., *Psychiatric Prediction and Military Effectiveness,* Research Report WRAIR–56, Walter Reed Army Institute of Research (Washington, D.C.: Walter Reed Army Medical Center, 1956), p. 11.
5 Albert J. Glass, "Psychotherapy in the Combat Zone," *American Journal of Psychiatry,* 110:10 (April 1954), p. 728.
6 Israel Zwerling, "The Mental Health Potential of Urban Life for Children and Youth," Manhattan Society for Mental Health Conference, 1961.
7 E. Lowell Kelly and Donald W. Fiske, *The Prediction of Performance in Psychology:* Office of Strategic Services, *Assessment of Men* (New York: Rinehart & Co., 1948).
8 Albert J. Glass, *op. cit.,* p. 284.
9 Irving L. Janis, *Psychological Stress* (New York: Wiley, 1958), see biblio.; David Kaplan and Edward Mason, "Maternal Reactions to Premature Birth Viewed as an Acute Emotional Disorder," *American Journal of Orthopsychiatry,* 30:3 (July 1960), pp. 539–52; David Kaplan, "A Concept of Acute Situational Disorders," *Social Work,* 7:2 (April 1962), p. 15; also David Kaplan, unpublished doctoral dissertation, "Predicting Outcome from Situational Stress on the Basis of Individual Problem Solving Patterns," University of Minnesota, December, 1960.
10 Leopold and Dillon, "Psycho-anatomy of a Disaster: A Long Term Study of Post-Traumatic Neuroses," *American Journal of Psychiatry,* 119:10 (April 1963).
11 Erich Lindemann, "Symptomatology and Management of Acute Grief," *American Journal of Psychiatry,* 101:2 (September 1944).
12 Marie Jahoda, *Current Concepts of Positive Mental Health* (New York: Basic Books, 1958).
13 David M. Kaplan, doctoral dissertation, *op. cit.*
14 *Ibid.*
15 *Ibid.*

ADEQUATE FAMILY FUNCTIONING

Paul H. Glasser and Lois N. Glasser

1 For a fuller discussion of the case study method and its use in this project, see Paul H. Glasser: "Changes in Family Equilibrium

During Psychotherapy," *Family Process* 2, 2 (September 1963).
2 Taken from the definition of a competent family by Reuben Hill, J. Joel Moss, and Claudine G. Wirth's: Eddyville's Families. (Chapel Hill, N. C.: Institute for Research in Social Science, 1953.)
3 This is closely related to the concepts of Charles Horton Cooley (the "looking glass self") and George Herbert Mead (the "I" and the "me" and the "generalized other"). More recently Hess and Handel have proposed a similar concept for families, namely "establishing a satisfactory congruence of images through the exchange of suitable testimony." See Robert D. Hess and George Handel: *Family Worlds.* (Chicago: University of Chicago Press, 1959.)
4 Members of the helping professions have recognized this phenomenon for many years, especially in the setting of the child guidance clinic. Further, Caplan points out that the emotional climate within the family may be healthy for some members and not for others. Rapoport and Rosow describe a similar phenomenon among families of mental patients. See Gerald Caplan: "An Approach to the Study of Family Mental Health," mimeographed document (Cambridge, Massachusetts: Harvard University School of Public Health, 1957); and Rhona Rapoport and Irving Rosow: "An Approach to Family Relationships and Role Performance," *Human Relations*, 10, 3 (August 1957).
5 p. 215, Rapoport and Rosow. See above footnote.
6 Other terms have been used for this phenomenon, such as adaptability. For one description of its components, see Ernest W. Burgess and Paul Wallin: Engagement and Marriage (Chicago: J. B. Lippincott Co., 1953), Chapter 19, "Adaptability." For a publication revealing its importance in the prediction of marital adjustment, see Eugene Litwak, Gloria Count, and Edward M. Haydon: "Group Structure and Interpersonal Creativity as Factors Which Reduce Errors in the Prediction of Marital Adjustment," *Social Forces*, 38, 4 (May 1960).
7 See Evelyn Duvall: *Family Development* (New York: J: B. Lippincott Co., 1957).
8 See, for example, Elizabeth Bott: "Urban Families: Conjugal Roles and Social Networks," *Human Relations*, 8, 4 (November 1955); or Paul H. Glasser: "Family Organization During Psychotherapy," dissertation, University of North Carolina, Chapel Hill, June 1961; or Hess and Handel (footnote 3).

CHANGES IN FAMILY EQUILIBRIUM DURING PSYCHOTHERAPY

Paul H. Glasser

1 Robert Cooley Angell, *The Family Encounters the Depression* (New York: Scribner, 1936); R. S. Cavan and K. H. Ranck, *The Family and the Depression* (Chicago: U. of Chicago Press, 1938); T. D. Eliot, "Bereavement: Inevitable but Not Insurmountable," in H. Becker and R. Hill (eds.), *Family, Marriage and Parenthood* (Boston: Heath, 1948), pp. 641–668; T. D. Eliot, "Handling Family Strains and Shocks," in Becker and Hill, *ibid.*, pp. 616–640; R.

Hill, J. J. Moss, and C. G. Wirths, *Eddyville's Families* (Chapel Hill, N.C.: Institute for Research in Social Science, 1953); R. Hill, *Families Under Stress* (New York: Harper & Row, 1949); M. Komarovsky, *The Unemployed Man and His Family* (New York: Dryden, 1940); E. L. Koos, *Families in Trouble* (New York: Kings Crown, 1946); W. W. Waller, *The Old Love and the New: Divorce and Readjustment* (Philadelphia: Liveright, 1930).

2 E. W. Burgess and P. Wallin, *Engagement and Marriage* (Philadelphia: Lippincott, 1953); E. W. Burgess and S. Cottrell, Jr., *Predicting Success or Failure in Marriage* (Englewood Cliffs, N.J.: Prentice-Hall, 1939); H. J. Locke, *Predicting Adjustment in Marriage* (New York: Holt, 1951); L. M. Terman and M. H. Oden, *The Gifted Child Grows Up* (Standford, Calif.: Stanford U. P., 1947); L. M. Terman, *Psychological Factors in Marital Happiness* (New York: McGraw-Hill, 1938).

3 E. R. Duvall, *Family Development* (New York: Lippincott, 1957).

4 F. L. Bates, "A Conceptual Analysis of Group Structure," *Social Forces*, 36 (1957), 103–111; F. L. Bates, "Position, Role, and Status: A Reformulation of Concepts," *Social Forces*, 34 (1956), 313–321; E. Bott, "Urban Families: Conjugal Roles and Social Networks," *Human Relations*, 8 (1955), 345–384; P. G. Herbst, "The Measurement of Family Relationships," *Human Relations*, 5 (1952), 3–35; R. D. Hess and G. Handel, *Family Worlds* (Chicago: U. of Chicago Press, 1959); M. W. Kargman, "The Clinical Use of Social System Theory in Marriage Counseling," *Marriage and Family Living*, 19 (1957), 263–270; R. Linton, *The Study of Man* (New York: Appleton-Century, 1936); R. Rapoport and I. Rosow, "An Approach to Family Relationships and Role Performance," *Human Relations*, 10 (1957), 209–221; T. R. Sarbin, "Role Theory," in Gardner Lindzey (ed.), *Handbook of Social Psychology*, Vol. 1, *Theory and Method* (Cambridge: Addison-Wesley, 1954), pp. 223–258; G. A. Theodorson, "Elements in the Progressive Development of Small Groups," *Social Forces*, 31 (1953), 311–320; R. H. Turner, "Role Taking, Role Standpoint, and Reference-Group Behavior," *American Journal of Sociology*, 61 (1956), 316–328.

5 N. Ackerman, *The Psychodynamics of Family Life* (New York: Basic Books, 1958); E. Chance, *Families in Treatment* (New York: Basic Books, 1959); J. A. Clausen and M. R. Yarrow, "Mental Illness and the Family," *Journal of Social Issues*, 11 (1955), 3–65; E. J. Cleveland and W. D. Longaker, "Neurotic Patterns in the Family," in A. H. Leighton, J. A. Clausen, and R. N. Wilson (eds.), *Explorations in Social Psychiatry* (New York: Basic Books, 1957), pp. 167–200; F. Cote, T. E. Dancey, and J. Saucier, "Participation in Institutional Treatment by Selected Relatives," *American Journal of Psychiatry*, 110 (1954), 831–833; S. Fisher and D. Mendell, "The Spread of Psychotherapeutic Effects from the Patient to His Family Group," *Psychiatry*, 21 (1958), 133–140; L. L. Geismar and B. Ayres, *Patterns of Change in Problem Families* (St. Paul, Minn.: Family Centered Project, Greater St. Paul Community Chest and Councils, 1959); A. Kaplan and L. Wolf, "The Role of the Family in Relation to the Institutionalized Mental Patient,"

Mental Hygiene, 38 (1954), 634–639; T. Lidy, G. Hotchkiss, and M. Greenblatt, "Patient-Family-Hospital Interrelationships: Some General Conclusions," in M. Greenblatt, D. J. Levinson, and R. H. Williams (eds.), *The Patient and the Mental Hospital* (New York: The Free Press, 1957), pp. 535–544; M. L. Moran, "Some Emotional Responses of Patients' Husbands to the Psychotherapeutic Course as Indicated in Interviews with the Psychiatric Caseworker," *American Journal of Orthopsychiatry*, 24 (1954), 317–325; T. Parsons and R. R. Fox, "Illness, Therapy, and the Modern Urban American Family," *Journal of Social Issues*, 8 (1952), 31–44; C. G. Schwartz, "Perspectives on Deviance—Wives' Definitions of their Husbands' Mental Illness," *Psychiatry*, 20 (1957), 275–291; J. P. Spiegel, "The Resolution of Role Conflict within the Family," in Greenblatt, Levinson, and Williams, *op. cit.*, pp. 545–564; L. C. Wynne, I. M. Ryckoff, J. Day, and S. I. Hirsch, "Pseudo-Mutuality in the Family Relations of Schizophrenics," *Psychiatry*, 21 (1958), 205–220.

6 Every family must evolve persistent patterns of expectations and behavior among its members if it is to endure for even a relatively short period of time. In addition, there must be internal role consistency, consistency of family roles and norms and actual role performance, and compatibility of family roles and norms with societal norms. A family in such a state is in equilibrium. When one or more of these conditions are not met the family is considered to be in a state of disequilibrium or crisis. Two family-crisis periods are described in the larger study; (1) when the patient is in the acute stage of mental illness and (2) when the patient is in intensive, insight psychotherapy.

7 This report covers the last three stages of family organization. The seven role areas are as follows: (1) sexual practices; (2) social activities; (3) household provision; (4) household management; (5) child care and control; (6) authority patterns; (7) maintenance of morale.

8 In two of the cases the patient was hospitalized for a short period of time prior to the beginning of outpatient psychotherapy.

9 Each of the families attempted to hide the patient's symptoms and the possibility of mental illness from other relatives, friends, and neighbors prior to the beginning of treatment.

10 The distinction between family diagnosis and the treatment of the family as a group is an important one. The former often may be necessary while the latter may or may not be the treatment of choice.

11 In one of the families studied, following the beginning of treatment with the patient, the spouse became acutely ill, and finally had to be hospitalized in a psychiatric institution.

12 For a discussion of the criteria to evaluate interaction patterns as well as means to characterize the family as a problem-solving group, see the author's dissertation: *Family Organization During Psychotherapy* (unpublished doctoral dissertation; Chapel Hill, N.C.: University of North Carolina, 1961).

MENTAL HEALTH AND THE FAMILY

Clark E. Vincent

1 An unpublished list of these 59 laws has been compiled for interagency use.

2 *Catalog of Federal Programs for Individual and Community Improvement,* Washington, D.C.: Office of Economic Opportunity, 1965.

3 Many of the historical notes in this chapter are derived from conversations with Dr. Bertram S. Brown, Deputy Director of the National Institute of Mental Health, and from a number of his published and unpublished papers. See B. S. Brown and H. P. Cain, "The Many Meanings of 'Comprehensive': Underlying Issues in Implementing the Community Mental Health Center Program," *American Journal of Orthopsychiatry,* 34:5 (October, 1964), pp. 834–839; L. D. Ozarin and B. S. Brown, "New Directions in Community Mental Health Programs," *American Journal of Orthopsychiatry,* 35:1 (January, 1965), pp. 10–17.

4 A. Deutsch, *The Mentally Ill in America,* New York: Columbia University Press, 1949.

5 Clifford W. Beers, *A Mind that Found Itself,* New York: Doubleday, 1921.

6 Kingsley Davis, "Mental Hygiene and the Class Structure," *Psychiatry,* 1:1 (February, 1938), 55–65.

7 A little-known fact is that Congress appropriated no money for the first year's operation of the National Institute of Mental Health, which had to be financed by a grant for about 40 thousand dollars obtained by Dr. Robert Felix from a private foundation.

8 The organizational predecessor of the Mental Hygiene Division was the Mental Hygiene Section authorized by the federal government in 1930 to administer the program of two "narcotic farms" established in 1929 at Lexington, Kentucky, and Fort Worth, Texas.

9 Historians who may someday document in detail the fascinating development of the federal government's role in the mental health field will find it inseparable from the professional career of Dr. Robert H. Felix. His dedicated leadership throughout more than 30 years began in 1931 with the first allocation of federal funds for a program related to mental health—the treatment of narcotic addiction. As the first director of the NIMH, his administration spanned all the program innovations during nearly 20 years of the growth of the NIMH from $40,000 in the form of a private grant to an annual budget of more than $250,000,000. His leadership ended (as director but not as consultant) in 1964 with his retirement to become a medical school dean only after he had witnessed congressional approval and funding for what may well become the most significant of the many ideas for which he was a major prime mover—the comprehensive community mental health center.

10 *Action for Mental Health,* final report of the Joint Commission on Mental Illness and Health, New York: Basic Books, 1961.

11 See bibliography in John P. Spiegel and Norman W. Bell, "The Family of the Psychiatric Patient," in *American Handbook of Psychiatry*, Vol. 1, ed. by S. Arieti, New York: Basic Books, 1959, pp. 114–149; and in the bibliography in Yi-Chuang Lu, "Contradictory Parental Expectations in Schizophrenia," *Archives of General Psychiatry*, Vol. 6 (March, 1962), pp. 219–234.

12 Theodore Lidz, George Hotchkiss, and Milton Greenblatt, "Patient-Family-Hospital Interrelationships: Some General Considerations," in *The Patient and the Mental Hospital*, ed. by Milton Greenblatt, Daniel J. Levinson, and Richard A. Williams, New York: The Free Press, 1957, pp. 535–543.

13 Talcott Parsons and Renée Fox, "Illness, Therapy and the Modern Urban American Family," in *Patients, Physicians and Illness*, ed. by E. Gartley Jaco, New York: The Free Press, 1958, pp. 234–245. See also Joseph Greenblum, "The Control of Sick-Care Functions in the Hospitalization of a Child: Family Versus Hospital," *Journal of Health and Human Behavior*, 2:1 (Spring, 1961), pp. 32–38.

14 See Reinhard Bendix and Bennett Berger, "Images of Society and Problems of Concept Formation in Sociology," in *Symposium on Sociological Theory*, ed. by Llewellyn Gross, Evanston, Ill.: Row-Peterson and Co., 1959, pp. 92–118.

15 For a report of this and related studies see Marvin B. Sussman and Lee Burchinal, "Kin Family Network: Unheralded Structure in Current Conceptualization of Family Functioning," *Marriage and Family Living*, 24:3 (August, 1962), pp. 231–240.

16 Eugene Litwak, "The Use of Extended Family Groups in the Achievement of Social Goals: Some Policy Implications," *Social Problems*, 7:3 (Winter, 1959–1960), pp. 177–187; "Geographic Mobility and Extended Family Cohesion," *American Sociological Review*, 25:3 (June, 1960), pp. 385–394; "Occupational Mobility and Extended Family Cohesion," *American Sociological Review*, 25:1 (February, 1960), pp. 9–21.

17 Dennis H. Wrong, "The Oversocialized Conception of Man in Modern Sociology," *American Sociological Review*, 26:2 (April, 1961), pp. 183–193.

18 Most of the content of this section is adapted from the first part of the author's "Familia Spongia: The Adaptive Function," *Journal of Marriage and the Family*, 28:1 (February, 1966), pp. 29–36.

19 William J. Goode, *The Family*, Englewood Cliffs, N.J.: Prentice-Hall, 1964, p. 2.

20 The changes in his interpretations are evident in comparing the content of the following: William F. Ogburn, *Social Change*, New York: Viking Press, 1922; William F. Ogburn, "The Changing Family," *Publications of the American Sociological Society*, Vol. 23, 1929, pp. 124–133; William F. Ogburn and Clark Tibbitts, "The Family and Its Functions," in Presidents' Research Committee on Social Trends (ed.), *Recent Social Change in the United States*, New York: McGraw-Hill, 1933, Vol. 1, pp. 661–708; and William F. Ogburn and M. F. Nimkoff, *Technology and the Changing Family*, New York: Houghton Mifflin Co., 1955, pp. 15, 45–48, 129–130, 244–247.

21 See, for example, Franz C. Muller-Lyer, *The Family*, New York: Alfred A. Knopf, 1931; and Herbert Spencer, *Principles of Sociology*, New York: D. Appleton-Century Co., 1897, Vol. 1, pp. 653, 681—683.

22 For a cogent review of the major "traditionalists" and "philosophical conservatives" who reacted to the individualism of the French Revolution legislation with efforts to strengthen the family and reconstitute the *ancien regime*, see Robert A. Nisbet, *The Quest for Community: A Study in the Ethics of Freedom and Order*, New York: Oxford University Press, 1953.

23 Pitirim A. Sorokin, *Social and Cultural Dynamics*, New York: American Book Co., 1937, Vol. V, p. 776; and *The Crisis of Our Age*, New York: E. P. Dutton, 1941, p. 18.

24 See Carle C. Zimmerman, *Family and Civilization*, New York: Harper & Row, 1947, pp. ix, 782–783, 802 ff.; and Ruth N. Anshen (ed.), *The Family: Its Function and Destiny*, New York: Harper & Row, rev. ed., 1959, pp. 3–19.

25 William J. Goode, *World Revolution and Family Patterns*, New York: The Free Press, 1963, chapter 1.

26 Ernest W. Burgess and Harvey J. Locke, *The Family: From Institution to Companionship*, New York: American Book Co., 1945.

27 Daniel R. Miller and Guy E. Swanson, *The Changing American Parent*, New York: Wiley, 1958, p. 198–202.

28 Bernard Farber, *Family: Organization and Interaction*, San Francisco: Chandler Publishing Co., 1964.

29 For an analysis of this change see Hyman Rodman, "Talcott Parsons' View of the Changing American Family," in *Marriage, Family and Society: A Reader*, ed. by Hyman Rodman, New York: Random House, 1965, pp. 262–286.

30 Talcott Parsons, "The Point of View of the Author," *The Social Theories of Talcott Parsons*, ed. by Max Black, Englewood Cliffs, N.J.: Prentice-Hall, 1961, p. 129.

31 Talcott Parsons and Robert Bales, *Family, Socialization and Interaction Process*, New York: The Free Press, 1955, pp. 10–11.

32 See footnote 19.

33 Karl Mannheim, *Ideology and Utopia*, New York: Harcourt, Brace & Co., 1957, p. 86.

34 Goode, *World Revolution and Family Patterns, op. cit.*, pp. 10–26.

35 For a critical review of some of the historical, methodological and theoretical issues involved in "functionalism," see *Functionalism in the Social Sciences*, ed. by Don Martindale, Philadelphia: The American Academy of Political and Social Science, Monograph 5, 1965.

36 W. F. Cottrell, "Of Time and the Railroader," *American Sociological Review*, 4:3 (April, 1939), pp. 190–198.

37 See P. E. Mott, F. C. Mann, Q. McLaughlin and D. P. Warwick, *Shift Work: The Social, Psychological and Physical Consequences*, Ann Arbor: University of Michigan Press, 1965, especially Chapters III and IV, pp. 64–146.

38 William F. Whyte, Jr., "The Wives of Management," *Fortune*,

October, 1951, and "The Corporation and the Wife," *Fortune*, November, 1951.

39 Alvin W. Gouldner, "Attitudes of 'Progressive' Trade Union Leaders," *American Journal of Sociology*, 52:4 (March, 1947), pp. 389–392.

40 Goode, *World Revolution and Family Patterns, op. cit.*, p. 14.

41 Lee Rainwater has commented on this predisposition to overloading as a concomitant of individualism and of regarding familial roles as secondary to roles in other social systems. "The [family] internal adaptation process presumably is guided by the demands that family members bring home based on their involvement with other institutions—career, teen-age peer group, school, etc. The family is seen by each particular institution—business sees the executive's family as an extension of him in his executive role; the school sees the pupil's family as an extension of the pupil in his learning role; etc. Because of the value placed on individual achievement and gratification, the individual often identifies more with the demands of the secondary institution in which he has a role than he does with a solitary family." (Personal communication with the author.)

43 See references cited in footnotes 15 and 16.

43 *The Report of the President's Commission on National Goals*, The American Assembly, Columbia University, November, 1960.

44 Jay Haley and Ira Glick, *Psychiatry and the Family: An Annotated Bibliography of Articles Published 1960–64*, Palo Alto, Cal.: *Family Process* (no date given).

45 Gerald H. Zuk and David Rubinstein, "A Review of Concepts in the Study and Treatment of Families of Schizophrenics," in *Intensive Family Therapy*, ed. by Ivan Boszormenyi-Nagy and James L. Framo, New York: Harper & Row, 1965, pp. 1–32.

46 M. B. Parloff, "The Family in Psychotherapy," *A.M.A. Archives of General Psychiatry*, Vol. 4 (May, 1961), pp. 445–451.

47 J. Haley, "Family of the Schizophrenic: A Model System," *Journal of Nervous and Mental Diseases*, Vol. 129 (October, 1959), pp. 357–374.

48 D. D. Jackson and V. Satir, "A Review of Psychiatric Development in Family Diagnosis and Family Therapy," in *Exploring the Base for Family Therapy*, ed. by N. W. Ackerman, F. Beatman and S. S. Sherman, New York: Family Service Association of America, 1961.

49 A. B. Hollingshead and F. C. Redlich, *Social Class and Mental Illness: A Community Study*, New York: Wiley, 1958.

50 See Zuk and Rubinstein, *op. cit.*, and the reviews of the literature cited in Haley and Glick, *op. cit.*

51 See the bibliography and review discussion of the work of L. C. Wynne, D. D. Jackson, J. E. Bell and others in Irving E. Alexander, "Family Therapy," *Marriage and Family Living*, 25:2 (May, 1963), pp. 146–154.

52 See Lloyd H. Rogler and August B. Hollingshead, *Trapped: Families and Schizophrenia*, New York: Wiley, 1965; and J. K. Myers and B. H. Roberts, *Family and Class Dynamics in Mental Illness*, New York: Wiley, 1959.

53 John P. Spiegel and Norman W. Bell, "The Family of the Psychiatric Patient," *op. cit.*

54 There are notable exceptions. See, for example, T. Lidz, S. Fleck, Y. O. Alanen and A. Cornelison, "Schizophrenic Patients and Their Siblings," *Psychiatry*, 26:1 (1963), pp. 1–18.

55 See Don D. Jackson, "The Study of the Family," *Family Process*, 4:1 (March, 1965), pp. 1–20.

56 For references concerning the earlier work of Fred L. Strodtbeck and Roland G. Tharp and some of the more current work of D. Wells Goodrich, Robert G. Ryder and others, see *Family Process*, 5:1 (March, 1966), pp. 1–20, 30–48.

57 Talcott Parsons and Renée Fox, "Illness, Therapy and the Modern American Family," *op. cit.*, pp. 234–245.

58 Talcott Parsons, "Definition of Health and Illness in the Light of American Values and Social Structure," in *Patients, Physicians and Illness*, ed. by E. Gartly Jaco, New York: The Free Press, 1958, pp. 165–187.

59 *Social Scientists Advisory Meeting, Working Paper: Summary of Deliberations, June 20–21, 1960*, U.S. Department of Health, Education and Welfare, Social Security Administration, mimeograph.

60 Alvin L. Schorr, "Family Policy in the United States," *International Social Science Journal*, 13:3 (1962).

61 Arthur W. Calhoun, *A Social History of the American Family*, Glendale, Cal.: The Arthur H. Clark Co., Vol. II, 1917, p. 334.

Index